RETAIL SERVICES

LEE PERLITZ · DAN HILL · MATTHEW COXHILL

RETAIL SERVICES

The McGraw·Hill Companies

Sydney New York San Francisco Auckland
Bangkok Bogotá Caracas Hong Kong
Kuala Lumpur Lisbon London Madrid
Mexico City Milan New Delhi San Juan
Seoul Singapore Taipei Toronto

The McGraw·Hill Companies

National Library of Australia Cataloguing-in-Publication Data

Author:	Perlitz, Lee, 1952–
Title:	Retail services / Lee Perlitz, Dan Hill, Matthew Coxhill.
ISBN:	9781743070741 (pbk.)
Notes:	Includes index.
Subjects:	Retail trade—Employees—Training of—Australia.
Other Authors/Contributors:	Hill, Dan, 1971–
	Coxhill, Matthew, 1963–
Dewey Number:	381.1071

Published in Australia by
McGraw-Hill Australia Pty Ltd
Level 2, 82 Waterloo Road, North Ryde NSW 2113
Publisher: Norma Angeloni-Tomaras
Development editors: Jess Ni Chuinn, Carolina Pomilio
Production editor: Claire Linsdell
Permissions editors: Haidi Bernhardt, Lisa Macdonald
Copyeditor: Janice Keynton
Proofreader: Pauline O'Carolan
Indexer: Olive Grove Indexing Services
Designer: Dominic Giustarini
Cover design: Em & Jon Gregory
Internal design: Lauren Statham
Typeset in AGaramond-Regular 11.5/15pt by diacriTech, India
Printed in China on 70 gsm matt art by 1010 Printing International

Contents

Chapter 3 • SIRXIND101 Work effectively in a customer service environment

PART 2 • MARKETING AND MERCHANDISING

Chapter 4 • SIRXMPR001A Profiling a retail market

Chapter 7 • SIRXSLS201A Sell products and services 207

PART 3 • RETAIL OPERATIONS

Chapter 8 • SIRXWHS101 & SIRXWHS302 Apply safe work practices and Maintain store safety 242

PART 4 • PERSONAL DEVELOPMENT

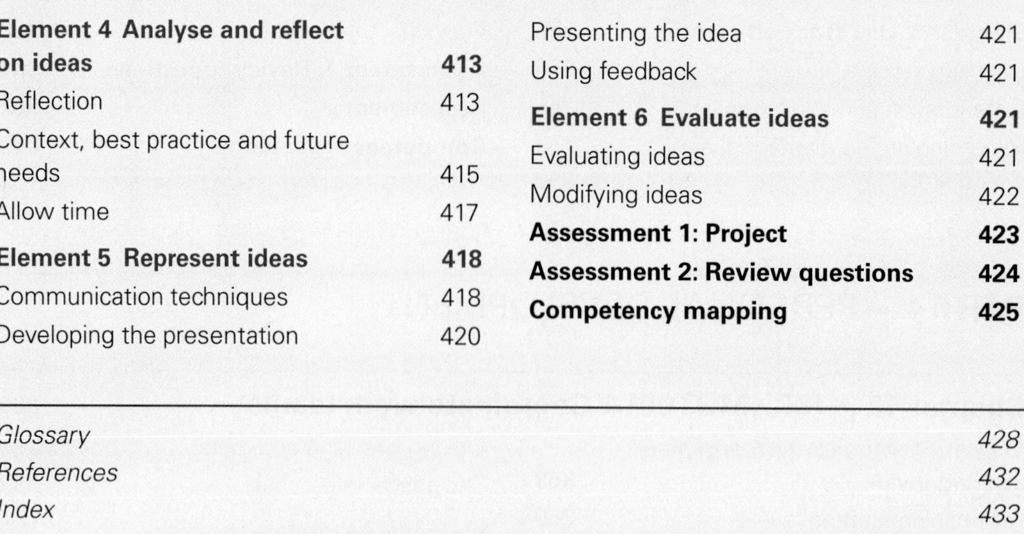

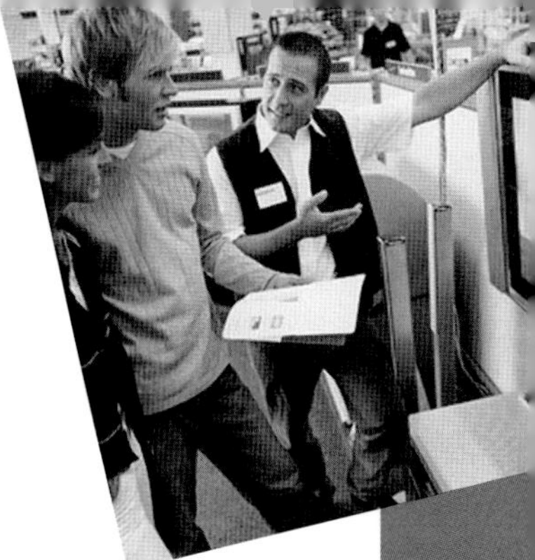

Preface

Retail has certainly changed in the last decade. While the bricks-and-mortar retailers had a modest increase of just 0.3 per cent in 2011, online and mail-order retail experienced a record turnover of an estimated $143 billion, a 15 per cent increase. M-commerce is now an attractive option for some 1.4 million Australians, choosing to shop on sites like eBay and Amazon via their mobile phones. So where does that leave the traditional retail shops we all grew up with?

The exciting news is that technology is not the enemy of bricks-and-mortar retail, but a companion to it. Australian retailers are reporting that while their online stores are performing well, new technology is making the in-store experience more inviting. The job of the 21st century retail employee is a collaborative effort between sales and inventory technology and good old-fashioned service.

Service is the cornerstone of a retail business. A good product line, convenient location, nicely presented store and effective stock controls will be less effective if the service experience is not up to customers' expectations. As a retail employee, the skills that set you apart are your abilities to listen, communicate empathetically, foster a safe and happy workplace, and solve complex customer problems. All of these 'soft skills' are drawn on daily and are the reasons behind the success of your workplace. You only need to put yourself in the position of a customer to realise the importance of a smile, a friendly response and accurate service.

Selling is a service, not just a verb. You don't sell *to* someone—they buy *from* you. Everything from your appearance, language and eye contact to your professionalism, product knowledge and experience are on sale. When a customer relates to you, they are more inclined to buy from you. The way you act and the attention you give to the smallest details will ultimately leave customers with a positive or negative experience; and retail profitability is *all* about repeat customers.

Retail can be a very satisfying career. Like any job, you get out of it what you put into it. So work safely, work with purpose, and above all, remember that your customers are the reason you are working. Happy retailing!

Lee Perlitz, Dr Dan Hill, Matthew Coxhill

Assessment information for trainers and assessors

Assessments in this text have been mapped to the units of competency from the January 2012 version release of SIRX07 Training Package. While every effort has been made to construct the assessments to apply to a broad range of contexts, ultimately you will have to make adjustments to meet the specific needs of your assessment candidates. Any adjustments will form the basis of a new version of the assessment for use at your RTO. As such, it is recommended that you keep copies of your contextualised assessments as per your RTO's compliance policy.

Acknowledgments

The authors would like to thank the following people for their contribution to this first edition of *Retail Services*:

- Amanda Hill, Terry Hill and Cheryl Henderson for their commitment to seeing the project completed.
- Local business owners and staff.
- J Harch, Liam Monaghan, Rachael Monaghan, Glen Kluck, Deajay Nielsen and Tania Murray for their feedback and participation.

In addition, McGraw-Hill would like to thank Deb Kerrison and the entire Retail team at the College of Retail Training in WA for reviewing the manuscript and providing invaluable feedback and advice throughout the creation of this textbook.

About the authors

Lee Perlitz

Lee Perlitz has more than 15 years experience as first a trainer and then director of several registered training organisations within the VET sector. Most recently Lee has run her own training and business consultancy, offering services such as compliance work for RTOs and writing assessments and resources to VET standards. She provides business mentoring and coaching to a variety of businesses, including retail operators, and in addition has spent many years working in sales and marketing, predominantly in the retail tourism sector. Lee is now the Skills Link Manager for the Queensland Tourism Industry Council, an organisation which has close links with Service Skills Australia. Lee can be contacted via www.lptraining.com.au.

Dan Hill

Dr Dan Hill has worked in the retail sector and in general business management for more than 16 years. His roles have ranged from sales, merchandising and buying to national sales management and general management with some of Australia's most respected retail and distribution organisations. He is the founder and CEO of SpecTraining, a registered training organisation in Queensland that specialises in the development of multimedia learning and assessment tools. Dan has an MBA and a PhD in the field of sociology and is co-author of *Vocational Training and Assessment*, (McGraw-Hill, 2011). Dan can be contacted at dan@spectraining.com.au.

Matthew Coxhill

Matthew Coxhill has broad management experience, having worked in management and training in various industries for more than 20 years. His roles have included sales and marketing, project management and general management positions and he is currently a director of Fishtail Education, a company which specialises in providing management, sales and business sustainability resources and training for a range of industries. Mattthew can be contacted at matthew@fishtail.com.au.

Online learning centre

www.mhhe.com/au/retail

The Online Learning Centre (OLC) that accompanies this text will help you get the most from your course. It provides a powerful learning experience beyond the printed page. Instructors have additional access to an instructor-specific resource area.

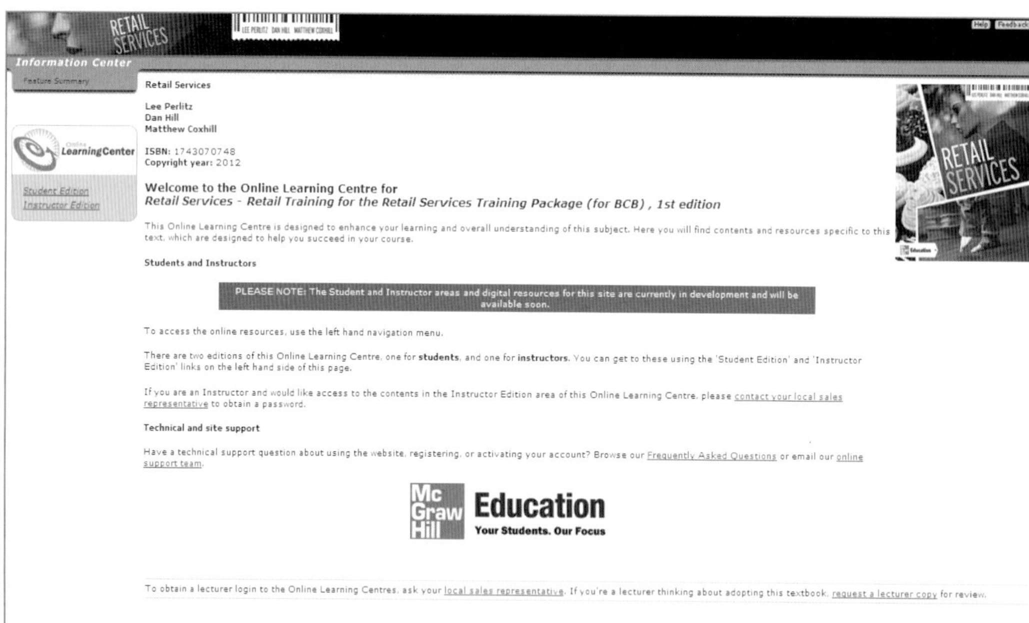

e-student

PowerPoint® presentations

A set of PowerPoint presentations summarise the key points of each chapter. They can be downloaded as a valuable revision aid.

RETAILSERVICES

Establish a rapport with customers

Learning outcomes

1.1 Establish rapport and relationship with customer and express a genuine interest in customer needs and requirements to enhance customer commitment, trust and credibility of store and to build return customer base.

1.2 Maintain professional ethics with the customer to promote store image and credibility.

1.3 Accurately clarify customer needs and preferences to maximise sales opportunities.

1.4 Maximise sales opportunities by use of add-on and complementary sales techniques

1.5 Give customer space and time to evaluate purchase decision, while using time to maximum advantage for customer and store.

1.6 Use effective methods to close sales.

Copyright © 2012 McGraw-Hill Australia Pty Ltd
PPTS to accompany Retail Services – Lee Perlitz, Dan Hill & Matthew Coxhill

CH 1 • 2

e-instructor

In addition to all student resources, instructors have additional password-protected access to:

Videos

These videos provide a practical insight into the Retail industry. They are ideally suited to enhancing practical skills by drawing together the underlying principles of the customer relationship.

Facilitator guide

The Facilitator guide provides practical assessment worksheets, which include instructions and observation checklists. It saves time for instructors and helps to provide consistency across teaching teams.

Artwork library

Illustrations and tables from the text are available in an online artwork library as digital image files. Instructors thus have the flexibility to use them in the format that best suits their needs.

eBook

To assist in flexible learning, *Retail Services* is available in print and eBook formats. Our eBooks enhance students' learning experience and assist with blended and e-learning strategies. Enjoy the convenience of accessing the eBook via computer, laptop or tablet, as well as interacting with the highlighting, note taking and search engine functionalities.

PART 1

Customer contact

Units covered in Part 1:

1. SIRXSLS303—Build relationships with customers
2. SIRXCOM101—Communicate in the workplace to support team and customer outcomes
3. SIRXIND101—Work effectively in a customer service environment.

Every business, no matter whether it is large or small, exists to make money. It makes money by selling its products or services to people who have specific requirements. These are customers.

How much money an organisation earns and how successful it is—and continues to be—depends entirely on how well it deals with customers and their specific requirements. There is no point in having a great location with fantastic products and competitive prices if the customer service component of the business is sub-standard. Customers wish to be acknowledged and treated with respect. They are willing to spend (often) substantial amounts of money to have their requirements met and if your organisation will not or cannot meet these requirements then they will find someone else who will.

Customer service is therefore the single most important aspect of any business and should never be neglected. However many businesses fail to fully understand the importance of this area of their operation and, as a consequence, lose customers to competitors with better service standards.

Figure 1.1 Poor customer service means sales may be lost

'**Excellence** is an art won by training and habituation. We do not act rightly because we have virtue or excellence, but we rather have those because we have acted rightly. We are what we repeatedly do. Excellence, then, is not an act but a habit.'—***Aristotle***

Always remember that while your organisation may be in business to earn money, without a steady flow of customers there is no business.

Looking after the customer should be the number one priority in any organisation. Staff must show an interest in their customers and take advantage of every possible opportunity to build a relationship with them to ensure that they keep coming back.

In Part 1 we will look at how to:

- build relationships with customers to keep them coming back
- interact with customers effectively
- promote and sell products and services to customers.

Note: as part of the activities and assessments in this course you will be required to put together a portfolio of useful information in various units of competency. This information will not only be a means of assessing your competence in the subject but will be a valuable resource that you can use and add to throughout your retail career.

Chapter 1

SIRXSLS303

Build relationships with customers

Customers are just people who come in to your shop or office and buy the things that you sell, aren't they? You're not trying to be their friends … it's unlikely you'll ever socialise with them … so why is it important to build a relationship with them?

A relationship is defined as 'the way in which two or more people or groups regard and behave towards each other' (see Oxford online dictionary—http://oxforddictionaries.com). What this means is that in order to build a positive relationship with a customer, a positive behavioural standard must be employed.

If your organisation is not interested in whether customers come back and do business with them on a regular basis, then building a positive relationship with them doesn't matter. If, on the other hand, your organisation cares about its image and reputation and wants customers to keep coming back and bringing their friends with them, then building positive relationships is essential.

Many organisations will spend substantial amounts of money on advertising and promoting their products and services—with some degree of success. Nothing, however, can compare with repeat business and word of mouth (**WOM**) recommendations—where a good customer will always shop with you and will bring their friends and family along too. Repeat business and WOM cost nothing (apart from initial relationship building) and have often proven to be the most effective form of advertising and promoting. It is a question of getting your customers to like dealing with you and spreading the word.

Good customer relationships are based on:

- honesty—can they believe what you are telling them?
- trust—do they believe you have their interests in mind?
- reliability—do you provide a consistent service and good quality products or services?

In this chapter we will look at how to establish long-lasting relationships with customers and give you the tools required to keep your customers coming back time and again.

ELEMENT 1
ESTABLISH RAPPORT WITH CUSTOMERS

The cornerstone to delivering customer service excellence is establishing a **rapport** and an ongoing relationship with customers. In establishing this rapport you are:

- showing a genuine interest in the customer's needs and expectations
- building up a level of commitment and credibility
- gaining their trust so that they will continue to do business with your organisation and
- ensuring the long-term future success of the organisation.

1.1 Establish rapport and relationship with customer and express a genuine interest in customer needs and requirements to enhance customer commitment, trust and credibility of store and to build return customer base.

1.2 Maintain professional ethics with the customer to promote store image and credibility.

1.3 Accurately clarify customer needs and preferences to maximise sales opportunities.

1.4 Maximise sales opportunities by use of add-on and complementary sales techniques.

1.5 Give customer space and time to evaluate purchase decision, while using time to maximum advantage for customer and store.

1.6 Use effective methods to close sales.

LEARNING OUTCOMES

LO

Who is the customer?

Before we look at what it takes to establish rapport and ongoing relationships with customers, let us first examine who a customer actually is.

A customer is someone who has a specific requirement for a product or service and seeks out a business that is likely to have that product or service in order to satisfy that requirement. Customers can be:

- new or prospective contacts—people who have not done business with you before but have the potential to do so. These people may be recommended to you by existing customers, may see your ads or promotional materials or may simply walk in off the street
- repeat customers—people who do business with your organisation regularly. It is important to keep these customers happy as they have a substantial influence on your business's continued success

- external and internal customers
  - External customers are people who come from outside your organisation and have no direct links with it. They simply walk in, off the street, or phone in with their needs. An external customer pays real money for your product, a fact that shows up on the organisation's bottom line.
  - Internal customers are, more often than not, people who work for or with the organisation. For example, employees who may receive products at a greatly reduced price, or as part of their employment benefits. Internal customers can also be other departments within the organisation—where goods or services are 'transferred' between departments and no money changes hands.

Now that we know who a customer is, how do we establish a rapport with them?

No matter who they are, each customer should be treated equally with care, courtesy and respect. The aim is to establish an atmosphere that a customer is happy to return to on a regular basis. Repeat customers are an excellent source of steady income and word of mouth **referrals** to other potential customers. Creating a harmonious relationship with others can be accomplished in a few simple steps as follows:

1. Be aware of your body language—Remember that people will not only listen to what you are saying but will also watch your actions and gestures, so keep any gestures you make and your tone of voice positive and friendly. Communication skills (including **non-verbal**) will be covered in detail in Element 5.
2. Create harmony with the customer by 'matching and mirroring' their own gestures—Mirroring the customer's gestures and tone of voice means behaving towards them in a way that makes them feel more comfortable. For example:
   - If they are soft spoken then don't speak to them in a loud voice—match their tone.
   - If they look as if they need space, then don't crowd in on them—give them room.
   - If they speak slowly then don't chatter away at a rapid pace—slow your speech pace down to match theirs.

   By matching their behaviour you are offering them a comfort zone—an atmosphere in which they can feel confident in their dealings with you. Opposing behaviour (speaking loudly and quickly if they are shy, retiring and soft-spoken people) will turn a customer off and you may lose not only a sale but the opportunity to build a long-term relationship with them. They simply will not like dealing with you.
3. Use excellent communication skills—As communication skills will be covered in detail in Element 5 we will look at this only briefly here. Establishing a positive rapport with customers depends to a large extent on how well you communicate with them. For example:
   - How interested are you in what they are saying?
   - Does your body language reflect that interest?
   - Are you genuinely interested in assisting them?
   - Are you actively seeking open communication?

This last point is very important. The type of questions you ask a customer can determine how well you establish a rapport with them. For example:

Table 1.1

Customer questions	
Do say:	**Don't say:**
What can I help you with today?	Are you right?
What in particular are you searching for?	That top is too expensive for you!
What size do you normally wear?	We don't have your size here.
How can I help you?	I'll be right over here if you need a hand.

Ignoring a customer completely when they walk in to your store is also a sign of bad communication. A smile and a friendly hello is all that is needed to make them feel welcome.

The most important thing to remember is that when all things are considered, the customer is the sole provider of every business. They represent the **revenue stream** that pays for everything else: your wages, rent for the premises, phone bills, stock, security, insurance just to name a few. You can have the very best products or services, have great accountants and managers to look after the business but this all means nothing without a steady revenue stream. This revenue stream is directly linked to all sales made and nothing happens until something is sold—to a customer. So making sure that the customer is happy with your products and services is vital to the success of the business.

Task 1.1

Over the next few days make an effort to establish a rapport with people you meet in shops or people at work that you don't know very well. Answer the following questions.

1. What methods of establishing a rapport did you use?
2. How successful were you? What worked well? What didn't work?
3. Discuss the impact that having a good rapport with people in your workplace will have on the working environment.

Professional and ethical behaviour

Establishing a rapport with customers is only part of what is necessary to build lasting relationships. It is also very important to present a professional and ethical image of both yourself and your organisation at all times. In developing professional and **ethical behaviour** you should:

Be personable, but not overly familiar

This means that you should act in a friendly manner towards customers without getting too 'chummy'. It is easy to cross the line with customers and say things that might be offensive so be friendly, but not best friends!

Use positive statements

It is important to always portray a positive image of yourself, your organisation and your organisation's products and services.

Never make negative comments about your organisation or its management to customers as this gives them a bad impression.

Using positive statements also means keeping a positive attitude about any situation or problem that may arise; customers do not want to hear what you can't do, they are more interested in what you can do. They are also not interested in what company policy states—they want to know how you can help them, so keep the conversation friendly and aimed at finding a solution that is acceptable to both the organisation and the customer.

Be honest in your dealings

Honesty in answering customer questions is critical in establishing long-term relationships.

- If you don't know the answer to a question then say so and tell the customer that you will find out for them.
- Never make up an answer as customers will (generally) believe what you tell them and will distrust you if what you have told them turns out to be incorrect or false.
- If a product or service does not perform a function that the customer requires, do not tell them that it does simply to get the sale. Such behaviour is not only unethical, but it could lead to customers making negative comments about your organisation to all of their friends and potentially to legal action being taken against you.

Use only confirmed appraisals of products and services

This follows on from the previous point in that you should only use correct and accurate information about the products and services you sell. Confirmed information and appraisals will generally come from the product manuals or from the supplier or manufacture.

Comply with requirements

Always make sure that you follow any organisational policies and procedures, and comply with any legislative requirements.

Dress and act professionally

It has been said that it takes a mere ten seconds for a person to form an opinion of you. They will look at you: how you are dressed and how you present yourself and will form an initial impression. They will then spend the next five minutes confirming that first impression. So when you first meet someone they will have formed an initial idea of whether they like you or not based almost solely on your dress and presentation—you have not yet had a chance to say a word. How you dress and act will, of course, depend on your work environment:

- You may be required to wear a uniform—in which case your organisation has complete control of your outward presentation and all staff will be presenting the 'corporate' image.

- The industry you are in may have varying degrees of formality. For example if you work in a surf shop your dress and customer approach may well be much more relaxed than if you worked in an up-market boutique where a single piece of clothing costs more than many people earn in a week.
- You may be required to work in settings that are industry related. For example working in a nursery—dealing with plants—may mean that you will need to wear outdoor clothing and boots. When working with food you will be required to observe strict hygiene regulations and will need to wear appropriate clothing: shoes, caps or gloves to ensure cleanliness.

Figure 1.2 Well dressed professional

In any case, customers will expect to see personal presentation in line with the industry they are dealing with and they will expect professionalism.

Useful websites:

Know This.com

www.knowthis.com/principles-of-marketing-tutorials/managing-customers/what-is-a-customer/

Ezine articles

**http://ezinearticles.com/?Interview-Questions---How-Do-I-Make-a-Great-FIRST-Impression-in-the-Interview?&id=2867390*

Task 1.2

1. Give at least two examples each of ethical and unethical behaviour that you have observed in a store (or that you have been involved in).

Ethical behaviour	
Unethical behaviour	

2. Discuss in each situation how this individual person's actions have impacted on their organisation.

Clarifying the customer's needs and preferences

In order to provide the best possible service to customers you must first understand their exact needs and requirements. It is relatively easy to talk a customer into buying specific products and more experienced sales people can even talk customers into buying things they don't really need. This type of selling however is negative as customers may walk out of your shop or office feeling as if they've been pressured and this may stop them from coming back. It is important to talk to customers to find out what they want and then to match your own products and services to those requirements.

This subject will be discussed in more detail in Chapter 7, Element 4. In brief however, customer needs and requirements can be clarified through:

- observation—watching what they are looking at as they wander through the shop
- appropriate questioning—asking the right kind of questions so that their needs are clearly understood
- active listening—actually listening to what they are saying as opposed to thinking about what you are going to try and sell them
- reassurance and confirmation—clarifying your understanding of what they have said to you. You can do this by restating what you have said or asking clarifying questions.

Then, too, clarifying their needs may involve understanding their specific preferences. Sometimes a customer may be a member of a loyalty club where they earn points or get discounts so they will always want to buy that specific product or brand. They may also simply prefer one product over another. Asking questions effectively can bring out any preferences they may have.

Briefly, customer needs and preferences may include:

- product type—for example, they may prefer Muesli over Weetbix, or sports wear over more corporate formal clothing
- brand—they may prefer Kellogg's over Uncle Toby's brand products, or Nike shoes over Converse
- size—they may prefer large economy-size packs for a family over a smaller sized package for a single person
- customer physical needs—they may require products or services that address physical needs, such as labels that include Braille text for the vision impaired, or safety caps on bottles for families with very small children, or special clothing or shoes for people with physical disabilities
- price—some people prefer to spend more to get lasting value while others may be on limited budgets and need to keep spending to a minimum.

All of these things, among others, must be clarified and understood before a product recommendation can realistically and successfully be made.

Maximising sales opportunities

In addition to understanding the customer's needs and requirements you must also—always—bear in mind that the organisation needs to make sales in order to remain successful. Sales of products and services are used to pay rent on the shop or office premises, staff wages, utility bills such as electricity, gas and phone and purchase of raw materials or stock for the shop so making the most of every sales opportunity is vitally important. Maximising sales opportunities could include:

Add on or complementary products and services

These are items that 'complement' (add to and fit with) the main product or service being purchased. For example, most often when you buy a hamburger at McDonalds they will ask, 'Do you want fries or a drink with that?' The fries and drinks are complementary products.

Selling up or down

This means selling the customer either something more expensive or even less expensive than they have originally asked for. For example:

- selling up—if the customer is buying a television you could try and sell them a bigger set, or one with more functions in order to earn more revenue for your organisation
- selling down—the same customer looking at televisions may walk away from the purchase if it is too expensive. In this case you could offer a set that is also very good but less expensive: it may be a smaller screen size, or it could have fewer functions. The idea is to still make the sale—even if it is worth less revenue.

Preferred products

Depending on the industry you are in, you may have a selection of 'preferred products'. These are products offered by your suppliers for which they will pay you a bonus or commission depending on the number of sales of that product that you make. For example Brand X supplier will pay you a bonus of 10 per cent of your sales if you sell at least 100 of these items whereas Brand Y supplier does not pay a bonus. It will therefore be your organisation's policy to sell Brand X over all other suppliers. Of course, if the customer specifically asks for a different brand then you must sell this to them.

Task 1.3

Choose three products or services from your own organisation or a local store and research them thoroughly. You will need this information for future tasks and assessments. Based on the three products you chose determine what complementary products or services you might be able to offer a customer. Also note how you might up-sell or down-sell these products or services.

Product	Complementary	Up-sell	Down-sell
1.			
2.			
3.			

Giving the customer space and time

Having made product recommendations in line with the customer's needs, you should then give them the time to consider your suggestions without pressuring them. Don't crowd or push them or you may lose the sale. Customers who feel under pressure could leave without making any purchase at all, or complain to your management. An unhappy customer can also impact on the organisation's image and reputation by making negative comments about you to their friends and families.

A purchase can often be very expensive and the customers will need time to justify the expense to themselves. Among other things, they will consider what the risks are in going ahead with the purchase, what would happen if the purchase goes wrong, whether they really need the product or could do without it, and whether they can trust the sales person selling them the product.

Taking a step back from them at this point will give them the time they need to be sure of their decision. This will also give them time to consider any additional or complementary products or services that you may have suggested.

CASE STUDY

Jemma Potts was moving in to her own flat for the very first time. She was very excited and was looking forward to going out and buying all the items she would need to set up her new home. Her parents provided her with some furniture and other items to get her started but she needed new towels, sheets and doonas for her bathroom and bedroom.

A week before she was due to move in to her new flat, she went to a local department store and, with a shop attendant's help, chose the items she thought she would need—they amounted to around $450 which was at the top of what she had budgeted. The shop attendant continued to bring out more and more items showing Jemma how well made they were and telling her that these items were essential for any household. Jemma told the attendant that she had reached her financial limit but nevertheless accepted some of the extra items.

The attendant continued to push for more sales and disregarded the non-verbal signs that Jemma was becoming frustrated and angry.

Despite Jemma's continued protests that she did not want any more items and that she was ready to pay, the shop attendant kept going—with the final result that Jemma walked out of the store without buying anything at all. In the end, not only did the shop attendant lose the sale but Jemma never went in to that store again.

Task 1.4

Using the above case study as your basis answer the following questions:

1. Why do you think the sales attendant lost the sale when everything was going so well?
2. What did the sales attendant do wrong?
3. How would you approach this sales situation? For example:
   a. How would you would go about finding out Jemma's needs and expectations?
   b. What behaviour would you display to show Jemma that you are willing to give her time and space to make choices and decisions?

Closing the sale

This subject will be dealt with in detail in Chapter 7. Briefly, however, when customers are ready to make the purchase they will, normally, send out non-verbal **buying signals**. They will, for example:

- get out their purse or wallet
- talk about the price
- ask about purchasing options
- ask when the product could be delivered
- move towards the cashier or register
- carry the item around the store with them
- talk about warranty.

These and other signals are signs that it is time to stop the 'selling' process and close the sale. If you keep trying to sell products beyond this point you may very well find that the customer will walk out—as in the case study above.

When you notice that the customer is ready to make the purchase you can ask questions to close the sale. For example:

- 'How will you be paying for this?'
- 'Would you like me to book that service for you now?'
- 'Shall I wrap that for you?'

You can also use silence to close a sale. When you have presented all the necessary information, stand back and let them decide.

To summarise

Establishing a rapport with customers is a question of showing a genuine interest in what they have to say, maintaining a professional and ethical image at all times and providing them with the products and services that match their requirements.

ELEMENT 2
APPLY EXPERT KNOWLEDGE

Over time you will become very knowledgeable about the products and services your organisation offers. Even though, during your first weeks in a new job, it may not seem so, the process of gathering knowledge and expertise can be surprisingly swift. This knowledge will grow and expand as you gain a greater understanding of your industry and as products or services change.

Product knowledge is an enormous asset that, if applied effectively, can mean the difference between a sale or not … or between a long-term relationship with a customer … or not.

Figure 1.3 Providing advice on products

LEARNING OUTCOMES

2.1 Provide customer with accurate information regarding product and service appraisals, correct statements and warranties according to legislative requirements.

2.2 Provide detailed knowledge of supplier or manufacturer information according to customer needs and commercial confidentiality guidelines.

2.3 Evaluate product range, accurately demonstrate features and benefits of products or services where appropriate and make recommendations to the customer to maximise sales potential.

2.4 Maximise customer interest in product or service through price negotiation where applicable and offer payment and credit options according to store policy.

2.5 Accurately calculate prices and discounts according to pricing determinants and store policy.

Providing accurate information

Accurate and reliable information is vital if customers are to make effective decisions. It is an essential component of any effort to influence customers in making decisions different to the ones they might have made had this information not been available. In the absence of accurate and reliable information people may make bad decisions which will lead to dissatisfaction, complaints and a loss of business.

In the previous section we looked at how to build a rapport with customers and learned that honesty and credibility were a large part of that process. Providing accurate information not only goes a long way towards building that credibility, it is also a **legal requirement**. You should never exaggerate what a product or service can do for the customer or tell them outright lies in order to make the sale. This is not only dishonest but could, under certain circumstances, lead to serious problems and to legal action being taken against you.

Providing accurate information means advising customers about a range of issues.

Transport, storage and handling of goods

This means advising the customer of the best way to transport their new purchase. For example, a fridge *must* be transported upright—it cannot be laid down on its back or side. Some audio or visual equipment must be transported in such a way as not to damage screens or other delicate equipment. You must also provide information about how a product should be stored. For example certain chemicals are poisonous and must be stored in a safe and secure manner. There may be specific hygiene instructions that must be followed when handling products, and so on.

Warranties

Many products, such as electrical equipment, offer 'warranties'. A warranty is a guarantee: a written assurance that some product or service will be provided or will meet certain specifications. It includes the assurance that, should the product or service *not* meet the specified requirements then the customer can expect an exchange or refund from the manufacturer or supplier. It is part of your role to explain the warranty details to customers so that they are aware of what recourse is available to them should the need arise.

Terms and conditions of sale

This relates to practical and legal issues. For example the terms and conditions of sale might address the following issues:

- how to return or exchange damaged or faulty goods
- warranty information including limitations of liability
- how and when the goods will be delivered
- what, if any, payment conditions apply.

An excellent example of a terms and conditions paper can be found at: www.taylormarine.com/conditions/index.html.

Full disclosure

It is a legal requirement that the customer be made aware of any issues, problems or conditions under which their purchase must be used. For example, some clothing items may shrink or discolour if not handled correctly. Customers must be made aware of how to wash and care for these items.

LEGISLATIVE REQUIREMENTS

Providing accurate information also means addressing any legislative requirements.

Almost every business, regardless of whether it is in the retail sector, hospitality, trades or professional industries, will be bound by government legislation of some sort. Government legislation will cover a range of different industries and issues and these have been put in place to safeguard not only the customer but the organisation and its staff as well.

This legislation will often give specific direction on how business is to be conducted within a given industry and organisation's belonging to that industry must comply with the regulations outlined there. These become part of the organisation's policies.

The Competition and Consumer Act (CCA) and fair trading laws

The *Competition and Consumer Act 2010,* (formerly the *Trade Practices Act*) is an act of the Parliament of Australia and applies to almost every aspect of a business. It covers such things as:

- advertising and marketing ethics
- price setting
- ethical conduct by the business operator
- consumer protection
- warranties.

Each state also has laws relating to unfair trading practices and these must also be observed (see Chapter 5).

Many organisations have compliance programmes that help them to identify and reduce the risk of breaches of the CCA. So when offering customers advice about products and services the Act must be kept in mind. This means being open and honest about the products or services, disclosing any negative features, explaining the safe use of the product, use-by dates and so on.

Environmental protection legislation

This means providing information about potential hazards involved with the use of the product or service. For example:

- safe disposal of chemicals
- what hazardous materials might have been used in the manufacture of the product
- water consumption levels needed by the product or service
- advice on waste management or recycling of the product.

Workplace Health and Safety (WHS)

This is related to the above point and covers issues dealing with health and safety in the workplace. For example:

- how to deal with security issues
- what to do in the event of accident or illness in the workplace
- maintaining a safe and secure workplace
- the responsibilities of both the employer and employee.

Privacy laws

Maintaining confidentiality of both the organisation's and the customer's details is mandatory. Giving away confidential information on your company or your customers can result in instant dismissal and legal action being taken against you.

Liquor and tobacco laws

Some industries, like the hospitality industry, are subject to legislation regarding the sale of tobacco and liquor and it is extremely important for staff working in these areas to know the governing laws. For example, it is against the law to sell alcohol or tobacco to persons under the age of 18 and organisations in breach of this law can be subject to heavy fines—they could even lose their liquor or tobacco licence. Then, too, smoking is prohibited in most public places today. So if you are employed in an industry that sells alcohol or tobacco such as a bottle shop, duty free shop or gift shop, or an organisation that serves food or alcohol, you must be aware of and comply with this legislation.

Task 1.5

1. Using the products you have previously researched find out if there are any legislative issues that need to be considered when selling those products or services.
2. Research your own organisation's products and services and collect any information on legislative requirements that apply. Keep this information in your portfolio.
3. Describe any WHS requirements that involve the products you have researched in terms of information you must supply to the customer, or how the products must be handled.

Sources of product knowledge

Providing accurate information means gathering knowledge and this can be accomplished in a variety of ways including reading through brochures and catalogues, talking to colleagues and customers, researching products and services on the internet among other methods. We will look at sources of information in detail in Chapter 7.

Providing detailed knowledge of supplier or manufacturer

There will be times when your customers may want information about the supplier or manufacturer of the products you sell. Reasons for this may be to enquire directly about:

- warranty claims
- return of products directly to the supplier (for repair or replacement)
- information about delivery of the product
- making complaints about the product or service.

Before providing supplier details to customers however it is necessary to consider the confidentiality and legal issues involved.

Sometimes, it will be permitted to provide this information. With large, well known manufacturers, their details are supplied with their product. For example all Toshiba products come packed in boxes that disclose company details. Smaller manufacturers may allow the organisations they supply to pass on their details so potential customers can contact them for after-sales service or additional accessories.

Sometimes it is not allowed to provide supplier information. For example, there may be a contract between the supplier and the distributor (your organisation) which specifies that the product be branded with the distributor's logo, giving the impression that it is an 'in house' product. Small suppliers, with no infrastructure to deal with direct customers, will rely on distributors to be their 'public face' and the agreement between the two companies will specify what information can be made public and what cannot.

As previously mentioned, confidentiality is an important consideration and needs to be weighed up against the customer's need access this information. You should always be guided by your organisation's policies in these issues.

Task 1.6

Project

1. Continuing to build knowledge and information on the products and services you have researched so far. Find information on:
   a. warranties
   b. how it is manufactured or produced (where possible)
   c. the uses of the product or service, flexibility and optional extras
   d. any legislative or WHS issues surrounding that product or service, its manufacturer or provider.
2. Add this information to your fact sheets on these products or services.

Evaluating product range

Evaluating product ranges and matching the right product or service to the right customer is a matter of knowing your product well, and you will learn this over time. Evaluating product range means considering:

1. the type of customer you are dealing with and what their specific needs and expectations are
2. the products or services that your organisation offers
3. how these products and services match up with what the customer wants
4. presenting the appropriate product or service to the customer by explaining how the product or service meets their requirements.

No two people are alike and the products that may suit one person, may not suit another. People will make choices based on their:

- economic background—some customers will not consider the price of an item, while others may be more budget conscious
- social background—trends and peer pressure can often influence a customer's choice of product or service

- age—young people will often have different tastes and requirements from more senior customers
- family status—a young single person may also have very different needs from a family with children
- physical or mental ability—the choice of product or service can also be influenced by a customer's physical or mental ability.

In every industry and sector of retail there are countless products and options, something to suit every taste and every customer. It is your job to find out exactly what it is that your customer wants and then find the right product for them.

If you listen carefully to what the customer is saying, ask questions to gain information and clarify your understanding, and watch the customer's body language you should have all the information you need to provide the customer with exactly what they want.

Features and benefits

As a rule customers are only interested in satisfying their needs and desires. They need to know what **benefit** a product will be to them and it is up to you to explain how your products or services will meet their needs. Every product has a range of **features** that most sales people go to great lengths to explain. Features are what a product or service has. Discussing only the features of a product or service however can be confusing to the customer.

Using the Apple iPod classic as an example; it has 160 GB of storage, a 2.5 inch (6.4 cm) display screen, it can shuffle your music and has a 'genius feature'. But what exactly does all that mean to the customer? What's in it for them? What benefit does the feature provide? You would need to translate the features of the product into something the customer can relate to. For example:

Table 1.2

Product features and benefits

Feature	Benefit
160 GB of storage	You can store up to 40 000 songs ... you never need to change CDs again! You can also store up to 200 hours of video and 25 000 photos, so all of your music and photos can be stored on a very small device that you can easily carry around with you.
6.4 cm (diagonal) display screen	Large screen size means you can easily look at photos and videos any time, any where
Shuffle option	Means you can either listen to songs or view pictures in the order you loaded them ... or have them shuffle for a different experience each time.
Genius feature	Genius finds other songs on your iPod classic that sound great with the one you're listening to, then makes a playlist for you. This means that you can listen to lots of songs that are similar to each other without having to sort them yourself.

A customer must be made aware of the features of a product, but while knowing the features of a product or service is very important, it is equally important to explain how these features will benefit the customer. Doing this well, can actually make the difference between getting the sale, or not.

Think about all the computer advertisements you see in the newspapers. They are full of features. To anyone but an avid computer user, the advertisement in Figure 1.4 might as well be in Latin. It is full of product features but no benefits.

BOLTEO 230X

- Intel I3 Processor. (2.93 GHz/1066 Mhz FSB/3 MB Cache)
- Genuine Windows 7 Professional 32 Bit
- 4 GB Dual Channel DDR3 SDRAM at 1333 MHz
- 320 GB SATA hard drive (RPM) (7200 RPM)
- Integrated Intel Graphics Media Accelerator X4500HD

Figure 1.4 Example of a computer advertisement

Why is it a good thing that this computer has Intel I3 processor or that it has 4GB dual channel DDR3? If you don't tell the customer what this means to them in terms of benefits, they won't buy it.

People don't buy products or services for what they are, they buy them for what they can do for them.

Features and benefits will be discussed in greater details in Chapter 7.

Maximising customer interest

A large part of a retail assistant's role is to make it easy for the customer to make the purchase decision. One of the best ways of doing this is to keep them interested in the products or services you are offering. You can do this by:

- involving them in the sales process—this means asking questions and listening to what the customer is saying. In the previous section we discussed evaluating and matching products to customer requirements. To maximise their interest in a product or service you need to continually match your product choice back to the customer's stated needs. For example: 'you mentioned that you want to be able to listen to music without always having to change CDs all the time. Our "music-maker" allows you to load thousands of songs into a single device so you never need to change CDs. You can even choose how and what you listen to by using the easy-to-use menu screen'
- letting them have a go—if the product you are suggesting requires a demonstration, let them have a try and show them how the various functions (if applicable) work
- providing background information—give the customer interesting information about the product or service: where it comes from, company background (for example, 'the company has been around for 120 years')
- giving them testimonials—tell the customer of others who have used the product or service and how they used or liked it.

Keeping a customer interested in a product or service is not difficult if you ask the right questions, listen to the answers and put forward products and services that match what they have asked for.

Overcoming objections

Objections often come from the customer not fully understanding (or wanting) what you have suggested. Equally it could happen because you have not fully understood or clarified their needs. If objections arise during the sales process you may need to ask further questions to underpin or clarify the customer's exact requirements and then either amend your product suggestion or explain how the product you are offering matches up with what they have asked for.

If you have conscientiously asked effective questions and listened to the answers you are given, if you know your product range well and can match the customer's needs to one of your products, then objections should be very rare. If they do nevertheless occur then it may be because the customer was only gathering initial information and had not intended to make a purchase at this time. In these cases thank the customer for their enquiry and assure them that you will be ready to help them when they do decide to make the purchase.

Accurately calculate prices and discounts

A business needs to make a **profit**. It can only do this if it successfully makes a sale. Unfortunately, in the process of making that sale, the business will also have expenses that need to be met and these expenses represent the cost of providing a product or service. The cost of providing a product or service takes into consideration:

- manufacturing and raw materials
- staff wages
- rent of premises and equipment
- and other running costs.

To the cost of providing or producing the product or service is added a profit margin. This could be a percentage or a set amount. For example the cost price of a product might be \$100. The organisation may choose to add a profit margin of 25 per cent on top of the \$100 cost price, or they may add the set amount of \$20.

So in the first instance the cost price is 'increased' by 25 per cent—the calculation is: \$100 × 1.25 = \$125. If the percentage profit margin was 36 per cent then the calculation would be: \$100 × 1.36 = \$136. If the cost price was \$124.75 and the profit margin was to be 15 per cent the calculation would be: \$124.75 × 1.15 = \$143.46.

In the second instance you simply add the set amount to the cost price. For example if the cost price was \$46.98 and management decided to add a profit margin designed to even out the price and keep pace with market trends and requirements they may add a set amount of \$8.02 making the sale price of the item \$55.

How big the profit margin is will be determined by individual organisations. The organisation, however, must keep in mind market trends and how much people will be prepared to pay (in general) for a given item. There is no point in adding a large profit margin only to find out that this makes your product much more expensive than your competitors—no one will buy it.

Task 1.7

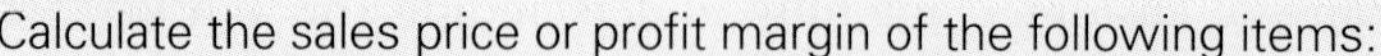

Calculate the sales price or profit margin of the following items:

Cost price	Profit margin	Sales price (show your calculations)
$2.05	15%	
$275.60	45%	
$45.80	20%	
$176.98		$220.00

The profit margin added to a product or service can, sometimes, be used to give discounts or make special offers. Some reasons for offering discounts or special prices could include:

- trade pricing—special discounts or prices given to people in related trades. For example hardware stores will often give special prices to carpenters or painters
- staff discounts—for people who work for the organisation. Staff discounts can often also be extended to the family members of staff
- loyalty programs—such as frequent flyer clubs, flybuys and other such programs. Loyalty programs offer customers the opportunity to accrue points for each purchase they make and when enough points have been accumulated, they can exchange these for products or services
- price matching—some organisations offer to match prices if a customer can prove that they have seen the same product with a competitor at a lower price
- special offers—often an organisation will run promotions to:
  - launch new products and services
  - attract new customers
  - sell old, out of season stock.

  In these situations the organisation will sell products at heavily discounted prices or will make offers of 'Buy 1, get 1 free' and so on.

- discontented customers—discounts and promotional items can also be used when dealing with discontented and complaining customers. It is never a good idea to offer discounts as a matter of course (see 'point to consider' below), but if a complaint is serious enough, a discount or special offer may appease the customer and help retain the organisation's good reputation. An offer of discount or special considerations should always be approved by your manager or supervisor.

A POINT TO CONSIDER

Promoting a particular product by selling it at a discounted price is not always a good idea. Discounts can cost your organisation more than you might think. Taking into consideration the costs of producing the product or offering the service, you can see from the table on the right, that with every percentage point that you give away in discount you are eating into your profit margin and therefore earning less money.

So if you were selling a product with a sale price of $500 at a 20 per cent discount, you would only be earning $400 and giving away $100. As profit margins can, sometimes, be quite small it is very important to calculate the sales price—or determine a discount level—very accurately. The organisation's management would not be very happy if, in our 20 per cent discount example above, the cost price of producing the product was $400 as you would have made no profit on the sale.

Table 1.3

Discounts and profit margins

Discount	5%	10%	15%	20%	25%
Sale price $	**$**	**$**	**$**	**$**	**$**
50.00	47.50	45.00	42.50	40.00	37.50
100.00	95.00	90.00	85.00	80.00	75.00
150.00	142.50	135.00	127.50	120.00	112.50
200.00	190.00	180.00	170.00	160.00	150.00
250.00	237.50	225.00	212.50	200.00	187.50
300.00	285.00	270.00	255.00	240.00	225.00
350.00	332.50	315.00	297.50	280.00	262.50
500.00	475.00	450.00	425.00	400.00	375.00
1000.00	950.00	900.00	850.00	800.00	750.00

GST

In addition to the above considerations it is also essential to remember that most goods and services in Australia attract a Goods and Services Tax (GST). The GST is a broad-based tax of 10 per cent on the supply of most goods, services and anything else consumed in Australia. GST is paid at each step in the supply chain, with businesses charging GST in the price of goods, services or anything else they supply. 'Supply chain' refers to the various stages a product or service goes through from initial production to the end consumer. For example an item of clothing may follow this path:

1. The cotton grower—grows the cotton and sells it to a spinning mill. The cotton grower adds GST to the price of the raw cotton.
2. The spinning mill—turns the raw cotton into yarn which is sold to fabric manufactures. The spinning mill adds GST to the price of the yarn.
3. The fabric manufacturer (or weaver)—uses the yarn to make fabric and sells it to a design house or clothing manufacturer. They add GST to the price of the fabric.

4. The clothing manufacturer—uses the fabric to make clothes and sells them to department stores or retail outlets. The manufacturer adds GST to the (wholesale) price of the clothes.
5. The retail store—sells clothes to the general public. They add GST to the (retail) price of the clothes.

If an organisation is registered for GST, it can claim input tax credits from the Australian Taxation Office, for any GST included in the price paid for goods, services or anything else bought for the business. This means that the GST liability flows along the supply chain and is actually included in the price paid by the consumer, who cannot claim input tax credits.

However, for GST registered organisations the liability to pay GST rests on the supplier of goods and services, not on the consumer. In other words, even if the business does not include the GST in the price of goods and services supplied, it is still liable to pay it to the ATO.

Table 1.4

Business example

Supply of goods	GST flows	GST collected
Lawrie, a timber merchant, sells timber to Trish, a furniture manufacturer, for $220 (including $20 GST).	Lawrie pays the $20 GST to the ATO.	$20.00
Trish uses the timber to make a table and sells it to Gus, a furniture retailer, for $440 (including $40 GST).	Trish is entitled to an input tax credit for the $20 GST included in the price paid to Lawrie. She offsets this $20 against the $40 payable on the supply of the table to Gus and pays $20 to the ATO.	$20.00
Gus sells the table to Owen, a consumer, for $550 (including $50 GST).	Gus is entitled to an input tax credit for the $40 GST included in the price paid to Trish. He offsets this $40 against the $50 GST payable on the supply of the table to Owen and pays $10 to the ATO.	$10.00
Owen purchased the table for $550.	Owen bears the full costs of the $50 GST as consumers cannot claim input tax credits.	Total:$50.00

Source: Adapted from ATO publication 'Guide to GST', www.ato.gov.au/businesses/distributor.aspx?menuid=0&doc=/content/00221985.htm&page=2#P36_2696.

From the consumer's point of view, if they wanted to work out how much GST they are paying for their goods and services they would divide the cost of the item by 11 which gives them the 10 per cent GST amount.

EXAMPLE: GOODS

Tom buys a watch for $110. This price includes 10 per cent GST. If Tom wants to work out how much GST was included in the price of the watch, he divides $110 by 11. This means the amount of GST Tom paid was $10.

EXAMPLE: SERVICES

Sue has her hair cut by a professional hairdresser for $33. This price includes 10 per cent GST. If Sue wants to work out how much GST was included in the price of the haircut service, she divides $33 by 11. This means the amount of GST Sue paid was $3.

GST exemptions

There are some types of supplies that are not subject to GST. These are called GST-free supplies and input taxed supplies. If a supply is GST-free, GST cannot be charged on the supply, but input tax credits may be available for anything acquired or imported for use in the enterprise.

GST-free supplies include, but are not limited to:

- most food
- exports
- most health services
- most educational supplies
- most child care services
- non-commercial activities of charities.

You Tube Video: *http://youtube/nBHMJgm7jZU, GST Basics—how to charge GST properly, from www.smallbusinessworks.com.au/index.php?*

Payment plans

For high priced items or where customers are on a limited budget many stores will offer a number of options to pay for the product or service in instalments. These options include:

LAY-BY

A 'lay-by' is essentially a contract where the customer pays a business for a product over a period of time rather than up front. With a lay-by agreement, the customer pays an initial deposit, followed by a given number of payments. The goods are held by the business owner until the customer has fully paid for them. A lay-by agreement must be in writing and should specify all the terms and conditions surrounding the lay-by of the goods, including any termination charge. If the customer decides to cancel a lay-by, the business may charge a termination fee but must refund all the money paid except for the termination charge. Of themselves, a business can only cancel a lay-by agreement if:

- the customer has breached a term of the agreement (such as missing a scheduled payment)
- they are no longer trading or
- the goods are no longer available due to circumstances outside the trader's control.

HIRE PURCHASE

Hire purchase is similar to lay-by in that the customer can pay for the product or service over a given period of time, but has the advantage in that the customer may use the goods while paying for them. They do not, however, own the products or services until they have been fully paid for. Hire purchase agreements are a great deal more complex than lay-by agreements, as the customer is granted access to the goods while paying for them. As the store is, essentially, extending credit to the customer, a full credit check is made and, subject to approval by whatever finance company is backing the hire purchase agreement, the customer can go ahead with the purchase and take the goods home.

Fees and charges

Fees or charges are sometimes applied for an additional service provided. For example, when a customer applies for store credit or enters into a hire purchase agreement there are administration costs that are incurred and these are often passed on to the consumer. If you are involved with these types of transactions you must be aware of all the fees and charges that should be applied.

Fees and charges can also be applied to:

- delivery services
- installation services
- loyalty club memberships
- advisory services.

Task 1.8

Research **terms and conditions**, as well as any fees or charges, that may apply to lay-bys or hire purchase in at least three organisations such as Harvey Norman or Target. Keep this information in your portfolio.

Store policies in relation to operational and sales issues

In most instances, businesses will have objectives that set the path for their promotional, operational and financial futures. More often than not they will forecast, in advance, the income they expect to make for a given period of time (from one to three years). Store policies help them achieve their revenue targets by ensuring that staff interact with customers to the required organisational standards and make the most of each sales opportunity.

These organisational requirements can relate to (but are not limited to) the following:

Payment and delivery options

These include lay-by facilities, hire purchase procedures and payment plans, charges for the delivery of goods to the customers and more.

Pricing and discount policies

As discussed, the price at which an organisation sells its products or services will be based on the cost of producing the product or providing the service plus a profit margin. How much is added as a profit margin will depend on what the market (consumer) is willing to pay for the product or service. Discounting is a practice that 'eats' into the organisation's profit margin and should therefore be approached with caution. Each organisation will have set policies on this issue.

Quality and continuous improvement processes and standards

The feedback received from customers should always be seen as an opportunity to improve the service offered them. This is an issue that should be looked at on a regular and continual basis so the organisation can grow and increase its business.

Quality assurance and procedures manuals

This follows on from the above point; according to feedback received and improvements made, benchmarks should be set for staff to follow in order to ensure a consistently high standard of service. These benchmarks and procedures could be provided to staff in the form of induction training, staff manuals or handbooks.

Replacement and refund policy and procedures

Policies and procedures are needed to ensure a consistent approach for staff to follow in case of complaints.

Confidentiality and security requirements

These are very important issues and, in this context, mainly concern the security of information within an organisation. Information about customers should always be kept confidential and never given out to people outside the organisation—possibly not even outside your department. The customer trusts your organisation with their personal details and expects that trust to be honoured. Equally, information stored in the organisation's filing system and computers should be kept confidential. It is important to keep files secure and out of sight when not being used. When not in use you should also log out of your computer to ensure that no one has access to your files while you are away from your desk.

Goals and objectives

Every organisation will have targets that they hope to achieve and all staff must play their part in helping to reach the goals and objectives set. This means that any procedures and policies must be followed. They have been put in place for a reason and when all staff do their part correctly then the organisation will be able to deliver a consistently high quality product or service to its customers while at the same time earning the revenue it needs to survive and succeed.

Preferred supplier policies

This information gives staff guidance on what suppliers are to be sold in preference over others.

ELEMENT 3
PROVIDE POST-SALES SUPPORT

It is important to remember that when a sale has been completed and the customer has left the store, that the sales process may not necessarily be over. After-sales support is every bit as important as getting the customer to buy the product or service in the first place.

After-sales support may involve making arrangements for delivery of the product or service, providing technicians and advice on how to install or use a product or service, or providing support in terms of:

- warranty work
- dealing with complaints about the product or service
- arranging and monitoring payment options.

LEARNING OUTCOMES

3.1 Accurately provide evidence of ongoing support as sale is concluded.

3.2 Accurately explain back-up service and reassure customer according to legislative requirements and store policy.

3.3 Provide customer with store or salesperson's contact details to provide line of contact and customer followed up according to store policy.

3.4 Accurately enter customer and transaction details into customer database.

Providing evidence of ongoing support

Providing customer service excellence is more than just a matter of smiling and engaging with a customer while selling them a product or service. It also means ensuring that the customer remains satisfied with not only the product or service, but with their decision to do business with you. One of the ways to ensure this service excellence is to let them know what ongoing support they can expect from you. This means providing accurate evidence of what the product or services features and benefits are—and also, explaining your support and back-up service.

Evidence of support and back up could include:

- delivery specifications—advising the customer about when and how their purchase will be delivered as well as whether the cost of delivery is included or not
- warranties—who to call if products or services are faulty or need repairs
- returns policies—some organisations will give a full refund, while others will only exchange goods. All businesses, however, *must* give the customer a full refund or exchange if:
  - their product is faulty
  - the product was incorrectly described or
  - the product does not do what its description states it should do.

- technical support or installation—customers may need to know who to contact for help with installation or set up of their products. They may wish to upgrade and need information about what options they have
- financial products and services—may include the ability to pay the product or service off over a given period of time. Financial arrangements may also include the store's policies on lay-by and flexible payments.

It is essential that after-sales support be explained accurately as giving incorrect or false information could lead to:

- disappointment and loss of trust for the customer
- loss of reputation for the organisation
- legal action against you or the organisation.

Be sure of what back-up services your organisation offers and don't make promises you are not able to keep.

Task 1.9

Using the detailed product information you have now accumulated from previous activities, discuss what back-up service might apply to the products or services you researched. In your written report address:

a. availability of the product or expected delivery time
b. is delivery of the product included in the price of the item
c. what technical support is available to customers
d. whether installation is included in the price
e. who and how can customers contact the organisation for follow up enquiries.

Providing customers with store contact details

After the sale, customers may wish or need to contact the store for a variety of reasons including (but not limited to) to:

- ask questions about their purchase
- request technical support or advice
- make further purchases or
- make a complaint.

Again, it is important to provide customers with accurate information and where possible, give details of which department they should contact for specific reasons.

Entering customer and transaction details into the customer database

A record of all customer contact transactions should, and in some cases *must*, be kept. Each transaction with a customer represents a piece of information—information that can be stored and used again at a later time for reasons we will outline below.

RECORDS YOU SHOULD KEEP

Records you *should* keep include:

- contact details, such as:
  - name, address, telephone and email
  - details about birthdays or special interests such as sport or hobbies
  - special preferences in terms of products or brands they like to use.
- purchase details, such as:
  - what they bought
  - when the purchase was made
  - how much they paid
  - reasons for the purchase.

Promoting an organisation and its products can be very expensive so a finely tuned and targeted approach can save a great deal of money and effort. Information the organisation collects about its customers can be used when the organisation plans special presentations or promotions on specific products. With the information on the customer database, the organisation can target only those customers who are likely to be interested in that product or service. They may be introducing new product and service ranges. Here, too, the organisation can save money and effort by aiming their information and marketing campaigns to specific customer groups. Sometimes an organisation will run events or offer tickets to events to their best customers in order to strengthen relationships. Information on the customer database about their preferences and interests can ensure that the organisation is not inviting people who prefer going to the ballet to a football match!

RECORDS YOU MUST KEEP

Records you *must* keep include:

- records of financial transactions—such as receipts for money received, invoices for incoming and outgoing money, tax payments and so on. These will normally be dealt with by the organisation's accounts department but you must be aware of what documents you need to complete
- records relating to transactions involving products or services that require a licence to purchase, including vehicles or weapons.

Whatever information needs to be recorded, it is important that this be done accurately as mistakes about payments made or product preferences can prove to be embarrassing for both the organisation and the customer.

Keeping customer records will be covered in greater detail in Element 6: 'Maintaining and utilising a customer database'.

To summarise this section, providing full customer service means:

- building a rapport and relationship with customers
- ensuring that customers get the products and services they have asked for

- ensuring that customers remain satisfied with the products, services and their relationship with you by supplying ongoing support.

Task 1.10

Customer service survey

1. Over the next few weeks, you should conduct a customer service survey. The purpose of this activity is to evaluate how well businesses in your area look after their customers. Each time you go into a shop or other type of business, take a moment to fill out the survey form over the page.
2. You will then need to submit a written assignment (minimum 1 500 words) outlining your findings and conclusions on the standards of customer service in your area.

Address the following issues in your assignment:

a. Show the statistical analysis of your survey. For example:
   'of the businesses surveyed 25% were small retail, 35% were large retail stores, 15% were in hospitality and 25% in the trade industry. Of these, hospitality showed the highest standard of good customer service; 85% of these establishments greeted me with a friendly smile and hello, the large retail stores, by comparison, only had a 15% rating in this area' and so on ...
   If you are able to show your statistics in graphs, this would be helpful.
b. Discuss the impact of good versus bad service on a business.
c. Of the businesses that delivered good service, what in particular did you like? Of the businesses that delivered bad service, what did they do to make you feel this and what should they have done?
d. Discuss what you personally believe constitutes exceptional customer service.

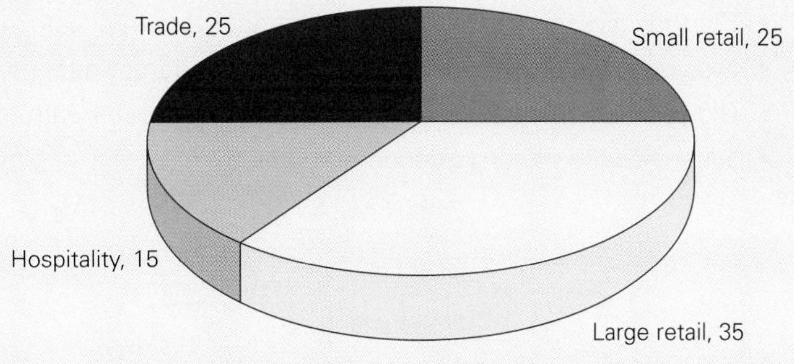

Figure 1.5 Sample statistical analysis

CUSTOMER SERVICE SURVEY

Type of business visited (tick relevant one)

Small Retail	☐	Large Retail	☐	Hospitality	☐	Fast Food	☐
Trade	☐	Supermarket	☐	Other: ______			☐

	Yes	No
• Did the staff acknowledge you when you walked in?	☐	☐
With a smile?	☐	☐
With a greeting?	☐	☐
• Was the store well presented – clean and tidy?	☐	☐
• Was the staff member well presented – clean and neat?	☐	☐
• Were you kept waiting?	☐	☐

• How long? (circle one) 1-5 minutes 5-10 minutes more than 10 minutes

• Did the staff make an effort to establish a rapport with you?	☐	☐
• Did they endeavour to find out your needs and requirements?	☐	☐
• Did they show a genuine interest in helping you?	☐	☐
• If unable to provide you with what you wanted did they try to offer alternatives?	☐	☐
• Did they offer any add on or complementary products or services?	☐	☐
• Did they give you space to make your decisions in private?	☐	☐
• Did you make a purchase based on their good treatment of you?	☐	☐
• Did you NOT make the purchase based on their bad treatment of you?	☐	☐

• What was the general attitude of the staff?

Excellent	☐	Very Good	☐
Good	☐	Satisfactory	☐
Unsatisfactory	☐		

General comments: ____

____

____

____

Make as many copies as you need. You may design your own questionnaire if you prefer.

Figure 1.6 Sample questionnaire

ELEMENT 4
PLAN SALES PRESENTATIONS

Sometimes making a sale is more involved or complex than a face-to-face transaction in a shop. At times you may be required to represent your organisation at a function or a trade fair at which you will be promoting the organisation and its products or services to large numbers of people. In this section we will look at how to plan for and prepare a **sales presentation** to groups of people.

LEARNING OUTCOMES

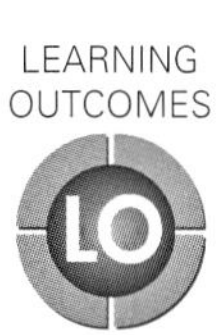

4.1 Plan presentation to complement product characteristics.

4.2 Select client group according to product characteristics and store merchandising policy.

4.3 Access promotional materials where required and distribute to client group.

4.4 Select and prepare a range of products or services for presentation to reflect store image, demographics and merchandising plan.

Planning a presentation to complement product characteristics

How to put together your presentation—what format it will take—will depend largely on the purpose of the presentation. The purpose could include:

- training—training sessions are often run by management to provide information on policies or procedures or to introduce new or changed product lines. The organisation's management might also provide ongoing professional development (PD) for their staff where new skills are taught, existing skills are further developed or new market or product trends are discussed.
- trade fair—these are events, outside of the organisation's premises, where the organisation and its products and services are promoted to the general public at large. Trade fairs can be extremely expensive particularly if they are interstate; by the time you have paid for airfares, accommodation, meals, staff wages, products and promotional materials to take to the fair and the fee for the fair itself you could spend many thousands of dollars. It is therefore essential that you plan such presentations carefully.
- client presentation—these might be in-store presentations to customer groups where products are demonstrated. For example, some hardware stores run weekend workshops where tradesmen teach customers how to build things or make repairs using specific products; art supply stores might run painting classes where specific products are used.

So the first thing you need to think about when planning a presentation is: who will you be presenting to? The next considerations in the planning process involve thinking about:

- appropriate product range—what exactly will you be promoting and why? Are you presenting to provide information only, or are you presenting to sell products?

- where the presentation will take place—will it be in-store, in a shopping centre, in a booth at a trade fair? How much space will you need? This will influence the number of products or display materials you can bring and how many people will need to be involved.
- what resources you will need—will you need support staff, printed information kits, promotional materials, a supply of products, and a cash float if you are selling products?

These are important considerations as they help in setting the scene for the presentation. For example if your presentation was to be on a new range of exclusive and expensive beachwear designed for 18–25 year old females, you would need to set the scene appropriately by addressing that specific market. You could do this by playing appropriate music, using the right decorations, appropriate use of staff and resources or selecting the specific beachwear that appeals to this age group.

Depending on the nature of the presentation it can cost substantial money so it is important to get it right! Preparing a well-rounded presentation also means having an in-depth knowledge of the characteristics of a product or service so that all the effort expended is not wasted because you can't answer questions about the product. Characteristics of a product could include:

- what the product is used for
- how many different functions it can perform
- different sizes (or colours)
- how long the product/service will last
- under what conditions it must be used
- any warranty
- any optional extras
- the variety of ways in which it can be applied
- any use-by date that customers should be made aware of
- if the item is currently in stock, or has to be ordered. If it must be ordered, what is the expected delivery time?
- the product's safety features
- the price range.

These are all important questions and you must be able to answer them should a customer ask. Providing customers with accurate and complete information about a product or service they are considering could be the difference between them actually making the purchase or not. So it is important to know as much as possible about the products and services you sell.

Selecting client groups

As discussed, the product or service being promoted and the purpose of the presentation will be influenced by the target market (or audience). For example, is the presentation mainly aimed at specific age groups, gender, socio-economic groups or ethnicity, or is it aimed at the general population? These considerations will determine what resources you will need for the presentation and the style and set up of the presentation.

Going back to our beachwear example, if this new range of clothing included skimpy bikinis and thongs, you need to be very targeted in your presentation approach. For example, while there is certainly no reason why senior citizens cannot wear a bikini, it is not normally the type of swim wear they buy, so targeting elderly ladies when selling this type of clothing is likely to be a failure.

Accessing and distributing promotional materials

Very often a presentation will mean that you will require resources that allow customers to sample the product or service or that will serve as a reminder of the product.

These 'promotional' items can include:

- giveaways such as pens, balloons and small samples of the product being promoted
- vouchers for discounts or free products
- written information such as brochures, pamphlets and posters
- promotional merchandise such as T-shirts, baseball caps, towels or water bottles
- business cards—always make sure that you have plenty of business cards available.

When preparing for your presentation you will need to ensure that you have an adequate supply of these materials as well as actual products (if appropriate) or make sure that you can easily access extra items if you run out. There is nothing worse than going interstate to a three-day trade fair with a supply of materials only to run out on the first day and have no way to replenish.

Task 1.11

Project

Using the product information you have previously researched (or you can use the results of your survey in Task 1.10) prepare a presentation for the following scenarios:

1. a staff training session at which you will share information about this product or service with colleagues who will also need to sell it
2. promoting the product or service in a booth at the local shopping centre on a Saturday morning
3. a presentation to management on the general customer service available in other stores and the results of your survey (Task 1.10).

In addition to preparing this presentation please provide information on what promotional items you intend to use and/or provide a copy of any presentation materials you would use (flyers, PowerPoint presentations etc).

Submit a written plan for each of these presentations to your trainer.

ELEMENT 5
IMPLEMENT SALES PRESENTATION

In the previous section we looked at how to plan a sales presentation by considering the audience, purpose of the presentation and product range. Implementation of the presentation should be undertaken with the same care and attention to detail.

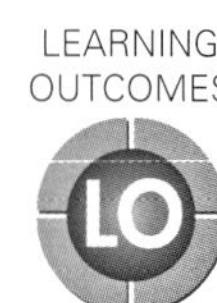

5.1 Ensure sufficient numbers of adequately briefed support staff, where required for a presentation.

5.2 Apply communication skills to effectively create interest, focus attention, and encourage customer interaction with individuals or groups.

5.3 Demonstrate products or services to create a buying environment.

5.4 Measure results of sales presentation according to predetermined criteria, review overall performance and results, and apply information to enhance future sales presentations according to store sales policy.

Ensuring sufficient numbers of adequately briefed support staff

As you have learned, a presentation can be very involved and complex. So depending on the nature and type of presentation to be undertaken other staff from your organisation may need to be called upon for support. These might include:

- administration staff for:
  - photocopying and producing promotional materials to be used at the presentation
  - ordering resources
  - booking flights and hotels
  - booking trade fair booths and exhibition furniture
  - transporting materials to venue.
- sales staff to help at the presentation to:
  - answer enquiries
  - demonstrate products
  - take shifts if the trade fair is over several days.

Having potentially spent substantial amounts of money on a presentation, or taken great care over the planning of a presentation, it would be a shame to waste this effort by not having sufficient back up and support to ensure a smooth and successful event.

Applying communication skills

Effective communication is the key to influencing customers in a positive way. If done well, you can create a desire in a customer to buy products and recommend your organisation to others. We will cover communication skills in great detail in Chapter 7, but for now, effective communication skills include being able to:

- establish a rapport with customers
- understand and use non-verbal language effectively
- listen with a positive attitude
- ask effective questions.

Effective communication skills will help you focus the customer's attention on the products and services you are selling and encourage a positive interaction with them.

Communicating effectively can also mean applying technical skills to create visually interesting displays and presentations. This might mean designing the space for the display or presentation or preparing an electronic presentation using computer software such as Microsoft PowerPoint.

Whether you are designing a space or booth, or a PowerPoint presentation, always keep your target audience in mind and create a display or presentation that will appeal to that specific age group, gender or socioeconomic group.

Demonstrating products or services

In almost all cases the main purpose of a presentation—or demonstration—is to make a sale. As mentioned previously it is important, during a presentation, to gain the customers interest. In addition to those methods already outlined, a successful product demonstration can be achieved by taking the various communication learning styles of your audience into consideration.

- *Explain* how your product can meet the customer's needs—appealing to the customer who takes in information best by listening.
- *Demonstrate* how the product works—rather than just telling them—appealing to customers who prefer to see how a product works.
- Get the customers *actively involved*—by letting them try it for themselves—appealing to those who best take in information by doing it themselves.

By using a variety of communication styles during your demonstration you are appealing to the widest possible audience.

Figure 1.7 Customer satisfaction survey

Measuring results of sales

Measuring results of a presentation is extremely important. You may have spent considerable money or effort on the presentation, so you need to make sure that this effort was worth it.

Results can be measured in several ways.

Conducting enquiry surveys

If, after a presentation, enquiry levels go up then this may be a good indication that it was successful. Asking customers where they heard about your company and its products is always an excellent method of measuring results. This should be done as a matter of normal business practice as the information collected can provide management with data upon which to base future decisions such as which products to introduce or withdraw from sale, what type of advertising or promotional activities work—and which ones do not. For example:

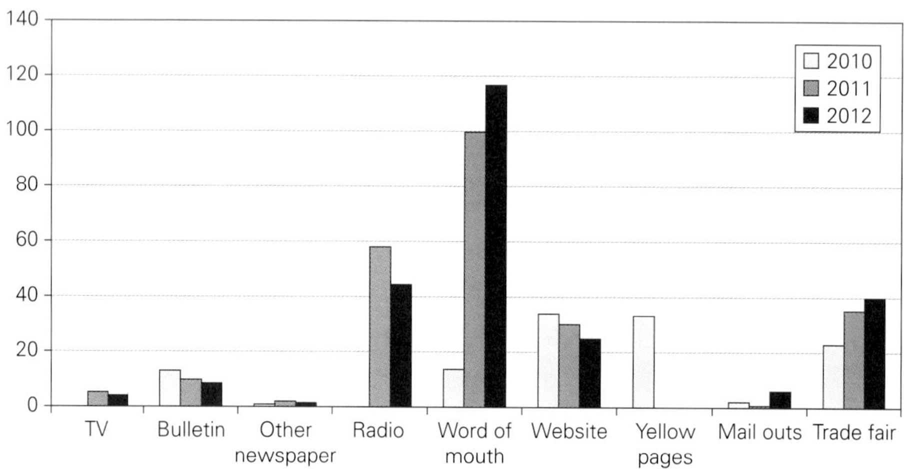

Figure 1.8 Example enquiry survey

The graph above shows that during 2011 and 2012 word of mouth was the main source of customer enquiry, whereas money spent on television and newspaper ads was less successful. It also shows that enquiries did come from a trade fair held each year, indicating that this was successful and that the company should continue to attend these fairs.

Measuring sales made since the presentation

This follows on from the above point. Revenue figures in the days and weeks after the presentation should show an increase if the presentation was successful.

Measuring increases in the customer database

Equally, while sales may not have increased, a measure of success could include an increase in the size of the company's database. New enquiries do not always mean a sale but they do mean more customers for the database and future targeting.

ELEMENT 6
MAINTAIN AND UTILISE A CUSTOMER DATABASE

As far back as the 1500s Sir Francis Bacon said 'Knowledge is power', and this is as true today as it was 500 years ago. Information is an extremely useful and valuable business resource as, if used effectively, it will allow an organisation to promote its products and services in the most cost-effective way. In this unit we will be looking at various methods of retaining customer records and how to effectively use this information.

6.1 Maintain customer confidentiality as required by store policy and legislative requirements.

6.2 Develop and maintain accurate customer records and store securely according to store policy and procedures.

6.3 Accurately identify and follow up regular customers according to store marketing policy.

6.4 Accurately utilise customer records to advise customers on products and services of possible interest.

6.5 Implement customer loyalty schemes where required according to store promotional activities.

LEARNING OUTCOMES

The importance of customer databases

Today, almost all organisations keep a customer database—but what exactly is a database and what is it used for?

A database is just that—a collection of data (or information). It is used to store customer details as outlined in Element 3: 'Provide post-sales support' and it fulfils a very specific purpose. Marketing and promoting an organisation and its products and services can cost a great deal of money. To be most effective these efforts should, ideally, be precisely targeted and you can only do that if you have captured accurate information on your customer base. This information could include (but is not limited to):

Suburb

where do your customers live? This information is useful if the organisation wants to run a promotion or event only for customers in the immediate surroundings

Age

what age groups is your business attracting? Knowing the age groups your customers fall into allows the organisation to promote products and services, or stage events, aimed at those specific age groups

Gender

are most of your customers male or female? This information can be used when promoting special events such as Mother's Day or Father's Day

Purchases made:

- What did they buy? This gives you information on which products are selling well, and which are not. This data can then be used to determine if you should increase the product range because it is selling well, or decrease it (or withdraw it completely) if it is not selling well.
- When did they buy it? Knowing when customers buy certain products can give you an indication of trends: peaks and troughs. For example certain products, such as beachwear, will sell better in summer than in winter. Knowing what the buying trends are and when trough periods will occur can help an organisation run promotions to increase sales during those specific periods or plan, financially, for the decrease in business.
- Why did they buy it? This information might give you ideas of what complementary products or services the customer might be inclined to buy.

Personal preferences

knowing what brand, size or colours your customers prefer will allow you to control your inventory. For example, if almost all of your customers buy a specific brand or size as opposed to other products you offer, then you can increase stock of the preferred product allowing you to make extra sales, and decrease stock of the less popular product, which means you spend less money on stock that doesn't move as quickly

Anniversaries and special dates

this information is useful for relationship building. If you are aware of special dates or interests in a customer's life you can send them cards, or invite them to events such as concerts or sports events that you might be sponsoring.

Accurate and detailed information can lead to very specifically targeted marketing which means a greater chance of success.

Utilising customer records effectively

As we have just discussed, a well set up and accurate database can be used to promote specific products to specific customer groups. Using the information stored in the database you can develop promotional activities and marketing strategies with pin-point precision.

With this in mind, identifying and following up with regular customers becomes a process that can be undertaken often and effectively. It allows the organisation to develop strategies for increasing sales during known trough periods as well as to develop client relationships by inviting customers with specific interests to events that they will enjoy and that will engender loyalty.

Maintaining customer confidentiality

When dealing with customer records you are often given information of a private or confidential nature. Customers place their trust in you when they provide you with their contact details and these should never be passed on to third parties without their express consent. Divulging information on customers or your organisation to outside parties can be grounds for instant dismissal from your job and you could even find that legal action may be taken against you. Having said that, it may sometimes be necessary to forward customer information on to third parties (such as government departments) for various reasons (such as taxation). In these cases an organisation may use application forms or notices that provide a space or tick box asking customers for permission to pass information to other companies or advising them that this may be a government requirement.

Developing and maintaining accurate customer records

When setting up and maintaining a database it is important to consider what the database will be used for and how it will be interrogated. The following are just some (but not all) of the issues to consider:

- determining the information you want to keep
- making sure it is easily accessible
- implementing measures to secure the information
- ensuring that the new database can integrate and work with other systems the organisation has in place
- updating information as soon as:
  - a transaction takes place
  - details of customers, products or other issues change
  - customers move away and are no longer viable.

Ensuring the database is easy to interrogate is also an extremely important consideration. There is not much point in having excellent information if it is difficult to extract. An effective database should allow the user to ask questions as needed by the organisation. For example, 'show me all my customers who…':

- live in a given postcode area
- have bought a specific, given product
- spent over a certain amount of dollars in the past twelve months
- have a birthday coming up this month.

Using a database in this way will allow the organisation to develop deep and effective relationships with their customers by understanding and acting upon their needs.

As mentioned previously customer records can contain information of a confidential nature, so the storage of this information must be done strictly to organisational policies and procedures. For example, computer records should be protected with individual login and password codes. Possibly, only certain specially authorised staff may be allowed to enter or amend information to ensure privacy. Paper-based records should be kept securely locked in filing cabinets.

Implementing customer loyalty schemes

An excellent way to build relationships with customers and gain their loyalty is to put in place a reward system of some sort. Some of these can be on a grand scale such as flybuys or airline frequent flyer clubs—others only need to be based around your own business. Customer loyalty schemes may include:

- customer clubs—where members get special offers such as:
  - first option on new products
  - invitations to events and launches
  - special offers for members only
- customer reward schemes—where customers who spend a given amount of money in the store receive a free or discounted product; for example, 'buy 10 books get one free', or 'buy 20 cups of coffee and get your next one free'
- credit or discount facilities—can also be used to encourage customers to continue shopping with your organisation.

Well-run programs have the power to generate substantial sales for a business. One major department store has turned its loyalty program around in recent years, introducing a loyalty card, which has 3.4 million members and contributes an enviable 66% of sales.

The starting point to any loyalty program must be to research, no matter what sort of business you're running. You need to clearly understand what you're setting out to achieve.

Too many businesses set unrealistic deadlines and rush to put a loyalty program into place in a bid to beat its competitors. It is important to take the time to consider what you're setting it up for.

- Are you trying to acquire new customers?
- Are you trying to retain current customers?
- Are you doing it to reward your best customers?

Only once you have explored your purpose fully can you design the program that will best suit your business objectives.

Relevant rewards

Loyalty programs can offer everything from discounts, cheap petrol, free products, invitations to VIP nights and 'buy-one-get-one-free' offers. Whatever your loyalty program offers it is important to make sure it represents value to customers and works in your favour. The offer needs to be:

- something the customer will aspire to
- authentic and honest in terms of why you are running the program and what your objectives are
- consistent—people can get confused if you change the program and the rules too often. Changes to conditions may also lead to legal difficulties where a customer may have agreed to join the loyalty program based on something that you subsequently withdrew.

Task 1.12

Looking at the organisation you work for (or have worked for) design a loyalty program that will encourage customers to use your products or services.

Task 1.13

1. Using all of the product information you have now gathered, create a database to collect information on (a) your customers and (b) your products.

Each database sheet should contain, at a minimum, information on the following:

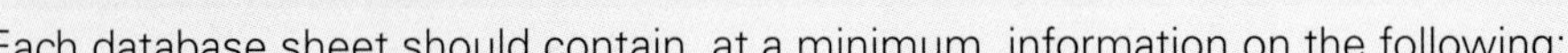

Customers: customer details as well as purchase details. These purchase details should include:

- what each customer purchased
- how much they paid for it
- when they purchased it
- reason for their purchase.

Products or services: finalised details of the products you have researched. This should include:

- characteristics
- warranty information
- prices and pricing options
- complementary products
- manufacturer/supplier details.

2. Produce a separate paper or spreadsheet that shows the relationship between the products you have in your database and the customers who purchased them.
3. Explain how you would use this information to:
   a. promote further products or services to your customers
   b. improve your service and/or the products you offer to customers.
4. Explain how you will maintain the confidentiality of this information.

ELEMENT 7
DEAL WITH DIFFICULT CUSTOMERS

Regardless of what sector of retail you are in or, indeed, what industry in general, there will always be times when you will be required to deal with difficult customers or complaints. How well you deal with these situations will determine whether the customer goes away satisfied or whether they go away and tell their family and friends how bad your service is (even if that is not true). In this section we will cover the tools you will need to deal with difficult situations.

LEARNING OUTCOMES

7.1 Acknowledge customer complaints and problems and reassuringly support difficult customers to produce positive outcome.

7.2 Use questioning and active listening to encourage customer to verbalise issue and minimise customer frustration.

7.3 Develop customer's confidence in the candidate and product or service to promote long-term trust and commitment to store.

7.4 Establish mutually acceptable resolution of complaint.

Acknowledging customer complaints and problems

A complaint, no matter how trivial it might sound to you, is legitimate in the eyes of the customer and must be taken seriously. Customers come into your organisation to do business. They have a need and they believe (or hope) that you will be able to fulfil that need. They are willing to pay for your time, effort and service and they expect your full and undivided attention. If they do not receive this attention or a satisfactory product or service, then they are not receiving value for their money and have every right to complain.

In dealing with complaints and problems, in the first instance it is important to acknowledge the customer and their right to complain. Ignoring them, or hoping that if you don't acknowledge the problem it will go away will often do just the opposite.

Using effective communication skills, as outlined in Element 5, is the key to dealing with all kinds of customers and issues. When problems or complaints arise it is important to define and clarify exactly what the problem is. Only when you fully understand the issues can you find a mutually acceptable solution. Using effective communication skills also means that the customer will know you have taken them seriously and will, normally, then be ready to discuss the issue in a reasonable manner. Dealing with complaints and difficult customers is part of every retailer's role—one that should be accomplished with tact and a graciousness that leaves the customer feeling valued.

Difficult customers may include:

- aggressive people with a 'no nonsense' manner who may be brusque and don't like wasting time

- assertive people who know what they want and can sometimes insist that they know best—even when they might not
- passive people who are easily led into making decisions that might not necessarily be what they want
- fussy people who 'nit pick' and find fault in all but the most perfect product or solution
- demanding people who insist on immediate attention and action
- rude people who display bad manners and behaviour
- exasperated people who become frustrated when they are unable to get what they want.

Regardless of the customer's own behaviour and manner it is very important that you remain calm and totally professional during all of your exchanges with them. Reacting negatively to rude or aggressive behaviour on the customer's part could lead to major conflicts that cannot easily (or ever) be resolved. So while it may be hard to do, never get drawn in to behaving in a negative manner yourself and remember that the customers are, themselves, reacting to a disappointment most likely caused by your organisation, and their actions are not meant against you personally but rather at the organisation.

Developing customer confidence

In order to find a mutually acceptable solution you will need to gain the customer's trust and confidence. You can do this by:

- being open and honest about what you can and cannot do to help them
- using positive communication skills. This means listening carefully to what they are saying, asking effective questions, watching the customer's body language, and using the appropriate tone of voice
- letting them know that you are interested in them and in finding a solution for them.

For a lasting relationship to build, the customer must be convinced that your products or services are the best ones for them, that they match their needs and that the organisation values them. This means:

- being above-board in all dealings with them
- delivering what you say you will deliver
- dealing with problems efficiently and promptly
- making allowances for their needs and, often, personality traits.

Establishing mutually acceptable resolution of complaint

Complaints are often mishandled because conflict has arisen. Conflict arises due to misunderstanding. It also arises when it seems more important to determine who is right and who is wrong. In the initial instance who is right or wrong is irrelevant—it's not a contest! The customer has bought a product or service in good faith and, for some reason, feels that they have not received what they have paid for. The first step towards resolving the conflict, therefore, should not be an argument with the customer. You need to foster good relations with your customer by displaying understanding and empathy. Steps in finding mutually acceptable solutions to problems could include the following.

STEP 1: LISTEN

At the time of the complaint the customer feels angry and frustrated—anything but valued. Time spent here in repairing the relationship with the customer will be time well spent. So take your time and don't rush them—listen to what they have to say. Listening carefully and completely to what your customer is saying without interrupting them will show that you are interested through your 'positive listening attitude'. (We will be looking at communication skills in a later chapter.) Most importantly, while their anger and frustration may be directed at you momentarily, don't take it personally. It is not meant personally and if you handle the situation correctly the customer will calm down and be reasonable.

STEP 2: TAKE OWNERSHIP OF THE PROBLEM

Take ownership regardless of whether you were involved in the problem or not! 'Passing the buck' at this point is not going to help matters. The customer approached *you*, so deal with it and do not pass them off with, 'It's not my problem' or 'The lady who handled this is not here now …'. At that particular moment in time the customer does not see you the individual, they see you the representative of the company, so it is you, the representative of the company, they expect to help them.

STEP 3: APOLOGISE

Apologise for the inconvenience that this particular issue has caused them and assure them that you will try to reach a satisfactory solution to it. It is important to note here, that you should apologise only for the issue at hand—do not allow the situation to escalate into a litany of everything that has ever gone wrong in their lives. Keep to the matter at hand.

STEP 4: USE NON-VERBAL LANGUAGE EFFECTIVELY

Make eye contact with your customer. Act and speak calmly. Try to remember that the complaint is often not meant against you personally. Arguing with the customer could result in a full-blown confrontation. Pause before making a response to your customer. This will give you time to collect yourself, to calm any irritation you might feel and will also give you a chance to work out how to phrase your response in the most appropriate way.

STEP 5: PAY ATTENTION TO THE CUSTOMER

Do not allow yourself to be distracted by things that do not involve the current situation. Try to put yourself in their place; empathise with them. Use expressions such as, 'I can understand why you would feel that way'. Be patient and understanding. Do not interrupt them. Once your customer has had their say, they will generally be a lot calmer and easier to reason with. The problem can then often be resolved in a civilised manner.

STEP 6: MAKE SURE THAT YOU GET ALL THE RELEVANT INFORMATION

If necessary repeat your understanding of the issue to the customer to get agreement that you understand clearly.

STEP 7: OFFER A SOLUTION

When you have all the relevant information and are able to, offer a solution that meets the expectations of the customer. Bear in mind that the objective is to retain the customer. If a solution is hard to reach, put the resolution in the customer's hands by asking, 'How do you feel the problem can be resolved to the satisfaction of both of us?' Then listen to what they have to suggest. For the most part the customer will be fairly reasonable.

STEP 8: BRING IN A NEUTRAL PARTY

If a satisfactory solution cannot be reached, you may need to bring in a higher authority to deal with the situation.

STEP 9: DOCUMENT THE PROCESS AND THE OUTCOME

Information about how a problem occurred and what was done to resolve it can be used to make improvements to procedures and policies.

The most important thing to remember, at all times, is to stay calm! Arguments solve nothing and only serve to aggravate an already tense situation. Communication skills are discussed further in Chapter 2.

There will be many instances during your working life in which you will have to deal with difficult people or need to resolve a problem. Staying calm at all times and listening to the customer's complaint without interruption are the most important methods in calming the customer down. Once this has been achieved then reasonable, two-way communication can proceed.

The same applies when dealing with other difficult situations such as demanding, fussy or vague customers. Always remember:

- stay calm and professional
- listen to what the customer is saying
- match their needs or requirements with your organisation's products, services or options to fulfil those needs
- present them in a clear calm voice stating exactly and accurately how your solution matches their needs
- give them time and space to consider your solution and give you feedback
- negotiate an agreement
- bring in a neutral third party if necessary.

ASSESSMENT 1: ROLE PLAY

<table>
<tr><td>Assessment instructions</td><td>Using the product information you gathered so far split in to groups of four and conduct a sales consultation with one sales person and three customers. Each person should be handed the product fact sheets prepared by their role play partners and spend some time familiarising themselves with those products so that they can play their part of the customer as effectively as possible.
Customers: Based on the product fact sheets you have been given, your role is to 'purchase' one of those products from the sales person. Explain—very briefly—what you are looking for and then answer any questions the sales person asks you. During the sales process:
• one customer will find something to raise an objection about (price, flexibility, availability, etc.)
• one customer will complain about having had to wait too long for service
• one customer will be an overseas visitor whose English language skills are poor.
Spend a little time prior to the role play to determine who plays which role. In each role play, respond to the sales person as if in a real sales situation.
Sales person: Your role is to make a sale to three separate customers, based on your chosen products. The customer will briefly explain what they are after, but it is up to you to fully confirm their needs and then to get them to make the purchase by using effective communication skills. Ensure that you:
• get full contact details from the customers and their purchases (as you will need this information for a later task)
• endeavour to build a rapport with each customer
• offer complementary products
• provide as much information about the product and its supplier as you can. This will include providing information (if applicable) on:
– legal issues concerning the product
– terms and conditions of use
– availability and delivery options
– product or service characteristics
– features and benefits
– costs and payment options.
• deal with each customer individually, dealing with any problems or issues that may arise during the sales process.</td></tr>
<tr><td>Evidence required</td><td>• Completed Facilitator observation checklist (McGraw Hill website).
• Copies of all product flyers.</td></tr>
<tr><td>Range and conditions</td><td>• This assessment can take place either in the workplace, where the assessor will observe as you deal with store customers, or in a simulated environment (in the classroom) where the role play will take place as outlined above.
• You will be required to deal with and make sales to, at least, the three customers as outlined above.
• Each person in the group must have the opportunity to play the part of the sales person.
• Each role play should take no longer than fifteen minutes.</td></tr>
</table>

Materials and resources required	Access to a real or simulated work environment.
Assessor intervention	Your assessor will go through the assessment instructions with the class prior to commencement. You may ask questions at any point during the completion of the assignment prior to submission.
Reasonable adjustments	In the event that you have difficulty understanding the assessment tasks due to language or other difficulties, your trainer will attempt to make reasonable adjustments to the assessment paper in order to afford you every opportunity to achieve competency.
Decision-making rules	Facilitator guide/McGraw Hill website provides benchmark answers and checklists.

ASSESSMENT 2

Assessment instructions	Using the presentation you prepared in Task 1.11 you should now deliver this presentation to your class, or if in the workplace, to a group of colleagues. The presentation should be delivered in the form of a staff training session at which you will share information about the chosen product or service with your 'colleagues'. Ensure that you include information on: • product or service characteristics • any legislative or legal issues surrounding the use or purchase of this product/service • opportunities to up-sell or sell complementary products or services • after sales support • manufacturer or supplier information.
Evidence required	• Facilitator observation checklist • Copy of presentation documents (PowerPoint presentation, handouts, etc.).
Range and conditions	• Your presentation should be no more than fifteen minutes. • You must use at least one presentation aid: electronic presentations, whiteboard, butcher's paper, handouts or any other presentation aids that are suitable.
Materials and resources required	Access to computer/internet/appropriate software.
Assessor intervention	Your assessor will go through the assessment instructions with the class prior to commencement. You may ask questions at any point during the completion of the assignment prior to submission.
Reasonable adjustments	In the event that you have difficulty understanding the assessment tasks due to language or other difficulties, your trainer will attempt to make reasonable adjustments to the assessment paper in order to afford you every opportunity to achieve competency.
Decision-making rules	Facilitator guide/McGraw Hill website provides benchmark answers and checklists.

COMPETENCY MAPPING

Element		Performance criteria		Task	Assessment	Refer to page
1	Establish rapport with customers	1.1	Establish rapport and relationship with customer and express a genuine interest in customer needs and requirements to enhance customer commitment, trust and credibility of store and to build return customer base.	1.1	1	4, 5
		1.2	Maintain professional ethics with the customer to promote store image and credibility.	1.2	1	7
		1.3	Accurately clarify customer needs and preferences to maximise sales opportunities.	1.4	1	9
		1.4	Maximise sales opportunities by use of add-on and complementary sales techniques	1.3	1	10
		1.5	Give customer space and time to evaluate purchase decision, while using time to maximum advantage for customer and store.	1.4	1	12
		1.6	Use effective methods to close sales.		1	13
2	Apply expert knowledge	2.1	Provide customer with accurate information regarding product and service appraisals, correct statements and warranties according to legislative requirements.	1.5, 1.8	1	14–17
		2.2	Provide detailed knowledge of supplier or manufacturer information according to customer needs and commercial confidentiality guidelines.	1.8	1	17
		2.3	Evaluate product range, accurately demonstrate features and benefits of products or services where appropriate and make recommendations to the customer to maximise sales potential.		Assessed in Chapter 7	18–20
		2.4	Maximise customer interest in product or service through price negotiation where applicable and offer payment and credit options according to store policy.	1.7	1	20
		2.5	Accurately calculate prices and discounts according to pricing determinants and store policy.	1.7	1	21–24

Element			Performance criteria	Task	Assessment	Refer to page
3	Provide post-sales support	3.1	Accurately provide evidence of ongoing support as sale is concluded.	1.9	1	28–29
		3.2	Accurately explain back-up service and reassure customer according to legislative requirements and store policy.	1.9	1	28–29
		3.3	Provide customer with store or salesperson's contact details to provide line of contact and customer followed up according to store policy.	1.9	1	29
		3.4	Accurately enter customer and transaction details into customer database.	1.13	1	29–30
4	Plan sales presentations	4.1	Plan presentation to complement product characteristics.	1.11	2	33–34
		4.2	Select client group according to product characteristics and store merchandising policy.	1.11	2	34
		4.3	Access promotional materials where required and distribute to client group.	1.11	2	35
		4.4	Select and prepare a range of products or services for presentation to reflect store image, demographics and merchandising plan.	1.11	2	35
5	Implement sales presentation	5.1	Ensure sufficient numbers of adequately briefed support staff, where required for a presentation.		2	36–37
		5.2	Apply communication skills to effectively create interest, focus attention and encourage customer interaction with individuals or groups.		2	37
		5.3	Demonstrate products or services to create a buying environment.		2	37
		5.4	Measure results of sales presentation according to predetermined criteria, review overall performance and results and apply information to enhance future sales presentations according to store sales policy.		2	37–38
6	Maintain and utilise a customer database	6.1	Maintain customer confidentiality as required by store policy and legislative requirements.	1.13	1	39–40
		6.2	Develop and maintain accurate customer records and store securely according to store policy and procedures.	1.13	1	40–41
		6.3	Accurately identify and follow up regular customers according to store marketing policy.	1.13	1	41

continued

Element		Performance criteria		Task	Assessment	Refer to page
		6.4	Accurately utilise customer records to advise customers on products and services of possible interest.	1.13	1	41
		6.5	Implement customer loyalty schemes where required according to store promotional activities.	1.12	1	42
7	Deal with difficult customers	7.1	Acknowledge customer complaints and problems and reassuringly support difficult customers to produce a positive outcome.	1.14		44
		7.2	Use questioning and active listening to encourage customer to verbalise issue and minimise customer frustrations.	1.14	1	45
		7.3	Develop customer's confidence in the candidate and product or service to promote long-term trust and commitment to store.	1.14	1	45
		7.4	Establish mutually acceptable resolution of complaint.	1.14	1	45–47

Required skills and knowledge	Task	Assessment	Refer to page
Required skills			
Selling techniques, including: • opening and closing techniques • identifying buying signals • strategies to focus customer on specific merchandise • add-ons and complementary sales • overcoming customer objections.	1.4	1	10, 11, 13, 19, 21
Presentation skills.		2	33–38
Conflict resolution.	1.14	1	44–47
Verbal and non-verbal interpersonal communication.	1.1		6
Accessing relevant product information.	1.3		14, 15, 16
Literacy and numeracy skills in regard to: • reading and understanding product information • reading and understanding store policies and procedures • recording client and sales information • calculating prices and discounts.	1.5, 1.6		14, 15, 16, 17, 21, 26–27

Required skills and knowledge	Task	Assessment	Refer to page
Required knowledge			
Store policies and procedures, in regard to: • establishing, maintaining and utilising customer records • updating and maintaining customer mailing lists • methods of maintaining customer confidentiality and secure storage of customer details • pricing, including GST requirements • price negotiation and payment and credit options • resolving customer complaints.	1.7, 1.13, 1.14	1	21, 29–31, 39–43
Store and area merchandise and service range.	Covered in Part II		
Relevant legislation and statutory requirements.	1.5	1	16
Relevant industry codes of practice.	1.2		16
OHS requirements such as: • manual handling • plant and equipment • hazardous substances and dangerous goods • workers compensation.	1.5		16
Customer types and needs, including: • customer buying motives, customer behaviour and cues • individual and cultural differences, demographics, lifestyle and income • types of customer needs, e.g. functional, psychological.	These topics will be covered in Chapter 7 Sell products and services		

continued

Required skills and knowledge	Task	Assessment	Refer to page
Critical aspects for assessment and evidence			
Consistently applies store policies and procedures.		1	14
Consistently develops customer commitment to store and builds return customer base.	1.9		14, 18, 19
Consistently maximises sales opportunities.	1.3		10
Consistently and accurately applies detailed knowledge of manufacturer and supplier supply.	1.8		17
Consistently uses effective questioning, listening and observation skills.			throughout
Consistently and effectively plans, prepares and conducts sales presentations and briefs support staff.	1.11	2	33–38
Consistently evaluates personal and or team sales performance to maximise future sales.	This topic will be covered in Chapter 7 Sell products and services		
Consistently and accurately establishes, records and maintains customer records and details.	1.13	1	39–43
Consistently resolves customer complaints.	1.14		44–47

Chapter 2

SIRXCOM101

Communicate in the workplace to support team and customer outcomes

Communicating effectively is, without a doubt, one of the most important skills that you will learn. The key to dealing successfully with other people, whether they are colleagues or customers, is to not only gain an in-depth understanding of their needs and expectations but to ensure that your own are also understood. Reaching a full understanding of another person's needs leaves little room for error or misunderstanding and conflict can often be avoided simply by listening attentively to what others have to say.

Effective communication is an extremely important subject and will be covered in many of the units in this book to greater or lesser extents. Please view the repetition of any information provided as an opportunity to anchor this knowledge so that communicating effectively becomes second nature. This is a skill that you will use each and every day and using it effectively can mean the difference between a successful and satisfying work life and an unhappy, unproductive one.

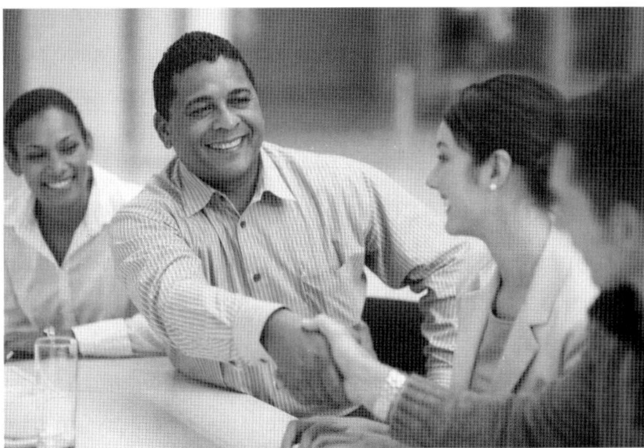

Figure 2.1 Working in a happy team

ELEMENT 1

COMMUNICATE FACE-TO-FACE WITH CUSTOMERS

Research has shown that it only takes between three and ten seconds for a first impression to be formed. This means that a customer coming into your store will look at you and make up their mind in as little as three seconds whether they like you and want to deal with you, and therefore your organisation, or not. In such a short space of time, you may not have even had the chance to speak to them so it is important to make that first impression count. You can do this by presenting a positive, professional image and behaving in accordance with store policies and procedures. In this section we will provide you with the skills and knowledge you need to achieve the following learning outcomes.

LEARNING OUTCOMES

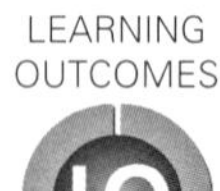

- 1.1 Maintain a welcoming customer environment that reflects store branding and market position and is in line with store policy and procedures.
- 1.2 Greet customer warmly according to store policy and procedures.
- 1.3 Create effective service environment through verbal and non-verbal interaction according to store policy and procedures.
- 1.4 Use questioning and active listening to determine customer needs.
- 1.5 Demonstrate confidentiality and tact.

Maintaining a welcoming environment

As stated above, a customer will gain an impression of you and your store in a very short space of time, so those first few moments when they come in are critical to making them feel welcome. Ensure that the shop is clean and tidy and that display racks and shelves are fully stocked.

Smile and greet the customer when they walk in. You may be busy serving someone else but a warm smile will let them know that you have seen them and will attend to them as soon as possible. People are often quite happy to wait patiently as long as they feel they have been acknowledged and a small greeting will do just that.

Working in accordance with store policies and procedures

Most organisations will have **policies and procedures** that outline how staff are to respond in given situations. These policies and procedures are developed and implemented in order to ensure that staff are working to the organisation's standards. They are also put in place to make sure that staff observe all legislative and legal requirements an organisation may be subjected to. Policies and procedures of an organisation can include (but are not limited to) information on:

Customer service standards

Including:

- building rapport and relationships with customers
- interpersonal communication skills
- dealing with customer complaints about products or individual staff (dealt with in the next section).

Marketing and sales

Including:

- store appraisal—ensuring that the shop or office looks clean, tidy and inviting at all times. This could include:
  - making sure all signage is correct and up to date
  - clearing away any packing boxes.
- merchandise and service range of the store—this means:
  - ensuring that there is a large enough range of products for customers to choose from
  - ensuring there are sufficient quantities to meet customer demand for popular products
  - setting up displays that entice the customer to buy
  - placement of products to encourage customers to purchase them.
- selling techniques—training staff in the art of making and maximising sales.

Human resource management

Including:

- induction process—ensuring that staff are aware of and understand:
  - organisational standards, procedures, code of conduct and duty of care
  - interaction with other members of the organisation
  - their job descriptions and responsibilities.
- staff supervision, including:
  - monitoring team performance to ensure they are working to the desired standards
  - discipline—as and when needed to correct bad or inconsistent behaviour
  - grievance handling of staff-related issues
  - allocating duties and responsibilities to staff according to their strengths and organisational needs.
- meetings to update staff on organisational issues and requirements
- lines of communication to staff and management.

Relevant legislation and statutory requirements

Including, where applicable:

- *Competition* and *Consumer Act*
- tobacco laws
- lottery legislation
- liquor licensing regulations
- sale of X- and R-rated products
- sale of second-hand goods
- trading hours
- transport, storage and handling of goods
- WHS (workplace health and safety) and duty of care
- EEO (equal employment opportunity) and anti-discrimination practices
- relevant industry codes of practice.

It is very important to be informed about legislation and statutory requirements of your industry, as non-compliance with these issues can mean legal action being taken against your or the organisation you work for, or loss of licence or registration.

While many of these policies may seem far removed from communicating with customers directly, all of them in fact have an impact on how an organisation deals with its customers.

CASE STUDY

The owner of a local BBQ equipment retailer had a *sales policy* which required staff to 'make sales at all costs'. They were given KPIs (key performance indicators) each month which indicated how many sales they were expected to make. They were told that their jobs depended on them achieving these KPIs.

This resulted in some very sloppy sales being made with staff either glossing over or entirely leaving out conversations over terms and conditions and safety instructions of the products they sold. Their thinking was that telling the customer anything negative about a product and its use might stop them from buying it.

In one case neglecting to explain the correct method of lighting a gas BBQ to a novice user resulted in serious consequences. The new owner proudly invited friends and family to a BBQ lunch, left the gas turned on for far too long before lighting the burners and was seriously injured in the resulting gas explosion.

Duty of care and the store's obligation to provide full and correct information were ignored in this case with catastrophic consequences to the customer and the organisation. The customer had to undergo several skin grafts for burns to his face and hands and sued the retailer for a substantial amount of money.

Using communication skills to create a service environment

As mentioned in the opening of this section, communication is one of the most important skills you will ever learn and if done well can lead to a successful life.

Task 2.1

Reflection

Take a moment to reflect on the communication experiences that you have had when going into retail shops—times when you have encountered staff who were bored, unhelpful and non-responsive in comparison to staff who were friendly, courteous and helpful.

1. Give examples of good and bad experiences and explain your feelings during each encounter.
2. Describe what you would do to make a customer feel welcome in your store.

Communication takes place in a variety of different ways: we communicate when we are talking to people by explaining, questioning and listening. We also communicate silently in the gestures we make and the way in which we use our voices. Combining all of these well is the key to successful communication.

EFFECTIVE QUESTIONING TECHNIQUES

Asking questions effectively is an important skill—a skill that makes the difference between having a conversation with a customer and interrogating them. To make the best recommendation to a customer you first need to ask the right kind of questions. Question types include the following.

Open questions

This type of question should be asked at the beginning of any conversation when you are gathering initial information. An open question generally begins with the words: *what, why, which, where, when* or *how* and can rarely be answered in just a word or two. The customer will usually give you a fairly detailed answer to the question, 'What kind of computer did you have in mind?' while if you ask, 'Do you want to buy a computer?' the customer might simply answer, 'Yes'.

To follow through on the computer example, you might start off by asking the customer some open questions:

- 'What sort of business are you in?' This question will give you an overview of how a computer might be used in their specific business.
- 'What will you be using the computer for?' This question will let you know to what extent they plan to computerise their operations and may affect the sophistication of the equipment they need.

- 'What kind of software will you need?' The answer to this question will determine the type and range of software options you recommend to them.

There would be many more questions that you would need to ask the customer before you could go ahead and make a product recommendation.

Clarifying questions

During the initial conversation, or at the end of the conversation to summarise your understanding, you can use a clarifying question. This is used to ensure that you and the customer are on the same page or to get additional information, for example:

- in summarising: 'So what you are saying is that you would like [repeat your understanding of the customer's needs]. Is that correct?' The customer will then either confirm your understanding or correct you.
- in getting additional information: 'You mentioned that you would like your computer to have desktop publishing software. Will you be using this to produce promotional materials?' The answer to this question may lead to additional, complementary sales or give you a better understanding of how the customer will be using the computer.

Clarifying questions are extremely useful in ensuring that your recommendations to the customer are on the mark in terms of their needs.

Leading questions

A leading question is often used by sales people; they lead the customer into making a purchasing decision and, potentially, influence them to buy one of the organisation's preferred products. For example:

- 'So you agree that the iPhone is a better option for you than the Blackberry?'
- 'The Toshiba laptop suits what you are looking for better than the HP. Don't you agree?'

As you can see, the response to a leading question will generally be much shorter than to an open question. They also provide an opportunity to influence the customer into choosing one product over another—preferably one of your preferred products.

In the two examples above, specific companies were highlighted for agreement. The iPhone was put forward as the better option, as was the Toshiba laptop. Both options are still available to the customer and the ultimate choice is, of course, theirs. By asking leading questions, however, you can often influence the customer to buy a product that is not only good value but may earn you extra revenue. (We will cover maximising revenue opportunities in Chapter 7.)

Closed questions

Closed questions should be asked when you have enough information or are ready to wind up the conversation. A closed question will generally get you a 'yes' or 'no' answer—or a very short one. Closed questions usually start with the words: *do, can, is, will* or *are*. Use this type of question when you are summarising or closing the sale. For example:

- 'Is this what you had in mind?'
- 'Can I do anything else for you?'
- 'Will you be paying for that by credit card or cash?'

Task 2.2

Role play

Using the computer example in the paragraph on pages 59–60, perform the following role play exercise.

To begin, split into pairs, one sales person and one customer, and using the above questions as a starting point, the 'sales person' should gather information from the 'customer'. The sales person should continue asking questions until they have gathered as much information as possible in order to make a solid product recommendation. Each person should have the opportunity to play each role.

1. Alternatively, the customer can use a product of their own choice with the sales person, again, asking appropriate questions to find out as much as possible. Make a note of the *types* of questions you asked (open, clarifying, leading or closed).
2. Discuss how useful the questions were in getting the information you needed.

EFFECTIVE LISTENING SKILLS

Equally as important as asking effective questions is the ability to focus on the customer and *really* listen to what they are saying. More often than not, when someone is talking to you, you are already thinking of what you are going to say to them in reply, or you are thinking about what you are going to do this afternoon when you get home. You are doing anything but really listening to the customer.

This can not only lead to misunderstanding (because you haven't been paying attention) but also to a dissatisfied customer because they feel you have not taken them seriously.

The customer has come in to your store or office to get information and, hopefully, buy a product or service. It is part of your role to help them do that—so you need to develop a positive listening attitude. To do this, ensure that you:

- focus your attention on the customer
- do not let yourself be distracted by other staff or events happening around you
- maintain eye contact with the customer and use open body language to show that you are interested in them
- ask clarifying questions to ensure you have understood the customer correctly.

Task 2.3

> Following on from Task 2.2, to show how attentively you were listening, write down everything you can remember your 'customer' telling you about their product needs.

NON-VERBAL COMMUNICATION CUES

As well as using the spoken word in the communications process it is also important to learn to read non-verbal language. It is possible to *say* one thing and be *thinking* something completely different. For example, colleagues at work might say that they think you are doing a good job but be privately thinking that you are not. Learning to read a person's non-verbal language is an essential skill of an effective communicator.

Non-verbal language is made up of all the subconscious signals that are sent out together with spoken communication. For the most part you may not even be aware of the fact that you are doing this and that you could potentially be undermining your own efforts by (unknowingly) appearing untrustworthy or insincere. Non-verbal communication can be *positive*—indicating openness, honesty and sincerity—or it can be *negative*—indicating insincerity and untrustworthiness. Non-verbal communication can be demonstrated in a number of ways. **Body language** is an important part of non-verbal communication and includes:

Eye contact

Maintaining eye contact with a person you are talking to indicates that you are interested in what they are saying. It is a good sign of positive listening skills. When someone won't look you in the eye when you are talking to them, it makes you feel uncomfortable and could lead to misunderstandings and conflict.

Gestures

Gestures can indicate what you are really thinking. For example covering the mouth while speaking may be an indication that a person is not being entirely truthful, while a person who is crossing their arms and leaning away from you is indicating that they uncomfortable in your presence or have something to hide.

It should be noted, however, that gestures in isolation can be misread. A person crossing their arms may not necessarily be lying, they may simply be cold. You should therefore look for groups, or 'clusters' of gestures. For example, a person scratching the back of their neck *and* not looking you in the eyes probably has something to hide or is not telling the truth.

Tone, pitch and rate of speech

The way the voice is used—the tone of voice, the pitch of the voice and the rate of a person's speech can also be an indication of their true feelings. The tone of a person's voice can indicate boredom, arrogance, joy, enthusiasm and a great many other emotions and feelings. Equally the pitch of their voice and rate of speech can be a great indicator of how they are feeling; the higher the pitch and the faster they speak the more agitated a person might be. Lower pitch and slower speech might also indicate that their patience is running out. This must, again, be looked at in context; a person might naturally have a high-pitched or loud voice and speak quickly and not necessarily be angry. Being aware of these types of non-verbal communication, however, can help you read a person's mood and react accordingly.

Culturally specific communications and customs

In today's world of international travel and relations, we deal with people from other countries and cultures on an almost daily basis. It is important to understand that certain behaviour and gestures that are acceptable to you, might not necessarily be acceptable to those from other cultures. So when dealing with customers or colleagues from other cultures it is a good idea to keep gestures to a minimum and speak in a neutral and courteous tone of voice.

Task 2.4

In this task you will be interviewing your partner about their family, their job or their cultural background (choose one) to demonstrate your listening skills.

Split into pairs and spend ten minutes (each) interviewing your partner about their cultural background, their job, family or upbringing. Pay attention to their non-verbal language to read between the lines of what they are saying—or not saying—and what they might be feeling. You are not allowed to take written notes.

1. When you have finished the interviews, present the information you have received to the class.
2. Comment on any non-verbal signals you observed and what they may have indicated.

Task 2.5

Watch the following YouTube videos and answer the questions below.

'Body language'

http://youtube.com/ZfNoVo0F25E

1. What signs would you expect to see if a person was being untruthful?
2. Describe how eye cues might provide indicators of a person's sincerity.
3. Can you gauge a person's true feelings and meaning by observing only one isolated gesture?
4. Describe how understanding non-verbal language can help you in dealing with customers.

'Body language: The meanings of hand gestures'

http://youtube.com/PYclD4KWKe4

5. How many of the gestures shown in this video were you able to interpret correctly?

Using appropriate language

Good communication skills will not only depend on the things already discussed but also on your ability to use the appropriate language and level of formality when dealing with colleagues and customers. Consideration needs to be given to:

Famliarity with the person

Communication will differ greatly depending on how well you know the person you are talking to. With someone you know very well you can use less formal means of addressing them or talking to them; using their first name, being less formal in your tone and language, or having a joke. With a person less well known you may need to adopt a more formal and professional approach. While it might be fine to call a younger person by their first name and joke around it is not always acceptable to address a senior person in this manner. They should be addressed by their title and surname; for example 'Good morning, Mr. Smith', unless they invite you to do otherwise.

Your relationship with the person

Once again, depending on the nature of your relationship, it is acceptable to have a friendly and relaxed manner with colleagues, suppliers and well known customers. Always remember, however, that your own personal and your organisation's reputation depend on your level of professionalism, so a courteous and professional manner should therefore be adopted when dealing with all staff (particularly senior staff) and customers in general.

Cultural differences

In the retail industry it is not unusual to be dealing with people from all walks of life and from all corners of the world, so when communicating, particularly with people from other cultures, it is important to:

- consider their level of English—don't use long difficult words and use short sentences that are easily understood
- if you are constantly dealing with people from other countries, it is a good idea to learn about forms of address or other customs that you could adopt to make them feel more comfortable
- be aware that some people may have physical or mental disabilities and adapt your communication style accordingly.

Your surroundings

It is important to be aware of your surroundings when talking to customers or colleagues. It is unprofessional to joke and banter overly much with other staff or long-term customers when you are within earshot or view of new visitors to your organisation.

Maintaining confidentiality

The importance of confidentiality in the workplace cannot be stressed enough. It is the responsibility of every employee to treat all information relating to the organisation, its staff and its customers as private. Whatever you see and hear in the workplace must remain in the workplace and no information should be shared with or given to outside parties (unless permission has been given to do so).

Confidentiality is important for a number of reasons relating to the sensitivity and security of information:

- Any information relating to recruitment, compensation, and management of staff is naturally sensitive. In the wrong hands, this information could be misused to commit fraud, discrimination, and other violations.
- Customers will often be asked to give you their contact details such as phone, email or home address. They trust you with this information and expect that you will keep these details private. Then, too, information about what they buy and how much they pay is very useful to the organisation—but this information should never be passed on to parties outside of the company.
- Some organisational information (such as financial or security information) is extremely sensitive and in the wrong hands can lead to breaches in an organisation's security through fraud, theft or robbery.

Breaches of confidentiality can be quite serious and may lead to your instant dismissal from your workplace. It is therefore very important that you observe your organisation's policies and procedures on confidentiality and privacy.

Task 2.6

Scenario

You have been working with your organisation's customer list this morning, putting them into categories of top, regular and occasional customers. The organisation has asked for this to be done so that they can undertake a major marketing campaign aimed at those customers who have made significant purchases over the past twelve months.

During the course of the morning you notice that staff members from a competitor's store have come in to browse around on a number of occasions. As 'ghost shopping' is an accepted practice in retail—you think nothing of it. At noon you leave the store in the hands of a colleague for a few minutes to buy some lunch and as you won't be very long, you leave the confidential customer information and marketing campaign plans on the counter underneath some other papers where you believe they will be safe.

Upon returning you notice that the store is quite busy and rush to help your colleague serve customers. Once things have quietened down again you eat your lunch and then go to resume your work with the customer lists. To your dismay you find all the relevant documents are missing and a search of the immediate area shows that they have not accidentally been moved—they are gone. You remember that your competitors have been in the store several times that morning.

1. Given that it is *likely* that a competitor now has this information—what damage could this do to your organisation?
2. What would be the likely consequences of this incident to you personally?
3. Describe the steps you should have taken to avoid the loss of this information.

ELEMENT 2
USE TECHNOLOGY TO COMMUNICATE WITH CUSTOMERS

Using technology to communicate is very different to communicating face-to-face. When you are talking to a customer in person there is a great deal of non-verbal communication going on. Their gestures and facial expressions allow you to determine a person's true feelings and gain a complete picture of their needs and expectations. When you are communicating with customers on the telephone or other technological means, this is not always possible and you may need to rely on other skills to help you build a rapport with them.

LEARNING OUTCOMES

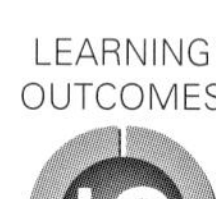

2.1 Answer telephone according to store procedures.

2.2 Use questioning and active listening to identify caller and establish and confirm requirements.

2.3 Use telephone system functions according to instructions.

2.4 Use email, social networking sites and other technologies to receive and process information and customer requests in line with store policy and procedures.

2.5 Record and promptly pass on messages or information.

2.6 Inform customer of any problems and relevant action being taken.

2.7 Perform follow-up action as necessary.

Dealing with telephone calls

As telephone calls may well be the first contact that a customer has with your organisation, you will need to convey a professional and welcoming manner in order to make the customer feel comfortable about doing business with the organisation. Most organisations will have standards and procedures for dealing with incoming calls and these might relate to how and when to answer a call as well as the process for taking and distributing messages.

In general, however, there are a number of tips for dealing effectively with incoming calls. These include, but are not limited to:

- answering all calls promptly—many organisations will have Quality Assurance (QA) programs that outline the standards to which each given task should be completed. QA often extends to the way in which a telephone call should be answered, including answering within a certain number of rings (usually no more than three rings), and with the company-approved greeting—for example, 'Good morning, ABC Retail Store, this is Abbey'
- using a friendly, courteous tone of voice—remember that a great deal can be communicated by the way you use your voice, so a bored or uninterested tone of voice can turn a customer off before they have even spoken to you
- speaking clearly and concisely—callers can come from all walks of life and from all over the world and may not understand you if you mumble or speak too quickly
- listening—always let the caller finish speaking before you answer their query or transfer them. It is discourteous to interrupt a customer or pass them on to someone else before they have finished telling you what they are after. Once they have finished speaking, repeat the details back to them (if necessary) to ensure that you have understood them correctly
- answering their query promptly and giving them as much information as you can
- passing them on to someone who can help them—if you cannot. In doing so, tell the customer who you are passing them on to, and give details of the customer's query to that person so that the customer doesn't need to explain it all again.

Figure 2.2 Using the telephone in a professional way

RECORDING PHONE MESSAGES

If there is currently no one there who can answer a question, you may need to take a message and tell the customer that someone will get back to them as soon as possible.

When taking a message record as many details as possible. These could include:

- who the message is for
- the time and date of the call so that the person for whom the message is intended knows how long ago the customer phoned

- details of the caller, such as name, company (if applicable) and phone number
- the reason for the call. This is important so that the intended recipient of the message can be prepared when they return the call
- expected outcome (if applicable). For example, if the caller is inquiring about the progress of a complex order, the intended recipient can follow up and get the answer before returning the call.

There are a number of different ways in which you can take messages, including writing pad, telephone message slips (example shown in Figure 2.3), electronic messages such as computer diary or database programs, and SMS.

Telephone message pads normally come in books with up to six individual messages per page. These are usually self-carbonating pages so that a copy of the message taken remains in the book for future reference if needed.

Telephone message			
Message for: **Abbey Gibbs**		Date: **15 / 10 / xxxx**	
Received by: **Tony McGee**		Time: **11:30 am**	
Name of caller: **Jeff Bridges**			
❑ Returned call	❑ Urgent	❑ **Please call**	❑ Will call again
Message: **Called about his book order. Wants to know if it has come in yet.**			

Figure 2.3 Example of a telephone message sheet

When taking messages, always remember to get as much detail as possible so that the customer is not inconvenienced by having to provide information over and over again—and so the recipient of the message can be well prepared when they return the call.

Task 2.7

You work as a receptionist at Abbey's Bookstore and have taken the following phone calls. None of the people the callers wanted to speak to were in. Please record their messages on the message slips below.

Today is 15 June.

1. Jessica Graham called at 10.30 am to speak to Abbey about a large order of atlases for her school. They were ordered two weeks ago and she has not heard anything since then. She wants to know what is happening with the order. Her phone number is 0499 888 777.
2. Kristy Braddon from Charlie's Restaurant in Brisbane called at 11.25 am to speak to Jo Flannigan who looks after Abbey's large cookbook section. Kristy is after the new Heston Blumenthal cookbook which is due to be released next week. Her number is 07 5555 2233.
3. Louis Sanchez called at 3.45 pm to talk to someone in the accounts department. He was returning a phone call to him and did not know who called or what it was about but mentioned that the message left said it was urgent. Mr Sanchez's phone number is 0418 999 999.

Telephone message

Message for: Date: / /

Received by: Time:

Name of caller:

❑ Returned call ❑ Urgent ❑ Please call ❑ Will call again

Message:

Telephone message

Message for: Date: / /

Received by: Time:

Name of caller:

❑ Returned call ❑ Urgent ❑ Please call ❑ Will call again

Message:

Telephone message	
Message for:	Date: / /
Received by:	Time:
Name of caller:	
❑ Returned call ❑ Urgent	❑ Please call ❑ Will call again
Message:	

USING TELEPHONE SYSTEMS EFFECTIVELY

An organisation's communication with customers, staff, suppliers and other outside parties will depend to a very large degree on a telephone system which allows it to make and receive calls, send faxes and a great deal more. There are a large variety of telephone systems available, all of which offer numerous functions designed to make communications easy and efficient. Depending on the size of the organisation a system may have as few as one telephone line or hundreds and each telephone system will have a variety of useful functions. Dealing with phone calls efficiently is a matter of knowing the functions and uses of your telephone system which could include:

- voice mail—which allows callers to leave a message if they are unable to speak to the person to whom they are calling and allows staff to leave 'extended absence greetings' when they are away from their office for long periods of time. For example, if your organisation closes over a long holiday period such as Christmas you could leave a message on the voice mail system advising callers that the store will be closed between certain dates.
- on hold—which allows you to 'park' a telephone call while you get information for the caller, or answer a second phone call. Once you have the requested information you can then take the call back off hold and return to the conversation. You would use this function, rather than just putting down the receiver while you get information, because by putting the call on hold you are blocking out anything the caller might hear than if you simply put the receiver down on the desk.

- transfer—which allows you to transfer a telephone call from one phone line to another. This might need to happen if a call were put through to you by mistake, if you are unable to help the caller and want to put them through to someone who can or if you have finished your conversation and the caller asks to be put through to another person.
- speakers—which are a very useful function if you wish one or more people in your office to hear the phone conversation, or if you want to continue working while speaking on the phone. Speakers are built into many telephones and can be used to talk to someone without the need for holding the receiver in your hand.

Other technology used in communication

Telephones are not the only technological means of communicating. Other forms of communication offer instant messaging facilities and the ability to include documents, photos and can include the following.

- SMS—or Short Message Service, is an excellent way of sending messages quickly and efficiently. Depending on the urgency of the situation information can be passed on to the recipient instantly rather than writing the message on a message slip and waiting for them to pick it up
- Email—is another excellent and instant method of passing information. It has the advantage that you are able to attach documents that might be needed when the recipient calls the customer back
- The internet—offers a variety of ways in which you can communicate with customers—for example websites, blogs and social networking pages such as Facebook—which allow an organisation to post information about their company and its products and services. These facilities often offer customers the ability to comment or submit enquiries or orders online.

Task 2.8

Role play or workplace observation

This task can be undertaken either in the classroom or in the workplace. You will be required to handle a range of telephone enquiries during the course of this task. You will deal with at least three incoming calls from customers making product or service enquiries. In a classroom situation, make up any necessary details.

During the course of dealing with these enquiries you will also be required to take messages for recipients who are not there to take the call themselves. You must also deal with any difficulties that come up in the appropriate manner and ensure that you inform customers of any problems and relevant actions you will take to solve the problem.

Your assessor will observe how you deal with the calls, based on the checklist below.

In dealing with incoming phone calls the student:	Yes	No
1. Answered the telephone using a professional greeting (minimum): • good morning / afternoon • stated name of company • stated their name.		
2. Dealt with the customer enquiry in a professional, courteous manner		
3. Answered questions in detail		
4. Transferred customer to other staff member: • advising who they would be transferred to • passing all relevant information on to other staff member.		
5. Recorded messages in full detail		
6. Passed messages on to absent staff in a timely manner		
7. Used technology effectively to record messages: • used email, calendar or database to record messages • sent messages on to appropriate staff using this technology.		
8. Dealt with difficulties by: • informing the customer of the problem involved in delivering the product/service or answering the enquiry • informing the customer of what action would be taken to solve the problem • performing follow-up actions, recording message for other staff or following up personally.		

ELEMENT 3
COMMUNICATE WITH CUSTOMERS AND COLLEAGUES FROM DIVERSE BACKGROUNDS

Recognising social and cultural **diversities** and dealing with cross-cultural misunderstandings is an important issue. In our everyday lives, it is unlikely that we will deal only with people of similar nature, background and ideals as ourselves. We come into daily contact with many different people. They are our customers and our colleagues or managers and we need to recognise and accept their right to their own beliefs and customs and, where practical, to make allowances for their differences and disabilities if we are to interact harmoniously with them.

LEARNING OUTCOMES

3.1 Value and treat customers and colleagues from diverse backgrounds with respect and sensitivity.

3.2 Consider cultural differences in verbal and non-verbal communication.

3.3 Use gestures or simple words to communicate where language barriers exist.

3.4 Obtain assistance from colleagues or supervisors when required to facilitate communications.

Treating cultural differences with respect and sensitivity

It could be argued that respect must be earned—and in certain circumstances this may be right. In a retail situation, however, respect must be shown to colleagues in order to maintain a harmonious work environment and to customers as the sole providers of the revenue that keeps the organisation in business.

Showing respect and sensitivity to the people you come in to contact with on a daily basis is a matter of professional courtesy. People are all different and it is these differences that allow an organisation to grow and thrive. However, differences can also lead to misunderstandings and conflict so it is important to understand the nature of diversity in the workplace.

'Diverse' refers to a range of characteristics, including:

AGE

People often talk about the generation gap, for example that between 'Baby boomers' and 'Generation X or Y', and discriminate against them because of their age—'You're so young ... what would you know?' or 'You're too old to understand'—and, what is worse, will not employ someone because they are either too young or too old. It is, in fact, against the law to discriminate against a person for this reason (or any of the reasons listed below). People of all ages can make substantial contributions to the workplace. Young people have fresh ideas and lots of energy that they can share, whereas older staff members have a lot of experience and expertise that they can pass on

CULTURAL BACKGROUND AND RACE

A person's cultural or racial background can have an impact on the way in which they work and reasonable allowances should be made for them. For example people of certain cultural backgrounds may have strict dietary requirements, may not be allowed to consume alcohol or may have to observe certain religious or traditional customs. These are not reasons to discriminate against them or make fun of them. Different cultures are what make Australia the cosmopolitan country that it is, and we can learn a great deal from those of other backgrounds

DISABILITIES

Disabilities come in many different forms: a person might have a learning disability such as dyslexia; they may have a physical disability such as blindness, deafness or something temporary such as a broken leg or arm; or they may have a mental disability. Whatever the case, people with disabilities can contribute substantially to the workplace and should be treated with the same courtesy and respect as everyone else

FAMILY STRUCTURE

This relates to a person's family situation and their reasons for wanting to be in the workforce. For example, a woman whose children have all grown up and are now independent may wish to re-enter the workforce to find something fulfilling to do. Conversely in a family with small children the mother may need to go to work to make financial ends meet. In some cases it is the mother who goes to work and the father who stays at home to look after any small children. Again, whatever their circumstances or reasons for wanting to work these people have a great deal to offer a workplace team

GENDER

Both men and women have unique views on a range of different topics—all of which will have valid points and are worth considering in a team environment. Discriminating against someone because of their gender or sexual preference is not only against the law but is short-sighted, as solutions to problems may only be a simple matter of a looking at the issue from a different perspective.

LANGUAGE

Having multilingual people on your work team can provide many advantages where they can help with translations and interpreting where necessary. It can also cause misunderstanding where words or phrases are used incorrectly or accents are so strong that it is difficult to understand what a colleague from another language background is saying. Care, patience and tolerance should be shown to such colleagues to help them integrate more fully into the work environment.

All of these points are reasons to *celebrate* our differences and the talents and values that each can bring to the workforce. The different traditions, habits and points of view that are brought to the table through diversity are things that can help us grow and expand our own personal horizons as well as our organisation's success.

Overcoming communication problems in a diverse work environment

When dealing with people from diverse backgrounds it is inevitable that communication problems will arise. Some of these problems may be due to physical disabilities when communicating. For example, someone who is hearing impaired may not be able to hear instructions given to them correctly (or at all). Sometimes difficulties may arise because the other person cannot speak the same language. Whatever the reason for the difficulties, adjustments can be made to the way in which you work to accommodate these problems:

- Offer written policies and procedures on how tasks should be completed.
- Equally, for those whose English is not very good, procedures laid out in graphics can help.
- Provide detailed induction programs for new staff. This might include demonstrating how tasks should be completed and watching them do the task to ensure they have it right, and providing them with a mentor or 'buddy' for a given period of time.

There are a few other simple things to keep in mind when dealing with colleagues or customers from different cultural backgrounds.

- Use simple gestures in greeting. A smile, handshake or wave signify beginnings and endings of conversations or meetings and let people know visually what is happening. Adjustments will depend on the issue at hand; for example, for a person with a hearing impairment, maintain respectful eye contact and nod your head in understanding so the other person knows you are paying attention, and speak slowly and clearly so that they can read your lips
- Give simple directions or instructions when asked for information. Keep sentences short and to the point. Don't use long or difficult words. If possible show what is required so that the person you are talking to can not only hear the answer to their question but also see what they are supposed to do
- People who do not speak your language are not deaf, so shouting the words or speaking in a louder voice will not help them to understand you any better. Speak in your normal voice and add hand gestures or even draw pictures if necessary to make yourself understood.

Where to find assistance

If, despite all your best efforts, you still have difficulties, you may need to try other methods to make communication possible. These might include:

- using sign language, gestures, showing or demonstrating what you want to express. For example, showing a drinking movement with your hands if you are thirsty
- getting help from colleagues who are familiar with the customer's language. You might have friends or relatives who can speak another language who can help out if you telephone them
- outside organisations, including:
  - interpreter services
  - diplomatic services
  - local cultural organisations
  - appropriate government agencies
  - educational institutions
  - disability advocacy groups.

  All of these options might be able to assist you in the communication process.

Task 2.9

1. Download the 'Diversity and Inclusion at Walmart' document from their corporate website (www.walmartstores.com/download/4889.pdf) and answer the following questions: (a) Refer to page 2, 'Message from Sharon Orlopp' and to the statement: 'When we are open to opinions and approaches that differ from our own, we open the door to growth and excellence—for ourselves, for our associates and for our company'.

Discuss this statement in terms of how it might relate to your own organisation or personal experience. How would being open to diversity affect you or your company?
(b) Refer to page 5, 'Our differences spark innovation'. Discuss how being open to a diverse environment would have contributed to the success and innovation talked about in this paragraph.

2. Junko works as a window dresser at the Simply Jeans clothing company, which owns stores in all states of Australia. She moved here from Japan three years ago and, while she is trying hard, her English language skills are not yet very good. The company nevertheless hired her as her skills as a designer were extraordinary. Several weeks ago Junko attended a management meeting with her supervisor to get information on requirements for the beginning of the summer season in the stores. The discussion was creative, lively and fast-paced—leaving Junko unable to fully understand what was required of her. She was embarrassed to admit that she did not understand and spent the next six days creating a brand new image for the summer fashion campaign that turned out not be what they had in mind.

As a consequence this caused a substantial delay in the campaign timeline as the work had to be repeated. The shops missed a specific window of opportunity that they had been aiming for, costing the company a substantial amount of revenue.

a. Should Junko have been allowed to participate in the meeting? Why, or why not?
b. Describe how this situation could have been avoided.
c. What can you do in your workplace to ensure that diversity is appreciated and accommodated?

ELEMENT 4
WORK IN A TEAM

Working for an organisation of any kind means that you will be working with other staff to ensure your organisation's objectives are met. These objectives may include increasing revenue or customer awareness, or providing the best possible customer service. Whatever the objectives, meeting them will require teamwork, cooperation and an understanding, on your part, of how your role impacts on the company as a whole.

LEARNING OUTCOMES

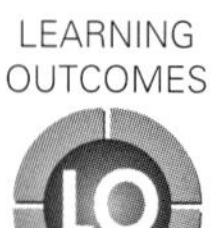

4.1 Demonstrate a courteous and helpful manner at all times.

4.2 Complete allocated tasks willingly, according to set timeframes.

4.3 Actively seek or provide assistance by approaching other team members when difficulties arise.

4.4 Identify and use lines of communication with supervisors and peers according to store policy.

4.5 Encourage, acknowledge and act upon constructive feedback provided by other team members.

4.6 Use questioning to minimise misunderstandings.

4.7 Identify signs of potential workplace conflict wherever possible and take action to resolve the situation using open and respectful communication.

4.8 Participate in team problem solving.

Ensuring a successful team environment

When working with a team of people it is very likely that others will depend on you completing your allocated tasks in order that they can get on with theirs. So the work you do has an impact not only on other staff in the organisation, but to successfully meeting goals.

For example, if your **allocated tasks** included opening the store in the morning, turning off the alarms and setting up the cash register, then other staff would be waiting for you to complete these tasks before they could begin their own tasks. If it was your job to produce and print out promotional flyers and lists for the organisation's chain of stores then sales staff would not be able to carry out these promotions properly until you had completed those tasks—potentially costing the organisation significant loss of sales.

It is therefore very important to understand your role within the organisation and work in cooperation with other staff to the required organisational and legislative standards. This may include requirements that you:

- demonstrate a courteous and helpful manner at all times—Working in harmony with colleagues creates a positive work environment and ensures that objectives and deadlines can be met. Behaving in a professional and courteous manner will also stand you in good stead should you need help or assistance yourself.
- complete allocated tasks willingly, according to set timeframes—As mentioned above, your part in a task or project may depend on other people doing their jobs correctly and on time—and others will be waiting for you to do the same. This is particularly true where the completion of a workplace project is the objective. There will be a sound reason for setting up a project: it might be to implement new procedures or to achieve a large specific task. Whatever that reason, there will usually be specific tasks allocated to team members in line with their strengths and expertise and timeframes in which each task in the project needs to be completed. One person holding up the process because they have not done their job correctly or completed it on time can hold up the entire team and project. This could have far-reaching consequences as the specific project may only be part of a whole strategy that management has put in place for business improvement and not finishing on time will not only hold up your team, but the whole organisation.

- give clear instructions—Should you be in a position where you are the one allocating tasks to more junior members of staff, it is important to give instructions clearly so that they know exactly what it is they are supposed to do. This extends to explaining policies and procedures to new staff members where applicable. Each person in the organisation's workforce should be aware of policies and procedures and the standards to which work must be completed.
- actively seek or provide assistance—by approaching other team members when difficulties arise. On occasion you may need help in completing a task. This may be because you are unfamiliar with the task, you have a large workload and are having difficulties completing everything, or you simply don't understand what needs to be done. In these cases it is important to ask for help rather than just go ahead on you own and perhaps get it wrong. Fixing a mistake can be more expensive and time consuming than asking for assistance and getting it right in the first place.
- identify and use lines of communication—with supervisors and peers according to store policy. This means understanding the roles and responsibilities of others in your organisation and communicating with them when required in the appropriate manner. This may also mean that you need to liaise with other departments, buyers or suppliers where necessary. Using the skills discussed earlier you can communicate at the appropriate level using the appropriate language.
- provide, encourage, acknowledge and act upon constructive feedback—Feedback is the act of giving or accepting a review of a person's performance. Feedback should always be constructive and encourage you or colleagues you are working with to improve the way you do things. As mentioned above, always ask for advice or assistance if you are having problems and ask for feedback on how you are performing. Equally if you are working with colleagues and you notice that they need assistance, offer positive feedback on how they might complete their allocated tasks more efficiently—without putting them down.
- use questioning—to minimise misunderstandings and confirm requirements. Communicating effectively is very important in a team environment: when tasks are allocated to you, ask questions if you have not fully understood an aspect of these tasks and confirm your understanding to make sure you have it right.

Task 2.10

Watch the YouTube Videos (1) 'Birds or People?' (http://youtube.com/jF80RqLkl6E) and (2) 'Teamwork' (http://youtube.com/FJVS__j_lio) and consider the following tasks.:

1. Discuss the advantages of working in a team in your organisation.
2. Discuss the consequences for your organisation of not working together as a team.
3. Refer to the display in 'Birds or People?'. Would this display have been possible without a great deal of cooperation?

Dealing with workplace conflict

Conflict between colleagues has the potential to completely disrupt the workplace and the team spirit and, if left unchecked, can weaken an organisation and perhaps even destroy it. To prevent what may start out to be a relatively minor issue from escalating into a major one, conflict situations need to be identified and dealt with.

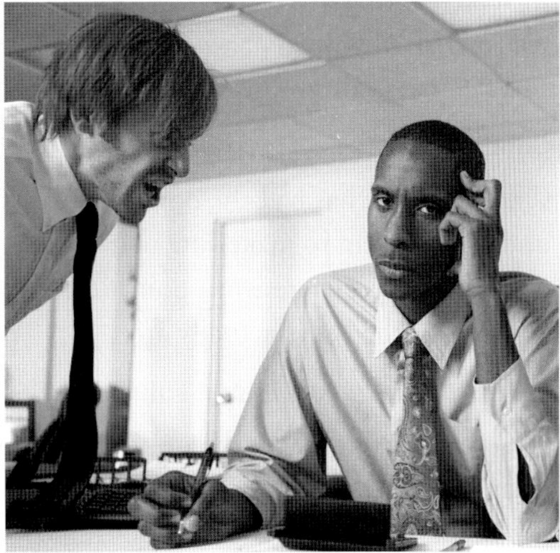

Figure 2.4 What do you do with an angry person?

Good conflict resolution skills include a willingness to meet the needs of others. The issues involved in the situation must certainly be discussed and addressed, but what about a person's human needs—the need, for example, to be a recognised and valued member of the team? These are important aspects of dealing with conflict situations and require good communication skills.

Causes of workplace conflict may include:

- poor communication or a lack of information from management
- changes to practices and procedures
- cultural misunderstandings
- colleagues vying for power
- staff dissatisfied with management
- weak leadership or change of leadership
- lack of empathy from colleagues or supervisors
- general unresolved complaints.

All of these issues can cause dissatisfaction and affect staff morale. If acted upon sensitively and quickly they can be resolved without any disruption to work. If they are ignored, however, then what may have started out as minor problems have the ability to completely break down the harmony within the workforce. This in turn can affect an organisation's productivity as staff become demotivated. Poor productivity will affect the organisation's revenue earnings.

Steps for solving problems and dealing with workplace conflict can include (but are not limited to) the following:

Listen to what the other party has to say

Their opinions and viewpoints are just as valid as yours and will be influenced by the way in which they have grown up and been educated, so just because they don't agree with you doesn't make them wrong—they may simply have a different perspective. Let them have their say—listen attentively and show empathy with them. Arguing with someone over who is right or wrong, or who is to blame for a situation, does nothing to solve the problem so leave that aside and try to stay positive.

Confirm details

Once everyone has had the opportunity to say what they think, confirm the details as you understand them to make sure that everyone is on the same wavelength and moving in the same direction. There is no point in moving forward if there are still misunderstandings about what the issues actually are.

Find a mutually acceptable solution

Negotiate a solution. Each conflict is going to require that compromises be made; decide what the really important aspects of the problem are and concentrate on those. Often a solution to a problem is drawn out unnecessarily because people focus and concentrate on side issues that are less important than the main issue at hand. Stick to the point and don't allow the issues to become clouded.

Use third-party mediation

If necessary (where a conflict cannot be resolved privately or quickly) it may be necessary to bring in a neutral party. This may be a supervisor or other colleague not directly involved in the problem at hand. This person would listen to all sides of an issue and offer a neutral solution.

Follow up

Once the solution has been found and agreed upon follow through and implement the measures arrived at, checking at various times during the implementation process that the solution is working and still acceptable.

Task 2.11

Scenario

You work at Jim's Electrical Store. As part of your role, you are responsible for making sure the shelves in your section of the store are always fully stocked and tidy and you take pride in the fact that this section is always up to store standards. One of your colleagues, however, is continually leaving stock lying around in untidy heaps or out of place when he has finished demonstrating products to customers. You have spoken to this person a number of times and asked him to put things back where they belong, but he simply laughs it off.

In the past few weeks this problem has become worse and you suspect that your colleague is now deliberately leaving stock lying around to annoy you. You feel very frustrated by this unprofessional behaviour and understand that something needs to be done to avoid a full-blown confrontation.

Describe, in detail, what you will do to deal with this situation.

ELEMENT 5
READ AND INTERPRET RETAIL DOCUMENTS

Communication is also about understanding and making efficient use of the documents your organisation gathers and stores. Retail documents can give detailed information on what products are or are not selling, allowing you to order stock appropriately. This, in turn, means that the organisation uses its resources and budgets in the most effective manner. Retail documents can also provide information on how well the organisation is performing financially—providing opportunities for improvement or updating and expanding skills and knowledge. Then, too, there are the daily documents you will need to access and use to do your job properly.

LEARNING OUTCOMES

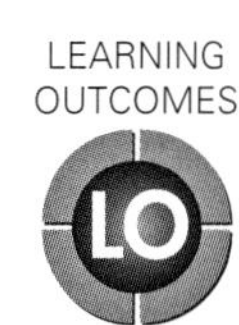

5.1 Identify and list a range of retail documents.

5.2 Read and interpret information from a range of retail documents.

5.3 Demonstrate appropriate application of information contained in retail documentation.

Types of retail documents

There are a great variety of retail documents that you may be able to access for information. In general they will include (but are not limited to):

- credit slips—which can take the form of slips given to customers who have returned an item in exchange for other goods, or gift vouchers
- lay-by slips—outlining customer details, the products they have laid away and their payment history
- manufacturer instructions—detailing the features and benefits of a product or service, how it is to be used and under what conditions. Manufacturer instructions are an extremely useful source of product knowledge

- planograms—that detail how a display is to be set up within the store or in a window. This subject will be covered in Chapters 5 and 6
- staff record forms—which are strictly confidential documents that provide staff contact details as well as their work history information
- stock sheets—which outline what products the store has in stock and how many of each item. This is useful when monitoring stock levels and re-ordering
- timetables—which could be used for a number of different reasons; for example, scheduling promotional activities and displays, staff rostering or rotating stock
- sales performance reports—which are very useful in determining how well the organisation is performing. These will usually provide information about such things as how each product is performing and what times of the year are busier than others. This type of information can be used for forward planning and determining what stock to carry (or not) as well as how much stock to carry.

Interpreting retail information

Depending on the type of document, you will gain information that will be useful to you in given situations. A credit slip, for example, will give you information on the dollar value of the credit and details of the customer to whom the credit applies. A planogram will give you details on what stock to display in the store, what shelves or racks to use, and the manner and layout in which it is to be displayed. Timetables and schedules will provide information on when to change these displays, or how staff are rostered to work. Stock sheets or inventories will let you know when you are running low on merchandise and need to order more.

Sales performance reports are, perhaps, the most useful retail documents as they provide detailed information about the organisation's performance. On the following page we have provided an example of a sales performance spread sheet and graphs.

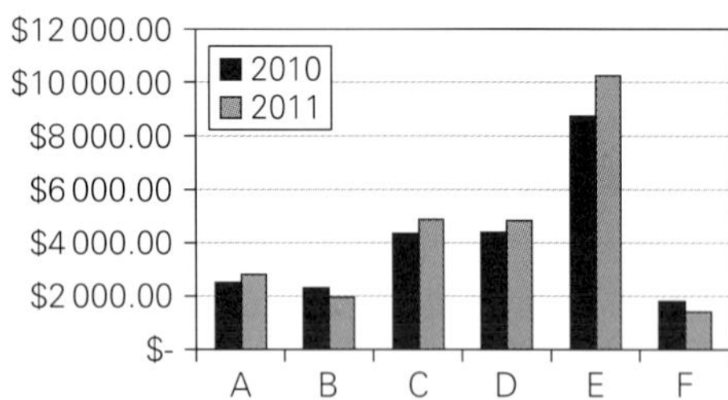

Figure 2.5 Products by total sales price

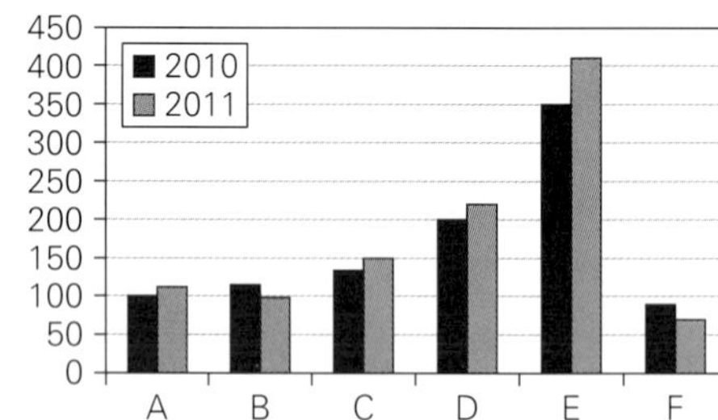

Figure 2.6 Products by type

Table 2.1

Sales performance report

Items	2010					2011					Total qty	Total cost	Total sales
	Qty	Unit price	Unit sales price	Total cost	Total sales	Qty	Unit price	Unit sales price	Total cost	Total sales			
Product A	100	$ 15.95	$ 25.00	$ 1595.00	$ 2500.00	112	$ 15.98	$ 25.00	$ 1789.76	$ 2800.00	212	$ 3384.76	$ 5300.00
Product B	115	$ 11.74	$ 20.00	$ 1350.10	$ 2300.00	98	$ 13.51	$ 20.00	$ 1323.98	$ 1960.00	213	$ 2674.08	$ 4260.00
Product C	134	$ 23.96	$ 32.50	$ 3210.64	$ 4355.00	150	$ 24.95	$ 32.50	$ 3742.50	$ 4875.00	284	$ 6953.14	$ 9230.00
Product D	200	$ 16.05	$ 22.00	$ 3210.00	$ 4400.00	220	$ 17.38	$ 22.00	$ 3823.60	$ 4840.00	420	$ 7033.60	$ 9240.00
Product E	350	$ 18.99	$ 25.00	$ 6646.50	$ 8750.00	410	$ 21.21	$ 25.00	$ 8696.10	$ 10250.00	760	$15342.60	$19000.00
Product F	90	$ 15.98	$ 20.00	$ 1438.20	$ 1800.00	70	$ 16.76	$ 20.00	$ 1173.20	$ 1400.00	160	$ 2611.40	$ 3200.00
Totals	**989**			**$ 17450.44**	**$ 24105**	**1060**			**$ 20549.14**	**$ 26125**	**2049**	**$ 37999.58**	**$ 33130.00**

As you will see from the spreadsheet and graphs above, they give details of product sales over a two-year period. In most organisations these figures will go back several years giving a very clear picture of which products perform better than others.

In the above example you can see that product E clearly stands out as the best seller over both 2010 and 2011, whereas Product F sells the least, and in fact is selling less in 2011 than in 2010.

The total cost of purchasing product E over the two year period was $15 342.60 and the total sales over that period were $19 000 so that product made a profit of $3 657.40 over that time whereas the profit made on product F was only $588.60 over the same period.

Using information such as this, management can make a decision on whether it is worth stocking product F in future.

Task 2.12

Using the spreadsheet and graphs above, answer the following questions:

1. Given that product E is the highest seller, which is the next highest?
2. What profit did the next highest seller make over the two-year period?
3. How many of product C were sold in 2010?
4. Which products actually sold less in 2011 than in 2010?
5. Would you continue to stock product B? Why, or why not?
6. Discuss what you could do to increase the sales of products not selling very well.

Reading and interpreting retail documents can provide a foundation for sound business decisions and give clear guidance on what is to be done in any given situation.

Terms and Conditions

Katies clothing store websites provide excellent examples of policy and terms and condition information.

A copy of Katies terms and conditions for online purchases can be found at:
http://www.katies.com.au/Buying-Online/Terms-and-Conditions.aspx

A copy of Katies returns policy for online purchases can be found at:
http://www.katies.com.au/Buying-Online/Returns-Policy.aspx

A copy of Katies privacy policy for online purchases can be found at:
http://www.katies.com.au/Buying-Online/Privacy-Policy.aspx

ASSESSMENT 1: WORKPLACE OBSERVATION

<table>
<tr><td>Assessment context</td><td>This observation is designed to assess your ability to communicate effectively with customers and colleagues. During the course of the observations you will be required to deal with situations as outlined by your trainer/assessor in accordance with the performance criteria of this unit (outlined at the end of the chapter).</td></tr>
<tr><td>Assessment instructions</td><td>Your trainer/assessor will observe how well you:
1. Customer interaction:
a. Greet customers on arrival in your store—creating a welcoming environment
b. Use verbal and non-verbal communication skills to establish a rapport with customers and find out their requirements
c. Maintain confidentiality and tact in your dealings with customers
d. Handle enquiries made by customers contacting you by telephone, email or other forms of technology
e. Pass on messages from customers to other staff
f. Interact with customers from diverse backgrounds:
i. Use appropriate levels of language and formality
ii. Use gestures and non-verbal language to develop an understanding of their needs
iii. Ask for assistance from colleagues or supervisors where necessary.
2. Colleague interaction:
a. Treat colleagues with respect and courtesy
b. Complete your tasks in a timely manner
c. Use appropriate communication skills to deal with problems or conflicts
d. Participate effectively as part of the workplace team
e. Seek and provide feedback from and to other staff
f. Understand the lines of authority within your organisation and communicate appropriately.</td></tr>
<tr><td>Evidence required</td><td>Completed observation checklist (located on McGraw Hill website)</td></tr>
<tr><td>Range and conditions</td><td>• Your trainer/assessor will set up a number of appointments to watch you in your workplace undertaking normal day-to-day duties.
• These observations may take place over a number of visits so you can demonstrate your skills and knowledge in all aspects of the unit competencies fully and on more than one occasion.
• For in-class students, this assessment can be undertaken as a role play, interacting with a variety of 'customers' played by other students.</td></tr>
<tr><td>Materials and resources required</td><td>Access to a retail work environment</td></tr>
<tr><td>Reasonable adjustments</td><td>In the event that you have difficulty understanding the assessment tasks due to language or other difficulties, your trainer will attempt to make reasonable adjustments to the assessment paper in order to afford you every opportunity to achieve competency.</td></tr>
<tr><td>Decision-making rules</td><td>Competency checklist (located on the McGraw Hill website).</td></tr>
</table>

ASSESSMENT 2: PORTFOLIO

<table>
<tr><td>Assessment context</td><td>A portfolio is an opportunity for you to gather information into a useful resource that will help you along your career path. In it, you will collect a range of workplace information designed to improve your knowledge of the industry in which you are working.</td></tr>
<tr><td>Assessment instructions</td><td>For this assessment you will be required to collect information on the following areas of a retail workplace. You will then be required to answer a range of questions relating to the information you have collected.

Information to collect includes:
1. Telephone system operating instructions
2. Website information on your organisation (including any blogs or Facebook information)
3. Policies and procedures dealing with:
a. customer service delivery
b. dealing with diversity in the workplace.
4. Staff handbook
5. Your job description
6. Documents on any team project work that you were involved in. This may include meetings about training, WHS issues, store management or similar.
7. A range of retail documents including:
a. staff rosters
b. merchandising plans
c. lay-by terms and conditions of your organisation
d. refund and returns policies and procedures of your organisation
e. telephone message pads.

Questions
1. Does your organisation have a policy or procedure for dealing with diversity? Give an example of how you would deal with a blind customer.
2. Describe a team project that you might have been involved in, in your workplace:
a. Describe how tasks were allocated (who to and reasons for choosing specific people).
b. Did you complete your allocated tasks on time? If not, explain why not?
c. Describe how the team members supported each other in the completion of the project.
d. Discuss the value of getting feedback on your performance in a team environment.
3. Describe the induction procedure in your organisation.</td></tr>
<tr><td>Evidence required</td><td>1. Copies of all documents outlined above.
2. Responses to questions outlined above.</td></tr>
<tr><td>Range and conditions</td><td>You may need permission from your workplace supervisor to collect this information.</td></tr>
<tr><td>Materials and resources required</td><td>No special requirements.</td></tr>
<tr><td>Reasonable adjustments</td><td>In the event that you have difficulty understanding the assessment tasks due to language or other difficulties, your trainer will attempt to make reasonable adjustments to the assessment paper in order to afford you every opportunity to achieve competency.</td></tr>
<tr><td>Decision-making rules</td><td>No special requirements.</td></tr>
</table>

COMPETENCY MAPPING

Element			Performance criteria	Task	Assessment	Refer to page
1	Communicate face-to-face with customers	1.1	Maintain a welcoming customer environment that reflects store branding and market position and is in line with store policy and procedures.	2.1	1	56
		1.2	Greet customer warmly according to store policy and procedures.	2.1	1	56–58
		1.3	Create effective service environment through verbal and non-verbal interaction according to store policy and procedures.	2.4, 2.5	1	59–64
		1.4	Use questioning and active listening to determine customer needs.	2.2, 2.3, 2.4	1	59
		1.5	Demonstrate confidentiality and tact.	2.6	1	65
2	Use technology to communicate with customers	2.1	Answer telephone according to store procedures.	2.8	1	66–68
		2.2	Use questioning and active listening to identify caller and establish and confirm requirements.	2.8	1	59–64
		2.3	Use telephone system functions according to instructions.		1, 2	70
		2.4	Use email, social networking sites and other technologies to receive and process information and customer requests in line with store policy and procedures.	2.8	1, 2	71
		2.5	Record and promptly pass on messages or information.	2.7	1, 2	67–68
		2.6	Inform customer of any problems and relevant action being taken.	2.8	1	66–71
		2.7	Perform follow-up action as necessary.	2.8	1	66–71
3	Communicate with customers and colleagues from diverse backgrounds	3.1	Value and treat customers and colleagues from diverse backgrounds with respect and sensitivity.	2.9	1, 2	73–74
		3.2	Consider cultural differences in verbal and non-verbal communication.		1	74–75
		3.3	Use gestures or simple words to communicate where language barriers exist.		1	73–75
		3.4	Obtain assistance from colleagues or supervisors when required to facilitate communications.		1	73–75

continued

Element		Performance criteria		Task	Assessment	Refer to page
4	Work in a team	4.1	Demonstrate a courteous and helpful manner at all times.		1	77–78
		4.2	Complete allocated tasks willingly, according to set timeframes.	2.10	1, 2	77–78
		4.3	Actively seek or provide assistance by approaching other team members when difficulties arise.		1, 2	77–78
		4.4	Identify and use lines of communication with supervisors and peers according to store policy.	2.11	1	77–78
		4.5	Encourage, acknowledge and act upon constructive feedback provided by other team members.		1, 2	77–78
		4.6	Use questioning to minimise misunderstandings.		1	77–78
		4.7	Identify signs of potential workplace conflict wherever possible and take action to resolve the situation using open and respectful communication.	2.11	1	79–80
		4.8	Participate in team problem solving.	2.11	1	79–80
5	Read and interpret retail documents	5.1	Identify and list a range of retail documents.		1	81–83
		5.2	Read and interpret information from a range of retail documents.	2.12, 2.13	1	81–83
		5.3	Demonstrate appropriate application of information contained in retail documentation.	2.12, 2.13	1	81–83

Required skills and knowledge	Task	Assessment	Refer to page
Required skills			
Communication and interpersonal skills, including: • negotiating • questioning and listening • resolving conflict • using positive and inclusive language.	2.2, 2.3, 2.4, 2.5	1, 2	59–65, 73–80
Literacy skills to: • read and interpret workplace documentation, such as store policies and procedures and retail documents • record messages.	2.12, 2.13	1, 2	81–84
Technology skills to operate information and communications technology, including: • email • social networking technology • telephone system.	2.7, 2.8	1, 2	65–71

Required skills and knowledge	Task	Assessment	Refer to page
Required knowledge			
Functions and procedures for operating telephones and other communication equipment.	2.8	1, 2	65–71
Goods and services provided by the store.		1	56–58
Location of store departments.		1	
Store policy and procedures in regard to: • allocated duties and responsibilities • code of conduct, including sensitivity to diversity • internal and external customer contact • verbal and non-verbal presentation.	2.2, 2.3, 2.4, 2.5, 2.6, 2.9	1, 2	59–65
Critical aspects of evidence			
Provides a welcoming environment by treating customers in a courteous and helpful manner.		1	56
Uses effective questioning and active listening techniques to communicate with customers, while maintaining an awareness of the need for discretion, tact and confidentiality.	2.2, 2.3, 2.4, 2.5	1	59–64, 73–75
Interprets and communicates information to customers, supervisors and peers both face to face and via other electronic communication equipment.	2.7, 2.8	1, 2	59–71
Accesses, comprehends and processes information according to store policy and procedures.	2.12, 2.13	1, 2	65
Follows routine instructions and seeks advice and assistance if required.		1	75, 77–78
Participates actively and positively within a workplace team.		1	76–80

Chapter 3

SIRXIND101

Work effectively in a customer service environment

Figure 3.1 Offering customer service

Working in a **customer service environment** means ensuring that each person who comes in to your store leaves again having had their needs attended to. Doing this *effectively* means serving them in such a way that they will come back to do business with you again—time after time—because they are truly satisfied with the service they received.

Working effectively in a customer service environment is about more than dealing with customers however. It is also about ensuring that your workplace operates efficiently (so that customer service can be offered in the best way), and supporting your colleagues to make sure they are also in a position to work to the standards required by the organisation.

ELEMENT 1
WORK WITHIN ORGANISATIONAL REQUIREMENTS

Each workplace will have set standards and procedures which have been put in place to make sure staff know what to do, how to do it and when to do it—to a consistently high level. Making sure that you work to these standards is important to maintaining the store's reputation and efficiency levels.

1.1 Identify and read organisation's requirements and responsibilities and seek advice from appropriate people where necessary.

1.2 Interpret staff rosters and provide sufficient notice of unavailability for rostered hours according to workplace policy and procedures.

1.3 Develop and use a current working knowledge and understanding of employee and employer rights and responsibilities.

1.4 Comply with relevant duty of care and legal responsibilities, and support organisational culture.

1.5 Identify roles and responsibilities of colleagues and immediate supervisors

1.6 Identify standards and values considered to be detrimental to the organisation and communicate this through appropriate channels.

1.7 Identify, recognise and follow behaviour that contributes to a safe and sustainable work environment

LEARNING OUTCOMES

LO

Understanding organisational requirements

As mentioned above most organisations will have certain requirements that relate to the way in which they want work completed. These may be entirely internal requirements, or they may be based on legislative or industry requirements. It is very important to understand these requirements and follow them at all times.

In brief, an organisation's requirements may include understanding:

- access and equity principles and practice—ensuring that all people within your organisation are treated equally with no discrimination.
- business and performance plans—understanding what the organisations goals and objectives are and helping towards achieving them.
- ethical standards—dealing honestly and openly with customers, colleagues and management.
- legal and organisation policies, guidelines and requirements—ensuring that you are aware of your role and responsibilities both in a legal sense and follow procedures to the required standards. This includes observing workplace health and safety procedures.

- modes of communication—communicating with customers, colleagues and management in the most appropriate way, whether it is face to face or by way of written communication or reporting.
- interaction with other team members and management—ensuring a harmonious and cooperative work environment.
- quality and continuous improvement processes and standards—looking out for areas that can be improved.

Some of these can be found in the organisation's Staff Handbook, or in their Policy and Procedures Manual. In either case, these documents should give you clear guidance on the company's expectations of you. We will look at some of these areas in greater detail as we move through the chapter.

SEEKING ASSISTANCE

There may be times during a normal working day when you may be unsure of what to do. In these cases do not 'make it up as you go along' and hope that you have got it right! If in doubt there are people you can ask for help and assistance. These may include other colleagues, supervisors or managers. Asking for help is not a sign of weakness or incompetence. You cannot know everything there is to know about an organisation—especially if you have just joined it. Asking questions is a sign that you are interested in your work and shows that you want to do your job correctly.

Task 3.1

Look up the policies and procedures in your organisation and answer the following questions:

1. How are toxic chemicals (such as cleaning agents) to be handled and stored?
2. What is the procedure for processing the banking at the end of the day?
3. Who do you need to contact in case of an emergency or incident at work?
4. What is the procedure for closing the shop at the end of the trading day?
5. What is the procedure for dealing with a refund?
6. What is the procedure for dealing with an aggressive, complaining customer?

Staff rosters

All organisations will have a given set of tasks that must be performed every day if the business is to operate smoothly. These tasks may need to be undertaken in a certain order or to given standards. So it is important that you are available to work in line with the organisation's **staff roster** as others may be depending on you to complete your tasks correctly and on time, so that they can get on with theirs. Rosters provide staff with a schedule of working hours for the week, fortnight or month ahead and generally display the number of hours, days of the week and start and finish times each staff member is scheduled to work over that period.

The **Retail Award** requires that an employer post staff rosters on a notice board where all employees can access it. Full time staff are *generally* rostered to work 38 hours per week, whereas casual or part-time staff undertake shifts of less than 38 hours.

TYPES OF SHIFTS

Shift work is a type of work scheduling system that generally requires you to work outside normal morning to late afternoon times (such as 9 am to 5 pm, five-day-a-week schedule). Many jobs require staff to work in shifts, particularly in businesses that are open 24 hours a day or that require round-the-clock security or maintenance. These can include supermarkets, airports as well as many retail stores today. Types of work shift schedules include fixed, split and rotating shifts.

Fixed shifts

On a fixed shift, you work the same number of hours, starting and stopping at the same times, for a specified period of days. These types of shifts are typically used in static systems, where staff work the same shifts regularly. An example of a fixed shift is a nightshift, where you are permanently assigned to work the same hours each night and don't ever switch over to dayshifts.

Split shifts

Staff who work at two or more different times each day are on split shifts. The 'split' refers to daily *unpaid breaks* taken in between paid shift work. An example of a job that uses a split shift schedule is in hospitality where a waiter in a hotel restaurant may be rostered on to work the breakfast service early in the morning, then go home (the unpaid split) and return in the evening to work the dinner service (which would be the second part of the shift).

Rotating shifts

Rotating shifts means that staff work at different times based on a pre-planned pattern. For example, you could work the morning shift for three consecutive days in a row and then move forward to working the afternoon shift for three days, on a rotating basis.

EXAMPLE: ROSTER—GENERAL RETAIL INDUSTRY AWARD 2010

Week beginning: 15/01/20xx

Award title: General Retail Industry Award 2010	**Minimum shift length (part-time):** 3 hours **Minimum shift length (casual):** 3 hours	**Maximum hours of work without a meal break:** 5 hours (employees working 10+ hours are entitled to 2 meal breaks)	**Rest breaks:** 1 × 10 minute paid break for shifts of 4–7 hours: 2 × 10 minutes paid for shifts of 7+ hours

ALL STAFF NOTE: You must take your break as rostered below. Ensure you have at least 30 minutes off if working more than 5 hours.

Employee's name		*Alison Clark*	*James Martin*	*Jillian Anders*	*Mike Johnson*		
Monday:	Start	*9.00 am*	*9.00 am*				
	Meal break	*12 noon*	*1.00 pm*				
15../1../......	Finish	*5.00 pm*	*5.00 pm*				
Tuesday:	Start	*9.00 am*	*9.00 am*				
	Meal break	*12 noon*	*1.00 pm*				
16../1../......	Finish	*5.00 pm*	*5.00 pm*				
Wednesday:	Start	*9.00 am*	*9.00 am*				
	Meal break	*12 noon*	*1.00 pm*				
17../1../......	Finish	*5.00 pm*	*5.00 pm*				
Thursday:	Start	*9.00 am*	*9.00 am*				
	Meal break	*12 noon*	*1.00 pm*				
18../1../......	Finish	*5.00 pm*	*5.00 pm*				
Friday:	Start	*9.00 am*	*9.00 am*	*9.00 am*	*9.00 am*		
	Meal break	*12 noon*	*1.00 pm*	*12 noon*	*1.00 pm*		
19../1./......	Finish	*5.00 pm*	*5.00 pm*	*5.00 pm*	*5.00 pm*		
Saturday:	Start	*9.00 am*	*9.00 am*	*9.00 am*	*9.00 am*		
	Meal break			*12 noon*	*1.00 pm*		
20../1../......	Finish			*5.00 pm*	*5.00 pm*		
Sunday:	Start			*9.00 am*	*9.00 am*		
	Meal break			*12 noon*	*1.00 pm*		
21../1../......	Finish			*5.00 pm*	*5.00 pm*		

Source: http://www.fairwork.gov.au/resources/templates/pages/industry-specific.aspx

Task 3.2

Looking at the staff roster above answer the following questions:

1. What is the minimum shift length for a part-time employee?
2. What is the maximum number of hours an employee can work without a meal break.
3. If an employee was working for a shift of longer than 7 hours, how many rest breaks would they be entitled to?
4. How many meal breaks are employees entitled to if they are working for more than 10 hours?
5. If available, submit a copy of your own work roster to your trainer and explain:
   a. Do you work full time, part time or casual?
   b. Describe what hours you are generally required to work.
   c. What procedure must you follow if you are unable to attend a work shift?

Rights, responsibilities and legal obligations

In addition to understanding policies and procedures there are certain rights and responsibilities that you must be aware of in order to work efficiently. These rights and responsibilities relate not only to the employee but to the employer as well.

While in the workplace an employee's rights and responsibilities may include:

- attendance and punctuality—making sure that you attend work in line with your rostered hours, or advising your supervisor should there be some reason why you are unable to work as required
- maintaining confidentiality and privacy of the business, client and colleague information
- knowing and understanding the terms and conditions of own employment and role within the organisation
- obeying all lawful orders and instructions given to you
- understanding the legal ramifications of discrimination and sexual harassment in the workplace; you may not discriminate or harass others in your workplace, nor should you allow this to happen to you
- the right to union representation
- understanding the industry awards or agreements under which you are employed
- not knowingly cause harm or damage to any person or workplace equipment
- attending all training programs supplied by the employer.

Employer rights and responsibilities extend to:

- taking responsibility for providing a safe environment free from discrimination and sexual harassment according to relevant state or territory and commonwealth anti-discrimination legislation

- the right to counsel or dismiss employees if they:
  - are negligent, careless or cause an accident
  - commit a criminal offence or
  - commit acts of disloyalty, such as revealing confidential information.
- establishing evacuation procedures in the event of an emergency
- establishing policies and procedures to provide guidance on a range of situations, including grievance and conflict resolution, robbery, threats, chemical spills and fire training for staff on
  - use of new equipment
  - workplace health and safety issues
  - company policies.
- career succession plans that help grow and expand staff knowledge and therefore their worth to the organisation.

Many of the conditions under which you are employed will be covered in your workplace contract or staff handbook and can also be found in the relevant industry awards (for example the General Retail Industry Award 2010 on the Australian Industrial Relations Commission website, www.airc.gov.au/awardmod/awards/general_retail.pdf).

Roles within an organisation

Small organisations may only have a manager and a small number of casual employees and duties are split fairly equally among these few people. Larger retail organisations, such as department stores, however will have a steeper **organisational hierarchy**. Roles found in these organisations can range from the store's general manager (or managing director) who has overall responsibility for the entire organisation and oversees the main operational issues, to department heads who are responsible for looking after their section of the store. This may include maintaining the presentation of their area and managing the sales staff in their departments. Additionally a larger organisation may have accounts staff who look after payroll and all other financial details of the organisation, there may be a stores supervisor who looks after the warehouse (storage) area of the organisation where stock is kept until it is needed on the shop floor. The 'stores' area may also include drivers who look after delivering products to customers.

Each role within the organisation will have specific duties to fulfil and will contribute to the company's goals and objectives.

Depending on the organisation, there may be specific procedures and protocols to adhere to. These may relate to channels of communication; as a casual employee, for example, you may not have direct access to a head of department or general manager and will need to communicate with them through your supervisor. Communication between colleagues and supervisors, however, should be frequent as feedback received from customers or suppliers about product and service performance can help the organisation continually improve.

Set out in Figure 3.2 is a typical organisational chart.

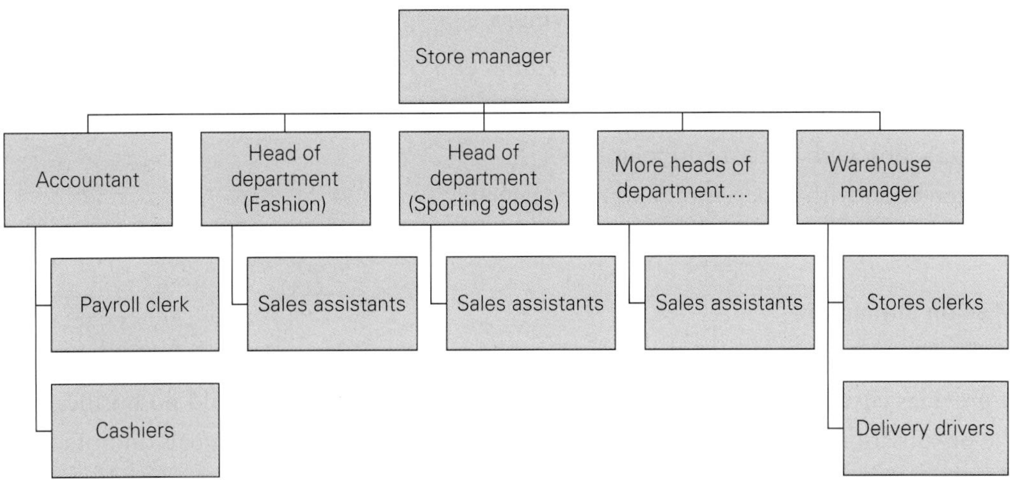

Figure 3.2 A typical organisational chart

Supporting the organisational culture

All of the above are issues and areas that support the organisational culture and understanding them helps establish a safe, harmonious and efficient work environment.

A working knowledge of the organisation's culture also means that staff are able to contribute to achieving the organisation's goals and objectives so it is important to be aware of such things as the following.

CHAIN OF COMMAND

The chain of command determines who has the authority to make decisions, who is responsible for given areas of the organisation, and the methods by which you can approach them with ideas, suggestions and feedback.

Organisational structure

You should understand the various departments within the organisation, the functions they fulfil and your own position and role within this structure and interdepartmental communication channels.

Duty of care

You must understand your responsibilities in terms of dealing with colleagues, suppliers and customers. Duty of care is a very serious issue. It means that a legal obligation is imposed upon you to observe a standard of reasonable care when performing tasks that could, potentially, harm others.

For an excellent description of duty of care obligations and legislation see the WorkCover Authority of NSW website:

www.workcover.nsw.gov.au/healthsafety/Pages/Dutyofcare.aspx

Organisational goals, values and behaviours

Understand the workplace policies, procedures and quality assurance manuals relating to:

- contact with customers
- interaction with other team members
- interaction with supervision and management
- job descriptions and responsibilities.

Mission statement

A mission statement is a short, simple, statement that outlines the purpose of an organisation. It provides customers with an inspirational overview of why they should do business with the organisation, and provides staff with a simple statement of what goals and objectives they can contribute towards. Examples of mission statements include:

Coca Cola

At the Coca-Cola Company we strive to refresh the world, inspire moments of optimism and happiness, create value and make a difference

Nike

To bring inspiration and innovation to every athlete in the world

Walt Disney Corporation

The mission of The Walt Disney Company is to be one of the world's leading producers and providers of entertainment and information. Using our portfolio of brands to differentiate our content, services and consumer products, we seek to develop the most creative, innovative and profitable entertainment experiences and related products in the world.

Looking at the mission statements above, can you see how they would help employees work towards achieving the company goals?

Detrimental work practices

No matter how efficient an organisation strives to be, there will always be practices that fall below the required standards and have a negative impact on the business. These may be caused by:

- human error—where staff inadvertently make mistakes or have not been shown the correct procedures
- worker carelessness—sloppy work on the part of employees
- poor maintenance—of equipment, machinery or premises—leading to errors or below standard work
- inconsistent work habits—where staff are simply not following procedures and no remedial action is taken
- haphazard risk identification and management—potentially leading to injury or damage.

The impact of detrimental work practices can be very negative to the organisation as a whole, leading not only to injury to staff or damage to property, but also damage to the organisation's reputation and standing in the community. It is therefore very important that all staff within an organisation work to the required standards and report any incidents of detrimental practices to supervisors wherever they are observed.

Task 3.3

Go the following 'Corporate Governance' in the Investor section of the Myer website: http://investor.myer.com.au/phoenix.zhtml?c=231681&p=irol-govhighlights. Download 'Code of Conduct' from the Governance documents and answer the following questions:

1. What are the three objectives of their code of conduct?
2. Under the code of conduct, what are the responsibilities of employees/contractors?
3. List at least four other policies the company has.
4. Who should you report breaches of the code to?
5. Describe the consequences of breaching the code of conduct.
6. List at least four things that the company holds as being confidential.

Contributing to a safe and sustainable work environment

Sustainability in the workplace is becoming ever more important. As people become more aware of our impact on the world around us, customers are actively seeking out suppliers who contribute towards sustainability. From a business perspective, sustainability is not only a matter of reducing the negative impact we have on the world around us and its resources, but it can also offer smart businesses significant savings where new and better systems are introduced.

What can you, as an employee, do to contribute to the smooth and efficient operation of your organisation? In addition to doing your job to the required standards there are a number of ways in which staff can make a difference to the organisation including implementing environmental protection procedures, such as:

- waste minimisation
- recycling
- reuse
- energy efficiency, e.g. electricity saving devices and practices
- waste disposal
- resource management
- water efficiency.

Task 3.4

Looking at your own organisation's policies and procedures discuss the following.

1. What areas of the organisation are subject to legislation and compliance?
2. Briefly describe your company's code of conduct and duty of care procedures.
3. How does your organisation ensure that staff are aware of their WHS roles and responsibilities?

ELEMENT 2
SUPPORT THE WORK TEAM

In any organisation—working in a harmonious and cooperative environment comes down to how well staff work together. Workplace conflicts can seriously undermine and damage that environment, so it is important that all staff work towards the common organisational goals and endeavour to establish good team work.

LEARNING OUTCOMES

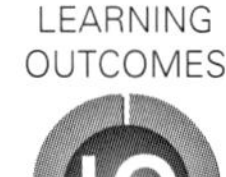

2.1 Display courteous and helpful behaviour at all times.

2.2 Take opportunities to enhance the level of assistance offered to colleagues and meet all reasonable requests for assistance within acceptable workplace timeframes.

2.3 Complete allocated tasks as required.

2.4 Seek assistance when difficulties arise.

2.5 Use questioning techniques to clarify instructions or responsibilities.

2.6 Identify and display a non-discriminatory attitude in all contacts with customers and other staff members.

Display courteous and helpful behaviour

Courteous behaviour does not mean that you have to agree with everything your colleagues say, just to avoid disharmony. Disharmony and conflict generally only occurs when discussions get overly emotional and feelings are hurt. In a professional work environment, it is important to remember that all staff members are entitled to present their points of view. While another person's points of view may be different to your own, it does not mean that they are wrong—just different. They will be influenced by that person's background, upbringing, educational levels and personal experiences and, so, are just as valid as your own. Therefore it's important to listen to what colleagues have to say with an open mind.

Points of difference can be negotiated to reach mutually beneficial outcomes and treating all people within your organisation with respect and courtesy goes a long way to establishing a close team environment—one in which ideas can be expressed freely without fear of being ridiculed. Always bear in mind that *golden rule: Treat others as you would expect them to treat you.*

Take opportunities to enhance the level of assistance

Displaying courteous behaviour also extends to offering help wherever and whenever it is needed. Often a person's workload can be quite large, and depending on how many additional issues a colleague may have to deal with in the course of their normal day, they may get overwhelmed by the many tasks they need to undertake. All staff within an organisation should, at all times, be working towards the same goal—going in the same direction. So offering to help a colleague will not only benefit that colleague, but yourself—in terms of getting your own part of a joint task or project completed and, in the end, the entire organisation.

Policies, procedures, standards and goals are developed at managerial levels, filtered through, discussed and implemented with and by department heads or supervisors who, in turn, implement these standards and procedures with their staff to ensure that the organisation's goals and targets are met; all staff heading in the same direction.

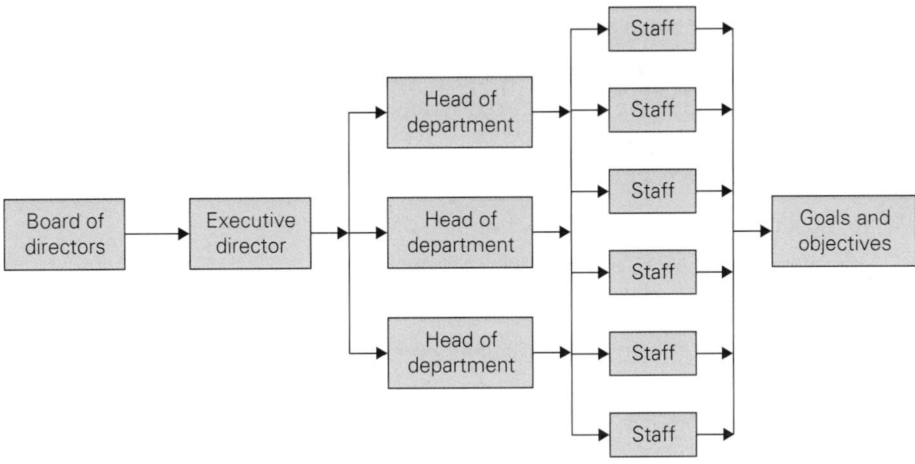

Figure 3.3 All levels of staff working toward the same goals and objectives

Complete allocated tasks

By looking at the graphic above, it becomes clear that each person within the organisation must do their part and ensure that they do their jobs to the best of their abilities. A large part of achieving goals and objectives is making sure that you complete all tasks allocated to you on time and to the required standards. As previously mentioned—others may be depending on you to do this so that they, in turn, can subsequently do theirs.

Task 3.5

CASE STUDY

Jeff is a sales representative for the Surfing Clothes and Boards Company. He is going to be representing his company at a Home and Leisure Show at the Show Grounds in two weeks and needs promotional materials to take with him. He has asked for brochures and 2000 small 'surfboard' giveaways with the company name and logo on them. These would be given away to potential customers to entice them in to one of the company's many stores around the state. A week before the event he checks with the company's administration staff, who were tasked with getting the giveaways produced, and found that they had not even been ordered yet. The administration clerk abuses Jeff and asks why he didn't do the work himself if it was so urgent.. ***and doesn't he know how busy admin staff are!?*** Jeff points out that it is administration staff's job to do this and that he would have done it himself if he had been told they were too busy.

A rush was put on this task, but in the end it was too late to get these items produced, imprinted with the company logo and packaged up. This left Jeff with only brochures to hand out and nothing to help him stand out from competitors. He had spent $8500 on hiring the booth and exhibition furniture at the Show as well as $2500 on promotional flyers that included a star burst announcing 'free mini boards' to each person who approached them at the booth. In addition to this, the company would have to pay wages for Jeff and one other staff member to attend the booth over the entire weekend.

Given the above scenario, discuss:

1. What impact the failure to complete the task may have on:
   a. Jeff's ability to promote the company effectively
   b. the company as a whole.
2. How could Jeff have ensured that this task was completed on time?
3. The administration clerk's attitude to completing the work.
4. What should they have done when they knew they wouldn't be able to complete the task?

Seek assistance when difficulties arise

Once again, there will always be times when you are unable to fulfil your duties to the required standards or in the allotted timeframe. Reasons for this could include:

- having too big a workload for you to cope with in general
- unforeseen circumstances taking up valuable time during the day such as equipment or machinery failure, or emergency situations that put additional pressure on staff

- staff absences—so someone else has to do their work
- extreme weather conditions affecting the workplace, or people's ability to make it in to work
- being unsure of exactly what is expected of you, or of procedures.

Always remember that everyone should be working towards the same goal, so asking for help is a sign that you want to do things correctly. If you are unsure of what to do, or how to perform a specific task, use questioning techniques to clarify instructions or responsibilities. Help can be sought from colleagues in the same department, team leaders or supervisors, or in some instances from outside experts.

Display a non-discriminatory attitude

It is against the law in Australia to discriminate against people because of their religion, race, language, gender, disabilities, family structure or age and there is legislation in place to ensure that discrimination does not happen.

Discrimination means treating someone unfairly or harassing them. The Human Rights and Equal Opportunity Commission administers federal laws that relate to breaches of human rights and discrimination. These laws are aimed at protecting people from discrimination of certain kinds in public life.

Discrimination can be direct or indirect.

- Direct discrimination—means that a person is very obviously being treated unfairly or regarded as unequal. For example, if an employer will not give a job to a woman just because she is a woman, this is direct discrimnation.
- Indirect discrimination—means having a requirement for the job that, although it is the same for everyone, is unfair to certain groups. Valid qualifications gained overseas but not recognised by an employer in Australia would be an example of indirect discrimination.

Legislation introduced by the Human Rights and Equal Opportunity Commission includes:

- *Age Discrimination Act 2004*—which states that people may not be treated less favourably on the ground of age in various areas of public life, including employment, provision of goods and services and education.
- *Disability Discrimination Act 1992*—which endeavours to eliminate discrimination against people with disabilities and promote community acceptance of them.
- *Racial Discrimination Act 1975*—which promotes equality before the law for all people regardless of their race, nationality or ethnic background and makes discrimination against people on this basis illegal.
- *Sex Discrimination Act 1984*—which promotes equality between men and women, eliminates discrimination on the basis of sex or marital status and endeavours to eliminate sexual harassment in public life.

In your daily work life you will be required to work with colleagues, and serve customers, from all walks of life and from all corners of the world. Showing respect is not only a matter of ensuring harmony in the workplace, but can open doors to other cultures and broaden your personal horizons.

Useful website:

Anti Discrimination Australia:

http://www.antidiscriminationaustralia.com.au

Task 3.6

CASE STUDY

Rui Yamamoto joined the company you work for 6 months ago as an IT assistant looking after the company's computer and database systems. Although he's a whiz with computers, his English language levels are not very good and he found it difficult to make himself understood. Many of the staff had taken to making fun of him because of this and Rui began to withdraw and become isolated from the team. The harassment continued with the result that Rui left the company and went to work for a major competitor who welcomed him into their team and treated him with respect and courtesy. Since starting there, Rui has upgraded their entire computer systems and databases with the consequence that they now have a fully functioning online shopping facility and are enjoying a huge increase in profits.

1. Were the actions of your staff in breach of discrimination legislation?
2. What could have happened as a result of this discrimination?
3. What could your team have done to make Rui feel welcome?
4. Discuss the impact of the team's actions on the company as a whole.

Is it Bias? Making Diversity Work

http://youtube.com/WlocPhxOzXk

Diversity Awareness and Sensitivity in the Workplace

http://youtube.com/aHIklj_GPoQ

ELEMENT 3
MAINTAIN PERSONAL PRESENTATION

A tidy store, with well stocked shelves and racks is very important to a store's image. Customers will take very little time deciding whether to come in to your store based on how well presented it is. The same also applies to the way in which customers view your personal presentation. While being at the height of fashion might be favoured by staff it is not necessarily corporate dress; depending on the store, short skirts, board shorts or torn jeans won't make much of an impression. When you are representing your organisation you must dress in accordance with their guidelines.

3.1 Observe appropriate dress code and presentation as required by the workplace, job role and level of customer contact.

3.2 Follow personal hygiene procedures according to organisational policy and relevant legislation.

LEARNING OUTCOMES

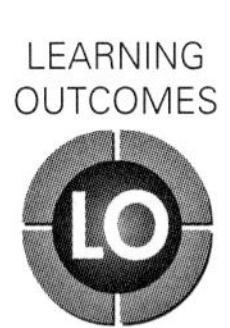

Personal presentation

Personal presentation is an important form of communication. How you dress and how you present yourself tells people a great deal about you—and it tells them in an instant! Remember: within a few short seconds of first meeting someone they will have evaluated you; they will look at your appearance and behaviour, they will observe your mannerisms, body language and grooming and will have made up their minds if they want to deal with you.

This first impression happens in every new situation without any conscious effort. A few seconds are not a long time, so the first impression a customer has of you will be visual and your personal presentation should be positive and professional.

Figure 3.4 A well-dressed and professional work team

DRESS CODE

Depending on the industry you work in and what role you fulfil within it, appropriate dress code is important.

Uniforms

Some retail organisations such as large banks or department stores will supply a uniform. It is very important that these be worn according to company guidelines as the uniform is linked to the company's image and reputation and should always portray a positive impression.

Corporate dress code (commonly referred to as 'business attire')

Where no uniform is provided, the organisation you work for might still require you to dress in a formal fashion while at work. This formal dress is called 'corporate' and usually means that you are required to wear a suit and tie, or at a minimum, a long sleeved shirt and tie, if you are male or fitted skirts, blouse and perhaps jackets if you are female. At the very least corporate dress means clean cut clothing that gives customers the right impression of an organisation's professionalism.

Industry specific or appropriate dress code

Once again, depending on the area of the retail industry you work in there may be specific clothing necessary to the job. In a department store's warehouse areas, for example, staff would probably be required to wear sturdy clothes that won't rip or tear when they are moving heavy boxes around. They may also need to wear safety boots. In the delicatessen areas of supermarkets, staff may be required to wear caps to keep back their hair, or gloves when handling food. Staff in surf shops need to attract the right customers so their dress codes may be somewhat more relaxed and in keeping with the products they offer.

Dress code also includes shoes and accessories. Shoes should always be clean and polished and, depending on the nature of your role, accessories such as jewellery should be kept discreet and to a minimum for the most professional impression.

POSTURE

Posture refers to the way in which you hold your body and affects both physical well being and appearance. Bad posture can damage a person's skeletal and muscular system or their internal organs and circulatory system. Posture also communicates the way people perceive you in professional terms. Bad posture indicates a lack of confidence and self-esteem and could give the impression of lazy carelessness.

So good posture is important not only to your health and well being but to the way in which people will react to you—how seriously they take you. Good posture means:

- standing up straight
- not slouching or hunching your shoulders when standing or sitting. Slouching is bad for the back and makes you look lazy and bored
- holding your head up high and keeping your shoulders back.

Good posture gives the impression of confidence, professionalism and a sense of self-worth that will make people pay attention to you.

CONFIDENCE

Self-confidence is important in almost every aspect of our lives, yet so many people struggle to find it. Self-confident people inspire confidence in others: in their colleagues, their supervisors or managers, their customers, and their friends. Gaining the esteem of others is one of the key ways in which a self-confident person finds success. Self-confidence can be portrayed in a number of different ways, some of which we have already discussed:

The way you dress

Smart clean clothes make you feel better about yourself and this shows in the way you act.

Your body language and tone of voice

A firm handshake and a clear strong voice will make a great deal of difference in the way people perceive you. A strong walk with confident strides is also the mark of a confident person.

Your posture

As mentioned above, good posture tells people that you are confident in yourself and in the organisation you work for.

Knowledge

An excellent knowledge of your products and services allows you to talk about them to customers or colleagues with confidence and authority.

All of these things and more can help you to be confident and professional in your job.

Personal hygiene

Personal hygiene is a matter of common courtesy when working with colleagues and customers. Nobody wants to see staff who have dirty hair or clothes and such behaviour is detrimental not only to your own image, within the workplace, but also to the company you work for. So it is important to ensure that your personal hygiene is of a high standard when going to work: shower before going to work and ensure that your hair, clothes and shoes are clean and in good condition.

Task 3.7

1. Go to the employee grooming guidelines in the Careers section of the Novotel Hotel website (www.novotelcairnsresort.com.au/intranet/employee_grooming.html) and answer the following questions:
   a. Why does the hotel have presentation standards?
   b. What sort of shoes are front office staff required to wear?
   c. What is the rule regarding wearing jewellery?
   d. Given the hotel's quality and image, do you think their presentation standards are reasonable? Give a reason for your answer.
2. Discuss the personal presentation requirements of your own workplace:
   a. Are you required to wear a uniform?
   b. Are the specific instructions on how to wear it?
   c. If you are not required to wear a uniform, what is the dress code of your organisation?
3. Discuss the importance of personal hygiene in the workplace.

ELEMENT 4
DEVELOP EFFECTIVE WORK HABITS

All of the things discussed so far help you gain a deeper understanding of organisational business practices—the reasons why organisations do the things they do, and why they require you to work to their set standards and benchmarks. These policies and procedures allow you to participate actively in the success of the organisation, display behaviour that contributes to a safe work environment and become an effective member of the team.

Figure 3.5 Results of ineffective work habits

LEARNING OUTCOMES

- 4.1 Interpret, confirm and act on workplace information, instructions and procedures relevant to the particular task.
- 4.2 Interpret, confirm and act on legal requirements in regard to anti-discrimination, sexual harassment and bullying.
- 4.3 Ask questions to seek and clarify workplace information.
- 4.4 Plan and organise daily work routine within the scope of the job role.
- 4.5 Prioritise and complete tasks according to required timeframes.
- 4.6 Identify work and personal priorities and achieve a balance between competing priorities.

Getting the job done correctly

In order to do your job to the very best of your ability you need to fully understand the organisation and its requirements of you. When you first start work you will, most likely, be given a job description (which details all of your duties), a staff handbook (which provides a brief overview of company policies) and an induction (which introduces you to other staff, the premises and some procedures). In some cases you may be paired up with a 'buddy' to help you through the first week or so of your new job, but quite often you are left to get on with work on your own.

As we have said all through this chapter, meeting organisational goals and objectives is a vital part of any role within that organisation. The company will have developed policies and procedures that set the standards and conditions that must be met if those goals and objectives are to be achieved. So it is important that you understand and act on information and instructions given to you in accordance with the procedures.

Basic workplace information can be found in a variety of places including:

Company business plans and strategies

Plans and strategies detail what the organisation hopes to achieve over a given period of time (usually one to three years).

Industry awards and agreements

These relate to personal job role and terms and conditions of employment. This might include information about such things as award wages, working conditions, leave entitlements and hours of work.

Employer and employee responsibilities

These are outlined earlier in the chapter. Under an Australian apprenticeship contract of training there are additional responsibilities for employers and employees. These might revolve around special employment contracts, supervisory and training arrangements, allowing time for studies and dealing with Registered Training Organisations.

An excellent resource for finding out about roles and responsibilities in Traineeships and Apprenticeships can be found at the website of the State Government Victoria: Department of Education and Early Childhood Development:

http://www.skills.vic.gov.au/__data/assets/pdf_file/0005/347999/A-Guide-to-Apprenticeships-and-Traineeships-Fifth-Edition-June-2011.pdf

Workplace policies, plans and procedures

These give details of how the company expects you to behave in relation to dealing with grievances, discriminatory behaviour, equal opportunity issues, harassment, hygiene and presentation, staff rosters and notification of shift availability or non-attendance, providing customer service to colleagues and customers, workplace ethics and staff counselling and disciplinary procedures.

Legal requirements of the organisation

You may be required to have an understanding the relevant legislation and statutory requirements, such as:

- equal employment opportunity (EEO) legislation
- work health and safety (WHS)
- privacy
- anti-discrimination legislation
- workplace relations.

In your daily work life you will be required to obey any lawful instructions given to you by supervisors—even if you don't agree with them. In these cases, where you don't believe the current methods are the best ones, there is a right way and a wrong way to go about stating your views. Don't disagree with your supervisor in public and be deliberately insubordinate. This will most probably result in a reprimand from the supervisor or the organisation's manager and could, eventually, lead to dismissal.

If you believe there are better ways of performing certain tasks, research your idea and think it through thoroughly. Then prepare a report based on your research outlining your suggestion, what additional (if any resources) might be required to implement the suggestion, and how your suggestion would benefit the organisation. In this way, your idea may get a fair hearing and may, indeed, be implemented.

Task 3.8

1. Review the General Retail Industry Award 2010 document at:
   http://www.airc.gov.au/awardmod/awards/general_retail.pdf
   Then answer the following questions:
   Part 3—Type of employment
   a. What are the maximum number of hours a part-time employee may work?
   b. What things must be agreed to, in writing, when a part-time employee commences work?
   c. Is a part-time employee entitled to annual leave and sick leave?
   Part 4—Classifications and wage rates
   d. What is the minimum weekly wage for a Retail Employee Level 2?
   e. Under what conditions is a meal allowance paid, and how much is the payment?
   f. List at least three allowances provided to employees under this award.
   Part 5—Ordinary hours of work
   g. Under clause 26.2, what is the ordinary spread of working hours on a Tuesday?
   h. What three things must a staff roster show?
      i. If you are working more than four hours, but less than five hours, are you entitled to a break? If yes, describe the break you are allowed.
2. Go to www.antidiscriminationaustralia.com.au and read the information on 'What is unlawful discrimination?' found on the home page. Answer the following questions:
   a. What descriptions are given for:
      i. sexual harassment
      ii. age discrimination
      iii. family responsibilities
      iv. race.
3. Click on the menu item 'Workplace bullying' and give the definition of workplace bullying.
4. What is the percentage indicated, in this information, of people in the workplace who are bullied?
5. List at least four types of bullying mentioned there.

The daily routine

All of the things we've covered may seem a little overwhelming and you may wonder how you will ever remember everything. Be assured—you will not need to know or memorise all of this information at once and your learning curve will go on for most of your career—as information, procedures and requirements continue to improve and change. This information will also be learned as you go about your daily work routine, which may include:

- interacting with customers
- interacting with supervisors and other staff members
- handling the telephone
- organising and maintaining work areas
- maintaining merchandise and display
- assisting other team members
- working within required timelines.

As you perform these tasks you will be shown the correct way of undertaking them and the more you do them, the more you will gain in confidence and professionalism.

PRIORITISING AND COMPLETING TASKS

Sometimes tasks need to be performed in a certain order or some tasks may be more important that others. In these cases you will need to look at your duties for the day and ensure that you are completing them in the right order or giving them the right priority.

For example, some of your daily duties might involve tidying stock on their shelves, opening the store, setting up the cash register with a cash float and unpacking newly arrived stock. There would be a certain order in which you would be required to perform these tasks; there is no point in opening the store to the public until you have set up the cash register. For security and safety reasons, you do not want to be handling large amounts of cash with customers already in the store. Equally, at the end of the day, you would not count the day's takings with customers still in the store. You would also want the shop to be tidy before letting customers in. Then, too, any instruction given to you by a supervisor would generally supersede any routine tasks that you have—but they will still need to be completed at some point during the day.

Task 3.9

1. Make a list of all the duties that you are required to perform each day.
2. Put these in order of priority—write them out as a schedule.
3. Give a brief outline of the standards to which these tasks must be performed.
4. Discuss the impact on other staff and across the organisation if you do not complete them on time or correctly.
5. Explain who relies on you completing your tasks in order that they may do theirs.

Work and personal priorities

The workforce in Australia is changing constantly. The birth rate is declining, people are living longer and the Australian population is ageing. The traditional family model is also changing; in the past one parent went to work while the other stayed at home looking after children. This is now less widespread as there are an ever-increasing number of single parent families, or families where both partners go out to work. This might be a lifestyle choice or out of necessity.

Jobs and work practices are also now different with an explosion of casual, part-time and shift work. For many people work has become more intensive and working hours are growing longer. So balancing work, family and lifestyle has become an important issue for more Australians, their families, businesses and government.

WORK/LIFE BALANCE

The workplace can become a very stressful place if the right balance is not found between the working day and private or social activities. Balancing work and personal priorities means finding time to study and develop your career, time to relax at home with friends or family, pursue cultural practices and much more.

Longer working hours put more pressure on families. It has been suggested that people working longer hours are more likely to experience stress and conflict between work and family responsibilities, and often have poorer coping mechanisms to deal with these issues.

Work-life balance policies are becoming more important, as they increase people's ability to participate in the workforce and be productive, while taking care of family and personal needs. Today programs designed to balance home and work life are being offered to employees. These can include:

- on-site day care for children
- the opportunity to work from home
- job sharing
- flexible hours.

These programs are slowly being promoted by some businesses as a means to improve their organisation's profitability by reducing staff absenteeism and turnover. Organisations who provide employee support programs also gain a competitive advantage when offering their staff enhanced working conditions. In doing so, they add value, loyalty and efficiency to their service and productivity.

ASSESSMENT 1: PROJECT

Assessment context	When working in the retail industry you will be required to work within certain organisational and legal parameters. This project is designed to assess your ability to work with organisational policies and procedures, and your ability to work with other team members. As part of the assessment you will need to work with at least one other person in your workplace, and hold at least two meetings at which you will be required to keep meeting minutes. You may need to ask for the cooperation of a supervisor, or colleague to undertake this project. For learners in a classroom environment, choose at least 2 partners for this project.
Assessment instructions	1. Choose three of your organisation's procedures for review a. Allocate one area to each team member for them to thoroughly review. b. For each one describe – The nature and purpose of the procedure – What staffing levels are required to perform the tasks involved in that procedure to the current standards – Who do these staff report to? – What, if any, rights, responsibilities and compliance issues are associated with each area under review – Discuss the current standards required by that procedure and what practices might be detrimental in achieving those standards – How can staff contribute to the successful completion of those tasks? 2. Hold at least two team meetings to: a. Allocate research areas as outlined in point 1a above b. At a second or subsequent meetings discuss the team's progress on the review process: – Is the review process on schedule? – Do team members need assistance and support to complete their reviews? – How are problems with the review solved? 3. Make suggestions for improvement. Once the review process has been completed, hold a final meeting to discuss the results and determine if the current methods are still valid, or should be amended. a. Discuss ideas for improvement b. Ensure you consider all aspects of making a change: – Will additional staff or resources be required? – How will this affect the organisation's budget? – How will your new ideas benefit the organisation?
Evidence required	1. Completed review report providing details (as outlined above) on all three procedures reviewed 2. Minutes of any meetings held 3. Report on suggestions for improvement.

continued

Range and conditions	• As part of this unit of competency you are required to demonstrate that you can work within tight timeframes. In completing this assessment you will therefore have two weeks to complete the project. Extensions are only possible in extenuating circumstances such as illness. • If in the workplace, you will require the cooperation of a small group of colleagues in order to hold the team meetings requirement of the assessment. • If in a classroom, you can form teams with your classmates.
Materials and resources required	• Access to workplace policies and procedures. • Access to facilities in which to hold team meetings.
Reasonable adjustments	In the event that you have difficulty understanding the assessment tasks due to language or other difficulties, your trainer will attempt to make reasonable adjustments to the assessment paper in order to afford you every opportunity to achieve competency.
Decision-making rules	You will be assessed on your ability to: • Read and interpret organisational documents • Identify practices that no longer work, and make suggestions for improvement • Determine correct staffing levels to complete given tasks • Discuss employer and employee rights, responsibilities and legal obligations • Work and communicate harmoniously with a team of people.

ASSESSMENT 2: REVIEW QUESTIONS

1. What organisational documents would you look up to find information about:
   a. Your rostered working hours
   b. Company uniform or dress code policy
   c. Your daily duties and responsibilities.
2. You are rostered on to start work tomorrow morning at 7 am. Part of your duties are to open the store and set up the cash register. Tomorrow is also the beginning of a new promotional campaign that has been advertised on television for over a week. You are feeling very unwell and will not be able to go in to work tomorrow. What will you do?
3. Describe why it is important for staff to follow duty of care and other legal obligations set by the organisation.
4. As a casual employee of a large department store you would have easy access to the store's General Manager whenever you needed to talk to him. True or false?
5. In your own words, describe how you would go about establishing a harmonious team environment.
6. It is acceptable to give out customer information to people outside your organisation. True or false?

7. Describe what type of behaviour would be considered harassment in the workplace.
8. Describe what type of behaviour would be considered discriminatory in the workplace.
9. What is a mission statement used for?
10. When in the workplace, what are an employee's responsibilities?
11. Describe why it is important to comply with the organisation's personal presentation and hygiene policies and procedures.
12. What are the employer's responsibilities to apprentices or trainees in the workplace?

COMPETENCY MAPPING

Element		Performance criteria		Task	Assessment	Refer to page
1	Work within organisational requirements	1.1	Identify and read organisation's requirements and responsibilities and seek advice from appropriate people where necessary.	3.1, 3.3, 3.8	1, 2 (AQ1)	91–92
		1.2	Interpret staff rosters and provide sufficient notice of unavailability for rostered hours according to workplace policy and procedures.	3.2, 3.8	2 (AQ2)	93–94
		1.3	Develop and use a current working knowledge and understanding of employee and employer rights and responsibilities.	3.3, 3.5	1	95
		1.4	Comply with relevant duty of care and legal responsibilities, and support organisational culture.	3.3, 3.8	2 (AQ3)	97–98
		1.5	Identify roles and responsibilities of colleagues and immediate supervisors.	3.3	1, 2 (AQ4)	96
		1.6	Identify standards and values considered to be detrimental to the organisation and communicate this through appropriate channels.	3.4, 3.8	1	98
		1.7	Identify, recognise and follow behaviour that contributes to a safe and sustainable work environment.	3.4	1	99
2	Support the work team	2.1	Display courteous and helpful behaviour at all times.	3.5	1	100
		2.2	Take opportunities to enhance the level of assistance offered to colleagues and meet all reasonable requests for assistance within acceptable workplace timeframes.		1, 2 (AQ5)	101
		2.3	Complete allocated tasks as required.		1	101
		2.4	Seek assistance when difficulties arise.		1	102
		2.5	Use questioning techniques to clarify instructions or responsibilities.		1	55–89
		2.6	Identify and display a non-discriminatory attitude in all contacts with customers and other staff members.	3.5, 3.8	2 (AQ8)	103

Element		Performance criteria		Task	Assessment	Refer to page
3	Maintain personal presentation	3.1	Observe appropriate dress code and presentation as required by the workplace, job role and level of customer contact.	3. 7	2 (AQ11)	105–6
		3.2	Follow personal hygiene procedures according to organisational policy and relevant legislation.	3.7	2 (AQ11)	107
4	Develop effective working habits	4.1	Interpret, confirm and act on workplace information, instructions and procedures relevant to the particular task.	3.5	1, 2 (AQ1)	108
		4.2	Interpret, confirm and act on legal requirements in regard to anti-discrimination, sexual harassment and bullying.	3.6, 3.8	1, 2 (AQ3,6,7, 8)	109–110
		4.3	Ask questions to seek and clarify workplace information.		1	55–89
		4.4	Plan and organise daily work routine within the scope of the job role.	3.9		111

Required skills and knowledge	Task	Assessment	Refer to page
Required skills			
Communication skills to: • ask questions to identify and confirm requirements • follow routine instructions through clear and direct communication • use language and concepts appropriate to cultural differences • use and interpret non-verbal communication.	3.5, 3.6	1, 2 (AQ5)	55–89
Literacy skills to: • interpret and follow workplace policies and procedures • process relevant workplace documentation.	3.1, 3.2, 3.3, 3.8	1, 2 (AQ1, 3)	91, 93, 95, 101, 108–110
Personal presentation skills to comply with workplace presentation and dress code.	3.7	2 (AQ11)	105–107
Planning and organising skills to manage tasks within workplace timeframes.	3.4	1	98, 101, 111
Problem-solving skills to solve routine problems.	3.4	1	98, 102, 111
Technology skills to select and use technology appropriate for a task.		1	55–89

continued

Required skills and knowledge	Task	Assessment	Refer to page
Required knowledge			
Industry awards and agreements that relate to personal job role and terms and conditions of employment.	3.2, 3.8		93
Employer and employee responsibilities under an Australian apprenticeship contract of training where applicable.		2 (AQ12)	95
Relevant legislation and statutory requirements, such as: • equal employment opportunity (EEO) legislation • work health and safety (WHS) • privacy • anti-discrimination legislation • workplace relations.	3.1, 3.6, 3,8	1, 2 (AQ6)	95, 97, 99, 103
Workplace policies, plans and procedures, including: • dealing with grievances • discriminatory behaviour • equal opportunity issues • harassment • hygiene and presentation • staff rosters and notification of shift availability or non-attendance • providing customer service to colleagues and customers • workplace ethics • staff counselling and disciplinary procedure.	3.2, 3.3, 3.7, 3.8, 3.9	1, 2 (AQ7, 8)	91, 97, 99, 103, 108–110, 111
Workplace organisational structure.	3.5		97
Critical aspects of evidence			
Identifies, locates and articulates the organisation's requirements, including goals and values.	3.3, 3.5, 3.8	1, 2 (AQ9)	91, 103, 108–110, 111
Demonstrates work practices that reflect the relationship between own role and organisational requirements.	3.4	1	96, 108–110
Demonstrates knowledge of workplace procedures for upholding employee and employer rights and responsibilities.	3.1, 3.6, 3.8	1, 2 (AQ10)	95, 103

PART 2

Marketing and merchandising

Understanding Part 2

This part of your textbook is all about exploring the business environment in which you will operate, the people in it and how to best target the right customers for your products and services. Units covered are:

4. SIRRMRB001—Defining a retail market
5. SIRXMER001—Merchandise products
6. SIRRMER002—Plan, create and maintain displays
7. SIRXSLS002—Sell products and services

Marketing

PART 2

Marketing and merchandising

Units covered in Part 2

This part of your textbook is all about exploring the business environment in which you will operate, the people in it and how to best target the right customers for your products and services. Units covered are:

4. SIRXMPR001A—Profiling a retail market
5. SIRXMER201—Merchandise products
6. SIRXMER202—Plan, create and maintain displays
7. SIRXSLS201A—Sell products and services

Selling products and services to customers and earning revenue for the organisation is the ultimate goal of all organisations—but first you need to get the customer into your store.

This is where marketing and merchandising come into play.

Marketing

Marketing is the process of understanding what customers want and endeavouring to provide it for them. In simple terms it involves:

- researching customer needs and expectations
- planning and executing the development of products and services appropriate to those needs

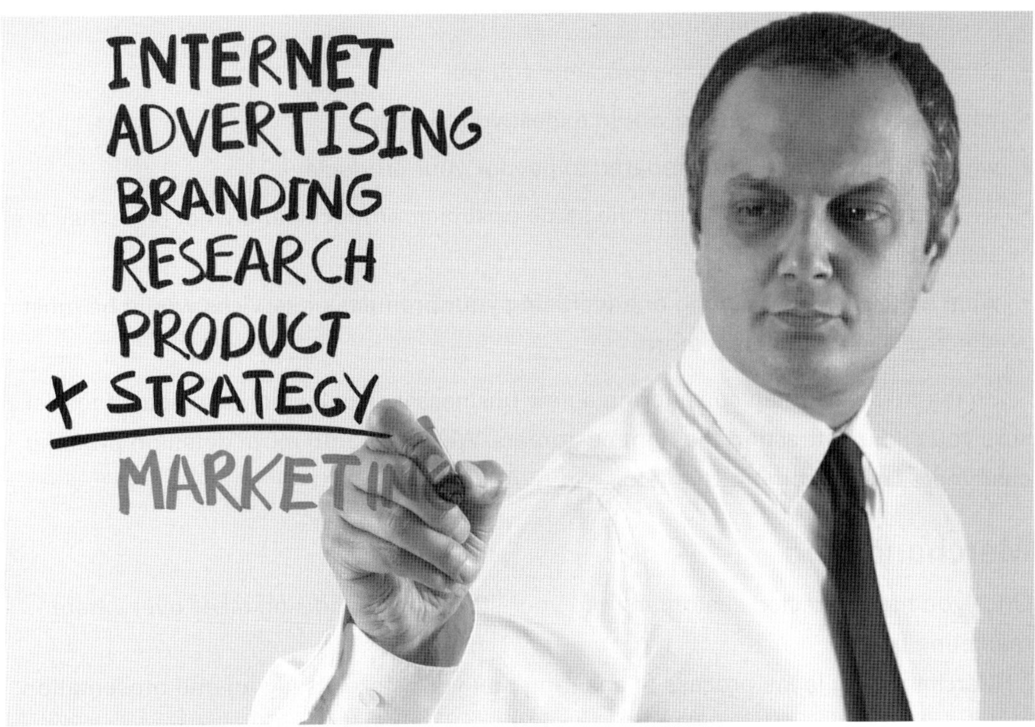

Figure 4.1 Marketing function components

> '**Make** it simple. Make it memorable. Make it inviting to look at. Make it fun to read.'—***Leo Burnett, advertising guru***

- providing competitive pricing for these products and services
- promoting them via such means as advertising, **promotional campaigns** and events
- providing a distribution point for the products and services so that customers can access them. In the retail industry, this would be your store.

In marketing, this process is known as the 4 Ps: product, price, promotion, place.

In times gone by most businesses were product-driven: 'these are the products I have to offer and people who want them will find me'. In today's competitive world this no longer works. Each business now has a great many competitors and not only in their own area—with the advent of the internet, customers are able to shop around the world. So if your store doesn't provide what they want, they will find someone else who can. Most businesses today, then, are consumer-driven: 'Tell me what products and services you expect from me, and I'll see if I can provide them for you'.

Effective marketing will tell you:

- who is most likely to want the products you sell
- what quality and range they would expect you to offer
- what price they would be prepared to pay for your products
- who else in your area is selling the same or similar products (and what price they are selling them for)
- what methods of promoting or advertising your products or services would be most effective and a great deal more.

So the first step when considering a new business is usually market research to make sure you end up attracting the right customers. We will go into more detail on profiling customers later in coming chapters.

Merchandising

Once you have attracted customers into your store, merchandising takes over where marketing began.

Merchandising is the process of ensuring that your store, its layout and presentation, and the stock you carry are attractive enough to encourage customers to buy.

This may include such activities as:

- ensuring that your store is always tidy and clean
- setting up attractive displays in the store window and inside the store
- grouping items to encourage customers to buy more than one product
- placing items that you particularly want to sell within easy reach or at strategic locations in the store (near the cash register).

All these things are methods of ensuring that your organisation will make the most of every sales opportunity.

Figure 4.2 A well laid-out shop floor

Chapter 4

SIRXMPR001A

Profiling a retail market

A successful business is one that knows its market well and caters to its specific needs; it carries stock aimed at its specific market, and its displays and store image are created to attract that market. But how do you know if you have a specific market? And if you do, how do you find out who they are? For that matter, what exactly is a **target market?**

Let us deal with the last question first: *what is a target market?*

A target market is comprised of customers who have the need or desire to buy the specific products or services that your organisation sells. For example the target market for a sporting goods store would be customers who are actively involved in sports and outdoor activities. To be most effective, this store would aim its promotional activities and advertising at this specific customer group.

Some organisations don't have specific markets and sell general products to the public at large—but even here there are differences. For example, Big W versus David Jones: both are department stores but cater to very different customer needs and expectations. The target market for Big W might be budget conscious shoppers whereas David Jones' target market would be those of greater financial means. The expectations of these two target audiences would be different too: Big W customers would expect low prices and value for money and, perhaps, quantity over quality. David Jones customers would expect top-quality merchandise for the top dollar they spend.

In order to be truly successful, the image a store projects, the merchandise it carries, the way it promotes itself and the presentation of its staff must be aimed at the right customers in the right way.

ELEMENT 1
REVIEW THE IMAGE OF THE STORE

Profiling your market means looking at the image your store projects and determining whether it attracts the right customers. Large amounts of money can often be spent on creating an image, but money is wasted if the design, layout and overall impression isn't right. In this section we will look at components of a store's image, how they are used effectively and how they promote to and attract customers.

LEARNING OUTCOMES

1.1 Analyse the components of the store image.

1.2 Access and analyse relevant store documentation in relation to store image.

1.3 Promote the store image in an appropriate manner.

Analyse the components of the store image

There are quite a number of different parts to a store's image all of which, combined, give a very distinct impression. These components include the following.

COMPANY LOGO

Thousands of dollars can be spent creating a company logo. It is the logo which, so often, is instantly recognisable as associated with a specific company. Consider the image of an apple with a bite taken out of the side: this should instantly bring the Apple Corporation to mind, or the golden yellow arches that symbolise a McDonald's restaurant. So it is important that the company logo be displayed prominently, and correctly, in line with the organisation's policies. Never use the company logo for purposes other than promoting the store and never without the company's permission. As stated, a great deal of money can be involved in creating an image and once established it can be destroyed by negative customer perceptions.

PRODUCTS AND SERVICES OFFERED

The image a store creates will also revolve around the products it sells and the services it offers. These should be reviewed on a regular basis:

- Are the products you offer still in demand with customers?
- Does the service you offer meet customer expectations?
- Do both of these (products and services) still properly represent who you are as a business?
- Are your product sales increasing or decreasing?
  - If they are *increasing*—what is the reason for this? Are you doing anything differently or better? What are customers saying?
  - If they are *decreasing*—what is the reason for this? Has anything changed for the negative and if so what will you do about it?

THE LAYOUT OF THE STORE

The layout of a store is very important. It should be easy for customers to see what you have to offer and for them to access those products. An untidy, cluttered shop looks cheap and does not encourage customers to come in, feel comfortable and browse. This is an important point because the longer a customer spends in your store, the more likely they are to buy from you.

MERCHANDISE DISPLAYS

Displays are created for a variety of reasons and should therefore be carefully constructed with their intended purpose in mind. Displays are created to:

Showcase the merchandise carried by a store

A window display is the first thing that most customers will look at before going in to a shop. Depending on the type of store and the nature of the products sold, the window might be crowded with a large variety of goods to show range or, in the case of an exclusive store, it may contain only one item thereby showcasing that products offered by this company are of extremely high quality and price. The display may influence whether a customer will go into the store or not.

Create a desire to purchase

Both window displays and in-store displays should be aimed at making a sale. Simply hanging a jacket on the end of a clothing rack does little to attract a sale, but if it is lit with a spot light and teamed with a blouse, scarf and accessories then the customer's eye is drawn to it and they can see how this jacket might be worn—creating the desire to try it on for themselves and buy it.

Encourage impulse purchases

Grouping products, as just mentioned, can encourage the customer to buy more than they actually intended. If the customer was only looking for a jacket, but saw how well the scarf, belt and necklace went with it, they may be tempted to buy those too. Another method of attracting impulse buys is to display items at strategic and unexpected locations within the store. Such displays draw the customer's eye and encourage them to pick up the products—and perhaps buy them. Supermarkets are particularly good at such impulse buy displays: every checkout station has a display of various small items that you might not otherwise have thought of buying but will pick up while you are waiting to pay; magazines, chewing gum, chocolate bars. Ask yourself: have you ever picked up one of these items while waiting in the queue and bought it? These might be very small purchases but when added up over the space of a week can represent considerable additional revenue.

Often, the way in which you display or merchandise your products can have an enormous impact on the revenue generated by the company: the more interesting your shop looks, the more customers are likely to come in.

TICKETS AND PROMOTIONAL PRICE TAGS

The price tickets you display in your store will also have an impact on its image. Large (loud) price tags *might* convey an image of low prices and large quantities, whereas smaller discreet price sale tickets might convey a very different image. The type of promotional ticket you use in your store will be dictated, largely, by the type of stock you carry and the type of customer you want to attract.

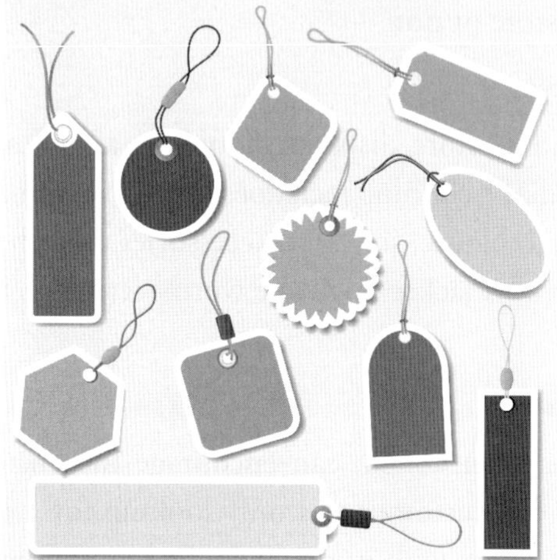

Figure 4.3 A variety of tickets and promotional price tags

PROMOTIONAL EVENTS AND THEMES

A further component of a store's image is often dictated by season or by special events. Christmas involves the most 'theming' on the part of almost every organisation: Christmas trees and decorations are put up, special displays are created and special stock may even be ordered. Other events that encourage stores to 'theme' and create special promotions include:

- Easter
- Mother's Day
- Father's Day
- Valentine's Day
- Melbourne Cup
- 'back to school'.

You can attract customers to your store by effectively presenting your specific products or services in appropriately themed ways.

Successful marketing and merchandising is as much about emotions—creating feelings in a customer—as anything else. Presenting a consistent image is the key that makes your organisation instantly recognisable and begins to create 'brand awareness' in your customers. The right image creates the right feel; it makes customers feel comfortable in your store and more inclined to buy.

Task 4.1

Over the next two weeks take a note of the atmosphere in each retail store you visit. Prepare a short report on the best shop you entered and the worst shop you entered, using the points outlined above. What was the difference between the two—what made you like one more than the other?

Task 4.2

1. Take some time to consider these brands and visit the websites provided below. Discuss:
   a. How consistently do they present their image in store and on the internet?
   b. What do you think of when you think of these brands?
   c. Have you ever bought products from these companies?
   d. What made you buy them, or made you buy from that particular company?

Brand	Website
McDonalds	www.mcdonalds.com.au
Coca Cola	www.coca-cola.com.au
Woolworths	www.woolworths.com.au
Nike	www.nikestore.com.au

2. Research other well-known brands and describe their image and how you relate to them.
3. Using the research that you have undertaken, discuss:
   a. how your own store's image measures up against the ones you researched
   b. how you would change your own store's image to create a better brand awareness.
4. Look at the photo on the right and describe what type of customers you think might be attracted to this store.

Figure 4.4 Retail store

Access and analyse relevant store documentation in relation to store image

Having an in-depth understanding of what customers are thinking about your store, how it is performing and what drives its success is essential. This means keeping accurate records and conducting regular research so that you are always able to stay a step ahead of the market and behave in a *proactive* manner, rather than having to *react* to something unexpected and unforeseen.

The following are some methods of documenting information about your store's performance.

CUSTOMER SURVEYS AND FEEDBACK

Conducting regular surveys with customers will provide valuable information on how your store is performing and is perceived by customers. This subject was touched on briefly in Chapter 1, but to expand a little on what was covered there, customer feedback can be gathered by means of:

Pre-prepared questionnaires

Customers can fill in a form with set questions while they are waiting to be served (or you might mail it out to them).

Customer forums or focus sessions

This type of feedback mechanism is very powerful as it allows you to discuss, in great depth, what customers actually think of your organisation, its image and the products and services provided. In these cases, you invite a select number of customers to your store, or other venue, and ask them to discuss a set of pre-prepared questions that you need answers to. The difference between giving the customers a form with questions to answer and holding a forum, is that you can then drill down in to the answers they give you and find out reasons why they react the way they do, and how they would see you improving. This type of feedback mechanism can lead to some surprising results and open up discussion that may not otherwise have happened.

Casual discussions with customers

The quickest and most effective way to find out what customers think of the store and its image is simply to ask them. There are numerous opportunities for you to engage in conversations with your customers; listen to what they are saying and take note of any areas of concern or suggestions for improvement.

MARKET RESEARCH

Market research should be conducted regularly. As mentioned earlier, an organisation can be either *proactive* or *reactive*. The difference between the two is that a *proactive* company knows what is going on around it; has done its research and recognised new and emerging trends within its industry or surroundings; and is prepared to deal with these trends as they come up, or even pre-empt them by taking the initiative before the event and be seen as a leading-edge company. A *reactive* company, on the other hand, is one that does not keep up to date with such issues and may then be unprepared for any changes that occur in its environment—it must react to the situation whether it likes it or not. We will look at research in much greater detail later in this chapter.

SALES REPORTS

Reports on how the company is performing are invaluable. Statistics kept over extended periods of time (over several years) can provide extremely useful information such as:

- which products consistently sell well and which ones do not—this information can then be used to determine the quantity of product you need to keep in stock to meet demand, or which products you should discard.
- trough and peak periods—this relates to certain times of the year when products will sell better than at other times. For example sales over the Christmas period will be higher than at others. This is usually a given fact, but what about other peak or trough periods: are there specific seasons applicable in your industry? Think about how products and displays change during winter and summer periods. An excellent example of this is the tourism industry where travel to Europe, for example, drops off dramatically during their winter season. The airlines know this to be a regular trend during October, November, January and February and will drop airfares considerably during that slow time to encourage customers to travel and ensure that aircraft seats are filled.
- performance against the company's key performance indicators (KPIs)—most companies will have set revenue targets that they need to achieve each year in order to remain successful. Regular reviews and reports can let management know whether these KPIs are being met or not. If they are not, then corrective action needs to be taken. This may involve gathering feedback and finding out why customers are not coming into the store or buying.

ORGANISATIONAL POLICIES AND PROCEDURES

Other important documents that will have a bearing on the store and its image are the organisation's policies and procedures. These will set out the manner in which work is to be carried out, and to what standard. They will address all issues that affect the way in which customers will perceive the store, its image and reputation. Policies and procedures of a typical organisation, in relation to store image, can include:

Maintaining stock levels

This means controlling the amount of stock the store will carry: never running short of products to sell, but also not having too many. Too much stock on hand can be as bad as not having enough stock, as this will cost money and if this stock is not sold subsequently then this will affect the store's cash flow.

Layout and accessibility of the shop floor

This means keeping walkways between racks and shelves clean and easy to navigate around. This is important for a number of reasons: first from a visual point of view—a well laid-out floor plan makes it easy for customers to find what they want and to see what you have to offer. Secondly, from a WHS point of view, in case of an emergency you must ensure that access into and out of the store is not blocked in any way.

Cleanliness and tidiness of the shop

This will impact on how attractive the store looks: if it is messy with stock in untidy heaps customers may not bother to come in. If the store is attractively laid out, with tidy shelves and racks, then customers are drawn in.

Customer service standards

Many organisations will also have policies and guidelines that set out how to deal with customers in a range of situations. They may cover such things as:

- how to greet customers—in person and on the telephone
- how to handle complaints
- how to deal with difficult customers
- who to turn to for assistance in solving problems and authorising deals.

These are only some of the issues that are covered by organisational policies and procedures and they may vary greatly from one industry to the next. Whatever these policies and procedures are, it is always important to follow them. They were put in place to ensure consistency of service and this is inextricably linked with the organisation's image.

Promote the store image in an appropriate manner

Other means of ensuring that the store is being perceived in a manner consistent with its image is the way in which it is promoted. Promotion can mean a number of things and is not necessarily restricted to standard advertising methods. Some of these include:

Word of mouth

The least costly and often most effective method of promotion is word of mouth; having your customers spread the word about you to their friends and families. Nothing can beat word of mouth for positive advertising; customers are telling others, in detail, how good your service is and how well the products they purchased are working for them. Equally, negative comments can have the exact opposite effect so it is important to ensure that a consistently high quality of service and product is made available to customers.

Banners, posters and tickets

Either inside the store or outside, banners and posters can be eye catching and should always be created with the company's image in mind.

Figure 4.5 Store banner

Promotional items and giveaways

Another effective way of promoting your store and its image is by providing customers with small giveaway items. These often include such things as balloons, pens, baseball caps and water bottles, but could also include items specifically made for your store to fit with its image. There are a number of promotional companies who produce such materials at reasonable prices.

Exhibitions and trade fairs

Opportunities present themselves at various times each year to participate in exhibitions or trade fairs. These may take the form of large fairs such as Home and Leisure Shows held at major venues around Australia, or specialised fairs for specific industries, or local shows in your own area.

www.homeleisureandlifestyleshow.com.au
www.melbournehomeandleisureshow.com.au
www.rncas.org.au/homeshow/site/index.php
www.supershow.com.au
www.travelxpo.com.au

Figure 4.6 Exhibition/trade fair

Photo courtesy of Coomera Anglican College

Sponsorships

Sponsorships are another method of promoting your store and its products. You will often see the results of major sponsorships when watching sporting events on television: major football and racing events all have sponsors and you will see these sponsors' names on billboards around the sporting event, on uniforms, T-shirts and caps. These major sponsorships can cost many thousands of dollars and are normally out of reach of most small companies. Sponsorships, however, are usually available for local events, sporting teams and activities and it can be a great boost to a store's image to be associated with and active in the local community.

Loyalty programs

Promoting your store and its image can also be accomplished by developing a loyalty program for your customers. A well-thought-out loyalty program that is of actual value to the customers and thereby encourages them to buy more products from you is well worth thinking about. A loyalty program does not have to be complicated or costly. Many stores have initiated programs whereby the customer is given a card which is stamped each time they make a purchase with the promise that their '*10th coffee (or book or other product) is free*'. This can be a great incentive and will keep customers coming back to your store as opposed to shopping with a competitor.

Paid advertising

Advertising is a generally accepted method of promoting a store and its products. A store might advertise for a number of reasons: they may have moved or just opened and want people to know where they are, or they may want to sell specific products at special prices and want to attract customers to come in and buy. Methods of advertising can include:

- media—such as newspapers, magazines, television, radio, cinema
- letterbox drops—distributing flyers into people's letterboxes can be a cost-effective and very targeted way of promoting. You can choose what areas the flyers are distributed to, thereby ensuring that you are reaching a local market
- publicity—an excellent method of promotion—if you can get it! Publicity is free advertising: if you have an interesting story to tell about your products or services, or will be putting on a special event that may be unusual or interesting you can let the local newspaper, television and radio know about it by way of a media release, and if they find the information you provide interesting enough, they will cover it for you.

Once again, when choosing the media for promotional purposes it is important to keep the target audience and the purpose of the promotion in mind. For example it would probably be a waste of money for Fred's Fishing Bait and Tackle Shop to advertise its specials in *Cosmopolitan* magazine.

Whichever method you choose to promote the store, however, it must fit with the image you are trying to present to customers. A substantial amount of money is often spent on promotional activities so it is important to make sure that the promotional dollar and effort are aimed at the people you actually want to attract.

Task 4.3

1. Research promotional companies to see the types of items that might fit with your store's image. You can start by looking at:
   www.creativepromotions.com.au
   www.promotionsonly.com.au
   www.completepromotionalproducts.com.au
2. Over the next two weeks take note of any advertisements or promotional activities you see around your area. These can be in local newspapers, or local events.
   a. Do these ads or events address specific needs and portray specific images?
   b. What did you like or not like about them?
   c. Did they tempt you to buy the product? Why, or why not?

Write a short report on what type of promotional giveaway might be useful in your store and which form of advertising you would use. Explain how your choices would benefit your store and the reasons why you chose those particular items and advertising mediums.

ELEMENT 2
RESEARCH MARKET DEMANDS FOR THE STORE

So far we have looked at the image your store portrays and how the components of that image can either entice customers to come in, or turn them away. Having a great store image is only part of what makes customers want to come in to your store—they also have to want what you are selling. There is little point in creating just the right image and atmosphere if you are not meeting market demands.

So where do you begin to find out the needs of the market?

LEARNING OUTCOMES

2.1 Select an appropriate area for research of market demands.

2.2 Use appropriate market research techniques according to store policy.

2.3 Plan market research according to store policy and procedures.

2.4 Collect, analyse and present data in an appropriate manner.

Select an appropriate area for research of market demands

Researching market demands can be a large and very complex process: what should you be looking for, what questions should you be asking, where do you find the relevant information, and once you have the information what should you do with it? Marketing research can give extremely in-depth answers and large companies will often spend many thousands of dollars on having research undertaken for them.

Does a small business really need to go into that level of depth? Not at all. Research into demand for your product can be relatively simple—you just need to know where to focus your research and to ask the right questions. For example, asking a customer 'Do you like my store?' would get you a very limited response, whereas if you asked them 'What do you like about my store?' you would get a more detailed answer. There are a number of areas that you can focus on for your research and before you begin you should be clear on what it is you want to know. Appropriate areas for research may focus on:

Location

If demand for your product is decreasing, or has never actually been high, you may need to look at the location of your store. Are you in the right area to attract customers who want what you sell? A clothing boutique in the middle of a technology park may not do very well!

Your consumer

Are you trying to attract the right customers? Trying to appeal to the wealthier strata of society with cheap products of questionable quality is as pointless as trying to appeal to those of lesser means by offering them extremely expensive goods, or trying to get confirmed 'couch potatoes' to buy gym equipment.

Product

Location and right type of customer aside, is there actually a demand for the product you are selling? If the products you are selling or the services you are offering do not meet customer needs and expectations or are not in line with current trends, then it is unlikely that you will sell them no matter what you do.

PRICE

You may have a perfect location and products that are exactly what customers want, but if you are selling them at prices outside of the market trends then you will have little success. A product is, essentially, only worth what someone will pay for it and if you have set your prices above the market average for that specific item or service, then customers will go to competitors whose prices are more in line with this market average.

LAYOUT

Conducting research into how your store layout impacts on customers can provide useful insight into why customers are, or are not, coming in to your store. They may find it difficult to negotiate around the many, many display stands you have, or find it hard to get an overview of what you are offering. If your store is too cluttered this may look cheap and untidy and repel the very people you are trying to attract.

ADVERTISING

An extremely important part of any research should be the effectiveness of any advertising you undertake. You may have spent a lot of money on creating and implementing an advertising campaign and then miss the chance of finding out how effective it was by not asking how customers found out about you. This is one of the simplest forms of research: when a customer phones or calls in to make an enquiry, ask them how they found out about your store or product. This simple question will let you know if your advertising dollars were well spent or not, and what you might do to improve the next campaign.

Planning and using appropriate market research techniques

These are all very important areas that you can focus on. You then need to employ the right technique to actually conduct the research. This can be accomplished in a number of different ways, many of which were covered on page 128 'Customer surveys and feedback', and include interviews, observations, surveys and questionnaires.

However you decide to conduct your research, it may be undertaken:

- with both existing customers and prospective customers
- in store, or externally with researchers standing in shopping malls or on the street asking passers by to answer some questions.

There are a number of things to consider when planning an effective program of market research. These include that you should:

1. determine exactly what it is that you want to know
2. determine the timeframe that you will be working with or towards
3. carry out the survey effectively
4. analyse and present data in an appropriate manner.

You will also want to act on the results.

1. DETERMINE EXACTLY WHAT IT IS THAT YOU WANT TO KNOW

Before you start any market research you need to have a specific purpose in mind otherwise the results may be of little real use. What are the issues you are facing, and what type of questions will get you the answers you need? It is important to be specific in your questions and to provide a range of options for answers. For example if you simply asked 'What do you think of our store layout?', you could get dozens if not hundreds of different answers and it would be extremely difficult to get a definitive outcome. Instead you should ask that question and give a range for the customer to choose from. This range could be a sliding scale from 1 to 5 (1 = excellent, 2 = very good, 3 = good, 4 = satisfactory and 5 = unsatisfactory). Alternatively you could have a range of other suitable options. The point is that instead of leaving it open to many different outcomes that are hard to collate, you restrict the answers to only five options. If necessary you can then leave space for additional comments the customer might like to make. Decide what it is you want to know, and develop appropriate questions with a reasonable range. Are you looking for ways to improve your product range? Then your questions should be centred on this issue, as in Table 4.1 overleaf.

Table 4.1					
Sample survey					
Question	**1**	**2**	**3**	**4**	**5**
Does our store offer a wide enough variety of products?					
Do we carry a wide enough range of sizes?					
Does our product range reflect today's fashion trends?					
What other lines would you like to see us carry? (Please tick appropriate box.)					
☐ Office wear (suits, blazers)					
☐ Evening wear					
☐ Sports wear					

Sit down with other stakeholders such as supervisors and colleagues and come up with a set of questions that will provide you with answers specific enough to be useful.

2. DETERMINE THE TIMEFRAME THAT YOU WILL BE WORKING WITH OR TOWARDS

The timing of a research program can be very important. If you are looking for improvements to be made in time for the next big holiday season, or for a specific promotional campaign, then the research needs to be undertaken well in advance. It takes time to conduct the survey, collate the results and act on any issues that need to be addressed. Set a schedule and stick to it.

3. CARRY OUT THE SURVEY EFFECTIVELY

At the specified time, conduct the survey. Get as many customers as possible to complete the survey. Remember, the more information you can get, the more accurate the picture and the better your decisions will be on what needs to be done. Do remember that if you are conducting your survey in a mall you may need to get permission from the centre managers.

Analyse and act on the results.

4. ANALYSE AND PRESENT DATA IN AN APPROPRIATE MANNER

The next, and most important, step in the process is gathering all the information and collating it. This means counting how many people responded and tallying their answers.

Imagine that 100 customers have completed the questionnaire given in Table 4.1. You can give percentages for each answer and produce a useful report of the survey results, which could include a series of graphs. This report should then be presented to supervisors or managers. For example:

Of the 100 customers surveyed about product range:
55 said the product range was excellent
5 said it was very good

5 said it was good
15 said it was satisfactory, and
20 said it was unsatisfactory

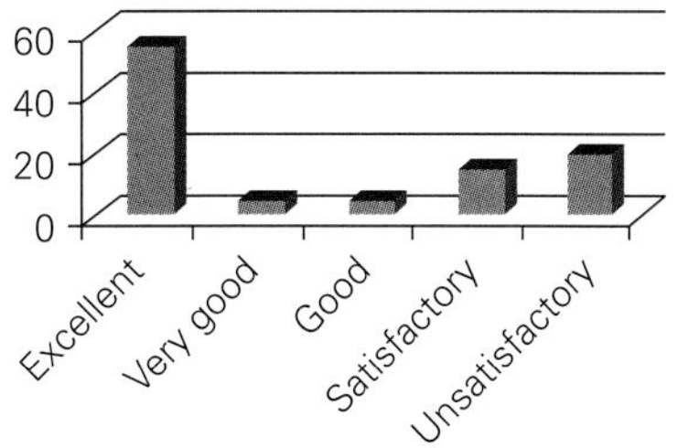

Figure 4.7 Product range graph

Of the same 100 customers surveyed about size range:
5 said the size range was excellent
10 said it was very good
10 said it was good
25 said it was satisfactory, and
50 said it was unsatisfactory

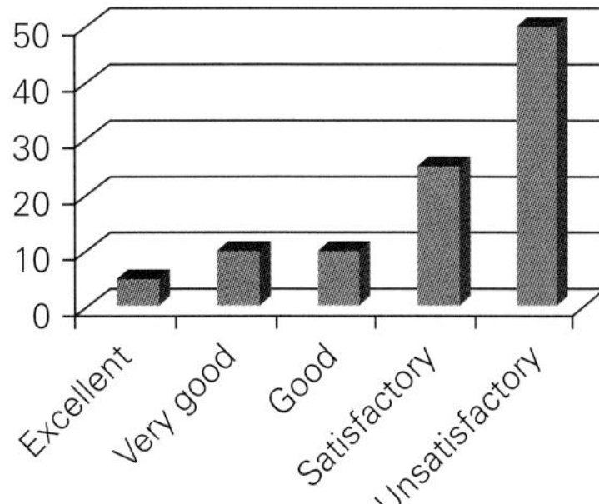

Figure 4.8 Size range graph

These results tell you that the majority of customers are happy with the product range you carry (so you won't need to do anything about that) but only 50 per cent feel you carry enough sizes (so you may have to do something about that).

OTHER FORMS OF DATA COLLECTION

In addition to undertaking a formal research program, there are other ways that you can gauge customer satisfaction levels and gain useful information. These can be sourced:

Internally

Customer orders, random surveys, complaints and returned goods can be used as indicators of what customers are saying or buying from you. Complaints and returned goods, while negative on the surface, should always be looked at as opportunities to make improvements. Looking at what they are complaining about, or what goods seem to be returned most, will give you a platform from which to initiate better product and service standards.

Externally

Sources such as the Australian Bureau of Statistics (ABS), books, newspaper reports and supplier information can demonstrate trends happening in your industry.

However you choose to carry out your market research a very important thing to bear in mind is the fact that far-reaching and long-lasting decisions may be based on the information you find out, so this information must be reliable, accurate and of sufficient quantity. What this means is that your research must be based on verifiable facts from authorised or first-hand sources and there needs to be enough of it to show the data as an actual trend. Asking one person a question, or using only one source for your research, means that you are making your assumptions based on only one opinion—which may or may not be correct or in line with current trends. Numerous sources all saying the same thing, on the other hand, are a clear indication of trends and decisions made on all this data will generally be sound.

Useful websites:

Survey monkey—allows you to develop and conduct your own surveys online:

www.surveymonkey.com

Formsite—will allow you to create forms and surveys to send out to customers:

www.formsite.com

Custominsight—will also guide you through developing a customer survey:

www.custominsight.com/survey-question-types.asp

Task 4.4

Use the websites above, plus any others that you might find, to:

1. develop a questionnaire for an issue in your store and conduct a survey
2. collate the results and prepare a short report on the results.

You will need to conduct at least twenty surveys to get a reasonable amount of data. Don't forget to get your supervisor's permission.

ELEMENT 3
PROFILE THE STORE'S CUSTOMERS

Profiling the market is taking a look at the wider market beyond the store. It gives you an overview of current trends and emerging markets, examines the products that you carry and customers' expectations of them, and looks at the areas of growth potential available to you. Profiling your store's customers, however, means taking a very close look at your customers to gain a greater understanding of them, to consider how you might better serve them, and to ensure that you are still meeting the demands of these important people.

Figure 4.9 Customers are all different

- 3.1 Research the demography of the store's customers.
- 3.2 Develop a demographic profile.
- 3.3 Access information about changing trends and relate to customer demands.

Research the demography of the store's customers

Understanding who your customers are is an important part of understanding what 'drives' your business. If you don't know who your customers are, where they come from, what their financial means are or what their expectations are, then how do you know if you are making the most of every possible opportunity?

We have previously given examples of a clothing boutique in the middle of a technology park, or Fred advertising his Fish Bait and Tackle Shop in *Cosmopolitan* magazine. The clothing shop may have opened there because the shop rent was cheap. Fred may have chosen *Cosmopolitan* because his wife likes it. Do you think that either of these businesses will be successful in their endeavours? Probably not, and the reason for this will be that they did not understand their market and made their decisions without the benefit of proper research.

Knowledge of the demographics of your customers is the first step to operating a successful business. What are demographics?

In very simple terms, 'demographics' refers to the statistical characteristics of a population. It includes features of the people who make up the population, such as the age, income, education levels, occupations, the type of home they live in, and whether they own their home or rent.

Demographics are extremely useful in the planning stages of any project from initial establishment of a business (are you locating it in the right place?) to deciding what new products to include in your range. Knowledge of area demographics can help you make important decisions: if you are planning to open a video arcade, will you open it in a area where most of the inhabitants are living in retirement villages, or are families with very small children? If you want to introduce exclusive evening wear to your clothing range, are there sufficient customers in the area who can afford them?

Develop a demographic profile

The type of customer that shops with you may be broken down into categories that will dictate the choices they make when buying products. We touched on this subject briefly in Chapter 3 when we discussed matching products with customer needs. Let's now look at how the demographics involved might impact on how a successful business operates.

Demographic profiles may include the following factors.

- Age may have an impact on the product range you might carry or the location of your business as shown with the video arcade example above.
- Family structures. Single people will have different needs and expectations to young families, families with many children or mature-aged people.
- Employment patterns and income levels may have an impact on how well your business does. If you locate your store in an area of high unemployment it may not do

as well as being located in an area where the community enjoys a stable employment record and has a steady income. Then, too, the level of income will make a difference to the type of customer you are dealing with and the products or services you offer.

- Education levels will have an impact on the decisions people make, their level of personal knowledge and their employability.
- Tourism will also impact on the way in which you do business. Are your customers mainly local and therefore offering the potential of repeat business, or are they tourists who are unlikely to come in to your store again? This may impact on the type of stock that you carry.
- Cultural and ethnic background may impact on your service and product levels as people from other cultures often have very specific and specialised needs. While non-Muslim populations might enjoy Halal meat, the best place to open a Halal butcher shop or restaurant would be in an area populated by Muslim people.
- Population size too can have a bearing on where you operate your business. Would David Jones or Myer open a department store in a town with a population of 568 people?

All of these factors will have an impact on how you locate, set up, stock and conduct your business. When you understand these things about your customers you can start to build a clearer picture of how to develop product offers and promotions around them. This is the secret to successful marketing.

Changing trends and how they relate to customer demands

Effective marketing not only means knowing all about your customers; it also means keeping an eye on trends and emerging markets so that you can be ready to take advantage of every new opportunity that presents itself. Companies that do not stay in touch with what is happening in their industry can be left behind and lose business as competitors, who move with the times and trends, continue to prosper. There are a number of areas that may have an impact on your industry and therefore on the way in which you service customers. These changing trends may include (but are not limited to):

Tourism

If your business depends on tourism:

- How will changing patterns of overseas visitors affect you?
- What impact will increases or decreases in the number of tourists have on you?
- How will you take advantage of and promote to new and emerging markets such as China and India?

Technology

- What effect do changes in technology have on your business?
- Does any new technology make it easier or harder to do business?

- Will you be required to adopt or provide this new technology? What will happen if you do not?

Selling approaches

- Is the way in which you sell to customers the most effective and efficient way?
- Are there new approaches or opportunities available?
- Can you sell your products or services online—opening your prospects to the world?

Leisure time

- Is your product or service aimed at people's leisure time?
- Do people today have more or less leisure time that previously?
- How does this affect the way in which you promote or sell to them?
- How can you adjust your product or service offerings to meet with and take advantage of new trends?

Environmental issues

Environmental issues have become very important over the last few years and there is a growing trend among customers to do business with companies that have a 'green' policy. In addition to developing environmentally sustainable business practices to meet legislative and customer demands, adopting such practices can also provide cost-saving benefits as you recycle or re-use materials rather than discarding them.

Discount operators

There is an ever-growing number of companies today who offer substantial discounts. Where you are competing with other shop owners you can combat this by either offering similar prices, or by offering better value and service to justify your higher prices. What do you do, however, about operators who can discount because they have no store presence: they sell solely via the internet?

- Does this type of competition impact on your business?
- If so, does your company have strategies in place to combat this type of competition?

Quality demands

As customers become more affluent, their demands for quality increase.

- Is this a factor in your own business?
- If so, how will you address it?

The business environment in which your store operates is an ever-changing one and it is important to your continued success to be aware of what is going on not only in your own industry, but in the wider business, social, economic, cultural and technological communities.

Sources of demographic information

There are a great many sources of demographic information available today. These include:

Primary sources

'Primary sources' refers to the research you undertake first hand according to your own specifications:

- customer surveys
- discussions with colleagues and suppliers
- sales performance reports
- financial reports.

Secondary sources

'Secondary sources' are research conducted by outside companies that you purchase or make use of for your purposes:

- Australian Bureau of Statistics (ABS)—provides in-depth information about Australia's population. This information is collected from a variety of sources including the Australian Census, Immigration reports and so on.
- Industry associations—your own industry association or governing body may have substantial background information about the products and services offered by the industry and the customers who purchase them.
- Local councils—will have very in-depth information about the population in their area.
- Chambers of commerce—will also have information about business sales and issues in its area of influence.

Task 4.5

1. Research
   a. Go to the Reports section of the Domain website:
   www.domain.com.au/public/apm/default.aspx?mode=research
   Type your postcode in the 'search' box and click on 'Demographics' to see a brief demographic profile of your suburb.
   b. Visit the Australian Bureau of Statistics website—www.abs.gov.au—and spend some time browsing through the various demographic reports you can find there to gain an understanding of the type and range of information available.
   c. Visit the website of industry associations relevant to your industry and familiarise yourself with the information they provide that might be useful in researching your target market.
2. Using the survey questionnaire you developed for Task 4.4, make amendments to it to obtain demographic information and re-survey your customers with this new form.
3. How might the information you have now gained impact on your organisation (if at all)?
4. Based on this new information, would you make any changes to the way you do business? If so, what would you change?

Task 4.6

Discuss the changing trends in your industry, using the points under 'Changing trends and how they relate to customer demands' above as your basis.

- How do these changes affect the way you do business?
- What, if anything, can you, or did you, do about them?
- What, if any, information do the sources listed in Task 4.5 provide to assist in recognising changes in trends and consumer demand?

ELEMENT 4
IMPLEMENT METHODS TO ATTRACT CUSTOMERS TO THE STORE

By now you should have an excellent knowledge of your customers, what they expect from you and how you can go about meeting their needs. Now all you have to do is *tell your customers* about the great service you offer!

In this section we will look at a variety of tools you can use to effectively promote your store and attract those all-important customers.

LEARNING OUTCOMES

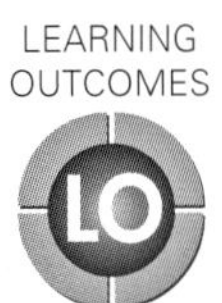

4.1 Access and analyse information about the customer (covered in the previous section).

4.2 Generate ideas to develop methods for attracting customers.

4.3 Select and develop a suitable idea in collaboration with others in the organisation.

4.4 Present and discuss the idea with relevant personnel.

4.5 Evaluate the idea to ensure that it meets the requirements for the target customers.

Generate ideas to develop methods for attracting customers

All of the knowledge you have gained about your customers and potential customers will give you a sound basis for developing promotional ideas to get them through your door.

Ideas on how to do this can be generated using a number of different techniques including:

- brainstorming—get together with colleagues to listen to a variety of ideas and discuss the pros and cons of each one
- visualising—think about ways in which the outcome can be achieved. For example, if you are promoting a new spring line in clothing you might visualise customers wearing your clothes to outdoor events, so you might then set up your window and in-store displays with the outdoors in mind

- telling or listening to stories that show how products or services have been used by people—this can give you some great and sometimes unusual ideas on who to promote them to
- making use of creative writing—when advertising or promoting in a written format (newspaper or magazine ads, flyers etc.), be creative in the way you present the product or service. Creative writing can paint excellent pictures of a product and how it can be used. It is important to note that written ads and promotional material should not be too long or wordy as people will not initially be attracted to promotional material with too much text. Keep your writing short and concise and aim to grab the customer's attention with a 'punchy' headline or title
- considering ads and campaigns that you, personally, like—look at how they may be used to suit your organisation
- considering combinations—there is no reason, other than possible financial considerations, that you need to restrict yourself to just one idea. By combining a number of ideas you can develop a fully-fledged promotional campaign that will reach your target market in multi-faceted ways. For example, you could develop ideas and themes around window displays, newspaper ads, banners, promotional giveaways and in-store theming, all coordinated and timed for maximum impact.

Useful websites:

Ad Cracker—provides some innovative ideas on how to generate creative advertising ideas, techniques and tools.

www.adcracker.com/index.htm.

Business Know-how—offers 31 low-cost ways to promote a business:

www.businessknowhow.com/marketing/24waysto.htm.

Select and develop a suitable idea in collaboration with others in the organisation

Once you have settled on an idea, or set of ideas, on how you will attract customers, it is important to ensure that all staff are comfortable with the ideas, 'on board' with them, and that the ideas are, in fact, viable. Start with basic discussions on:

- promotional medium—what format will work best for your promotion? Should you advertise in the newspaper, on television or radio? Will you need posters, special tickets or promotional giveaways?
- schedule—how long will the promotional campaign last? Will specific days of the week, or times of the day be more effective than others for running the promotion? How will you find this out?
- resources—what resources will you need to successfully run this campaign? Will you need to put on extra staff?

- cost—having established your basic promotional idea, medium and schedule, how much will this campaign cost? (Remember to include the cost of taking on any additional staff.)
- implementation—how will you ensure a smooth roll-out of the campaign? What are the roles and responsibilities of the staff involved in implementing the campaign? Will a timetable be put in place to make sure that each component of the campaign is delivered according to plan?
- expected outcomes—Have you developed a set of Key Performance Indicators (KPIs) to help determine the campaign's success? What are these KPIs based on?
- review process—What methods will you use to review the processes undertaken in this campaign? How will you know if the campaign has been a success? How will you use the information reviewed from the current campaign to make improvements for the future?

Looking at all of these issues and having a sound plan in place is the foundation to your promotional idea. The next step is to gain approval for it from the relevant supervisors or managers.

Present and discuss the idea with relevant personnel

With the promotional plan fully fleshed out you may need to get approval or authority to go ahead from other stakeholders. Ideally, in a small organisation, they will have been involved in the entire process, but this may not always be the case. Where approvals from relevant personnel may need to be sought these might include team leaders, supervisors or the organisation's manager.

In presenting the promotional idea to them it is important to be accurate and thorough—remember: you need them to give their approval. Presenting ideas for approval can be accomplished in a number of ways including:

- staff meetings—there are often opportunities to discuss 'any other business' at general staff meetings, or you may ask that time be allocated to you at the meeting as part of the agenda
- specially convened meetings—if the issue is important and interesting enough, a special meeting can be called to specifically discuss promotional ideas and campaigns
- written reports or proposals—that outline all of the points from the previous page:
  - purpose of the promotional idea and campaign
  - medium or mediums to be used
  - cost and additional resources
  - schedules
  - implementation plan
  - expected outcome.

When presenting an idea in written format only, you need to be very thorough and anticipate any questions the authorising stakeholders may have, as you will not necessarily be available to answer questions and they may base their approval solely on the written information you have provided.

Presentations may take the form of informal chats around the table, or formal presentations complete with graphs, spread sheets and PowerPoint displays. How this is done will depend entirely on your organisation, its structure and your place within it.

You will need to be ready to answer any questions that these stakeholders have, so make sure that you have thoroughly researched all aspects of your idea and can defend your decisions and recommendations where and if necessary. The successful outcome of your presentation may depend on this.

Task 4.7

1. Using the new survey information you collected in Task 4.5, develop a proposal for a promotional idea to attract this customer group into your store. Your proposal should include:
   - at least two different mediums—and reasons why you chose them
   - outline of the product you are offering
   - outline of the target customer group
   - a campaign schedule—over what period of time, when and how often the campaign will be run (if applicable)
   - any additional resources that may be needed for the campaign
   - approximate costs of running the campaign
   - Key Performance Indicators
   - the expected outcome of the campaign.
2. Present the proposal to your manager for their opinion and ask them to provide comments on your report.

Evaluate the idea to ensure that it meets the requirements for the target customers

In completing Task 4.7 you will have gained an understanding of the amount of work and the cost involved in generating a viable promotional plan, so you will also understand the importance of making sure you have it right before you actually go ahead with the plan. Spending time and money on promoting your store can be incredibly successful—or it could be a dismal failure. Which one will apply to your campaign will depend on how well you have done your research and laid the ground work.

BEFORE GOING AHEAD WITH THE FINAL PLAN

A final check before you make bookings, bring in extra staff and spend promotional budgets might include checking that:

- the promotion actually addresses the stated purpose
- all necessary approvals are in place
- budgets and resources are available
- any outside sources, such as advertising media, printers, entertainers and so on, are on schedule and have the right information
- any necessary bookings such as media space, shopping centre or exhibition booths and so on have been made and confirmed
- all necessary documentation is up to date, signed and securely stored.

AFTER THE CAMPAIGN

Once the promotional campaign has been completed there are further questions to ask:

- Were the KPIs met? Did the campaign generate:
  - › better customer response
  - › extra sales
  - › a greater awareness of your store and its products?
- Did the campaign stay within its allocated budget?
- What went right?
- What went wrong?
- Where could improvements be made in future?

Methods of gathering this information can include developing checklists and discussing the process with colleagues or supervisors and then writing a report of the outcomes. The answers to these and other relevant questions can then help to ensure that any future campaigns to promote business and attract customers will be more successful.

To summarise what you have learned: the image portrayed by your store, its components and the products and services you sell are all important aspects of a business—but these only work to your advantage if you understand who your customers are and what they expect of you.

Thorough research and a good understanding of your industry and the environment in which you operate, as well as the ability to stay up to date with trends and emerging technology and ideas, will stand you in good stead and give you an advantage over less well-informed competitors.

ASSESSMENT: PROJECT

Assessment context	This unit describes the performance outcomes, skills and knowledge required to profile a retail market. It involves reviewing the image of the store, researching market demands, profiling store customers and implementing methods to attract customers to the store. The purpose of this project is to assess your ability to understand your local market and develop ideas for attracting customers around this target market.
Assessment instructions	You have decided to open a new store at your local shopping mall. Before contacting the Shopping Centre Management you want to make sure that your business idea is sound and that there is a market for what you are offering. Using the knowledge you have gained throughout this unit, you will need to: 1. Describe the product or service you will offer. 2. Explain who you will discuss your ideas with to ensure you are getting the right advice. 3. Research demand for your product or service idea in terms of: – area demographics – competitor offerings – current market trends and changes in the industry 4. Who is your target market? Explain why you are targeting this customer group. You will need to develop a survey form to conduct some of this research. 5. Based on your target market, describe the components that will make up your store's image: – layout and access – design – level of formality. 6. Develop a promotional campaign designed to attract your target market (you will have a promotional budget of $10 000). Address all the points covered in the section headed 'Select and develop a suitable idea in collaboration with others in the organisation' (page 144). 7. Describe how you will review your plan for viability. 8. Hold a meeting with 'stakeholders' to discuss your plans and ideas and get their feedback. For students in the workplace these stakeholders can be made up of friends, family, work colleagues or your trainer. Classroom based students can hold meetings with classmates.
Evidence required	• Completed report outlining points 1–7 above • Any source research information such as: – demographic reports used – customer survey forms used—originals and collated final report – promotional mediums to be used. • Minutes of any meetings held with 'stakeholders' to discuss product offerings and promotional ideas.

Range and conditions	• You may base this project on any legal, legitimate business idea. The purpose of this assessment is to judge your ability to successfully determine who your target market might be and how you will attract them, so your business idea must be viable and aimed at a legitimate outcome. • You may be required to conduct your market research within the general population in your chosen area. If you are conducting this research in a shopping mall or other similar public area, be sure to gain any necessary approvals from centre managers or necessary authorities. • In order to achieve a reasonable picture of your idea's viability you will need to conduct at least 30 surveys. • You will have 2 weeks to complete this project.
Reasonable adjustments	In the event that you have difficulty understanding the assessment tasks due to language or other difficulties, your trainer will attempt to make reasonable adjustments to the assessment paper in order to afford you every opportunity to achieve competency.
Decision-making rules	You will be assessed on your ability to: • analyse components of your store's image • accurately profile your target market • develop promotional ideas methods designed to attract your target market • work with others in generating ideas and gaining feedback • present your information and plan in a well thought out report • work within resource and budgetary constraints • develop methods of reviewing successful outcomes.

COMPETENCY MAPPING

Element		Performance criteria		Task	Assessment	Refer to page
1	Review the image of the store	1.1	Analyse the components of the store image.	4.1, 4.2	AQ3	124–127
		1.2	Access and analyse relevant store documentation in relation to store image.	4.4		127–130
		1.3	Promote the store image in an appropriate manner.	4.3	AQ4	130–132
2	Research market demands for the store	2.1	Select an appropriate area for research of market demands.	4.4	AQ2	133–134
		2.2	Use appropriate market research techniques according to store policy.			135
		2.3	Plan market research according to store policy and procedures.			135
		2.4	Collect, analyse and present data in an appropriate manner.			136–137
3	Profile the store's customers	3.1	Research the demography of the store's customers.	4.5	AQ2	139
		3.2	Develop a demographic profile.	4.5	AQ2	139
		3.3	Access information about changing trends and relate to customer demands.	4.6	AQ2	140–141

continued

Element		Performance criteria		Task	Assessment	Refer to page
4	Implement methods to attract customers to store	4.1	Access and analyse information about the customer.	4.4	AQ2	142
		4.2	Generate ideas to develop methods for attracting customers.	4.7	AQ4	143
		4.3	Select and develop a suitable idea in collaboration with others in the organisation.	4.7	AQ4	144
		4.4	Present and discuss the idea with relevant personnel.	4.7	AQ6	145
		4.5	Evaluate the idea to ensure that it meets the requirements for the target customers.	4.7	AQ5	146–147

Required skills and knowledge	Task	Assessment	Refer to page
Required skills			
Interpersonal communication skills to: • carry out market research • generate ideas and discuss with relevant personnel through clear and direct communication • ask questions to identify and confirm requirements • use language and concepts appropriate to cultural differences • use and interpret non-verbal communication.	4.2, 4.3, 4.4, 4.5, 4.6, 4.7	AQ1, 2, 6	133
Literacy and numerical skills related to: • reading and understanding store policy and procedures • research • data analysis • generating reports.			124, 128, 129, 133, 135
Collaboration and teamwork.			144
Required knowledge			
Store policy and procedures in regard to: • accessing documentation • promoting store image.	4.3, 4.4, 4.5, 4.7	AQ2, 4	128, 129
Market research methods.			133
Evaluation methods.			135, 146
Creative thinking techniques.			143
Techniques in interpersonal communication.			145

Required skills and knowledge	Task	Assessment	Refer to page
Critical aspects for assessment			
Analyses components of the store image by accessing relevant store documentation.	4.1, 4.2, 4.3, 4.4, 4.5, 4.7	AQ1–6	124
Promotes the store image in an appropriate manner.			126, 129–130
Researches market demands using appropriate market research techniques.			133–137
Accurately profiles store customers.			139–141
Generates ideas for attracting customers to store.			143
Selects and develops a suitable idea in collaboration with others.			144
Presents and discusses idea with supervisor.			145
Evaluates idea to ensure that it meets requirements for target customers.			146
Implements the idea according to store policies and budgetary requirements.			146–147

Chapter 5

SIRXMER201

Merchandise products

In the introduction to Part 2, we introduced you to the basic concept of merchandising and how to arrange and display stock to its best advantage. **Merchandising** is about more than making a simple display of a product however. It also involves preparing and placing products in such a way that they present a logical flow to the store, are as safe and secure from theft as you can make them and that they are priced and described correctly and accurately.

In this chapter we will cover a range of subjects including how to deal with new merchandise and how to prepare display labels and price tickets, and we will take a brief look at maintaining displays.

Note on assessment: as this subject is closely related to Chapter 6—Plan, create and maintain displays, the main assessment for both units of competency will be undertaken upon completion of that chapter.

ELEMENT 1
PLACE AND ARRANGE MERCHANDISE

When new stock arrives in your store it needs to be unpacked and prepared for the sales floor. How you go about doing this will depend to a great extent on the store's policies and procedures but this might mean that you need to consider how the stock will be displayed, the size and type of labels and tickets to use and how you are going to ensure that the displays are maintained to ensure a balanced and fully-stocked appearance.

LEARNING OUTCOMES

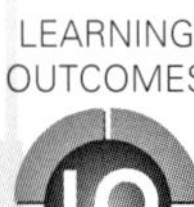

1.1 Unpack merchandise according to store policy and procedures and legislative requirements.

1.2 Place merchandise on floor, fixtures and shelves in determined locations according to WHS and other relevant legislative requirements.

1.3 Display merchandise to achieve a balanced, fully-stocked appearance and promote sales.

1.4 Identify damaged, soiled or out-of-date stock and take corrective action as required according to store procedure.

1.5	Place stock range to conform with fixtures, ticketing, prices or bar codes.
1.6	Rotate stock according to stock requirements and store procedure.
1.7	Ensure stock presentation conforms to special handling techniques and other safety requirements.

Unpacking and placing merchandise effectively

Depending on the nature of your store and the products it sells it is possible that you will receive deliveries of stock each day, so dealing with new stock will become an important part of your day. Dealing with arriving stock is not simply a matter of pulling things out of boxes and putting them on shelves. Unpacking merchandise should be done with care for a number of reasons including:

- stock control—when new stock arrives, it should be checked to ensure that everything ordered actually arrived, and in good condition
- maintaining the quality of the merchandise—removing the items from their packaging carefully ensures that you keep them clean and undamaged. Customers do not want to buy dirty or damaged goods and stock that has been broken or damaged after delivery cannot be returned to the supplier. This then leaves you with merchandise you will not be able to sell—a cost factor for the business, as it must still pay the supplier for the item
- familiarisation—unpacking stock gives you the opportunity to see what has arrived and become familiar with all the new items, ready to promote them to customers. As you know, product knowledge is a vital part of any sales person's role.

The arrival of new stock should never be allowed to interfere with the smooth operation of the store so wherever possible deliveries should be made through a loading dock or back entrance. If this is not possible then the stock should be moved directly out to a back room or storage area as soon as it arrives, rather than being left around the store.

The area you use for unpacking should provide enough space for you to work in efficiently with supplies such as price guns, tags and inventory forms within easy reach.

UNPACKING AND SORTING PROCESSES

To ensure that the unpacking and sorting of new merchandise happens smoothly and correctly you should:

- use safe manual handling techniques—when lifting heavy boxes
- check all stock against the supplier's invoice—as you unpack it, make a note of any missing items so that you can follow up with the supplier
- check that each item is clean and undamaged—if it is received in less than perfect condition you should be able to return it to the supplier and get a replacement or credit on your account

- sort the stock—into a logical order so that you know how it will be placed or displayed in the shop. Stock can be sorted according to:
  - type—sorting all items of a similar nature together for display purposes
  - brand—the store may have special areas for brand-named stock, so sorting by brand makes it easier to distribute the merchandise correctly and efficiently
  - size—depending on the nature of your store this might be done according to physical shape and size of the items or by clothing size
  - colour—similar or complementary colours are often grouped together to achieve a pleasing display in the store, so sorting them before taking them onto the shop floor can make the process easier
  - price—stock can also be grouped by price; sale items will often be located at specific points within the store so, again, sorting them in advance will make your task easier
  - customer need—some items sell faster and are more popular than others and, so, are also grouped and displayed more prominently in the store.
- price items—according to organisational requirements. Once items have been unpacked and sorted they will need to be priced. This may involve attaching labels or price stickers to each item and ensuring that the appropriate profit margin as well as GST (where applicable) has been added to the cost price. Most organisations will have product price lists that outline the sales price to be placed on each item they sell. Correct pricing is important and should be done in accordance with organisational and legislative requirements
- dispose of empty cartons and packing materials—in line with organisational and legislative requirements.

PLACING STOCK APPROPRIATELY

Placing stock on the shop floor must be done with care and due consideration. How will the stock be laid out? What fixtures, shelves and fittings will you use? What safety measures must you take? These and other questions are very important. For example, when placing new stock around the store you need to ensure that you don't overcrowd racks or shelves with too many items or items that are too heavy.

Too many items on a rack or shelf can make it difficult for customers to see the merchandise properly. Crowded shelves and racks often give a 'cheap' impression. This may discourage customers and they could leave the store without buying anything. Items that are too heavy could cause the shelving or the racks to collapse or break, potentially injuring staff or customers. Depending on the industry you are in, the store may have special instructions on correct loading of shelves or racks that will be dictated by government legislation or industry codes of practice.

It is also important to achieve a logical flow of traffic through the store. Each store will have specific areas that are 'hot spots' and 'cold spots'.

Hot spots—areas where more customer attention is focused than others. These hot spots are generally located at the store's entrance, at the cash register, and the area between the entrance and the cash register. This is where you would place popular, fast-selling items to draw customers in from the entrance, and encourage them to buy additional, accessory items that might be displayed around the register.

Cold spots—areas that are less frequented by customers and are generally found at the rear of the store. To ensure a steady flow of customers throughout the entire store, it is a good idea to place 'staple' items at the back of the store; items that are more *need-based* than *desire-based*. This encourages customers to come right in to the store.

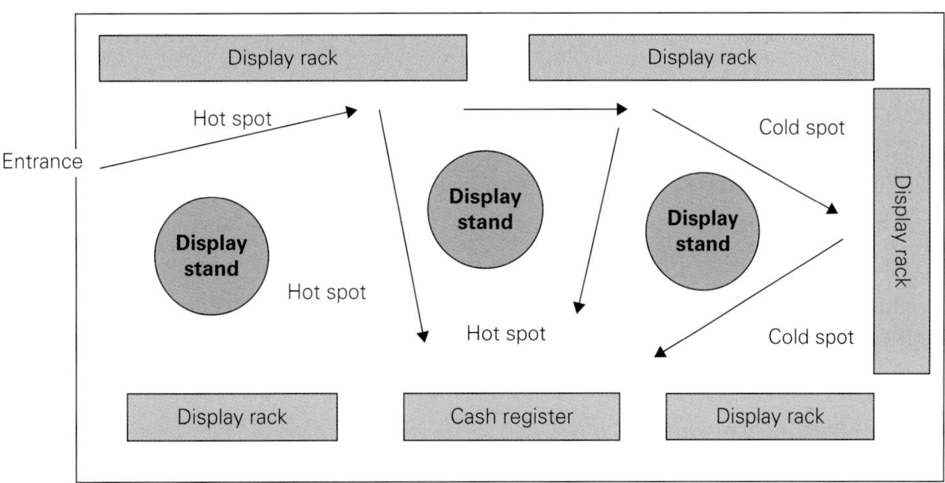

Figure 5.1 Hot spots and cold spots

As you can see from Figure 5.1, there are a number of ways in which a customer may navigate their way around a store. Placing fast-moving, popular stock in hot spots will draw them in, but you must then ensure that they move all the way around the store, and look at all displays and merchandise, by placing products in ways that will promote them and encourage customers further into the store. Displays will be dealt with in detail in Chapter 6.

ACHIEVING A BALANCED APPEARANCE IN YOUR STORE

It can take just a few short moments for a customer to gain a first impression of your store, so you have to make it count. The aim is to achieve a look that will attract customers into the store and encourage them to browse. A well-balanced, fully-stocked look can arouse customer interest and encourage them to come in. This is important, and can be achieved by setting up new displays, maintaining existing displays and keeping shelves and racks tidy and appropriately stocked.

Figure 5.2 Well laid-out shop floor

Figure 5.3 Crowded and cluttered shop floor

Look at the two photos in Figures 5.2 and 5.3 and ask yourself: which of the two would you prefer to go into? The store on the left has spot lighting to highlight stock, simple displays and lots of room for customers to move and browse. The photo on the right shows a store that is very crowded with merchandise, with narrow aisles and looks slightly untidy compared with the other photo. To be fair, it also is a discount store and has a good deal more stock and is aimed at a budget-conscious market whereas the store on the left is a one-off boutique with a completely different clientele. The comparison, however, shows that a great image can be achieved by keeping it simple.

MERCHANDISING PLANS

Many organisations, particularly those that are part of a chain, will have distinct plans that outline how merchandise is to be displayed in the store. They provide the store's sales staff with a 'blueprint' on a variety of issues such as colour and style of merchandise, how it is to be displayed and accessories to be used as well as fixtures and shelving to be used for each category of merchandise.

Examples of merchandising plans are shown in Chapter 6: 'Plan, create and maintain displays'.

Stock rotation

Stock rotation is a practice most commonly used in hospitality and retail—particularly where food products are sold. However it can also be very effective in general merchandising: if the way in which you display and promote your merchandise never changes, then customers may be discouraged from coming in—if they think they've already seen all you have to offer they won't want to waste their time coming in again. So stock rotation happens for a number of reasons including the following.

Task 5.1

1. Research a number of store layouts by taking note when you go shopping over the next week or so. Look at the difference between department stores and boutique shops, and the difference between department store types such as Myer and David Jones, and Kmart and Big W. Answer the following questions:
   a. How do displays and layouts differ between department stores and boutiques?
   b. How do displays and layouts differ between the different types of department stores?
   c. How can you use this information to improve the traffic flow and merchandising in your store?
2. Design a layout for your own store indicating your hot and cold spots and describing the type of products you would place in each spot. Give reasons for your placement choices. Also consider:
   a. What type of fixtures will you use?
   b. How will you ensure that the merchandise is not too heavy or overcrowded for the fixture?
   c. What type of signs or tickets will you use?
3. Look at the shops in your local shopping centre or mall. Take photos, if permitted, and submit them to your trainer indicating which ones you felt had a well-balanced look and which ones did not. Explain the reasons for your choices and comments.

   The YouTube Video 'Legend Studios Visual Merchandising 101' (http://youtube.com/2IxVEq5-_iM) provides an excellent overview of visual merchandising.

Health and hygiene legislation

Many food items have 'sell by' or 'use by' dates and it is important to ensure that these products are sold before these dates expire first, from a health and hygiene perspective, and second from a profitability perspective. If a product is still on the shelf after its sell-by date then it will have to be disposed of, as food poisoning can be very harmful to customers. There is also a cost to the store, which has paid for the stock but not sold it. Stock rotation protects both customers and the store's investment. There are a number of steps you can take to promote stock rotation:

1. FIFO (First In, First Out). This is a foundation rule of stock rotation: use the oldest items first.
2. Put newly received goods to the back of the store or shelf to promote FIFO.
3. Record the receipt date and use-by date on goods as they are received.

4. Record use-by date on non-perishables when they are opened.
5. Record production-date and use-by dates on any food that is prepared, that will not be served immediately.

Effective merchandising practice

Stock rotation can also be used effectively to refresh the look of a store, or to encourage customers to look through the entire store. Often, particularly in the case of supermarkets or stores that a customer frequents on a regular basis, the customer knows exactly what they want and where, within the store, these items are located. This means they go straight to the products they want and don't look at any of the other items for sale. To discourage this practice stores will often move their stock around so that the customer will have to search for the items they want and thereby look through the entire store—possibly picking up things they would not normally have seen. From a customer's perspective this can be a little annoying—but from the store owner's perspective it is a method by which they can encourage additional sales.

Dealing with damaged, soiled or out-of-date stock

It will be part of most store policies to check and rotate stock on a regular basis. At these times it is also a good idea to check if stock items are damaged, soiled or out of date, although you should keep an eye on this at all times.

Damaged stock—can be the result of careless unpacking of newly arrived goods or careless handling of stock by staff or customers. In either case, unless you have very special arrangements with the supplier, you will not be able to return these goods to them.

Soiled stock—can, again, be the result of careless handling by staff or customers. In some cases stock items can be cleaned and no harm is done, at other times however the item will have to be removed from sale as it cannot be brought back up to the required standard.

Out-of-date stock—is simply stock that has not sold within a given period of time. In the case of food or other perishable items, this will be dictated by use-by dates; in other cases this might be dictated by fashion and current trends. Depending on the nature of the products, out-of-date stock should either be disposed of (in the case of food items), or rotated in such a way as to make room for newer, faster-selling items.

You might also rotate damaged, soiled or out-of-date stock to the front of the store and offer it at special discount prices to encourage sales of these items. Whatever the item is, and however you dispose of it, you must always remember that it is an item in your store's inventory and must therefore be removed from that inventory in line with your organisation's policies and procedures. This may involve finding the item in the inventory list and entering the date on which it was removed from normal stock rotation, the reason why it was removed and what was done with it.

Depending on the size and sophistication of the organisation, inventory maintenance can be achieved in a number of ways, including handwritten lists that are updated when required, spreadsheets using software such as Microsoft Excel or Access, or purpose-built software programs such as 'Inflowinventory'.

Figure 5.4 Example of inventory management software

Programs such as this will keep track of incoming and outgoing stock and control your inventory without too much effort.

Useful website:

A free download of Inflowinventory is available at: www.inflowinventory.com. Download it and see what a product inventory system can do.

Task 5.2

Using the work you did in Task 5.1 point 2 (design a layout for your store):

1. Discuss how you would ensure rotation of your stock to comply with any legislative requirements, or to merchandise your products in the most effect way.
2. Develop a rotation schedule. What would your rotation schedule be based on?
3. Describe how you would deal with damaged, soiled or out-of-date stock.

Special handling and safety requirements

Depending on the nature of the products you sell there may be special procedures involved in unpacking, storing and displaying them. For example, a store that sells any kind of toxic chemicals (such as a pool shop or hardware store) will need to ensure that these chemicals are stored and labelled correctly and placed in the store with health and safety considerations in mind. Equally, a store dealing with children's toys will need to ensure that their products are packaged and displayed in such a way that small children will come to no harm when handling them. Handling techniques involved in dealing with such products may vary according to stock characteristics and store policy.

Heavy, bulky stock will need to stored and moved on to the shop floor carefully, taking care to observe WHS issues. The same applies to perishable goods which also need to be handled in line with legislative requirements.

Each store will have policies and procedures in dealing safely with products that could, potentially, present a risk to customers and staff. For example, heavy and bulky stock must be stacked on floors or shelves so that it will not fall and injure people. Correct manual handling techniques must also be used when moving such stock to avoid back injuries or muscle strain. Perishable items must be handled in a hygienic manner and be stored in accordance with food safety regulations. The store's policies and procedures may be based on in-house decisions, industry codes of practice, legislative requirements or a combination of all three.

Pricing requirements

According to the fair trading act of each state, you must tell customers the full cash price they are required to pay for any given product. Under the law, it is an offence to state only part of the price without also specifying the total amount to be paid, and the full price must include any applicable GST. So, for example, you cannot promote a product by stating that the customer only needs to pay a $100 deposit—without stating that the full price is $1 000. Attaching more than one price label to a product can also be misleading to customers. Whenever an item has more than one price marked on it, it is illegal to sell it for more than the lowest price label attached. It is also an offence to falsely inflate the price of an item to give the impression that it has, subsequently, been discounted or is on sale. For example if an item normally costs $59.95 you cannot put a price sticker on it saying that the original price was $89.95 and is now on sale for $59.95.

Keeping safety in mind

It is very important to look after your safety and the safety of customers and visitors to your store. Here are some of the important things to remember if you are receiving, unpacking, displaying or storing merchandise.

- Always use correct manual handling techniques.
- Use a safety knife for opening boxes and cartons to avoid serious injury from cuts, and always cut away from your body when using a safety knife.
- Check that shelves and fixtures are safe and steady before displaying stock on them.
- Don't block entrances, doorways or aisles when unpacking boxes.
- Don't leave packaging materials or cardboard anywhere in the store—remove all packaging materials from the floor and fixtures immediately. Blocked entrances and packaging materials left lying around represent a trip hazard and could cause injury. They could also get in the way during an evacuation in case of an emergency and so would represent a breach of legislation in relation to WHS matters.
- Cardboard boxes and cartons should be flattened and taken to the recycling depot.
- Non-recyclables should be placed in the appropriate waste receptacles.

ELEMENT 2
PREPARE DISPLAY LABELS AND TICKETS

Display labels, signs and tickets are used in the retail industry to provide pricing and promotional information. This information can be provided in a number of different ways from small price stickers to large posters and promotional banners. In the same way that an attractive, well-coordinated display can portray a given image, so too can the type and quality of the tickets and signs used to promote products; too much information on a promotional sign and customers are unlikely to stop and read it, put too little information on and busy customers are unlikely to follow up by coming into the store.

Good promotional signage and tickets grab the customer's attention and tell them just enough to pique their interest, encouraging them to come in and make a buying decision.

LEARNING OUTCOMES

2.1 Prepare labels and tickets for window, wall or floor displays according to store policy.

2.2 Prepare tickets using electronic equipment or neatly by hand according to store procedures.

2.3 Identify soiled, damaged, illegible or incorrect labels and tickets and take corrective action.

2.4 Use and maintain electronic ticketing and labelling equipment according to design specifications.

2.5 Place labels and tickets visibly and correctly on merchandise.

2.6 Replace labels and tickets according to store policy.

Preparing price labels and tickets

The preparation of labels, signs and tickets will need to be done with organisational policies and procedures in mind. This might mean considering:

- company logos to be used (if appropriate)
- what colour the labels or tickets should be in order to blend in with (or stand out from) given displays and store image
- how big or small the tickets and labels must be
- what information must be included on the ticket
- the method of creating the sign, label or ticket
- where in the store or window the sign, label or ticket will be placed.

You also need to know what type of label or ticket may be needed. Types of tickets, signs or labels could include such things as:

- shelf tickets—these are price tags attached to the shelf on which the product is displayed. They can be either slotted in to a fitted space, or hung from the shelf so that it looks like a tag

- written labels—while most stores use pricing guns to produce their labels and tickets, some stores do use handwritten labels. If the hand-written method is used it is important to ensure that the handwriting is clear and easy to read.
- swing tickets—these are used primarily in the retail clothing industry and are normally attached to the inside back collar of the clothing item. They will, generally, include the brand name of the item, its size and price.
- bar coding—this is a form of pricing that allows the store to capture a range of data about the product and makes it easy to track and control the inventory. Without a public bar code reader, however, it does not let the customer know the price of the product.
- price boards—these are commonly used in the hospitality industry or retail food industry. They are generally large signs outlining a range of items and their prices. They are, for example, often found on takeaway shop walls.
- posters or promotional signage—these can be quite large and are used to promote special offers, discounts or themes within a display.

Whatever the choice of label, ticket or sign it is important to ensure that it is in line with the store's image and that it is correct and not misleading.

While each store will have its own policies about the subject there are a number of general do's and don'ts that you should bear in mind when preparing tickets and labels for your store.

Things that you should do

- Use simple language—wherever possible to make it easy for customers to understand at a glance
- Allow 'white space'—between words and letters that is enough to avoid a crowded look to the sign. White space is the amount of *blank space* left on a sign and makes it easier for people to read.

Source: www.swingtags.com.au.

Figure 5.5 Assortment of tags

Figure 5.6 Window sign

Figure 5.7 Price board

- Ensure accuracy—the information on all labels, tickets or signs must not be misleading in any way and must not misrepresent your store or the product involved. Ensure that all grammar, spelling and prices are correct
- Highlight features and benefits—to the customer
- Keep the information clear, concise and 'punchy'—to grab the customer's attention
- Include a 'call to action'—if preparing signs or tickets. 'Call to action' is a marketing device that encourages customers to make a buying decision *now*. A **call to action** can include such statements as:
  - *Hurry—last day of sale!*
  - *Don't miss out—only 3 left*
  - *Sale ends Sunday*
  - *15 per cent off today only*

Things that you should *not* do

- Use handwritten signs—unless it fits in with a specific theme—handwriting can be difficult to read
- Include too much information—A label, ticket or sign that has too much written on it is hard to read, difficult to understand and most customers will not take the time to stop and read the information
- Use colours and styles that distract—from or are contrary to the overall theme of the store or its image
- Ignore legislative obligations—by providing information that is incorrect or misleading.

PRICING EQUIPMENT

Price stickers and labels can be created using a number of different methods including:

Pricing guns

A pricing (or label) gun is used to place price tags on items. The gun can be customised to imprint any price onto the sticker quickly and efficiently, which makes it useful in supermarkets, department stores and other retail stores. Pricing guns can be used to dispense sticky labels, which are great for products that are packaged in boxes, packets, tins or cans; and tags, which are mainly used for pricing items of clothing, where the tag is pushed through the cloth of the garment. This type of pricing method requires a specific tagging gun.

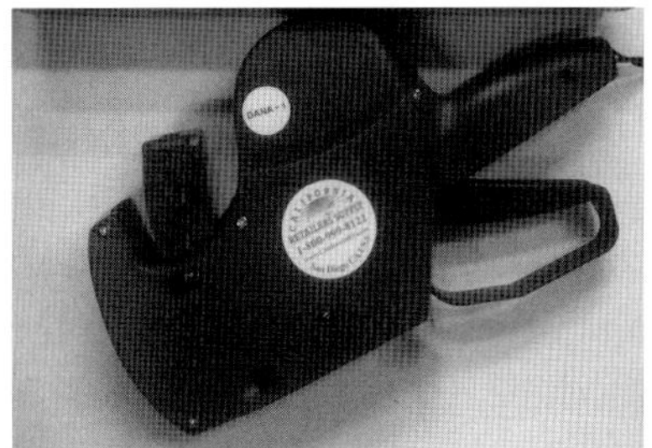

Figure 5.8 Pricing gun

Label dispensers

Label dispensers can be used to produce a range of different types of label including opaque and transparent labels. They are relatively easy to set up, with the label roll threading easily through the printing device. The information printed out on the label is controlled by computer software so it is possible to create a wide variety of different looks and images for the label.

Barcodes

Barcodes are an excellent method of pricing stock. There are many benefits to using barcode pricing systems including:

- keeping track of stock—fast-selling items can be quickly identified and reordered automatically
- identifying slower selling items—and taking action to prevent a build up of inventory
- monitoring the effects of merchandising changes or stock rotations—allowing fast-moving, more profitable items to occupy the best space
- predicting seasonal fluctuations—very accurately by using historical data on stock sale trends.

Not only do barcode systems provide detailed and up-to-the minute information on how the business is performing and how its stock is moving; barcode technology also allows the organisation to track individual customers through loyalty programs showing trends in customer preferences. This then allows the store to market and promote their products in the most effective way.

Figure 5.9 Barcode printer

Useful websites:

Shop Supplies

www.shopsupplies.com.au/shop/category/

Label Power

www.labelpower.com.au/main/home/

USING AND LOOKING AFTER PRICING EQUIPMENT

To ensure minimum problems and the longevity of pricing equipment, it is recommended that this equipment be cleaned and maintained frequently. Adhesive from labels, ink, dust, and other foreign objects can build up over time, and this can affect the function of the machine. Each individual piece of equipment will have its own cleaning and maintenance instructions provided by the manufacturer. It is important to make sure that the equipment is only used and stored as per its instructions. Not doing so could damage the equipment and void any warranty that might have been applicable. Depending on the nature of the equipment, it could also be a breach of WHS and organisational policies and procedures to use pricing equipment incorrectly. For example; tagging guns have very sharp needles and are used to 'inject' plastic price tags through clothing labels. If used incorrectly they could cause serious injury and, if it were proven that the equipment had not been used according to manufacturer instructions, legal action may be taken against the person responsible for the injury.

Task 5.3

Over the next couple of weeks, look at different signs, labels and tickets when you go shopping. Take photos of ones you like and don't like and submit them to your trainer. Explain what you liked or didn't like about them and what you would do to improve them.

1. Write two tickets for products from your store, or products of your choice. These products are 'on sale' and you should include a call to action to encourage sales.
2. Prepare at least two tickets for stock in your workplace using electronic equipment. Present these to your trainer with a short explanation of what equipment you used and describe how this equipment is maintained and stored in your workplace.

MAINTAINING STORE IMAGE

While a great deal of money, effort and resources can be spent on creating an image for the store, this can quickly be undermined by the smallest things. Things like damaged, incorrect or soiled tickets and signs can spoil the effect of a display or well-laid-out store and can discourage customers from coming in. Maintaining the store's image is therefore a very important part of any retailer's role.

Many stores will have opening and closing procedures for their staff. These procedures will include such things as processes for unlocking the store, setting up the cash register and so on. They may also include instructions on checking the store's image each day before opening up to the public and checking:

- to ensure the shelves and racks are tidy and that there are no boxes, products or other items lying around on the floor
- all promotional signs to ensure they are up to date, properly placed and in good condition
- that all shop surfaces are cleaned and polished
- that there is a sufficient quantity and variety of stock available on the shop floor
- that any sale items or preferred products are prominently displayed.

These are all important tasks in ensuring the store's image is maintained at all times. During the course of a busy day items are handled by customers and may then be out of place and look messy. A table full of jeans or shirts may need to be tidied and items refolded, clothing may have slipped from hangers and be lying on the floor, items may have been

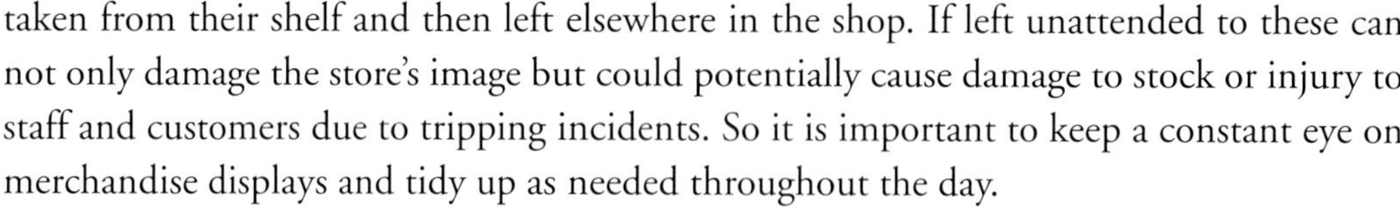

taken from their shelf and then left elsewhere in the shop. If left unattended to these can not only damage the store's image but could potentially cause damage to stock or injury to staff and customers due to tripping incidents. So it is important to keep a constant eye on merchandise displays and tidy up as needed throughout the day.

Task 5.4

Looking back over the stores that you have visited and researched over the past few weeks, separate them into stores you liked and stores you didn't like and answer the following questions.

1. How did the labels, signs and tickets contribute to or distract from the overall image of the store?
2. What kind of tickets, signs and labels did they use in each case and did this, and the way they were displayed, play any part in your like or dislike of the store's general image? Explain your reasons.
3. What would you do to improve the image of the store you liked least?

Produce a short report giving your answers for your trainer. If you have photos to support your opinions please submit them with your report.

Correct placement of tickets and labels

I went into a store to buy a set of [panty] hose. The hose section was beautifully organised. The packages were lined up in custom sized bins. Opened packages were discarded. The store price tags were all neatly affixed to the top right-hand corner of each package … right over the size information! So customers had to peel off the price tags with their fingernails in order to find out that critical piece of information. I couldn't be bothered. I bought my hose at another store. I've seen price tags over back cover copy on books. I've seen price tags over bar codes (so the product wouldn't scan). I've seen price tags over warning labels for children's toys. Train your employees on the proper placement of price tags. Poor placement will lose you sales.[1]

This is a quote from a customer who, quite rightly, points out the importance of correct label placement. Price tickets and tags are placed not only to let the customer know how much a product item costs, but often also to supply additional information and to make the buying decision easier, so placing pricing information to its best advantage is important.

The purpose of tickets, signs and labels is to provide information about specific products and services. This being the case, it is important to make sure that the information on these tickets, signs and labels is clearly visible, current and relevant to the product to which it refers.

Looking at the price tickets and signs in Figures 5.10 to 5.12, you can see that they have been placed directly above or next to the products to which they refer—without detracting from the actual product. They also provide several pieces of information in a short and sharp fashion:

- The sign in Figure 5.10 tells us that you can buy two games for only $40 but that you should hurry as the sale ends soon. This is a **call to action**—if you don't buy it now you might miss out on an excellent bargain.

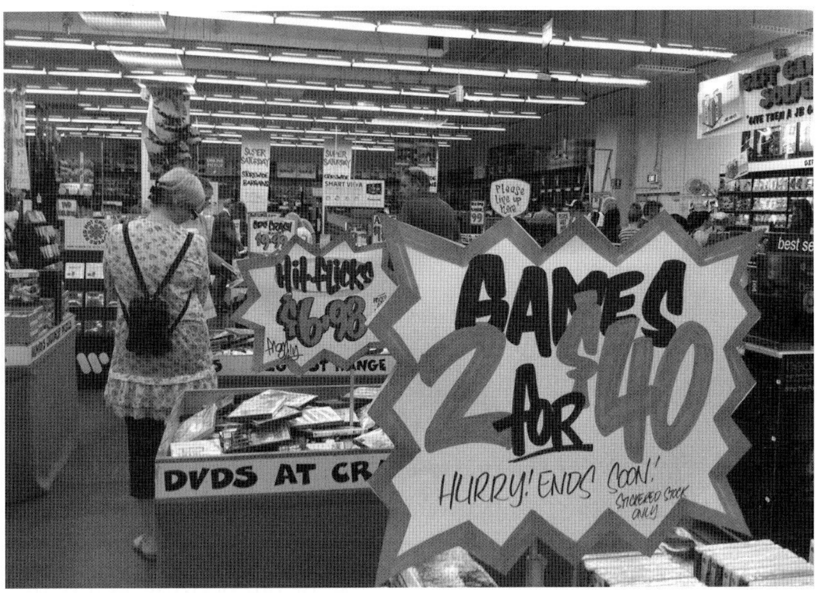

Figure 5.10 Tickets and signs offering product information in a variety of situations

Figure 5.11 Discount sign for famous brand name item

Figure 5.12 Discount information by price comparison

- The sign in Figure 5.11 tells us that you will get a 25 per cent discount off a famous brand name item. It does not tell you the price, but in this case this is acceptable as each individual item on display also has a small price ticket around the footing showing the price to which the discount will apply.
- The sign in Figure 5.12, again, offers discount information by way of price comparison: the normal price is $9.95; the reduced price is $7.95. The other sign in the photo lets us know that the sale is only on for three days—another call to action. The signs are placed directly with the products they are promoting so there is no room for confusion.

The same principle applies to price tags and stickers that are applied directly on to the product. As indicated in the customer quote in the introduction to this section, care needs to be taken over where the price tag or sticker is placed. For example don't stick the price over an important piece of product information such as size or operating instructions. This type of information is important to customers and will generally help them determine whether they will buy that particular product or not.

Each store will have set methods for applying price stickers and tags. It may be that they require you to place price stickers in the top right hand corner of each item to ensure a consistent look and approach to pricing. But a certain amount of common sense must be used: if there is an important piece of information printed in the spot where you would normally place the sticker then, with permission from your store manager or supervisor, you should consider placing the sticker in that general area—but not directly over the vital piece of information.

The same applies to clothing price tags where a plastic tag or pin needs to be inserted into the material of the item. You should never insert these directly into the cloth of the garment itself as this could, potentially, damage the item. Always insert the tag or pin either into a clothing seam or in the label at the back of the collar.

Placement of signs can also be used to create interest; in Figure 5.13 a window sign is used to announce a sale but it obscures the actual products to arouse curiosity and encourages the customer to go in to the store to see what is on sale.

Figure 5.13 Arousing customer curiosity by obscuring the products with a SALE sign

Replacing and maintaining correct pricing and product information

Having spent a good deal of money on the store's image it should not be spoiled by allowing torn or damaged signs and tickets to remain in view. If a sign or ticket is damaged, replace it and if the sale has ended or the prices shown on the signs no longer apply, remove them.

Maintaining correct pricing and product information is not merely a matter of ensuring that the signs, tickets and labels are neat and tidy, it is also a matter of observing legislative requirements to ensure that the organisation is not in breach of any laws or regulations. These can include industry codes of practice and fair trading laws.

INDUSTRY CODES OF PRACTICE

Aside from in the food industry there are no hard and fast regulations relating to the labelling of products. According to the Australian Retailers Association, labelling in Australia is not governed by any *one* law so retailers may need to look at more than one law to ensure that they are compliant with all packaging and labelling requirements of their particular products or services. Guidance can be provided by relevant industry associations. The Australian Retailers Association, for example, provides a 'Principles of Labelling Policy', which provides guidance on labelling practices. Among other things this policy states:

For public policy purposes labelling should:

- meet minimum health, safety and environmental requirements;
- be clear, simple and legible;
- inform consumers of how the product should be used most effectively;
- minimise compliance and ongoing costs; and
- be sufficiently flexible to allow for modifications, provided these are consistent with the desired outcomes of the labelling requirements, for example, when the required information does not fit on small or unusually shaped product.[2]

Task 5.5

Go to the Australian Retailers Association website, read the 'Principles of Labelling Policy' (www.retail.org.au/index.php/articles/policy/2237) and answer the following questions:

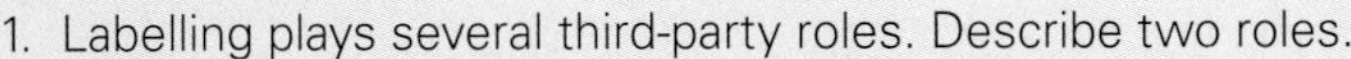

1. Labelling plays several third-party roles. Describe two roles.
2. How do labelling policies differ from other regulatory approaches?
3. Labelling can play several roles. Which one does the ARA state is the most prominent?

FAIR TRADING LAWS

There are a number of legal considerations that a store may need to observe and be aware of under various consumer and competition laws. These include the *Competition and Consumer Act* and state competition codes.

Competition and Consumer Act (CCA)

The Australian Competition and Consumer Commission (ACCC) promotes good business practices for a fair and efficient marketplace. It provides businesses with information about federal competition, fair trading and consumer protection laws and is responsible for administering the *CCA*. This law, formerly known as the *Trade Practices Act 1974*, ensures that trading in the marketplace is fair both for your business and your customers. The *CCA* covers unfair market practices, industry codes of practice, mergers and acquisitions of companies, product safety, collective bargaining, product labelling, price monitoring, and the regulation of industries such as electricity, telecommunications, gas and airports.

Useful websites:

ACCC—Product Labelling:

www.accc.gov.au

Product Safety Australia:

www.productsafety.gov.au

State competition codes

Each state and territory also has its own competition codes, with consumer protection provisions much the same as those in the CCA.

Useful website:

Australian Consumer Law (state and territory laws)

www.consumerlaw.gov.au/content/Content.aspx?doc=other_consumer_laws.htm

What all this means is that there are rules and regulations that *must* be followed when dealing with your customers and your competitors, and in the way in which your organisation presents its products and services. Your organisation will have policies and procedures in place that ensure that any legislative requirements are met.

Task 5.6

1. Go to the ACCC website page, www.accc.gov.au/content/index.phtml/itemId/655127. Browse through the information you find there to familiarise yourself with the site. Download the information you find on:
   - *Competition and consumer law—an overview for small business*
   - *Australian Consumer Law: what you need to know—business snapshot*

   Keep these documents in your portfolio of useful information.
2. Research your own organisation's policies and procedures on maintaining correct pricing information.
   a. How do they go about ensuring that all tickets and signs are correct?
   b. What is the procedure for dealing with soiled, damaged or illegible labels and tickets?

Other useful government websites:

Overview of fair trading laws—Business.gov.au:

www.business.gov.au

Australian Competition & Consumer Commission (ACCC):

www.accc.gov.au

ELEMENT 3
MAINTAIN DISPLAYS

Promotions can be held at different times during the year and for a variety of reasons—the most obvious being Christmas, Easter, Mother's Day and Father's Day. However, promotions can also be held to move surplus stock or to create interest in new stock or brands just introduced. Whatever the reason for the promotion, a major method of promoting these seasons and products is to create a display.

Much of this information will be dealt with in great detail in Chapter 6: Plan, create and maintain displays.

LEARNING OUTCOMES

3.1 Reset and dismantle special promotion areas.

3.2 Assist supervisor in selection of merchandise for display.

3.3 Arrange and face up merchandise as directed and according to layout specifications and load-bearing capacity of fixtures.

3.4 Identify, reset or remove unsuitable or out-of-date displays as directed.

3.5 Identify optimum stock levels and replenish stock according to store policy.

3.6 Maintain display areas in a clean and tidy condition.

3.7 Remove excess packaging from display areas.

Resetting and dismantling promotional areas

Promotional displays are, by their very nature, temporary and meant only to attract the attention of customers to products and services which are the focus of a current marketing campaign or promotion. This means that displays must be rotated or changed on a regular basis—and it must be done without too much disruption to the operation of the business.

Displays and special promotional areas are not restricted to shop windows and can be:

Interior displays

Interior displays are within the store itself; on tables, shelves or mounted on other wall fixtures. They could be grouped in a specific area around a special display stand or mannequin. These displays are generally accessible to the public, who may pick up stock and leave it in an untidy pile. Such displays must therefore be tidied and reset at regular intervals during the day to ensure that the right image continues to be portrayed. Interior displays can also be suspended from ceilings; signage and other promotional materials will often be hung from ceiling panels during special events or promotions.

Exterior displays

Exterior displays appear in shop windows, at trade fairs or promotional booths within a shopping mall. These displays can be more complex and lavish as customers do not

Figure 5.14 Internal shop display

generally have access to these display areas and you can bring in a range of accessories or props to underpin the image you are looking to promote.

Regardless of whether the display is inside the store or in a window it must be maintained to ensure that it is tidy, in keeping with the store's desired image and relevant to the promotional campaign that it is focused on.

When the time comes, the display must also be dismantled with minimum impact on the store's operation or customer convenience. Each store may have set times to set up and dismantle displays, such as early mornings before the store gets busy, or late afternoons just before closing. A few general rules to observe, however, include:

- using lifting equipment or correct manual handling procedures where heavy items are involved
- taking care when removing items from high shelves. Where possible use a step ladder and never climb on the shelves to remove stock from high areas
- remove and store props and stock soiled by the display in line with your organisation's policy and procedures.

The main aim in the process is to cause as little disruption as possible to the business.

Selecting merchandise for display

To ensure that the display is as effective as possible it is necessary to choose the merchandise carefully and, where necessary, follow the organisation's merchandising plan (example shown in Chapter 6 pages 194–195). Things to consider include:

Focus of the promotion

Depending on the nature of the promotion, stock should be chosen accordingly: Valentine's Day would include gifts of a romantic nature; Melbourne Cup might mean displays of high fashion, hats and accessories.

Range

This is an important factor; too many items in the display will give a cluttered untidy look, too few and there may not be enough to interest the customer. An exception to this rule is that if the display is to promote one specific item, then this may be displayed on its own to great advantage. With the proper lighting, accessories and layout, a single item in a shop window can appear very intriguing and expensive (regardless of its actual cost).

Colours

The right mix of colours is also very important and the store's merchandising plan will often provide guidance on this issue. Colours should be chosen that complement each other and that show the customer how different items of different colours can be mixed and matched—encouraging them to buy more than one product.

Accessories

The correct use of accessories can mean the difference between making a sale or not. They can also generate additional sales. Using a belt, scarf or necklace to display an item of clothing can show customers how attractive that item could be made to look and they will often buy the accessories as well in order to recreate that look.

Task 5.7

1. While shopping over the next week look at how the various stores use range, colour and accessories to promote their products. Take photos of displays you liked and describe why you felt the use of products, range, colours and accessories worked to make the display attractive.
2. In your own workplace, and with permission from your supervisor, create a small in-store display of a range of products using accessories and tickets to enhance them.
   a. Over the next week *maintain* your display and replenish stock as needed.
   b. Take photos of your display each day and submit these to your trainer.
   c. At the end of the week dismantle the display in line with organisational procedures.
   d. Ensure that you observe all necessary legislative and organisational requirements when putting your display together.

Arranging merchandise

Arranging merchandise for display should be done according to the layout specifications provided in the merchandising plan and the load-bearing capacity of the fixtures on which they will be displayed. On page 154, 'Placing stock appropriately', we discussed the importance of placing stock so that it can be accessed easily, safely and in line with any promotional campaigns.

To do this effectively you must decide what fixtures are to be used. These can include:

- clothing racks
- display tables
- gondola shelving
- cabinets and counters.

Each will have a specific purpose and load bearing capacity—which means that will hold only a certain amount of weight before it becomes unsafe.

Figure 5.15 Clothing rack

Figure 5.16 Display counter

Figure 5.17 Gondola

Figure 5.18 Display rack

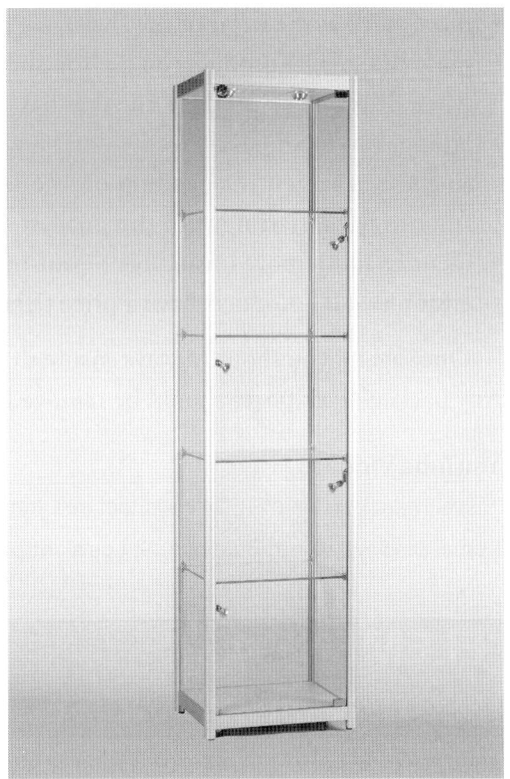

Figure 5.19 Display cabinet

Figure 5.20 Display tables

When placing and arranging merchandise for display:

- maintain sufficient stock—on the shelf to satisfy customer demand and provide a fully-stocked look. You may need to check fast-selling stock frequently
- do not stack products—on top of each other. This will ensure that products do not fall and can be reached by customers and staff

- place stock at the front of the shelf—so that displays look attractive
- place the smaller products on the top shelves and the larger items on the lower shelves—when displaying a product line that has several sizes on shelves
- arrange product lines correctly—on hangers according to colour and then on racks from smallest to largest. Depending on the rack used, sizes should go from left to right or front to back, starting with the smallest size
- identify and remove unsuitable or out-of-date displays—at regular intervals
- ensure that all products have a price ticket or barcode.

Once again, you should always ensure that the display is tidy, clean and free from clutter. Any packaging or boxes should be removed once the display has been put in place.

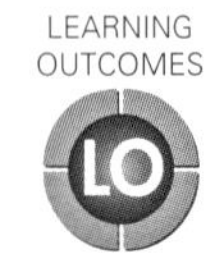

YouTube Videos:

'Visual Merchandising 101 Displays that sell' (http://youtube.com/oYZ7bJGrdFE)

'Visual Displays—Ziezo Boutique, St Louis' (http://youtube.com/zh2Fqr-mFvE)

ELEMENT 4
PROTECT MERCHANDISE

An important part of your role as a retail assistant will be to ensure the safety of your stock and to do everything possible to minimise theft. This subject, too, will be covered in depth in a later chapter.

LEARNING OUTCOMES

LO

4.1 Identify and apply correct handling, storage and display techniques according to stock characteristics and legislative requirements.

Characteristics of a product

Further to the characteristics of a product outlined in Chapter 1 page 34, products can be grouped in relation to how they must be handled within the store. For example, when dealing with perishable goods you must ensure that the stock is not past its use-by date, and that it is stored at the correct temperature to keep it fresh and ready to be consumed. Perishable goods not handled correctly can prove extremely hazardous to a person's health and issues such as food poisoning can lead to serious consequences. Equally, stock that is very expensive or made from rare or costly materials must be stored and handled in such a way that the material is not damaged, soiled or left open to theft. So, when caring for the merchandise in your store, you need to be aware of its particular characteristics and do all possible to ensure safety from a number of perspectives.

Protecting merchandise

Protecting merchandise is an issue that has two distinct facets: protecting yourself and customers from harm due to careless handling of stock and protecting the organisation's stock from damage or theft. Good store management can be an effective tool against such loss or damage. Some of these store management methods include:

SAFETY ISSUES

The store's WHS policies and procedures should be observed at all times when handling stock:

- remember to always use correct manual handling procedures when lifting or moving heavy or awkward stock
- ensure that any risks and hazards inherent on the premises or surrounding products are minimised and controlled:
  - all toxic chemicals, whether they are on sale or used to clean the premises or equipment, should be stored and labelled in line with that product's safety directions
  - all food stuffs must be handled, labelled and stored in accordance with hygiene regulations
  - all small items must be stored or displayed in such a way that they are not a hazard to children who may swallow them, and cannot be easily stolen
  - all merchandise must be dealt with, stored and displayed according to its handling instructions.
- do not stack shelves so high that items will fall on customers or staff when they try to reach them, and never put heavy items on high shelves
- clear away any packaging or labelling equipment to avoid injury to staff and customers.

METHODS OF MINIMISING THEFT

Shoplifting is an enormous problem in today's retail market. This subject will be dealt with in great detail in Chapter 8: 'Maintain store safety', however a few areas that can assist in keeping merchandise safe are:

- checkout areas—the store lay out should be designed so customers will need to pass the cash register area and staff to leave the store
- register—never leave the register unlocked or unattended
- keep the store neat and tidy—full displays and tidy shelves allow staff to see at a glance if something is missing, damaged or soiled
- use mirrors—in appropriate spots throughout the store to eliminate blind spots in corners that might hide shoplifters
- use locked cabinets—keep small, expensive items in locked cabinets or behind the counter. Cabinets can be unlocked if customers want to take a closer look at an item, but always ensure that you lock them back up afterwards
- dressing areas—these should be watched at all times. Many stores limit the number of items taken in by each customer or give them tags indicating how many items they take in to the dressing enclosure

- use alarms—on any unlocked exits and close or block off unused checkout aisles to prevent customers from leaving unnoticed
- signs and posters—reinforcing security messages should be used. Post anti-shoplifting signs like 'Shoplifters will be prosecuted' in clearly visible locations.

USING CUSTOMER SERVICE METHODS TO PROTECT MERCHANDISE

In addition to the methods outlined above there are a number of customer service-related things you can do to protect merchandise without being too obvious. For example:

- make sure that there are sufficient employees rostered on to work at any one time
- greet every customer as they enter the store. This fulfils two distinct purposes; firstly it should satisfy the organisation's requirements for customer service excellence, and secondly it lets the customer know that you are aware of their presence
- make yourself available to customers and never leave the store unattended
- give customers a receipt for every purchase. Make it a store policy to require receipts for cash refunds
- implement a policy and procedure for inspecting any large bags brought in by customers. You may want to put signage in place stating that the store 'reserves the right to inspect all bags before leaving the store'
- if you notice suspicious activities, alert other employees immediately. Many stores have a security code to alert staff of possible shoplifters. If you notice a person in your store behaving suspiciously, approach them and ask if they are finding everything they need. Mention that you will be near by should they need your help. People intent on shoplifting will, generally, not do so if they feel they are being watched
- staff should watch price tags and be on the lookout for price switching. Ask for a price check if something seems out of place
- shoe boxes, handbags, baskets with lids and other products easily opened should be inspected by staff to ensure that they do not contain other merchandise.

Task 5.8

1. Watch the YouTube Video 'Theft prevention' (http://youtube.com/aQmLhyot19w) and complete the following:
   - The statistics mentioned in this video relate to shoplifting in the USA. Research the statistics that apply to shoplifting in Australia.
   - What three key components of theft prevention are mentioned?
   - Describe some of the things you should look for in customer behaviour.
   - What is 'ticket switching'?

2. Look around your own store and think about the ways in which you can protect and secure your merchandise.
   a. Are valuable stock items properly secured?
   b. Are items displayed in such as way as to cause no harm or injury to staff and customers?
   c. Have you displayed your merchandise to its best advantage and in a way that it will not be damaged?
   d. Do you store hazardous substances or other items safely?
   e. What precautions do you take against theft?

Protecting your store's merchandise is an extremely important part of your job, whether it is from theft or damage. Each item your store sells has cost money and this money must be recovered by way of selling those items. Products that are lost, stolen or damaged cannot be sold and therefore represent a financial loss to the store. Too many of these can spell financial troubles for a store and your job will depend on the store remaining successful and financially sound, so always remember to look after the merchandise as outlined in your store's policies and procedures.

The store's success will, largely, also depend on the image that it projects. Remember, it takes just a few short seconds to make a first impression so handle store merchandise with care, display it to its best advantage so that customers are encouraged to come in and browse, keep the store looking clean and tidy (this means tickets and signs too!) and be attentive to what is going on in your store. By doing these basic, simple things you can contribute towards your store's success.

Endnotes

1. http://clientk.com/2008/11/19/the-positioning-of-price-tags
2. www.retail.org.au/index.php/articles/policy/2237.

ASSESSMENT: WRITTEN QUESTIONS

Assessment context	As a retail consultant you will be required to demonstrate your knowledge of your industry and its operations on a daily basis. These questions are designed to assess your competence in a number of operational areas.
Assessment instructions	Answer each question as fully as possible—giving as much detail as you can. This will help your assessor/trainer determine your understanding of the subject.
Evidence required	Completed questionnaire.
Range and conditions	– This is an open book assessment – You will have one hour to complete all questions – Your assessor/trainer may vary the conditions of the assessment in accordance with workplace or classroom requirements – You must answer all questions correctly in order to be deemed competent in this subject.
Materials and resources required	No special requirements
Reasonable adjustments	In the event that you have difficulty understanding the assessment tasks due to language or other difficulties, your trainer will attempt to make reasonable adjustments to the assessment paper in order to afford you every opportunity to achieve competency.
Decision making rules	In order to ensure consistency assessment responses will be judged against the indicative answers provided in the assessor's guide. These indicative answers provide a guideline only for what the assessor is looking for. Alternative answers are, of course, acceptable but must demonstrate a sound understanding of the subject in question.

Questions

1. Discuss the importance of unpacking merchandise correctly and give an example of how stock in your particular store is handled when it first arrives.
2. Describe what issues you must consider when deciding what fixtures to use when placing merchandise in to the store.
3. Describe the process you would undertake if you identified damaged or soiled stock, tickets or signs.
4. Discuss the reasons why it is important to rotate stock. Give an example of when you might do this in your store.
5. List at least two different pieces of pricing equipment used in your workplace and describe how you maintain and store these.
6. Describe how tickets and signs are produced in your workplace. Give an example of the type of information that would typically be included on a promotional sign.

7. Describe why it is important to maintain correct pricing and information on your store's merchandise.
8. Discuss the possible legal implications of giving incorrect or misleading information on a sign or ticket.
9. Describe why it is important to maintain the store's image.
10. Discuss the importance of keeping your store tidy and the possible consequences of not doing so.
11. Discuss at least three methods of protecting your store's merchandise.
12. Give a detailed description of at least one promotional display your store has recently undertaken: what was the aim of the promotion, what kind of stock did it promote, what sort of tickets or signs were used, how was the display set up, was the promotion successful? How could you tell?
13. What part did you play in the promotion in question 12?
14. Discuss the importance of lifting heavy or awkward objects correctly and give an example of the possible consequences of not doing so.
15. You have just received a shipment of liquid chlorine for sale in your pool shop. Describe what you will do to ensure that the product is handled, stored and displayed correctly.
16. Using the boxes here and overleaf write tickets to promote:
    a. A three-day sale on DVDs—$5.95 each.
    b. Winter stock sell out—50 per cent off the marked price. Famous brand names are available (make these up according to your store's own stock)—Sale ends on Sunday.

Box A

Box B

COMPETENCY MAPPING

Element			Performance criteria	Task	Assessment	Refer to page
1	Place and arrange merchandise	1.1	Unpack merchandise according to store policy and procedures and legislative requirements.	Covered in Chapter 6	AQ1	153
		1.2	Place merchandise on floor, fixtures and shelves in determined locations according to WHS and other relevant legislative requirements.	5.1, 5.8	AQ2	154
		1.3	Display merchandise to achieve a balanced, fully-stocked appearance and promote sales.	5.1	Covered in Chapter 6	155, 156
		1.4	Identify damaged, soiled or out-of-date stock and take corrective action as required according to store procedure.	5.2	AQ3	158
		1.5	Place stock range to conform with fixtures, ticketing, prices or bar codes.	5.1	AQ2, 15 Covered in Chapter 6	160–165
		1.6	Rotate stock according to stock requirements and store procedure.	5.2	AQ4	156
		1.7	Ensure stock presentation conforms to special handling techniques and other safety requirements.	5.1, 5.8	AQ2, 10, 14, 15	157, 159, 160

Element		Performance criteria		Task	Assessment	Refer to page
2	Prepare display labels and tickets	2.1	Prepare labels and tickets for window, wall or floor displays according to store policy.	5.3	AQ5, 6, 16	161–163
		2.2	Prepare tickets using electronic equipment or neatly by hand according to store procedures.	5.3	AQ5, 6, 16	163
		2.3	Identify soiled, damaged, illegible or incorrect labels and tickets and take corrective action.	5.6	AQ3	165
		2.4	Use and maintain electronic ticketing and labelling equipment according to design specifications.	5.3	AQ5	164
		2.5	Place labels and tickets visibly and correctly on merchandise.	5.4	AQ5	164
		2.6	Replace labels and tickets according to store policy.	5.6		168
3	Maintain displays	3.1	Reset and dismantle special promotion areas.	5.7	Covered in Chapter 6	171
		3.2	Assist supervisor in selection of merchandise for display.	5.7		172
		3.3	Arrange and face up merchandise as directed and according to layout specifications and load-bearing capacity of fixtures.	5.7		174–175
		3.4	Identify, reset or remove unsuitable or out-of-date displays as directed.	5.7		165
		3.5	Identify optimum stock levels and replenish stock according to store policy.	5.7		165
		3.6	Maintain display areas in a clean and tidy condition.	5.7		165
		3.7	Remove excess packaging from display areas.	5.7		165
4	Protect merchandise	4.1	Identify and apply correct handling, storage and display techniques according to stock characteristics and legislative requirements.	5.8	AQ10, 11, 15	176–179

continued

Required skills and knowledge	Task	Assessment	Refer to page
Required skills			
Use and maintenance of manual and electronic labelling and ticketing equipment.	5.3	AQ5	160–164
Completing tasks in a set timeframe.	5.7	Covered in Chapter 6	
Literacy and numeracy skills in relation to: • reading and interpreting store procedures and guidelines • machine or manual preparation of labels and tickets • reading and understanding manufacturer instructions.	5.3, 5.6	AQ5, 6, 8, 12	160–164, 169

Required skills and knowledge	Task	Assessment	Refer to page
Required knowledge			
Store policies and procedures, in regard to: • merchandising, ticketing and pricing of stock • correct storage of stock • store promotional themes, including advertising, catalogues and special offers • location of display areas • availability and use of display materials • stock rotation • stock replenishment • merchandise range • scheduling for building or rotating displays • correct storage procedures for labelling and ticketing equipment and materials.	5.1, 5.2, 5.3, 5.7, 5.8	AQ1, 2, 4, 5, 7, 9, 10, 11, 12	155, 157, 160–16, 171
Correct manual handling techniques for protection of self and merchandise.	5.1, 5.7	AQ14, 15	159
Principles of display.	5.1, 5.7	Covered in Chapter 6	
Elements and principles of design and trends in retail design.			
Relevant WHS regulations, including: • manual handling • hygiene and sanitation • hazardous substances • labelling of workplace substances.	5.7	AQ14, 15	157, 159

Required skills and knowledge	Task	Assessment	Refer to page
Required knowledge			
Relevant legislation and statutory requirements.	5.5, 5.7	AQ7, 8, 10, 14, 15	157, 169
Relevant industry codes of practice.		AQ7, 8, 10, 14, 15	169

Required skills and knowledge	Task	Assessment	Refer to page
Critical aspects for assessment			
Applies store policies and procedures and legislative requirements in regard to displaying, merchandising, ticketing, pricing and storage of stock.	5.1, 5.2, 5.6, 5.7	AQ7, 8, 10, 14, 15	157, 165, 171, 174
Displays merchandise on floor, fixtures, shelves and display areas, in determined locations, according to special manual handling techniques and other safety requirements.	5.1, 5.7, 5.8	Covered in Chapter 6	155, 171, 174
Prepares display labels and price tickets for merchandise with regard to store policies and procedures.	5.3, 5.6, 5.7	AQ3, 5, 6, 7, 8, 16	160, 161
Operates, maintains and stores a range of ticketing equipment according to: • store policy and procedures • industry codes of practice • manufacturer instructions and design specifications.	5.3	Covered in Chapter 6	160–164, 169
Arranges correct pricing and information on merchandise according to store procedures, industry codes and government requirements.	5.3, 5.5, 5.7	AQ3, 5, 6, 7, 8, 16	157, 167
Identifies damaged, soiled or out-of-date stock and takes corrective action as required by store procedures and legislative requirements.	5.1, 5.7	AQ3, 7, 8	158
Maintains display areas and replenishes stock as required according to store procedures and legislative requirements.	5.2, 5.7	Covered in Chapter 6	165, 171, 174
Performs correct manual handling, storage and display techniques according to: • stock characteristics • industry codes of practice • WHS legislation and codes of practice.		AQ1, 2, 10, 14, 15	157, 159

Chapter 6

SIRXMER202

Plan, create and maintain displays

A display serves one main purpose in a store: to showcase products and invite customers to come in and buy them. While displays, be they internal or external, will have a relatively short lifespan, they will nevertheless have an enormous impact on whether customers come in to the store to shop or not. An attractive, well laid-out display will be enticing and customers will stop to look at it, and come into the shop to investigate further. A display that is overcrowded, messy and carelessly thrown together will do the opposite.

So, if a display is to be successful, there are a number of things to consider when developing the display idea. Many stores, particularly those belonging to large chains, will use merchandising (or display) plans that set out exactly

Figure 6.1 Example of a creative, well-balanced display

Figure 6.2 Example of a crowded and cluttered display

what is to be displayed, where and how. These are often developed by merchandising professionals who may then visit individual stores to put the displays up. These plans can be very detailed and often it is left up to the store's staff to put the display up themselves—in strict accordance with the plans. This is done so that all stores belonging to that chain have a cohesive look and all project the image set by the company. Remember; the company may have invested a substantial amount of time, effort and money in creating its brand or image, so everything that happens within it must be in keeping with that image.

ELEMENT 1
IDENTIFY REQUIREMENTS FOR DISPLAYS

Displays are set up for a variety of reasons. The store might be promoting a new line of products, a specific holiday, or it may simply be a matter of a regular display change according to a **scheduled rotation**. Whatever the reasons, there are a number of considerations involved in putting together a successful display.

LEARNING OUTCOMES

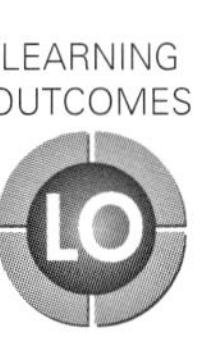

1.1 Identify purpose, audience and products for each display.
1.2 Identify organisational requirements and research relevant information where required.
1.3 Identify available budget and resources required to create the display.
1.4 Identify and consider constraints or factors that may affect the creation of the display.

Purpose and audience for display

The first considerations when planning a display are: what is its purpose, and who is it aiming to attract?

PURPOSE

This is an extremely important point: what exactly is the store hoping to achieve with the display? Is it hoping to attract new customers in to the store? Is it trying to promote new product lines that have been introduced? Is it holding a promotion to increase the number of people who come in to the store, or to generate more sales?

The purpose of a display will dictate what products are to be showcased, how they are to be showcased and when. For example, if a store has recently signed an agreement to carry Billabong clothing, then they would develop a display around that specific brand to let customers know that these are now available. They would display only Billabong clothing and have appropriate signage in their windows for the duration of the promotion. Equally, if they were having a massive sale of old or discontinued stock in order to get rid of it and stimulate additional revenue, they might not have anything in their window display at all—just a very large sign outlining a 'Massive stock clearance—3 days only!' This may be enough to entice customers into the store.

AUDIENCE

This, too, is an important issue: who is the organisation aiming the display at? For the most part displays will be targeted at the public at large, with no specific group in mind. There are times, however, when the store may wish to attract particular groups of people. For example, they may wish to attract people from specific age groups, cultural or ethnic backgrounds, business or leisure backgrounds, or genders.

Task 6.1

Over the next week take note of window displays that you see and complete the grid below with details about the store, the products being displayed and your impressions of the purpose of the display and the audience at whom the display is aimed.

Store	Products being displayed	Purpose of display	Audience

Organisational requirements

As well as thinking about purpose and audience you will need to consider the organisation's requirements when planning a display. This may mean:

- staying within a given budget
- keeping the company's image and reputation in mind
- thinking about the availability of materials
- taking organisational constraints into consideration.

Depending on its style and purpose you may need to seek information that will help in the design phase of the display; information that may give you new ideas and creative inspirations, guidance on company image, or emerging trends in display materials and equipment. Such information may be sourced from colleagues, direct observation, the internet, magazines, the company's marketing personnel, technical personnel or even written reports.

Task 6.2

Discuss what information sources you might use when designing a display for your own organisation.

Factors that will impact on the display

No matter how carefully you plan, there will be **constraints** that will impact on the way your display is put together. Some of these may be:

- availability of materials—accessories to be used to enhance the display
- budget—how much will you have to spend on materials, display equipment, tickets or signs
- product characteristics—size or volume of the products to be displayed in relation to the space available for the display
- space—including how much room you will have to work with, whether you will have to deal with an unusually shaped space, and whether the display is indoors or outdoors
- staff—will you have assistance in putting the display up? Sometimes it may be necessary to have help holding things for you while you pin them in place or helping to move heavy objects and items
- time—how long will it take to put the display up, and when is the best time to do this without disrupting the store's operations?

You will also need to consider what **resources** you might need to complete the display. These resources may impact on the budget that has been set for the display, so they should be chosen with care and only used if really necessary. Resources may include:

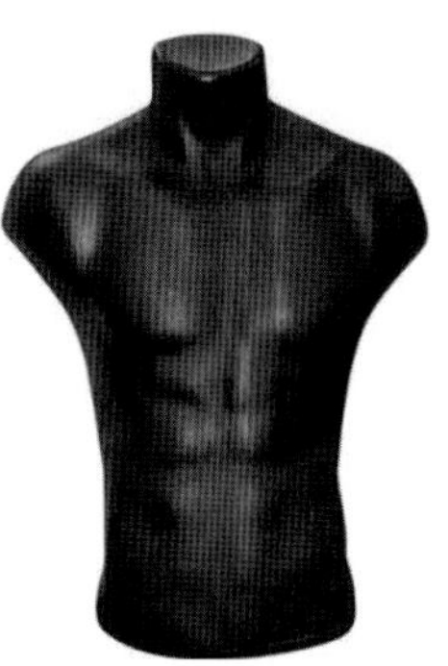

Figure 6.3 Mannequin torso

- equipment and technology—such as spot lights or turntables
- fixtures and fittings—such as mannequins, torsos, display stands or tables
- labels and tickets—as outlined in Chapter 5
- new or recycled materials—display materials left over from previous displays can sometime be used over a number of campaigns
- accessories—that can be used to enhance the product, show how it can be used or worn, and encourage additional sales
- unique eye-catchers—such as frames, photos or unusual objects that draw the customer's eye. An excellent example of an eye catcher, once seen, was a large tree branch suspended from the window ceiling across which the fabric shop had draped a variety of coloured fabrics. It was extremely effective. The photo in Figure 6.4 shows an example of a window using eye-catchers; these planks, rails and rope give the impression that the mannequins are on a boat—showcasing their leisure wear.

Figure 6.4 Window with eye-catchers

Always remember, however, that overcrowding a display with accessories may distract from the actual product being promoted—which should be the main focus of the display.

ELEMENT 2
DEVELOP DISPLAY IDEAS

Knowing the purpose and target audience of a display will give you an idea of what it should end up looking like. As we mentioned earlier, to be successful a display must catch the eye of passing customers and invite them to come in and browse or buy.

LEARNING OUTCOMES

2.1 Generate ideas for the display using creative thinking techniques.

2.2 Test ideas against display and organisational requirements.

2.3 Discuss display options with relevant personnel.

2.4 Modify display ideas and refine according to feedback and confirm with relevant personnel.

Generating ideas

Displays need to not only showcase products, they must do so as creatively as possible—capturing the eye and imagination of passing customers. The more inventive and eye catching the display, the better the chances that busy shoppers will actually stop to look.

But it can sometimes be difficult to keep display ideas fresh and inviting, so here are a few techniques for coming up with creative ideas:

- brainstorming—sitting with colleagues and simply throwing out ideas. These ideas can then be tested for feasibility when the best ideas have been chosen
- creative writing, telling stories, visualising or drawing—to set out a story for the display to follow. This could generate a series of themed displays that can generate interest for weeks or even months
- product association—thinking about how the customer might associate your products with an activity. For example the Billabong brand name may bring to mind sun, sea and surf for active people, so an idea for a display of this brand might revolve around a beach theme
- looking at photos or magazines—for themes and inspiration.

The ideas you have and the concept you choose will also be influenced by whether displays are indoor or outdoor, what kind of lighting will be available so that you can highlight products, whether there will be any requirements for sound or music, or whether the display will be static or moving.

Whatever idea you eventually decide upon, it must be tested against the organisation's requirements and its image. It must:

- be aesthetically pleasing and so should be well-balanced with a logical flow to the products on display, drawing the eye from one product to the next
- fit in to the allocated space so as not to take away from valuable floor selling space
- suit the store's image or brand and meet its standards
- be within the allocated budget
- conform to work health and safety requirements. No part of the display may pose a danger to staff or customers; items should be secured so that nothing can fall on people, or become a trip hazard
- not take up too much staff time
- meet with store policies and procedures, including housekeeping and waste disposal procedures.

Confirming and modifying display options

Feedback is an important part of the planning process and other people will have opinions and may need to authorise or approve the final plans. You may need to run your ideas past managers, team leaders or even external personnel with visual merchandising experience. These external personnel may be staff from head office who have developed the merchandising (or display) plan that you are working from.

You can gather feedback or approvals from these colleagues by getting together as a group to discuss the display options. You might also discuss the plans with relevant personnel one-on-one, or request feedback in writing so that you have a written record of their ideas and suggestions.

Task 6.3

You have been asked to develop a display for a product of your choice.

1. Provide a number of different themes and ideas (at least three) for the display that will properly showcase the product you have chosen.
2. Describe what sources of information and inspiration you used to come up with your ideas.
3. Explain who was involved in the idea generation process with you, and with whom you confirmed the display ideas and options.
4. Describe what organisational issues you needed to consider to ensure that your display idea was in line with requirements.

ELEMENT 3
PLAN AND BUILD DISPLAYS

Building a successful, creative display takes more than just picking a range of products and then putting them in a window. To achieve a well-balanced look, in keeping with the company image and the ideas generated, a merchandising (or **display) plan** is required.

LEARNING OUTCOMES

- 3.1 Develop ideas into simple display plans.
- 3.2 Source resources, materials and products to meet plan requirements.
- 3.3 Create displays following display plans.
- 3.4 Seek assistance from relevant personnel where required.
- 3.5 Review display and make refinements as required.

The display plan

With an idea for the display firmly in mind, you now need to plan how this display will be created using **basic principles of design** which include the following.

Colour palette

The colour palette that you will use should be chosen by colour-matching the items to be displayed with any background materials or accessories that are being used.

Flow of product

You should ensure that products are grouped in a logical fashion, or are placed into the display in such a way that the eye is led from one product to the next.

Use of space

Ensure that the allocated or available space is used as effectively as possible. Remember—a cluttered and crowded display can be confusing to potential customers as there are too many items to look at, whereas a display with a few well-chosen items can draw a customer in to the store. An excellent example of this is shown in the two photos at the beginning of this chapter; one is overcrowded with men's clothing while the other shows only two outfits. Which store would you go into?

Accessories

Accessories should be carefully chosen so that they enhance the products on display but do not overshadow them. For example, if you are displaying a dinnerware set, then placing a vase of flowers or set of wine glasses on the display table will enhance the dinnerware. If, however, you placed a large antique candelabra that was worth more than the dinnerware set on the table this would detract from the actual product being promoted.

Budget

You must consider the **budget** for the display—broken down into components showing how much will be spent on items such as decorative items, accessories, tickets and signs.

Eye catchers

The prudent use of 'eye catchers', as discussed earlier in the chapter, is basic to the design of a display.

A display plan can be a simple drawing or sketch such as the one shown in Figure 6.5, or can be a complete set of photos and sketches that outline each aspect of the store's displays and merchandising.

Figure 6.5 A simple hand-drawn display plan

The examples over the next few pages, include the:

1. colour palette of the clothing to be displayed
2. clothing palette showing the actual items the store is to display and carry in stock
3. store layout, detailing what items should be displayed and where
4. layout and palette for a window display.

The plan should be detailed and provide clear instructions on how, where and when the display is to be set up.

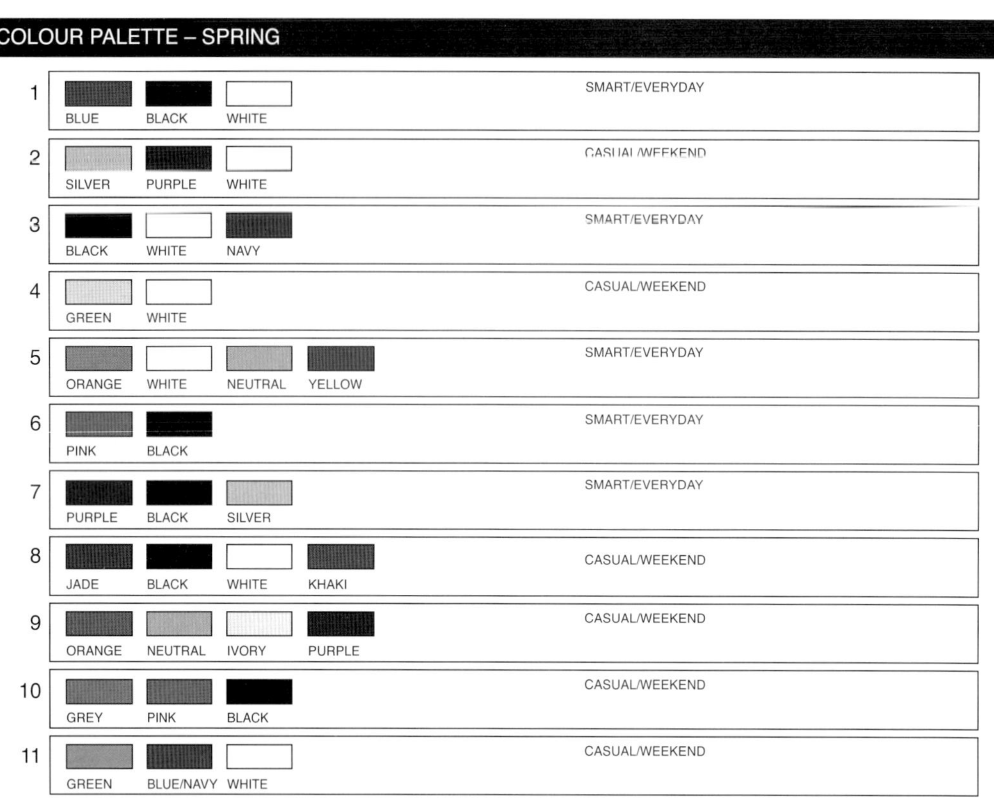

Figure 6.6 Merchandising plan: colour palette

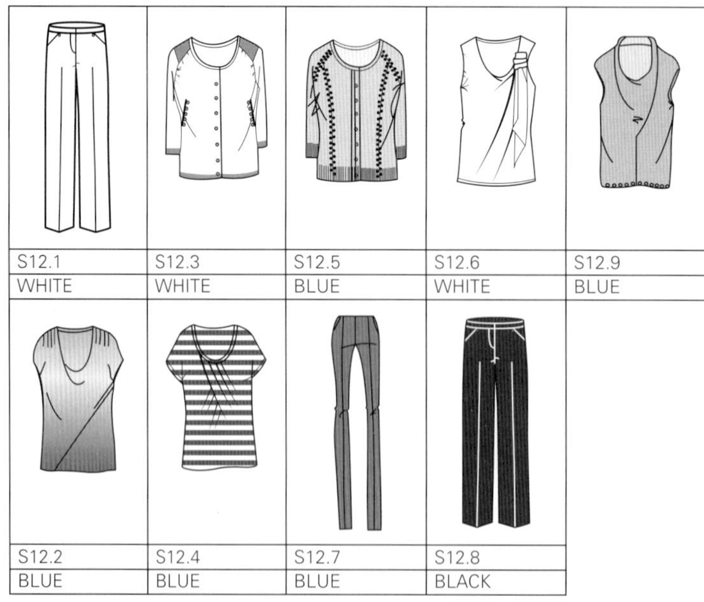

Figure 6.7 Merchandising plan: clothes palette

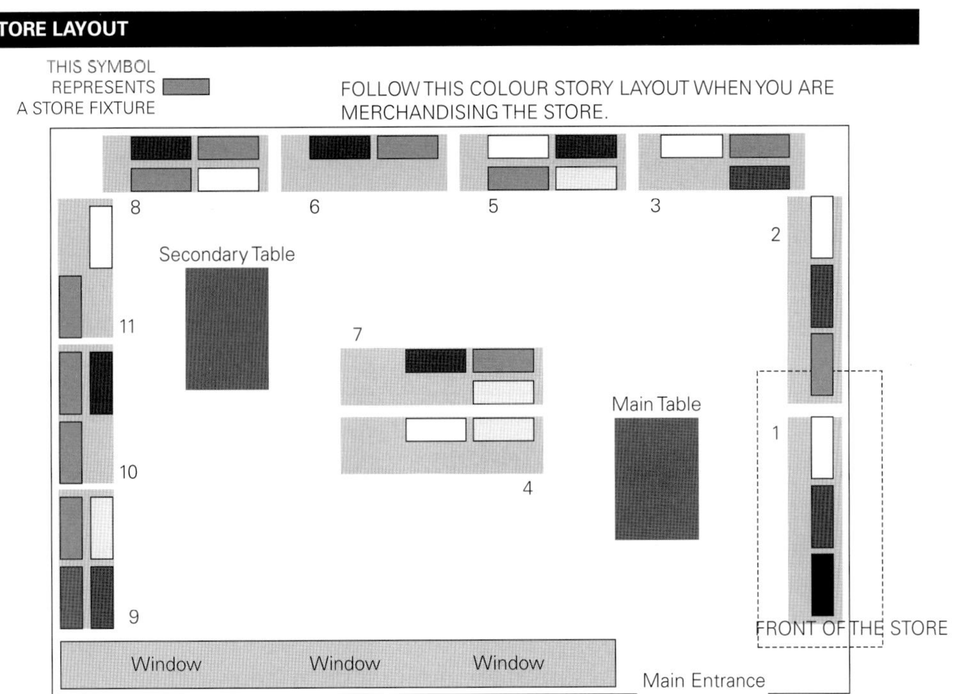

Figure 6.8 Merchandising plan: store layout

Figure 6.9 Merchandising plan: window layout

Task 6.4

1. Using the work you did in Task 6.3 produce a detailed display plan for at least two of your ideas.
2. Show your display plans to your supervisor or a colleague and request feedback from them about your ideas.
3. Take a note of their comments and discuss how you will incorporate any suggestions they made.
4. Present your display plans and the feedback you received (in a short report) to your trainer.

Resources and display materials

The display plan will list the various product items and materials that will be needed to create the display. Some of these will be things that are needed to set up the display and hold things in place and could include (but are not limited to):

- pins—for form-fitting clothing onto mannequins, or pinning items onto boards or frames
- fishing line—used to 'invisibly' suspend items from the window ceiling
- staple guns—for attaching items securely to boards, floors or other display
- tape—for sticking things in place
- pricing guns or labellers—for producing tickets and pricing signs.

Other resources may be more specialised and costly. These will need to be sourced and such sources could include companies that specialise in display materials and equipment (such as mannequins, racks and display stands). Materials may also be sourced from within the organisation. In a department store, for example, you can borrow accessories from different departments to complement the look you want to achieve. You may have interesting, eye catching objects at home that you can use to attract attention. Finally, you may also borrow items and accessories from neighbouring stores to use in your display. In these cases you would normally put a small sign near the item you have borrowed indicating that it was 'Provided courtesy of …' and the name of the store that loaned it to you.

Task 6.5

Research and gather sources of display materials for your portfolio of useful information. Examples are:

- Shop Supplies: www.shopsupplies.com.au
- Display Master: www.displaymaster.com.au
- Chas Clarkson: www.chasclarkson.com.au.

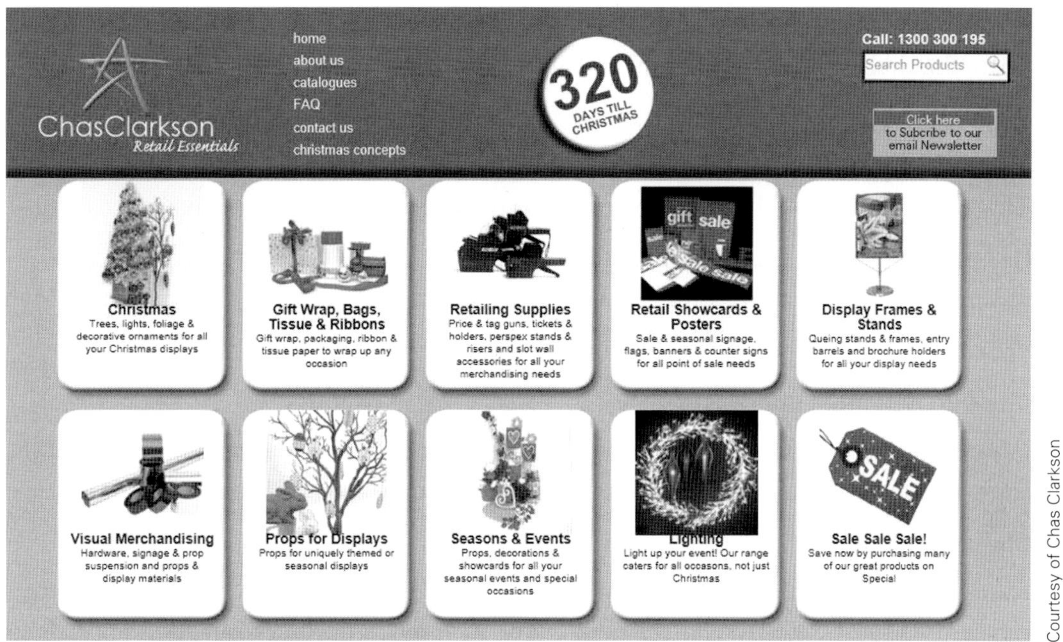

Courtesy of Chas Clarkson

Figure 6.10 Chas Clarkson screenshot

Creating the display

Once all of these items and materials are collected you can then begin to put the display together using your display plan as your blueprint. In doing so, there are a number of things to remember:

Work to the display plan

If the display is in a shop window, work your way from the furthest away point, to the window exit. If it is an in-store display, work in the most efficient manner according to the store space allotted.

Work neatly and carefully

Take care to avoid making too much mess, or breaking or damaging items or property.

Clean away waste as you go

Sometimes boxes, wrapping and materials can spill out into the shop area and this may pose health and safety problems.

Iron clothes

If your display involves items of clothing, ensure that the clothes are neat and pressed—never display badly wrinkled clothes as they give a very poor impression of the store.

Store any product boxes

Boxes should be stored out of sight, but within easy reach so that items can be put back in when the display is taken down.

Place tickets and signs in appropriate places

Tickets and signs should be near the products they relate to, to avoid confusing customers.

Use pins with care

If you are using pins to form-fit clothing onto mannequins or torsos, be careful in your placement of these pins so that the clothing items are not damaged.

Don't disrupt store operations

Put up the display during a time of day that does not disrupt the normal operation of the store. Before or after normal opening hours is best if this can be managed.

Check lighting

Most windows will have spot lights that are used to highlight various products. Lighting can be used most effectively to create mood or atmosphere and pick out specific products for showcasing. Check that lights are actually aimed at the products or, perhaps, at an eye catcher, rather than into a blank space or corner.

Set out below are some display examples.

Figure 6.11 Display examples

Seek assistance from relevant personnel

There may be instances when you will need assistance from colleagues or other staff when setting up a display. This might be when there are heavy objects to lift into or out of the display. You may also need help holding items in place when they need to be pinned or tied up to a prop. When asking for assistance ensure that the staff member involved is not needed elsewhere in the store.

Review and amend the display

Review your work at various times in the set up process; stand back from the display and check that it is in line with the display plan. Also check that there is a pleasing flow and that no pins, boxes or other waste are showing. Anything that doesn't fit or work well in the display can generally be fixed more easily during the process, than when the display is completely finished. Waiting until the end to check your work could, potentially, mean having to undo work to get at any offending items.

It is also a good idea to get a colleague or supervisor to review the display before you finish, to get a second opinion on the display content and flow and whether there is any waste material such as packing paper, bits of fishing line or pins still in view that you might have missed. More importantly it is a good idea to have someone else check your work, in progress, to ensure that it correctly follows the display plan.

Task 6.6

Discuss why it is important to involve other staff members in the creation of effective displays.

ELEMENT 4
MAINTAIN DISPLAYS

With the organisation's image and reputation at stake, it is important to make sure that any display you have set up is maintained and in good condition at all times. An untidy display that is falling apart gives a bad impression of the store and discourages customers from coming in. Equally, a display that never changes can get boring so stock within that display may need to be **refreshed**, or you may add extra items, on a regular basis to keep interest high.

LEARNING OUTCOMES

4.1 Regularly clean and tidy displays and replace products as necessary according to display plans.

4.2 Make changes or alterations to the display as appropriate.

Keeping displays clean and tidy

Window displays are relatively easy to keep clean and tidy as customers do not have access to these areas and they can therefore be left for longer periods of time without maintenance.

In-store table displays on the other hand are within the customers' reach and they will often pick up items and leave them lying again in untidy heaps. In these cases a great deal of maintenance is needed to keep the display looking fresh and tidy.

IN-STORE DISPLAYS

In-store displays should be checked and tidied on a regular basis throughout the day. This might mean:

- re-folding or repacking—items that have been picked up and carelessly left lying
- replenishing—items if sales have been made from the display. Keeping displays replenished gives a fully-stocked impression and looks inviting
- dusting or polishing—items that have been handled by customers. Fingerprints or smudges can make items look unattractive so they need to be cleaned regularly
- cleaning display—surfaces, including dusting and polishing glass shelves or tables as well as steel, wooden or chrome fixtures.

WINDOW DISPLAYS

Even though window displays will need less maintenance than in-store displays, they should nevertheless be checked each day to ensure that they are still clean and in good condition. You should:

- remove any insects—that might have fallen on the display floor. Dead flies in a display can be very off-putting
- check that all spotlights are still working properly—and replace any burned out bulbs
- check that everything is as it should be—in accordance with the display plan, and that nothing has fallen down.

Amending displays

Displays should never be left for too long without being changed or refreshed. The idea behind a display is to arouse customer curiosity and interest and get them to come in and buy the items they have seen on display as well as any additional products they see once they have browsed around in the store. So keeping a display static for too long will become boring—customers will have seen it many times as they pass and will not bother to look any closer. If the display is changed or amended regularly, however, their interest is sustained and they will continue to look at what you have to offer.

Task 6.7

Using your own store as an example:

1. How often do you need to tidy in-store displays?
2. How often do you rotate or change window displays?
3. Why do you think it is necessary to change displays on a regular basis?

ASSESSMENT 1: PROJECT

Part 1: Plan merchandising: creating display plans

Assessment context	As part of your role in a retail store you may be called upon to assist in the merchandising of products and maintaining promotional displays. In this project we will assess your ability to undertake the necessary steps to do this with confidence. It will be necessary for you to undertake this project in a workplace situation, either as part of your traineeship, or as part of a vocational placement scheme. If a workplace assessment is not possible, your assessor may devise a manner in which this project can be simulated. This assessment also covers the requirements outlined in Chapter 5—**SIRXMER001A: Merchandise products**
Assessment instructions	To complete this project you will need to design two merchandising displays: • one internal (table) display, and • one window display. These may be for a specific promotional purpose, or a simply a change of stock in your store. In order to accomplish this you will need to develop display plans. In your plans: 1. Discuss the purpose and target audience of the displays. 2. What organisational constraints and requirements may impact on your display ideas? 3. What other staff members will be involved in: a. generating the ideas b. giving approvals and authorities c. setting the display budget d. providing feedback and suggestions? 4. What tickets or signage will you need for the display: a. what style of tickets or signage will you use? b. how will these be produced? (what equipment will you need?) 5. What resources will you need for the display, and where will these be sourced from?
Evidence required	1. Two detailed display plans. 2. A short report answering the points 1 to 5 above.
Range and conditions	• Display must use at least three different display fixtures (e.g. shelves, racks, mannequins). • As working to deadlines is an important aspect of creating displays, you will have one week in which to complete these plans. No extensions will be granted.

Materials and resources required	In order to prepare the display plan you must have access to; • in-store and window display areas • stock for the displays • pricing, ticketing and display equipment • accessories to be used in enhancing the display.
Reasonable adjustments	In the event that you have difficulty understanding the assessment tasks due to language or other difficulties, your trainer will attempt to make reasonable adjustments to the assessment paper in order to afford you every opportunity to achieve competency.
Decision-making rules	You will be assessed on your ability to: • accurately identify the purpose and target audience for the displays • take the organisation's requirements and constraints into consideration when developing your display plan • generate creative ideas for the displays in cooperation with other staff members • identify the resources that you will need to complete the displays • develop fully detailed display plans.

ASSESSMENT 2: PROJECT

Part 2: Putting the display plan into practice

Assessment context	In Part 2 of the display project you will be required to actually assemble and maintain the displays (from Assessment 1) over a period of one week. You will need permission from your store manager to do this. If you are not permitted to use a store window, due to head office merchandising plans, ask if a small area of the store or back storerooms can be used to accomplish the same thing. This assessment also covers the requirements outlined in Chapter 5—**SIRXMER001A: Merchandise products**.
Assessment instructions	Using the display plans you developed in Assessment 1, you should now put these plans into practice. 1. Prepare tickets, signs and labels for your display using at least two different pieces of ticketing or labelling equipment. 2. Set up your displays in accordance with your display plans. 3. Over the next week ensure that your displays are maintained regularly. 4. Review your displays during that week, and make any adjustments or changes you feel necessary to keep them fresh and interesting.

continued

Evidence required	1. A short report on: • how you produced any tickets and signs, and what equipment you used • how you spent your display budget • what steps you took to maintain your displays • what assistance you received from staff members during the set up of the displays • how you reviewed your display ideas once they were fully set up. 2. Photographs of the displays at various intervals: • during the set up • on completion • three photos per day for the duration of the display, taken at different times of the day, to show how the displays were maintained. Photos must be time and date stamped.
Range and conditions	• As working to deadlines is an important aspect of creating displays you will have one hour to create the in-store display, and two hours to create the window display. • You will require the permission of your workplace supervisor to undertake this task.
Materials and resources required	• Access to in-store and window display areas • Access to stock for the displays • Access to display resources, equipment and materials as per your display plan.
Reasonable adjustments	In the event that you have difficulty understanding the assessment tasks due to language or other difficulties, your trainer will attempt to make reasonable adjustments to the assessment paper in order to afford you every opportunity to achieve competency.
Decision-making rules	You will be assessed on your ability to: • set up displays that accurately reflect the needs of the target audience • follow the display plans accurately • stay within the display plan budget • maintain the condition of your displays • use resources and materials in accordance with your display plans • set up your displays within the allocated space and timeframe.

COMPETENCY MAPPING

Element		Performance criteria		Task	Assessment	Refer to page
1	Identify requirements for display	1.1	Identify purpose, audience and products for each display.	6.1	1	187
		1.2	Identify organisational requirements and research relevant information where required.	6.1, 6.2	1	188
		1.3	Identify available budget and resources required to create the display.		1	189
		1.4	Identify and consider constraints or factors that may affect the creation of the display.	6.3	1	189
2	Develop display ideas	2.1	Generate ideas for the display using creative thinking techniques.	6.3	1	190
		2.2	Test ideas against display and organisational requirements.	6.3	1	191
		2.3	Discuss display options with relevant personnel.	6.3, 6.4	1	191
		2.4	Modify display ideas and refine according to feedback and confirm with relevant personnel.	6.4	1	191–192
3	Plan and build displays	3.1	Develop ideas into simple display plans.	6.4	1	192
		3.2	Source resources, materials and products to meet plan requirements.	6.5	1	193, 196
		3.3	Create displays following display plans.		2	194–195, 197
		3.4	Seek assistance from relevant personnel where required.	6.6	2	199
		3.5	Review display and make refinements as required.	6.6	2	200
4	Maintain displays	4.1	Regularly clean and tidy displays and replace products as necessary according to display plans.	6.7	2	200
		4.2	Make changes or alterations to the display as appropriate.	6.7	2	201

continued

Required skills and knowledge	Task	Assessment	Refer to page
Required skills			
Creative thinking skills	6.3	1	190
Interpersonal communication skills to: • communicate display ideas to others • seek and accept feedback through clear and direct communication • use language and concepts appropriate to cultural differences • use and interpret non-verbal communication.	6.3	1, 2	190, 191, 199
Representing ideas in the form of a simple display plan.	6.4	1	192–195
Observing when display needs to be changed, updated or altered.	6.7	2	199, 200
Maintaining display.	6.7	2	199, 200
Required knowledge			
Basic design principles, including: • colour • shape • use of space • flow of product.	6.4	1, 2	192–193
The audience for the display and what the display needs to communicate.	6.1	1, 2	187
A variety of display options.	6.3, 6.4	1, 2	192–195
Organisational requirements in terms of product display.	6.2	1	188
Critical aspects for assessment and evidence required			
Identifies the requirements for a new display.	6.3, 6.4	1	188
Creates a display plan that meets the requirements of the product, the audience and the organisation.	6.3, 6.4	1, 2	192–195, 197
Plans and builds the display plan and maintains the display.	6.3, 6.4	1, 2	192–195, 197

Chapter 7

SIRXSLS201A

Sell products and services

In previous chapters we looked at customer service excellence in terms of establishing a rapport with customers and finding out what their needs and expectations are. While making sure that customers are satisfied is very important, you must never forget that the aim of every business is to make money—and that means selling products and services to customers.

In any sales situation it is important to provide customers with accurate, detailed and honest information about the products and services they are interested in. This means that you must know as much about your products and services as possible so that you can provide this information and make the sale.

By listening to customers and doing your best to provide them with what they want, you establish a trusting relationship with them that can last for years. On the other hand, if you push customers into buying something they are not entirely happy with, you risk 'burning' them and they will not do business with you again.

In this chapter we will look at the skills you need in order to develop sound product knowledge. You will learn how to apply that knowledge, how to approach customers in the most effective way, to communicate with them and then to match the products and services you offer to those needs successfully—making the sales!

ELEMENT 1
APPLY PRODUCT KNOWLEDGE

Applying product knowledge means understanding the products and services your organisation offers and using that knowledge to match them with a customer's stated needs.

1.1 Demonstrate knowledge of the use and application of relevant products and services according to store policy and legislative requirements.

1.2 Develop product knowledge by accessing relevant sources of information.

LEARNING OUTCOMES

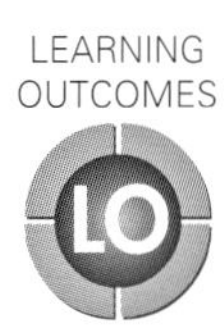

Does it really matter if every customer buys from you or not? If this one doesn't then surely there are plenty of other people who will! So why does it matter if you have a sound product knowledge? It is important because:

- the success of any business depends on making as many sales as possible
- customers spend their hard-earned money with you and deserve to receive value for their money
- keeping customers happy ensures that they come back again (and tell their friends about you) thereby building a solid and loyal customer base
- sound product knowledge avoids complaints about products or services that do not perform as the customer expected and avoids goods being returned
- sound product knowledge fulfils your duty of care towards the customer—giving them the best and most professional advice possible.

A reminder: product characteristics

When recommending products or services to a customer it is important to be aware of the uses of that product or service—its characteristics. You should know:

- what the product is used for
- how many different functions it can perform
- whether it comes in different sizes or colours
- how long the product or service will last
- under what conditions it must be used
- whether there are any special handling and storage requirements
- if there is a warranty
- whether there are any optional extras and, if so, how much they cost
- if it can be applied in a variety of ways
- if there a use-by date that customers should be made aware of
- if the item is currently in stock, or must be ordered (and if so, what the expected delivery time is)
- the product's safety features
- the price range.

Relevant sources of information

The above are all questions of importance to a customer and you must be able to answer them—but how do you know where to find this information? There are a number of relevant sources of information that may include:

INTERNET

A great deal of information is available via the internet. Most companies will have a website, and products supplied by them will generally have a web address printed on them. It is a good idea to browse the websites of main suppliers on a regular basis as these sites will provide you with the most up-to-date information about that particular product or service. It is also fairly simple to find information here via search engines (such as Google, Bing, Yahoo or WebCrawler).

When using the internet for research, you should always be careful, however, to make sure the information you download is from an *authorised* site. This means an official website that has been developed by the product or service principal, wholesaler or other official source (such as government or industry body). Anyone can upload information on any subject they choose onto the World Wide Web. They don't need to be an expert on the subject or even know anything about the subject at all, so the information on such a site may not be accurate. Be sure to verify any information before passing it on to customers or colleagues.

RELEVANT STAFF MEMBERS

Asking other staff members about a product or service is an excellent way of learning about it. Other staff often have first-hand experience of using the product, or they may have sold the product before or be a product specialist.

STORE OR SUPPLIER PRODUCT MANUALS

Depending on the complexity of the product or service, there may be a manual available which will give full details of the product characteristics.

PRODUCT LABELS

Labels will often give a description of an item's selling features, its ingredients, care and handling instructions and other relevant information.

STORE TOURS

Taking a good look at what your store has in stock and where items are located allows you to answer customer questions quickly and efficiently. There is nothing more unprofessional than not knowing if your store carries an item or not knowing where to find it.

GOVERNMENT OR COUNCIL WEBSITES

These authorities' websites provide up-to-date information about legal and legislative issues that all organisations and their staff should be aware of. They are also a source of formal, legal application forms such as liquor licenses for the hospitality industry, Blue Card or Working with Children application forms for the childcare industry, grant applications and many others.

LIFESTYLE PROGRAMS

Lifestyle programs on television can provide in-depth information about countless industries, products and services. Whole programs are devoted to such interest areas as fashion, technology, home improvements, arts and crafts and health and fitness.

These sources can often be referred to when advising customers about your products or services and will lend the information you provide them a higher level of credibility. They can also keep you up to date on the latest trends and emerging technologies.

TRADE MAGAZINES

There are a variety of trade or special interest magazines such as *Retail World* (www.eretailworld.com.au) that are filled with articles about their industry. Trade magazines are an important source of information about future trends, innovations and competitors and can also be used effectively when recommending products to customers. A useful website on what sort of magazines are available is: www.australianmagazinesubscriptions.com/industry_and_trade_magazines/index.html.

GENERAL MEDIA

In addition to the trade magazines mentioned above, there are a great variety of off-the-shelf magazines devoted to certain interest groups that can provide good information relating to your industry. They include magazines about information technology, gardening, home improvement, fashion, photography and arts and crafts.

Referring to articles published in reputable magazines can help with establishing credibility, especially if you can actually show the customer an article outlining the product or service you are offering them.

Task 7.1

1. Over the next few days list the programs on television that you believe contain information from specific industries, products or interest areas.
2. Research, in your local newsagent, what other magazines might be useful to the business sector. Make a list of likely magazines and next to them, write the industry that might be interested in that magazine for product information.
3. List which magazines would be useful in your current industry.
4. Research and list government or council websites that are useful to your organisation. Submit this information to your teacher. Use at least three sources of information and provide a list of the sources you used.

TRADE ASSOCIATIONS AND INDUSTRY BODIES

Most major industries will have governing bodies or associations that will provide up-to-date information about innovations within that industry, new government legislation, insurance and human resource issues and much more. Examples of just some of the associations and industry bodies in Australia are:

Council of Textile and Fashion Industry of Australia	www.tfia.com.au
Australian Information Industry Association	www.aiia.com.au
Mortgage & Finance Association of Australia	www.mfaa.com.au
Restaurant & Catering Australia	www.restaurantcater.asn.au

Internet Industry Association	www.iia.net.au
Australian Retailers Association	www.retail.org.au
Advertising Federation of Australia	www.afa.org.au

Task 7.2

1. Try these websites to see the type of information that is available to the relevant industries:

Australian Retailers Association:	www.retail.org.au
Master Builders Association:	www.masterbuilders.com.au
Real Estate Institute of Australia:	www.reiaustralia.com.au

2. Look up the industry body that applies to your own organisation and keep this information in your portfolio.

WHOLESALER OR PRINCIPAL PRODUCT LAUNCHES

Wholesalers and principals often hold functions to launch new products. You could potentially be invited to go to a breakfast or dinner at which the new product will be presented. These are an excellent way of finding out about new products.

Principals are the companies that manufacture, provide or produce the products that you sell through your organisation. For example, a computer store might sell Apple iPads—the products are manufactured by Apple, which is the principal. As they do not usually have shops or offices, or do not have many, principals will most often distribute their products to the wider market via agents or wholesalers.

Wholesalers are companies that act as a *middleman* between principals and retailers. For example in the food distribution industry:

1. the farmer will grow crops and is the principal (or primary producer)
2. his crop would be sold to a wholesaler (the local fruit and vegetable wholesale market)
3. the grocery shop (the retailer) would then buy the produce from the wholesale markets for their stores to sell to their customers.

WHOLESALERS' OR PRINCIPALS' SALES REPRESENTATIVES

The sales representatives of the companies you do business with can also be a source of product knowledge as they work for the principal (or wholesaler). They have very detailed knowledge of the particular products they supply, and can tell you many things about them. They will also be able to tell you about availability, adaptability to certain conditions and uses of their products. If in doubt, this is an excellent source of information.

These sources of information can help you out when your customers have requirements that are outside your personal knowledge base. It is important to keep yourself up to date

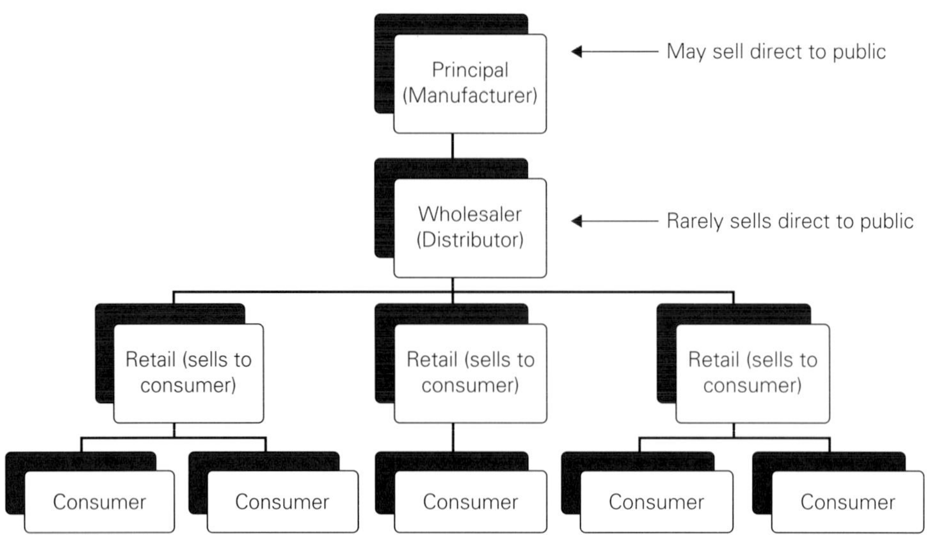

Figure 7.1 Pathway from principal to consumer

on new products, trends and legal or legislative issues to ensure your customers are getting the very best available products or services for their money.

Task 7.3

1. Research one product of the organisation you work for.
2. Write a one-page fact sheet on this product answering as many of the questions from the paragraph on 'Product characteristics' (page 208) as you can.
3. Use at least three sources of information and include a bibliography of these sources with your fact sheet.

Selling in accordance with store policies and legislative requirements

Often a sale can be very simple: a customer will come in to your store, browse for a while, choose a product and then pay for it at the cash register. Sometimes the customer may either ask questions about a product they are interested in, or require a demonstration of how it works. This is where solid product knowledge comes into its own: you will be able to confidently answer questions and show the customer how the product should be used. In doing this, however, you need to keep in mind not only store policies about selling to customers, but also any legislative issues or obligations.

STORE POLICIES

Store policies on selling to customers might dictate how you interact with the customer; how you greet them and how much time you are allowed to spend with any one customer.

Spending a long time with a customer who ends up not buying anything, or buys something of minor value, when other customers are waiting is an inefficient use of time and the company may well have a policy to guide you on this. They may also have policies on:

1. offering—**preferred products** over others (dealt with in Element 7 in this chapter)
2. requesting customer contact details—for marketing purposes
3. levels of authority for negotiating deals—with customers. Not everyone within the organisation may be allowed to negotiate discounts or deal with specific customer requirements, so you will need to know who you can turn to for assistance should a customer request a special deal or something outside of the norm
4. distribution of duties—and responsibilities to staff for specific areas of service. Depending on the industry you are in, the organisation may have specialist staff to deal with certain products or services, or may have specific staff to look after certain customer requests.

LEGISLATIVE REQUIREMENTS

Store policies on dealing with customers will almost certainly include the need to observe any legislative requirements associated with the industry you are in. In Chapter 1 we looked briefly at the legislative requirements of working in the retail industry. In addition to those mentioned, and depending on the industry you are in, there are a number of other legislative issues that you may need to keep in mind when selling products or services to customers. These include:

- lottery legislation
- industry codes of practice
- sale of second-hand goods
- sale of X- and R-rated products
- trading hours
- transport, storage and handling of goods.

The issues surrounding these areas of legislation will generally deal with information that must be provided to customers buying certain products, or may place restrictions on who can buy the product. Examples are given below.

EXAMPLE: LOTTERY LEGISLATION

Lottery legislation restricts who is allowed to conduct and benefit from lottery activities and explains how the integrity and fairness of lotteries is maintained. For an example of the legislative frameworks see the relevant government website for your state, or for NSW www.olgr.nsw.gov.au/promos_legltn_bkgrd.asp.

EXAMPLE: TRANSPORT, STORAGE AND HANDLING OF GOODS

In accordance with legislative requirements you may be obliged to advise customers on how they should handle the products they have purchased. Products that involve the use of chemicals must come with advice on how to transport, use and store those chemicals safely, and products that include sharp or complex machine pieces must come with an explanation and a demonstration on how to use them safely. Some products have specific care instructions and you will be required to provide relevant information. For example a customer who has just purchased an expensive cashmere jumper should be made aware of the fact that the garment will shrink if washed in hot water.

INDUSTRY CODES

Most industries have an association, or governing body, that provides advice and guidelines on legal issues of that industry, best-practice policies and procedures and guidelines for dealing with human resource or customer-related issues. In some cases they may have specific requirements for licensing or registration purposes. These must be kept in mind when dealing with customer requests.

A successful sales person is one who has not only taken the time to learn about the products and services their organisation offers but keeps in touch with new and emerging trends and offers the best possible advice to their customers.

ELEMENT 2
APPROACH CUSTOMER

There is a delicate art to customer approach which is sadly not observed in many retail environments today. Often, when you walk into a retail store staff may either ignore you or 'pounce' on you the moment you walk into the shop. Both of these 'approaches' can be negative.

In this section will take a look at the best way and time to approach a customer to maximise your service quality and the opportunity for making a sale.

Figure 7.2 Don't turn customers off

LEARNING OUTCOMES

2.1 Determine and apply timing of customer approach.

2.2 Identify and apply effective sales approach.

2.3 Convey a positive impression to arouse customer interest.

2.4 Demonstrate knowledge of customer buying behaviour.

Knowing when to approach the customer

The way in which you approach a customer entering your store or office will play a large part in making not only a successful sale, but also in establishing a rapport with what could become a loyal and long-term customer. Approach them too soon, and they may not have had time to get a general overview of what you offer. Don't approach them at all, and you run the risk of them walking out with a bad impression of your service levels and not having bought anything.

So, when is the right time to approach a customer who comes in to your store? This is a question that will be answered by your organisation's customer service policy, but there are some things that must be avoided, and a few general rules that you might follow.

THE APPROACH: WHAT *NOT* TO DO

Do not approach the customer the second they walk in to the store. Give them a few moments to get oriented and browse around. While it is normal practice in the retail industry for many store attendants to earn commission for sales they make, it is not good practice to pounce on customers as soon as they come in. Unless they have a very specific need, or know exactly what they want, the majority of customers will respond to an immediate approach with 'I'm just looking', 'I'm only browsing', or similar. A response like this leaves you with no graceful way to move forward into a sales situation.

Equally you should not ignore the customer. This shows a lack of interest in them and if you are not looking at the customer, you might miss a signal that shows that they need assistance or are ready to buy something.

Do not start the conversation with a *closed* question such as 'Can I help you?' A customer can simply say 'No' in reply, which again leaves you with nowhere to go. Use an open question, such as 'What can I help you with?'

THE APPROACH: WHEN AND HOW

1. When a customer enters your store, greet them in a friendly manner—smile and say 'hello'. This will show the customer that you have noticed them and that you are approachable. It is the beginning of establishing rapport.
2. Let them have a few moments to browse on their own. At the same time keep your eye on them and observe them to determine when you may approach them successfully.
3. Watch the customer's behaviour:
    - **a.** What are they looking at?
    - **b.** Are they spending a lot of time over a particular product?
    - **c.** Are they comparing products in the shop?
    - **d.** Are they discussing a particular product with a friend?
    - **e.** Have they picked something up and started to walk around the store with it?
4. If you notice any of this behaviour in the customer you should then approach them and ask if you can assist them. Ideally, you should approach the customer from the front—face on—with a smile, so that they can see you coming.
5. Have an opening comment ready for the approach based on what you have previously observed. For example, 'Those T-shirts are especially designed for us by a local artist. What do you think of them?' or 'I noticed you were looking at this hat, what can I tell you about it?' When you mention the product that the customer is looking at while also asking them an *open* question, they must respond to you in some way.

Effective sales techniques

Having approached the customer and successfully gained their attention you now need to know how to go about making that sale. This involves using sales techniques designed to arouse their interest in the product and to influence them to make the purchase. We will be looking at these techniques in more detail as we move through this chapter, but for now they include:

- understanding buying behaviour—knowing what motivates people to buy
- recognising buying signals—knowing when to stop selling to the customer and to let them make the purchase
- add-on and complementary sales—making the most of every sales opportunity to offer better service to the customer and maximise revenue to the store
- overcoming customer objections—recognising when a customer has issues with a product or service and finding ways to overcome them
- closing techniques—winding up the sales process and getting the customer to make the purchase.

CONVEYING A POSITIVE IMPRESSION

Delivering excellent customer service and, at the same time, earning revenue for your organisation is all about making a positive impression on the customer to not only arouse their interest in the product you are offering, but to keep them coming back.

Conveying a positive impression is a matter of listening to the customers, focusing on their requirements, asking effective questions to gather further details if necessary and then choosing products that you offer to match their stated needs. By using positive communication, knowing your product well and doing all possible to provide the customer with what they want, you are showing the customer that you are interested in their needs and are willing to help them.

Task 7.4

Role play

Set up the classroom—or find an environment—to resemble a retail environment. For those learners studying in the workplace, this role play can be undertaken as a workplace observation with your trainer.

1. Split into teams of four—one sales person and three customers.
2. Customers—walk into the office or shop at various intervals and browse through the products or brochures on show. When approached by the sales person, respond to them as you would in a normal retail situation.

3. Sales person—deal with the customers coming in to your store using your knowledge of customer service skills. Determine the correct moment to engage with and approach each customer and then endeavour to make a sale.
4. Each person in the class should have the opportunity to play the sales person's part.

Customer buying behaviour

To create a positive impression it is useful to have a general understanding of customer buying behaviour. What motivates them to buy? Why do they choose one product over another? What do they base their buying decisions on?

People buy for two very basic reasons; they have a *need*, or they have a *desire*. These are very different motivations. A *need* is something that is necessary to a person's physical or mental comfort. A person will *need* to buy food or pay rent. A sales person may *need* to use their car for business purposes and will therefore *need* to buy petrol and keep their car maintained. A *desire* is a different motivation. A desire-based purchase is something we don't actually need but *want* anyway. Impulse buys are driven by desire. You don't actually need a new pair of shoes but you *want* them, so you'll buy them. Buying the latest Xbox or PlayStation isn't really necessary but video games are your hobby so you go to the shop and buy one.

Decisions to buy products are either logically or emotionally based. Decisions to satisfy a need are made with the head (logic), while decisions to buy products to satisfy a desire are made with the heart (emotion). To make a successful sale you need to engage the customer's logic or their emotions.

NEED-BASED PURCHASES

These customers want things done quickly and they want them to work! You should take an efficient, no-nonsense approach, telling your customer exactly what the product or service will do for them. They won't want to waste any time so they will want you to meet their needs as quickly and efficiently as possible.

DESIRE-BASED PURCHASES

For many people even the process of planning and researching a purchase will be part of the total experience—especially if it is a large, expensive purchase like a car, furniture or holiday. In this situation you need to appeal to the customer's emotions and they should be completely involved in the process. They will need to feel that they are spending their money wisely and you should continually reassure them of this and allow them to take their time over the decision.

So, depending on the customer's reason for buying, your approach could be efficient and to the point, or enthusiastic with lots of interaction.

Task 7.5

Scenarios

1. Look at the following scenarios and determine if the customers are buying to satisfy a need or a desire.

Scenario	Product	Need or desire?
A mother is buying back-to-school gear for her 8-year-old child	School shoes	
A teenage girl is going to a birthday party	New dress	
A business owner is upgrading the way they maintain their customer database	Computer and software	
Young single person shopping for the coming week	Groceries	
A father buying something to keep his young son occupied during the holidays	PlayStation	

2. Choose two of the scenarios above and describe how you would approach and involve the customer buying those particular products or services. Submit your answer in writing.

ELEMENT 3
GATHER INFORMATION

As mentioned, making a sale can often be as simple as taking a customer's money at the cash register. There are certain industries, however, where the sales process may be very complex and will require good communication skills so that you can find out exactly what the customer wants. For example, in the information technology industry where you are selling computer systems and software, there are so many choices and options that a customer may become confused. They may not be familiar with different types of equipment or know which software to use for specific purposes. There may also be a great deal of money involved in these purchases. In such cases it is important to fully understand the customer's exact requirements. This takes excellent communication skills.

Communication skills were covered in detail in Chapter 2, however, in this section we will guide you through the process of asking the right kind of questions and observing a customer's non-verbal language—looking for signs that they are ready to buy, or are not yet satisfied.

LEARNING OUTCOMES

- 3.1 Apply questioning techniques to determine customer buying motives.
- 3.2 Use listening skills to determine customer requirements.
- 3.3 Interpret and clarify non-verbal communication cues.
- 3.4 Identify customers by name where possible.
- 3.5 Direct customers to specific merchandise.

Applying effective communication skills to gather information

As you learned in Chapter 2, asking the right type of questions can get you detailed information on a customer's needs and expectations. Equally, listening closely to what they are saying and being aware of their non-verbal language can be an indication of their readiness to buy—or lack of readiness. It could also indicate signs of dissatisfaction with the information or service received so far.

When gathering initial information about customer needs, it is a good idea to ask open questions and then listen to the customer's responses, asking follow up or clarifying questions as you gather more information. As you begin to build a picture of what it is your client wants, you can begin to match their needs to products or services that your organisation offers.

Task 7.6

Questioning practice

Matching products to customer needs will be dealt with shortly—for now, however, go back to Chapter 2 and review the information on 'Using communication skills to create a service environment', then undertake the following task:

- Split into pairs.
- Each person should think of a favourite holiday destination. It must be either a capital city or a country.
- In turn ask each other the right type of questions to find out the other person's choice of holiday place.
- Each person may ask only four questions.
- You are not allowed to ask where the place is.
- Trainers may substitute other product or service options for the holiday destination, but only four questions may be asked.

Debrief

1. Did you manage to find out the holiday destination of your partner?
2. What type of questions did you ask?
3. Were your questions as effective as you had hoped they would be?
4. What other questions could you have asked to get better answers (if applicable)?

Use the customer's name

Most people are attuned to the sound of their own name. Have you ever been to a party or a business function where there is a buzz of noise around you? You only concentrate on hearing what is being said in your immediate group—until someone at the other side of the room says your name and your 'antenna' automatically tunes in to hear what is being said!

A person's name is important to them and they will usually respond well when being addressed personally. But simply saying to the customer 'What's your name?' is very abrupt and might prompt the negative response of 'Why do you want to know!?' So how do you find out? If we work from the standpoint that a person's name is important to them, then in giving them your name first you are giving them something of value and they will, in turn, be more inclined to give you theirs. For example, 'I'm sure that we can find the right product for your requirements. By the way—my name is John, how may I address you?'

If the sales process is already well underway you might have had to check the customer's driver's licence or credit card which will also give you their name.

Task 7.7

Discuss other ways in which you can find out the customer's name.

ELEMENT 4
SELL BENEFITS

A customer doesn't buy a food blender because it has 'six speed settings'—they buy it because they are passionate about cooking, and a blender with six speed settings will allow them to prepare different foods in different ways and help them prepare gourmet meals. While these two things both amount to the same thing, it is the perception that will make the difference between making a sale and not making a sale: one of these descriptions is a *feature* and the other describes the *benefit* that this feature represents. 'Six speed settings' (a feature of the blender) means very little unless you explain how these settings will impact on the budding chef's ability to prepare food—'easily, with a greater variety of food and with perfect precision' (a benefit of them having that particular feature). In this section we will be looking at the skills and knowledge you will need to successfully match products and services to customer needs.

LEARNING OUTCOMES

4.1 Match customer needs to appropriate products and services.

4.2 Communicate knowledge of a product's features and benefits clearly to customers.

4.3 Describe product use and safety requirements to customers.

4.4 Refer customers to the appropriate product specialist as required.

4.5 Answer routine customer questions about merchandise accurately and honestly or refer to senior sales staff.

Matching products and services to customer needs

No two people are exactly alike. We are all shaped by various influences on our lives and will view ourselves and the world around us according to very specific measures. Some of these are our:

- education—the level of education a person receives will have an impact on their quality of life and the decisions they make
- upbringing—this often dictates a person's values and outlook on life
- socioeconomic background—this might influence a person's needs in terms of what they can or can't afford in life and the level of their expectations
- cultural background—cultural values play a large part in how a person sees the world and what values they hold dear, and will influence their reaction to the environment in which they find themselves
- life experience—as a person moves through life they gain experience and learn valuable lessons that will influence decisions they make
  - age—a person's stage of life will also greatly influence their view of the world. For example, a 19-year-old man may have very different opinions, outlooks and needs from a 60- or 70-year-old man
- family structure—young single professionals will have different needs and expectations of their lifestyle and the world around them from middle-aged parents with small children, or mature-aged 'empty nesters'
- physical or mental abilities—a person may also be influenced by limited or excessive physical or mental ability; a person who is wheelchair-bound may have different needs to someone who is not.

Note: Please note that these examples are generalisations only and do not necessarily reflect how a person will turn out or what their expectations of life might be. They are presented here as examples of how the conditions under which a person grows up and lives might influence their lives, their needs and expectations.

These influences will then also have an impact on our personal needs when we are buying goods or services.

Imagine that you work in a furniture store such as Freedom Furniture or IKEA. Let us look at how these different influences and factors might impact on various customer types buying a new sofa.

Matching products to customer needs becomes a matter of:

- fully understanding what motivates customers—are they buying to satisfy a need or desire?
- communicating effectively with them—asking them questions in a way that engages them and allows them to feel that you are taking their needs seriously and really listening to what they have to say

- knowing the characteristics of your products and services—having a detailed understanding of the products and services you sell and how they might suit or be made to fit in with the customer's stated requirements
- presenting the product or service—you feel best matches the customer's needs by explaining its features and describing how these features will benefit them and do what they have asked for.

Table 7.1

Matching customer needs with products

Customer type	When buying a new sofa might look for:
Young single person, on a trainee wage, moving into a bed sitter	Sofa bed, small enough to fit into limited space and reasonably priced
Family with two children (three and eight years old) and two dogs	A large, comfortable sofa to fit entire family. Hard-wearing fabric that is easy to keep clean. Removable covers that can be washed in a machine
Elderly couple in their 60s. The husband has a bad hip	Comfortable cushions, not too soft so that it is difficult to get up from, solid arm rests to lean on
Young professional man on a good salary moving into a new flat on his own	Good quality and modern that projects a stylish image

Task 7.8

As with the example in Table 7.1, describe what these customer types might look for in a car or in a holiday hotel.

Customer type	New car	Holiday hotel
Young single person, on a trainee wage		
Family with two children (three and eight years old) and two dogs		
Elderly couple in their 60s. The husband has a bad hip		
Young professional man on a good salary		

Describing product use and safety requirements

Depending on the products you sell, you may also have an obligation to describe the correct use of the product as well as any specific safety requirements. This is particularly true of any products or services that have the potential to cause harm or injury or that could be damaged if not operated correctly. For example, if the customer has purchased an electric tool, show them how to turn it on correctly and safely, how to use it correctly and how to turn if off and store it correctly.

Describing product use and safety requirements is not only good customer service, it may also be an organisational and legislative necessity.

The consequences of not abiding by this requirement could range from minor inconvenience to customers, when products break or don't work the way they are supposed to, to catastrophic, where customers are injured or even killed if they are not made fully aware of how a product should be used safely. In extreme cases your organisation (or you) could be subject to legal action. Care must be taken when discussing these aspects of any product or service that you are selling.

The YouTube video 'How to use a drill safely' (www.youtube.com/watch?v=tWimYthkI9o) is an excellent example of how to provide information on the safe use of a product. While you may not need to go into quite this much detail, it gives you an idea of how clear instructions can be given.

Features and benefits

As mentioned in the opening paragraph of this section, a customer will buy a product or service for the benefits they derive from using it. Explaining the benefits of a product is an important aspect of the sales process, so let's spend some time looking at the difference between features and benefits, and why this matters.

To best describe the differences we will use the example of the Bolteo computer from Chapter 1 (page 20). Looking at the advertisement for this product can be extremely confusing and you would need to be an expert in computer technology to understand it. The facts presented here give you no real reason why you should buy the product. The ad provides a range of features—but does not describe the benefits of those features.

1. Would you buy this product simply on the strength of the information given in this ad?
2. Would you need someone to explain what it all means?

BOLTEO 230X

- I3 Duo E7500 Processor. (2.93 GHz/1066Mhz FSB/3MB Cache)
- Genuine Windows 7 Professional
- 4GB Dual Channel DDR3 SDRAM at 1333 MHz
- 320GB SATA hard drive (RPM) (7200RPM)
- Integrated Intel Graphics Media Accelerator X4500HD

Figure 7.3 Bolteo computer advertisement

So what is the difference between a feature and a benefit? As we saw in Chapter 1, a feature is something that a product or service has. A benefit is a description of how a feature will *help* the customer. Table 7.2 uses the Bolteo computer as an example.

Table 7.2

Features and benefits

Feature of the BOLTEO 230x	Benefit of having that feature
I3 Duo E7500 Processor. (2.93 GHz/1066Mhz FSB/3MB Cache)	This is the brain of the computer. It allows you to process large amounts of information at the same time; you can open multiple windows and work on different projects without having to shut one down to work on another. *Benefit: It saves you time and improves your work efficiency*

Features and benefits	
Feature of the BOLTEO 230x	**Benefit of having that feature**
Genuine Windows 7 Professional	This is the computer's 'operating system'. Without this you would have a blank screen when you switched your computer on. This is your doorway to all the software and programs within the computer. It also provides you with access to external areas such as the internet. *Benefit: it gives you access to programs that let you produce Word documents, spreadsheets, graphics, photos and much more.*
4GB Dual Channel DDR3 SDRAM at 1333 MHz	This is what is known as the computer's 'mother board'. It is, essentially, the engine that makes the computer work. It also holds the computer's random access memory (RAM)—the bigger the number (i.e. 4GB, 8GB), the more random memory it has and *the faster it will work (benefit).*
320GB SATA hard drive (RPM) (7200RPM)	While it is on, the computer works with RAM to undertake the various tasks you ask of it—but RAM does not actually store the information. This feature, then, is where all the files are stored. Again, the higher the numbers, *the more information you can store on it (benefit).*
Integrated Intel Graphics Media Accelerator X4500HD	This is a specialised piece of technology that enhances a computer's ability to reproduce graphic images. It is great for people who like playing computer games, or for professionals who *need to reproduce high quality images (benefit).*

So in looking at the features against the benefit descriptions you can begin to see how explaining the benefits of the products features would be more likely to influence a customer to buy it.

Task 7.9

1. Below is a list of features. Write down what you believe the benefits are in the space provided.

Feature	Benefit
Product: Digital camera	
16 megapixels	
15 x optical zoom	
Product: Food processor	
Stainless steel attachments	
2-litre processing bowl	
10-year motor warrantee	
Non-slip feet	

2. Using the product you researched in Task 7.3, list its features and benefits here. Include any instructions for correct and safe use of the product.

Feature	Benefit	Instructions on use

Task 7.10

Watch YouTube video 'Retail Sales Training: How to Sell Features and Benefits' (www.youtube.com/watch?v=L2TUi4kNW0I) and answer the following questions:

1. Is price always the deciding factor when a customer purchases a product?
2. What is the difference between a feature and a benefit?
3. Why should you focus on selling benefits to a customer?

Seeking assistance

During the sales process most customers may ask about a great many things that relate to price, discounts available, quality of the product or availability of the product. Having spent time developing your product knowledge, you should be able to answer most of these routine questions.

Developing product knowledge is an important part of any sales person's role. As you have now learned, the ability to satisfy customer needs is essential to the success and growth of any business. There will be times, however, when a customer will make a request that you, personally, are unable to fulfil. This may be because you don't know enough about that specific product, service or subject, or it could be because what they have asked for is outside your own level of authority to grant or provide.

In those cases you may need to refer the customer to someone else within the organisation. If in doubt, don't make up an answer or make a promise that you are not sure about. Customers can be referred to senior staff members who have more experience, expertise or authority to handle a specific request or to staff with specialised product training.

ELEMENT 5
OVERCOME OBJECTIONS

When selling to customers it is useful to understand that an objection is not the same thing as a complaint. An objection is a reason why a customer might not want to buy what you are trying to sell them. It's important not to be discouraged by this and assume that it means you've lost the sale. It may simply be that there is some aspect of the information you have provided that is still not quite right or does not suit them. It will be part of your role to determine what their particular objection is and to find a solution to it.

LEARNING OUTCOMES

5.1 Identify and accept customer objections.

5.2 Categorise objections into price, time and merchandise.

5.3 Offer solutions according to store policy.

5.4 Apply problem solving to overcome customer objections.

Categories of objections

When a customer objects to some aspect of the sales process or the product you must never 'push' to complete the sale as this will only annoy the customer and they may leave without buying. You need to find out the nature of the objection, and these can fall into a number of different categories. The nature of the objection will determine how you solve the issue. Objections can revolve around:

Price

The product or service that you are offering may be too expensive and out of their price range. In this case you may need to find a less expensive option, give them a discount (if store policy allows for this) or talk to them about payment plans and options. Equally, the product you have offered might be too cheap. If they are looking for a good quality product they may not mind spending additional money for that quality and not be prepared to sacrifice this for the sake of some cost savings. In this case offer them the quality they are after—they will soon tell you if this is too expensive.

Quality

Another reason why customers can object is that the quality of the product or service offered does not match their expected standards. As mentioned above, price is not always the deciding factor on whether a customer will buy a product or not. People do not mind spending extra money if they receive value for their money and are able to purchase a product that meets their requirements in terms of quality.

Availability

This can be an important issue for some customers. They may want their product or service immediately and if it is not available and they are being asked to wait then they may not go ahead with the purchase. In this case it may be difficult to solve the situation: you could, should your store have several branches, make phone calls to see if you can find one somewhere else or perhaps call the manufacturer or supplier to see if you can get one quickly.

When immediate delivery of a product or service is not an option customers are normally happy to wait—for a reasonable amount of time. If the time you quote them is too long then, again, they may not be prepared to wait and you will have to negotiate this with them.

Solving objections

In order to solve an objection made by the customer and get the sale you need to apply problem-solving skills.

- Listen closely—to what the customer is saying, paying particular attention to any negative comments they are making.
- Look for options—to overcome their objections. This will take an in-depth knowledge of your products and organisational policies and procedures so you know what you have to offer them as an alternative and, importantly, if it is within company guidelines to offer it.
- Present the benefits—of your product or solution to them, explaining or repeating how it matches their needs.
- Gain their agreement—throughout the conversation by asking them clarifying questions.

ORGANISATIONAL CONSTRAINTS

The important thing in trying to overcome a customer's objection is to make a sale. You must nevertheless keep any organisational constraints in mind and not over-step your authority or company policy. The manner in which you solve the problem may be constrained by the organisation's policies and procedures on various issues. For example, they may have strict policies against offering discounts, as this erodes their profit margins, or they may have specific procedures regarding delivery of products that you may not ignore, as it may add an extra cost to providing the product or service.

Then there are resource implications to almost everything involved in making a sale: the amount of time you spend with a customer in trying to solve a problem is a cost factor. Your time is worth money and while you are spending time with them, you are not dealing with other customers or tasks. Anything you give away in order to make the sale costs money, whether it is a discount, a 'free' giveaway product or an extended payment plan. If the cost of making the sale ends up being higher than the value of the sale then it is not worth pursuing it.

When deciding what you should offer the customer in order to get a sale you should always keep your organisation's policies and procedures in mind.

Task 7.11

Scenario

You have spent some time with a customer who has come in to your HiFi store to buy a new sound system for his home. You have shown him five different options, all of them top quality and very expensive, in the hope of making a good sale for your organisation. You notice that the customer is very interested in these options but is reluctant to make a decision. He has glanced at the less expensive options a number of times during your presentations and as you continue to talk about his choices he moves closer and closer to the door.

1. What category of objection might this customer have?
2. What is likely to happen if you continue with your current sales presentation?
3. What can you do to gain the customer's interest and get a buying decision?

ELEMENT 6
CLOSE SALE

The most important step in the sales process is actually getting the customer to make the buying decision, and there are very specific steps to closing the sale. In many sales situations a sale is a simple matter of taking the customer's money once they have made a choice. If you've spent a substantial amount of time talking to a customer, finding out about their needs and presenting them with a product that matches those needs, how do you know when to wind up—or close—the sales process and *stop selling*? Many sales have been lost because the sales person did not stop selling when the time was right. In this section we will look at recognising buying signals and methods of asking for the sale.

LEARNING OUTCOMES

LO

6.1 Monitor, identify and respond appropriately to customer buying signals.

6.2 Encourage customer to make purchase decisions.

6.3 Select and apply the appropriate method of closing the sale.

Recognising buying signals

'Buying signals' are visual clues that a customer has made a decision and is ready to buy. Learning to recognise them and acting on them is an important selling technique and, when you are making a sale and presenting a product to a customer, your timing in closing the sale is critical. If you try to push for the sale too quickly, before they are ready, you can turn a customer off and they will leave without buying anything. Equally, if you take too long and keep talking when they are ready to buy, the customer could lose interest and walk away. This is known as 'un-selling' where a customer who had decided to buy your product changes their mind due to the sales person's over-zealousness or unnecessary sales pitch.

In Chapter 2 we discussed non-verbal language—the silent messages a person sends out that give us clues to what they are really thinking and feeling. Buying signals are filled with non-verbal language. They are the signs that a customer subconsciously sends out when they've made up their mind and it is these that you should look for if you want to successfully close a sale.

From the moment they walk into your shop or office a customer will be giving signs that indicate they *are*, or are *not yet*, ready to buy. These signals could indicate that they are:

- just wandering around with no real interest in products or intention to buy
- interested in a particular product, but not currently anxious to buy it
- very interested and might well buy it if you can answer a few questions
- ready to buy *this, now*!

Buying signals for all of these will be very distinctive and easy to recognise if you know what to look for.

NON-VERBAL SIGNALS: *NOT* READY TO BUY

The non-verbal signals that a customer is *not* ready to buy include:

- avoiding eye contact—with you. when you look at them and they immediately look away. They probably do not need assistance right at this moment
- making 'not now' excuses—when you ask a customer if you can assist them and they say 'just looking' or otherwise indicate they don't need help, smile and leave them, giving them space to continue browsing
- casual handling of the product—some shoppers may casually pick up different products and drop them back in untidy heaps after looking at them briefly. This is often a sign of a bored browser.

In all these cases, keep an eye on them and be ready to assist, as they may also change their minds when something catches their interest.

NON-VERBAL SIGNALS: READY TO BUY

The non-verbal signals a person sends out when they *are* ready to buy might include:

- spending considerable time looking at one product type—the longer a person looks at one product type, the more likely they are to buy it. They are investing their time, which is a sure sign of interest
- looking around for somebody to help them—if you see them looking around, catch their eye. If they hold your glance, smile and move in to help them
- asking questions about the product—when you offer your assistance, they may ask detailed questions about the product. These may include questions about price, which is a strong buying signal. If they ask about the functionality of the product, they may well have a checklist of things they are looking for, so ask for details of their requirements

- using possessive language—when they pick up the product, they may get a sense of already owning it. Ask how they will use it and let them try it out. Listen for language that indicates possession, for example, 'This will look great in my living room!'
- asking another person's opinion—when they ask a friend what they think about the product, they are probably thinking about buying the product and are looking for approval
- getting ready to pay—if they bring out their wallet or purse, this is a very strong signal for you. Go over to them and ask if you can help.

Methods of closing the sale

One of the most difficult steps in the sales process for new sales people is closing a sale. Some sales people may find it difficult, or even a little embarrassing, to ask the customer to make a decision or to pay for the product. But the close doesn't have to be as difficult as it seems. If you presented the product well and responded to any objections, the close should follow naturally and the customer should be ready to buy without too much persuasion. The most effective method of closing the sale is to simply ask for it. By asking closing questions such as 'How will you be paying for this?', 'How many would you like?' or 'When would you like this delivered?' you are winding up the process and asking the customer to make a decision.

The important thing to remember when you recognise any buying signal is to *stop selling* and close the sale! Many sales are lost because the sales person, full of enthusiasm, keeps on talking and presenting information. The customer is ready and waiting, but becomes frustrated by the sales person and eventually changes their mind and leaves.

Task 7.12

CASE STUDY

Catherine is in Australia on holidays. She is leaving for home (the USA) in two days and has bought souvenirs for friends and family at home. In addition to these she needs to buy a special present for her mother who will be celebrating her 50th birthday shortly after she gets home. She has decided to buy her something typically Australian—a piece of opal jewellery.

Catherine is told that the souvenir shop around the corner from her hotel offers some lovely pieces and she makes her way there. Once there she begins to browse the shelves for appropriate gifts but the store is enormous and she does not know where to begin looking for the things she wants so she looks around for assistance. She notices two sales people by the perfume counter who are laughing and joking with each other but does not manage to catch their eye.

She spends twenty minutes wandering around on her own until a sales person finally approaches her. Catherine explains that she is looking for a number of gifts plus something special for her mum but has a very limited budget. The store attendant begins to take her around the shop showing a large variety of products.

Catherine decides to buy three items for friends and a lovely opal watch for her mother. She takes out her purse and asks if the store accepts MasterCard, but instead of taking her to the checkout counter, the store attendant pulls out further products, explaining their features in great detail.

Catherine listens politely and asks a few questions to be polite but she looks pointedly at her watch a number of times and moves in the direction of the counter. The sales person, however, comes along all the while talking about how wonderful a particular watch (more expensive) would be compared to the one Catherine chose. Having long since made her choice, Catherine is most offended by this comment as she is on a limited budget and the watch she has chosen is the best she can afford. Thoroughly frustrated, she puts down the products she had intended to buy and leaves the store having purchased nothing.

1. What buying signals did Catherine display?
2. What non-verbal language did Catherine display?
3. What did the sales people do wrong?
4. Describe, in detail, how you would have handled this customer.

ELEMENT 7
MAXIMISE SALES OPPORTUNITIES

The final thing that we will look at in this chapter is how to ensure that you make the most of every sales opportunity. The most important issue in any business is how to make as much money as possible. As you have learned, the revenue an organisation generates pays for the shop rent, utilities bills, purchase of new stock and *your salary*.

There are a number of ways in which you can ensure increased revenue.

LEARNING OUTCOMES

LO

7.1 Recognise and apply opportunities for making additional sales.

7.2 Advise customers of complementary products or services according to each customer's identified need.

7.3 Review personal sales outcomes to maximise future sales.

Opportunity to make additional sales

Serving customers and making sure that they are satisfied is extremely important to any organisation. Earning maximum revenue for the organisation, however, is just as important (if not more so) and it is part of every sales person's role to take advantage of every opportunity to increase sales. This can be done in a number of different ways including by selling:

- preferred products
- add-ons or complementary products.

PREFERRED PRODUCTS

Depending on the type of industry you work in, and the organisation you work for, there may be a range of 'preferred products'. These are products you get from your regular suppliers who will pay your company an incentive, or bonus, for high volumes of sales, which means that the more of this particular product you sell, the more of an incentive they will pay your organisation. For example, a company that supplies you with stock for your shop may normally charge you $9.95 per item that you order from them. As an incentive for you to make more sales and place larger orders with them, they may give you a discount for higher volume sales; if you order 1 000 items they will give you a discount of 10 per cent, if you order 2 000 items, they will give you a discount of 15 per cent and so on.

For obvious reasons, it will be your organisation's policy to sell these preferred products ahead of others that offer them no discount. It is therefore essential that you know these products very well. You must be able to point out the positive advantages of using this product (as opposed to a non-preferred product) quickly, clearly and convincingly. You want your customer to be happy with their purchase—but you also want to earn the maximum revenue that you can from the sale.

Preferred products are usually given preferential placement on display racks. They will be at eye level, with non-preferred products placed higher or lower on the shelves. There should also be a greater number of these products available. At all times, when asked for a particular type of product, you should offer your preferred products. Naturally if a customer asks for a non-preferred product, then you must provide them with it—but offer it together with the preferred product explaining its features and benefits for comparison.

COMPLEMENTARY PRODUCTS AND SERVICES

In addition to offering preferred products, another method of maximising sales is to offer complementary products. These are items, products or services that 'complement' the main product that is being purchased. Have you ever bought a pair of leather shoes, and the shop attendant asked if you needed leather polish to keep them clean and in good shape? They

Task 7.13

What complementary products could you offer to go along with your researched product (Task 7.3)?

Your product	Complementary product
	•
	•
	•
	•
	•

were offering a complementary product. Equally, when buying a hamburger the attendant may ask 'Do you want fries with that?' These are all efforts to increase the volume and revenue of the sale.

Reviewing sales outcomes

Many organisations will have targets, or key performance indicators (KPIs) for their staff to achieve in order to meet financial goals and obligations. This means that the staff must meet certain revenue or sales benchmarks during the week and their pay structure may be linked to these targets. It is important, therefore, to look at and review the way you approach sales on a regular basis. There are a number of ways that you can do this including talking to supervisors or other staff members and getting their advice and feedback on your sales methods and how you might improve them. You might also ask yourself the following review questions:

- Did you make a sale to every customer you approached?
- If yes, what do you think you did to achieve this result?
- If you did not make every sale, what, *if anything*, do you believe you did wrong?
- What areas are there for improvement in your performance?
- Is your product knowledge as good as it could be?
- How could you improve your product knowledge?

Asking these and other questions and acting on the results will help you grow in your role as a successful sales person.

Selling is an extremely important aspect of any business operation. The organisation is, after all, in business to make money. While good service is what keeps the customer coming back again and again and builds loyalty, it is the sale that makes the business successful and keeps it going from year to year. It is the sale that pays for new stock, upgrades in equipment, and your wages so it is in your best interests to get it right. By following these simple steps you should be successful with most customers:

1. Approach the customer when they are ready to talk to you.
2. Spend time to find out what they are looking for.
3. Match your products or services to their needs.
4. Address any objections they have.
5. Pick up on buying signals.
6. Close the sale.

ASSESSMENT 1: ROLE PLAY OR WORKPLACE OBSERVATION

Assessment context	This unit of competency applies to frontline sales personnel. It requires the recognition and demonstration of verbal and non verbal communication skills to determine customer requirements, sell the benefits of products and services, overcome objections and close sales. Personal evaluation is utilised to maximise sales in accordance with industry codes of practice, relevant legislation and store policy. In order to be deemed competent in this unit you must demonstrate your ability in these skills.
Assessment instructions	For this assessment you will be required to interact with at least three customers. 1. Choose a product or service that all participants are comfortable and familiar with to 'sell' during the role play. You will then need to do the following: a. Greet each customer in turn as they come in to the shop and watch for the correct time to approach them b. Engage them in conversation to establish a rapport with them and find out their needs and expectations c. Present your product or service to the customer explaining features and benefits and showing how this product or service matches their needs d. Describe how the product or service is used safely and to best advantage e. Answer any questions the customers might have f. Handle any objections the customers might raise and negotiate a solution g. Look for buying signals and close the sale at the appropriate moment h. Offer complementary products. 2. Review your own performance: a. How well do you think you handled the sales? b. In what areas could you improve?
In the workplace:	Your trainer will make an appointment with you to undertake this observation. You will need to interact with customers in your normal way, although your trainer may ask you to perform specific tasks in order to gauge your competence in certain areas of the unit requirements.
Classroom simulation:	Split into groups of four: one sales person and three customers. Each person must have the opportunity to play the role of the sales person. • **Sales person:** your role is to make a sale to each customer in turn in line with the instructions provided above. • **Customers:** you should all 'walk in to the store' at intervals and browse around. When the sales person approaches you, answer any questions they ask and react as if this was a normal sales situation. Choose one person to be 'difficult' asking lots of questions and objecting to aspects of the sale such as price.
Things you should know	• The store policy does not allow for discounting but does offer a 'buy one, get one free' (the free products are ones that have been in the backroom taking up space for a couple of years and the owners are keen to get rid of them). • Where a product is not available in the store immediately, the delivery time is generally two–three weeks.

Evidence required	Completed observation checklist
Range and conditions	This assessment can take place either: • on the job with the trainer observing the student dealing with a variety of customers or • in the classroom in a simulated role play where each student is given the opportunity to play the part of the sales person dealing with at least three customers in turn.
Reasonable adjustments	In the event that you have difficulty understanding the assessment tasks due to language or other difficulties, your trainer will attempt to make reasonable adjustments to the assessment paper in order to afford you every opportunity to achieve competency.
Decision-making rules	You will be assessed on your ability to address the criteria on your trainer's observation check list.

ASSESSMENT 2: REVIEW QUESTIONS

1. Using your own industry (or one that you are familiar with) as a basis, what specific sources could you access to develop your product knowledge?
2. Describe how you would go about finding out a customer's name
3. You have just started working for a new company. A customer has come in to buy a product you are not yet fully familiar with. They begin to ask you very specific questions that you cannot answer. What will you do?
4. Describe at least two categories of customer objection and give examples of how you could overcome them.
5. Explain why it is a good idea to regularly review your own sales performance.
6. Describe why it is important to observe legislative requirements when selling to customers.
7. Describe what industry codes of practice are and what importance they have in your industry.
8. Discuss methods that can be used to maximise sales and give an example of how your method could be applied.

COMPETENCY MAPPING

Element		Performance criteria		Task	Assessment	Refer to page
1	Apply product knowledge	1.1	Demonstrate knowledge of the use and application of relevant products and services according to store policy and legislative requirements.	7.3	2(AQ1)	208–213
		1.2	Develop product knowledge by accessing relevant sources of information.	7.1, 7.2, 7.3	2(AQ1)	208–213
2	Approach customer	2.1	Determine and apply timing of customer approach.	7.4, 7.5	1(AQ1a)	214
		2.2	Identify and apply effective sales approach.	7.4, 7.5	1(AQ1a)	216
		2.3	Convey a positive impression to arouse customer interest.	7.4	1(AQ1b)	216
		2.4	Demonstrate knowledge of customer buying behaviour.	7.5	1(AQ1a–g)	217
3	Gather information	3.1	Apply questioning techniques to determine customer buying motives.	7.6	1(AQ1b)	219
		3.2	Use listening skills to determine customer requirements.	7.6	1(AQ1b)	55–89
		3.3	Interpret and clarify non-verbal communication cues.	7.6, 7.7	1(AQ1b)	
		3.4	Identify customers by name where possible.	7.8	2(AQ2)	220
		3.5	Direct customer to specific merchandise.	7.9	1(AQ1c)	221
4	Sell benefits	4.1	Match customer needs to appropriate products and services.	7.9	1(AQ1c)	221
		4.2	Communicate knowledge of product features and benefits clearly to customers.	7.10, 2.11	1(AQ1c)	223
		4.3	Describe product use and safety requirements to customers.		1(AQ1d)	222
		4.4	Refer customers to appropriate product specialist as required.		2(AQ3)	225
		4.5	Answer routine customer questions about merchandise accurately and honestly or refer to senior sales staff.		1(AQ1e)	225

Element		Performance criteria		Task	Assessment	Refer to page
5	Overcome objections	5.1	Identify and accept customer objections.		1(AQ1f), 2(AQ4)	226
		5.2	Categorise objections into price, time and merchandise characteristics.	7.12	1(AQ1f)	226
		5.3	Offer solutions according to store policy.	7.12	1(AQ1f)	227
		5.4	Apply problem solving to overcome customer objections.	7.12	1(AQ1f)	227
6	Close sale	6.1	Monitor, identify and respond appropriately to customer buying signals.	7.13	1(AQ1g)	228
		6.2	Encourage customer to make purchase decisions.		1(AQ1g)	230
		6.3	Select and apply appropriate method of closing sale.	7.13	1(AQ1g)	230
7	Maximise sales opportunities	7.1	Recognise and apply opportunities for making additional sales.		1(AQ1h)	231
		7.2	Advise customer of complementary products or services according to customer's identified need.	7.14	1(AQ1h)	232
		7.3	Review personal sales outcomes to maximise future sales.		1(AQ1a–h), 2(AQ5)	233

Required skills and knowledge	Task	Assessment	Refer to page
Required skills			
Selling techniques, including: • opening techniques • recognising buying signals • strategies to focus customer on specific merchandise • add-ons and complementary sales • overcoming customer objections • closing techniques.	7.4, 7.13	1(AQ1a–h)	212–232
Verbal and non-verbal communication skills.	7.6, 7.7	1(AQ1b)	55–89
Handling difficult customers.			
Negotiation skills.			
Sales performance appreciation.			
Questioning, listening and observation.			
Verbal and non-verbal communication skills.			

continued

Required skills and knowledge	Task	Assessment	Refer to page
Required skills			
Literacy skills in regard to: • reading and understanding product information • reading and understanding store policies and procedures • recording information.	7.1, 7.2	2(AQ1)	208–214
Numeracy skills in regard to: • handling payment for goods • weighing and measuring goods.			
Required knowledge			
Store policies and procedures, in regard to: • selling products and services • allocated duties and responsibilities.	7.10	1(AQ1a–h)	212
Store merchandise and service range.	7.3	1, 2(AQ1)	208
Specific product knowledge for area or section.		1	208
Relevant legislation and statutory requirements.		1(AQ1d), 2(AQ6)	208–214
Relevant industry codes of practice.		1(AQ1d), 2(AQ7)	
Customer types and needs, including: • customer buying motives • customer behaviour and cues • individual and cultural differences • demographics, lifestyle and income • types of customer needs, e.g. functional, psychological.	7.5, 7.13	1(AQ1a–h)	214–217
Critical aspects for assessment			
Applies product knowledge and uses appropriate sales approach to sell the benefits of products and services, overcome objections and close sales.	7.3, 7.9, 7.10	1(AQ1a–h)	214–232
Uses questioning, listening and observation skills to determine customer requirements.	7.4, 7.6, 7.7	1(AQ1b)	Chapter 2
Consistently applies store policies and procedures in regard to selling products and services.	7.10	1(AQ1a–h)	212–214
Maximises sales opportunities according to store policies and procedures.		1(AQ1h), 2(AQ8)	231–232
Consistently applies industry codes of practice, relevant legislation and statutory requirements in regard to selling products and services.		1(AQ1a–h)	212–214
Evaluates personal sales performance to maximise future sales.		1(AQ2a–b), 2(AQ5)	233

PART 3

Retail operations

Units covered in Part 3:

8. SIRXWHS101—Apply safe work practices & SIRXWHS302—Maintain store safety
9. SIRXFIN201—Balance and secure point-of-sale terminal
10. SIRXINV002A—Maintain and order stock
11. SIRXRSK201—Minimise loss

In addition to effective marketing and customer service, a successful retail operation requires attention to detail and compliance with legal obligations. Details like maintaining appropriate stock levels, balancing point of sale terminals and compliance with your safety and security obligations provide a solid foundation for successful operations.

Online retailing, while removing the physical interaction with external customers, still relies on easy and safe processes to remain successful. For example, customers have the right to expect secure checkout facilities and easily understood sales terms and conditions as part of their experience. Additionally, working in an online retail context still requires basic adherence to personal health and safety standards.

Figure 8.1 Fresh, clear signage and merchandising are key features of effective retail operations

> 'If you're a big-picture guy, you're not in the picture. Retail is detail.'
> —***James Sinegal, co-founder of Costco***

As a retail worker you are in a position of responsibility, not only to your employer and customers, but also to yourself and your co-workers. This responsibility extends to include your personal safety and a duty of care to those working and shopping in your store, as well as the ongoing profitability of your employer.

In Part 3 we will look at how to:

- apply safe work practices
- maintain store safety
- balance a point-of-sale terminal (elective)
- maintain and order stock
- minimise loss.

Chapter 8

SIRXWHS101 & SIRXWHS302

Apply safe work practices and maintain store safety

When it comes to safety, consider the effect you have on those around you by the way you act and the way you approach your work. Being aware of your obligations under the Safe Work Australia guidelines and maintaining a positive approach to safety in the workplace will provide a healthier and happier workplace. Applying safe work practices covers the requirements for basic safety procedures and emergency safety procedures. The first element deals with the basics.

ELEMENT 1
APPLY BASIC SAFETY PROCEDURES

Avoidable accidents, injuries, illnesses, and deaths are a massive cost to the Australian economy. For this reason, practices relating to workplace health and safety are now included in every traineeship, apprenticeship and qualification in the vocational education system. The results so far have been a steady decrease in total numbers of work-related fatalities; however, injuries and illnesses have been affected only slightly. The aim for all workplaces is to reduce the risks to an acceptable level.

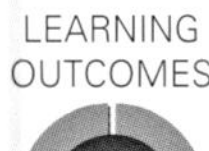

1.1 Follow safety procedures to achieve a safe work environment, according to all relevant WHS legislation, including codes of practice relating to particular hazards in the industry or workplace.
1.2 Clearly and accurately explain store WHS policy and procedures, and relevant WHS legislation and emergency procedures to team members.
1.3 Ensure access for team members to store WHS policy and procedures.
1.4 Identify and report unsafe work practices, including faulty plant and equipment according to store policy and procedures.
1.5 Manage dangerous goods and substances according to store policy and relevant legislation.

1.6 Identify potential manual handling risks and manage manual handling tasks according to store policy.

1.7 Report work-related incidents and accidents to designated personnel.

1.8 Model the implementation of WHS and emergency procedures to reinforce information and identify opportunities for training.

1.9 Participate in consultative processes and procedures for WHS.

A single workplace accident can result in a small retail business closing down and the loss of jobs and livelihoods for the owners, workers and their families. Applying basic safety practices has never been so important.

Following safety procedures—background

Every job has safety procedures whether they are obvious, like wearing hearing protection in noisy environments, or less obvious like wearing sanitised gloves when preparing take away food. These procedures are not just measures thought up on the spot to deal with complaints or to make things more comfortable. They are actually a result of years of refinement by lawmakers and standards bodies such as WorkCover—Authority of NSW, Safe Work Australia, Food Standards Australia and many more. Retailers operating businesses in Australia must meet the laws, regulations and standards produced by these organisations in order to keep their workers safe and be compliant with the law. Failure to do so could lead to accidents and injuries that could damage the reputation and financial bottom line of the business.

State-based workplace health and safety legislation has recently gone through one of the biggest changes in legal history—the national harmonisation of all state and territory legislations, regulations and codes of practice, along with a national compliance and enforcement policy.

The *Safe Work Australia Act 2008* (Cth) officially formed the national body responsible for bringing about the harmonisation: Safe Work Australia. Its job is to ensure that the state legislation progressed within the timeline and to form the compliance and enforcement policy (see www.safeworkaustralia.gov.au).

So what does this mean for you and other retailers around Australia? Well, initially, it means that workplace health and safety standards are the same around the country (more or less), so moving interstate to work will not mean learning new standards or procedures from scratch. Additionally, national retail operators can implement a single policy that covers their stores throughout Australia. No longer will they need separate policies and procedures for each state.

It also makes explaining the approach to WHS much easier. But there is still some work to finish before it is completed, so the following list is provided for you to identify the relevant legislation and standards in your region as of July 2012. Check your state or territory government website for the latest information.

Table 8.1

State-based workplace health and safety legislation	
QLD	*Work Health and Safety Act 2011* *Workplace Health and Safety Regulation 2008* Codes of practice are located at: www.deir.qld.gov.au/workplace/law/legislation/codes/index.htm
WA	*Work Health and Safety Act 2012* (pending at time of publication) Occupational Safety and Health Regulation 1996 (update pending) Codes of practice are located at: www.commerce.wa.gov.au/worksafe/content/About_Us/Legislation/Codes_of_practice.html
NSW	*Work Health and Safety Act 2011* *Work Health and Safety Regulation 2011* Codes of practice are located at: www.workcover.nsw.gov.au/lawpolicy/codesofPractice/Pages/default.aspx
SA	*Occupational Health, Safety and Welfare Act 1986* *Occupational Health, Safety and Welfare Regulations 2010* Codes of practice are located at: www.safework.sa.gov.au/show_page.jsp?id=5892
NT	*Work Health and Safety (National Uniform Legislation) Act 2011* *Work Health and Safety (National Uniform Legislation) Regulations* Codes of practice can be viewed individually at: www.worksafe.nt.gov.au
ACT	*Work Health and Safety Act 2011* *Work Health and Safety Regulation 2011* Codes of practice are located at: www.worksafe.act.gov.au/page/view/1403
TAS	*Model Work health and Safety Act 2011* *Model Work Health and Safety Regulations 2011* Codes of practice are located at: www.safeworkaustralia.gov.au/Legislation/model-COP/Pages/Model-COP.aspx
VIC	*Occupational Health and Safety Act 2004* *Occupational Health and Safety Regulations 2007* Codes of practice are located at: www.worksafe.vic.gov.au and search for 'Retail and Fast Food—Worksafe'

SAFE WORK PRACTICES

Safe work practices are designed to minimise the risk of injury when carrying out day-to-day tasks within a workplace. Table 8.2 identifies the four main categories for classifying work practices and provides examples of procedures that fall under each category.

Table 8.2

Safe work practices

Safety category	Examples of work procedures
Ergonomic	Hazard identification Personal safety procedures PPE (Personal protective equipment and clothing)
Physical	Emergency, fire and accident procedures Evacuation procedures (customers and staff) Manual handling Cash handling
Environmental	Handling dangerous goods Waste disposal Store security
Emotional	Issue resolution procedures Personal security Stress management

Ergonomic practices

Ergonomics is the study of work tasks in the work environment. You may have heard it mentioned when referring to the 'ergonomics' of a workstation (computer desk) in an office. This is only one example. Ergonomics can refer to the layout of a delivery dock or the use of a ladder when stacking shelves. In each case it refers to the personal hazards and risks identified with that task, in that particular context or environment.

Physical practices

The physical work practices are all those that involve movement of the worker. For example, lifting stock, moving around the store, counting back change to a customer and evacuating the store.

Environmental practices

Environmental practices are those involving interaction between the worker and their environment and could refer to handling chemicals, glare or heat through shop windows and daily waste disposal.

Emotional practices

Finally, the emotional practices are those affecting the mental wellbeing of the worker. Dealing with stress, conflict resolution and even bomb threats all relate to this category.

It is important not to get too concerned with categorising each procedure as they often overlap between categories. For example, store security procedures might involve an emotional, environmental *and* physical safety procedure. Just be aware that these categories help identify different safety concerns, which assists policy makers to cover a safety procedure more thoroughly.

Let's now look at some of the above examples in a work context to gain a better understanding of how you would follow and apply these procedures.

HAZARD IDENTIFICATION

Each area within your retail store will have **hazards** and **risks** to the health and safety of staff, customers and visitors. It is important to know what a hazard is and how you can manage and **control** that hazard in your work area to avoid dangerous **consequences**.

It is a requirement under the harmonised state WHS laws to have a risk identification procedure at your workplace. By identifying the risks, you can then work on controlling them and therefore reducing the likelihood of someone, including you, being harmed.

A simple but effective procedure is the regular completion of hazard identification and control forms. A high quality safety system will include procedures for how often, where and how hazard identification should take place. For example:

When: at the start of each shift

Where: within your work area

How: completed and implemented—including control measures. Handed to the store manager for filing.

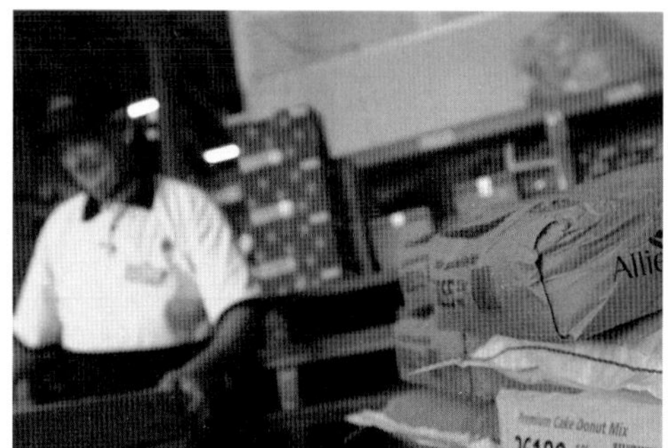

Figure 8.2 Take time to identify workplace hazards

Managing the hazards and their associated risks can be achieved through a suitable identification procedure like this, usually involving a hazard identification form similar to the one below:

Hazard identification and control form					
Date	*18/10/2012*	**Location**	*Warehouse*	**Name**	*Tina Couples*
Description of the hazard		*The industrial waste bin near the warehouse door is overflowing*			
Identified risks		*This is a fire hazard and presents potential health risks from vermin and old waste products*			
Control measure/s			**By whom**	**By when**	**Does this effectively control the hazard?**
Separate overflowing waste into bags and leave outside for collection			*Tina*	*10.00 am*	Y/N
Supervisor/Manager *(Sign when completed)*				**Name**	

While the specific reporting requirements may vary, it's vital that you and your fellow staff remain vigilant in the identification and reporting of hazards. Ensure you complete the forms provided by your employer in a clear and concise manner, in accordance with the store WHS policy.

Failing to report hazards can lead to harm or injury to you, a colleague, or even a customer. If an injury occurs at work where the person needs medical treatment, the retail operator must report it to the state WorkCover authority. (WorkCover is a government mandatory injury insurance requirement for businesses in New South Wales, Western Australia and Queensland. (In Victoria, the Australian Capital Territory and Northern Territory the authority is called WorkSafe, and in South Australia it is called SafeWork.) The authority may undertake an investigation. This directly affects the costs and reputation of the business and can have long-term repercussions for the employer *and* employees involved.

Harm does not have to be physical. Emotional, psychological or environmental harm are also a cause for concern in retail workspaces. So when you are identifying hazards, consider all the possible hazards in each category.

EXAMPLE

In *Lusk & Anor v Sapwell*, a case in Queensland in 2011, an older customer who was suffering from dementia sexually assaulted a young female worker out of sight of other workers and customers. It was found that employers only have to address risks in the workplace that are reasonably foreseeable, and that the worker must prove that the employer's breach of duty of care caused their injury. The employee was not able to work following the incident, and in the first case, was awarded $390 558 in damages (although this decision as to the amount was later reversed).[1]

APPLYING THE HIERARCHY OF RISK CONTROLS

Control measures can be more or less effective based on how they reduce the level of risk to you and others. Their effectiveness can be determined by where the control measure sits on the hierarchy of controls. The following table explains this six-step hierarchy.

Table 8.3

Hierarchy of risk controls

Control measure	Definition	Effectiveness
Elimination	Removing the hazard altogether so it no longer poses any risk	Highest
Substitution	Replace the hazard with something of a lower risk	High
Isolate the hazard	Restricting access to the hazard through the use of barriers, safety cones, tags, or locks	Medium
Engineering	Using devices or machinery to reduce the risk such as ventilation and safety switches	Medium
Administrative	Using policies and procedures to avoid the hazardous circumstance, e.g. training, posters, safe work procedure	Low
PPE	Personal protective equipment and clothing	Lowest

When you identify a hazard, you then need to consider the most reasonable way to control it. The terminology used in safety circles is to do what is 'reasonably practicable'. This means that you consider the likelihood that the hazard could harm someone and the level of consequences (such as hospitalisation or first aid treatment), and you determine what is practicable.

Practicability is usually a balance between what is possible and what is *financially viable*. It's easy to suggest a redesign of the back dock to remove the risk of falls from the loading bay, but if the cost is prohibitive for a small business, signs and procedures may be put in place instead.

PERSONAL SAFETY PROCEDURES

Personal safety procedures are any measures you need to take to reduce the risk of something harmful occurring to you. These include:

Keeping aware of your surroundings

Some terms you might hear include 'eyes on path', 'look up, down, left and right before proceeding', and 'spatial awareness'. All these terms aim to highlight the importance of being aware of the environment around you, which might include:

- gases and chemicals. Retail environments may include compressed gases and chemicals that, if released or spilled, could harm you
- spills that could lead to slips and falls
- overhanging stock or shelving
- protruding stock or fixtures
- broken air-conditioning
- dust
- direct sun and sun glare
- insects and vermin
- working in confined spaces
- manual handling tasks.

Conduct personal hazard identification

This may take the form of a procedure that the retailer implements or a task you conduct regularly for your own safety. Some industries (e.g. coal mining) require a personal hazard identification checklist to ensure that all common hazards are considered before doing any task. You should quickly review your surroundings and look for the hazards mentioned above.

Personal Protective Equipment and Clothing (PPE)

PPE is the equipment and clothing you should wear in a given environment to reduce the effects that hazards may have upon you. It is the lowest form of hazard control on the hierarchy of controls—but is still a line of defence against injury. The PPE you wear will depend upon the task you are performing. For example:

- warehouse or storeroom work—you might require a high-visibility shirt or vest, hard hat, gloves, steel capped boots, or even a dust mask
- manual labour—you may need to consider your manual handling aids such as forklifts, trolley or pallet jacks. You will also need to consider your hydration levels, so a water bottle may be a requirement
- shop floor sales/customer service—comfortable non-slip shoes.

Task 8.1

Complete a hazard identification and control form. For this activity you can use a form that exists in your workplace, or use the example in this section to create your own.

You can use your workplace, or a simulated workplace (training room), to conduct a fifteen-minute hazard identification walk-around. Remember, hazards can be ergonomic, physical, environmental or emotional—so try to find at least one of each.

Reporting unsafe work practices

Unsafe work practices can include:

- use of damaged or broken equipment
- using damaged packing materials or containers
- using ladders, trolleys, forklifts and pallet jacks incorrectly or with disregard for safety (riding pallet jacks or using forklifts as elevated work platforms)
- incorrect manual handling practices
- dealing with flammable materials near fire hazards
- use of sharp cutting tools in an unsafe manner (cutting towards your body)
- failing to clean up or barricade spills, debris and leaks
- unacceptable levels of stress.

It is everyone's responsibility to understand and implement store health and safety procedures to avoid unsafe practices like these. This is because the laws of each state and territory and the new federal standards require that businesses have WHS policies in place, and that all workers, contractors and visitors understand those policies in relation to their specific duty of care. Your duty of care is a basic tenet of occupational health and safety. So what is it?

DUTY OF CARE

Duty of care is a common law principle that has been developed over time through the courts of England and Australia. It refers to the obligations you have regarding the health and safety of those around you and vice versa. A duty of care is a legal obligation to have thought or regard for those who may be affected by your acts or omissions (an omission is failing to do something that may have prevented harm to someone). Implementing your duty of care means planning and taking measures that prevent workplace accidents, injuries and illnesses.

CASE STUDY

Lina Rowls started work in a busy coffee shop and coffee appliance retailer. A part of her basic induction was information regarding the business's safety procedures for fire evacuation. A simple walk-through was conducted and Lina signed her induction documentation to verify that she understood the procedures.

A few months later, an unserviceable coffee machine was being tested in the rear of the business premises. While the technician wasn't watching, the machine caught fire and released smoke into the service area, tripping the smoke detectors and causing the alarm to sound. At that moment, Lina was serving a customer in the front-of-house area and was startled by the alarm. She remembered the exits she was shown and made her way quickly out of the building via the front door—leaving her customer standing, puzzled, with a coffee plunger in his hands.

Did Lina have a duty of care to her customer? Should she have led her customer out of the store to safety? The simple answer is yes. The law requires businesses, and therefore their employees, to render assistance to those on its premises. Failing to do so could have resulted in the retailer, and Lina, facing stiff penalties under the law.

Under your duty of care, you should communicate any information that can impact upon the health and safety of people in your workplace. This may be in the form of a hazard report as documented earlier, or orally (see below).

SHARING THE INFORMATION

It makes sense to share information and procedures that could affect health and safety with your teammates. Some ways in which you can achieve this in your workplace include the following:

Regular meetings

Most retailers will have a regular staff meeting, either weekly or daily. Safety can be included on the agenda for these meetings and each staff member encouraged to have their say about potential hazards, unsafe practices they have observed, or safety messages they may have. They are also an opportunity for managers to share procedures with the staff.

Ad-hoc meetings

Where needed, you may conduct a short walk-through or training session with new staff regarding your workplace health and safety procedures.

Safety awareness sessions

Regular safety-specific sessions can be held to discuss recent safety concerns or changes in the layout or equipment in the store that may affect health and safety.

Safety shares

A 'safety share' is a request for workers to participate in a meeting by offering a recent story about a safety issue that they may have seen or been involved in. For example, if you had recently heard of a shop worker straining their back and having to go on sick leave, you can share the story so awareness of this potential hazard can be 'top of mind' for those at work that day.

FAULTY PLANT AND EQUIPMENT

Faulty machinery, equipment and stationary plant such as air-conditioners, cool rooms and refrigeration units represent a number of hazards including:

- environmental—hazards relating to the spillage or leakage of liquids and gases from the equipment
- physical—faults may lead to a build-up of toxins, bacteria could grow and spoil food and other perishable items, heat or cold could affect your ability to concentrate or cause you to feel poorly
- ergonomic—faults may hamper the normal operation which could lead to workers shortcutting the correct operating procedure and harming themselves or others
- emotional—failures or faults could easily lead to stressful situations or the need to act quickly to stem the damage. This can have a negative impact on your psychological state.

Ensure you report faulty equipment and plant as soon as it is noticed. Your workplace may additionally have a procedure for tagging the equipment with a 'faulty' or 'out of service' tag so others do not use it.

Handling and storage of dangerous goods

The requirements for handling and storage of dangerous goods are covered under the WHS legislation in each state. Dangerous goods are defined as:

> *substances or articles that present an immediate hazard to people, property or the environment. They are often highly concentrated substances like acids or contain large amounts of embodied energy such as explosives.*[2]

Dangerous goods must be labelled for identification and reported to the regulator for WHS legislation in that state. In retail, the more common dangerous goods would include those in the following table.

Table 8.4

Common dangerous goods		
Dangerous goods	**Examples**	
Flammable gases. Examples include butane and LPG that are often sold through retail outlets supplying camping or barbecue equipment	LPG cylinders BBQ lighters Cigarette refills/lighters Insect spray	FLAMMABLE GAS 2
Toxic gases. Waste storage can cause a build-up of toxic gases, as can working within a confined space	Carbon dioxide Methane Carbon monoxide	TOXIC 6
Oxidising substances. May be present in some cleaning products	Bromine Hydro peroxides Nitric acid	OXIDIZER 5.1
Combustible or flammable liquids. This can include goods with a high alcohol content	Acetone Ethanol Methane Vegetable oil	COMBUSTIBLE 3
Corrosives. Cleaning chemicals and acid-based products can be highly corrosive to human skin	Caustic soda Ammonium hydroxide Potassium hydroxide	CORROSIVE 8
Flammable solids. Solids which may easily ignite such as vegetable waste and some powders	Camphor Naphthalene	FLAMMABLE SOLID 4

Source: Courtesy of Australian Department of Infrastructure and Transport

SOURCES OF INFORMATION

If in doubt about the procedures required for handling any goods you should find out the relevant information before undertaking the task. There are five main sources of information regarding the safe handling of dangerous goods. In order, they are:

1. the material safety data sheet that accompanies the goods (MSDS)—by law, every dangerous good kept on site must have an MSDS supplied (usually by the supplier or manufacturer of the product). An MSDS covers everything from safe handling recommendations and PPE, to safe disposal and storage. They are vital resources for anyone handling dangerous goods. You can access information about MSDSs at www.msds.com.au.

2. the relevant dangerous goods standards—these fall under the WHS Acts or individual dangerous goods Acts and are accessible via the WHS authority website in your state.
3. product packaging—most dangerous goods will include basic safety information on the container in which they are originally supplied.
4. the WHS authority—this government body in your state will provide information regarding the safe use of these goods.
5. senior staff, supervisors and managers with experience—these can also offer helpful advice. However, their advice should always be compared with that of the MSDS to ensure that you are proceeding safely.

Task 8.2

Identify a dangerous substance in your workplace. List the following relevant information:

1. What is the substance known as?
2. Where is it usually stored?
3. Is the substance stored in accordance with its MSDS or manufacturer's instructions?
4. List one hazard associated with this substance.
5. What PPE should be worn when handling this substance (if any)?
6. Share this information with teammates, classmates or your trainer.

MANUAL HANDLING RISKS

Manual handling includes holding, pushing, pulling, lifting and carrying. Doing any of these tasks incorrectly can lead to injuries such as strains, overexertion, and long-term back pain. When handling items, be sure to consider:

- weight involved
- height of the task
- repetitive nature of the task
- the location (is it cramped or awkward?)
- whether there are existing handling instructions for the task.

To reduce the risks associated with manual handling, ensure that you:

- have the correct PPE. What should you be wearing to complete the task safely? Consider the use of gloves, a back brace or helmet
- have sufficient time to complete the task (don't rush)
- have adequate personnel to lift or move the object
- plan the task to take regular breaks if necessary.

This is a good time to refer to your store policy regarding manual handling. For more information, manual handling is also covered in Chapter 11, including the use of lifting, high access and heavy moving equipment.

INCIDENT REPORTING

It is a legal requirement for employers to report accidents where a worker has been injured and requires in-patient care at a hospital immediately after. In-patient care means that the person has had to be admitted to the hospital for treatment, and not simply seen in the emergency room. In the retail environment, that can include incidents such as:

- broken bones as the result of a fall or slip
- electrocution
- severe injury as a result of something falling from a shelf or rack
- cuts from box-cutting tools
- burns from fire or ice.

Workplace policies may also require staff to report *any* injury or illness at work that will affect performance or the worker's psychological state, including twisted ankles, cut fingers, bruising and light-headedness.

The responsibility for reporting the incidents will also be outlined in the policy. It could include the casualty's supervisor or store manager, witnesses to the incident and colleagues who may have witnessed the behaviour leading up to the incident.

WHAT TO DO WHEN REPORTING AN INCIDENT

It is vital that you stick to the facts only. It is very easy to make assumptions when you've witnessed something happen. It is our nature to try and figure out why things have occurred. For example, if we see a person clutch their chest and bend at the knees before collapsing, our immediate assumption is that they're having a heart attack. This, of course, is purely speculation. We are in no position to make that call. Even a trained medical practitioner would not state that the person was suffering a heart attack by merely observing these symptoms. So we should simply report what we see, and no more.

Take in as much information as you can under the circumstances. Ask yourself:

- What time is it?
- How long ago did the incident occur?
- Who was involved?
- What were the circumstances of the incident?

Read through the fields of the sample incident report over the page to familiarise yourself with the type of information you may be asked to recall. This, and other information, can then be transferred to an incident report and forwarded to the relevant person in your workplace, such as your store manager, HR (human resources representative, safety representative, supervisor, team leader or department manager.

TAKING PROMPT ACTION

When a hazardous event is identified or occurs in store it is critical to take action as soon as possible to prevent further harm to the victim or victims, onlookers or others. Rectifying the issue usually requires a higher level of action than the initial report.

INCIDENT REPORT

Complete a separate form for each incident, within three days of the incident occurring. Remember that failure to report an incident could result in someone else being put at risk in the future. This form should be used for each occasion of (tick):

☐ Injury of a customer on store premises
☐ Injury of an employee on store premises
☐ Illness identified, while on store premises, leading to medical treatment
☐ Near miss. An incident that had the potential to cause death or severe injury in the workplace
☐ Death of a person on store premises

<table>
<tr><td>Name of person completing the form:</td><td></td><td>Date of incident</td><td></td><td>Time of incident</td><td></td></tr>
<tr><td>Position title</td><td></td><td>Location</td><td></td><td colspan="2"></td></tr>
<tr><td>What was taking place when the incident occurred?</td><td colspan="5"></td></tr>
<tr><td>Other persons present at the time</td><td colspan="5"></td></tr>
<tr><td>Name/s of casualty/person involved (if known)</td><td colspan="5"></td></tr>
<tr><td>Description of event, including cause (if known)</td><td colspan="5"></td></tr>
<tr><td>Details of injuries</td><td colspan="5"></td></tr>
<tr><td>Type of first aid treatment administered (if any)</td><td></td><td>Property damaged (if any)</td><td colspan="3"></td></tr>
<tr><td>What actions did staff/volunteers take</td><td colspan="5"></td></tr>
<tr><td colspan="4">Has the incident been reported to the appropriate supervisor?</td><td>☐ Yes</td><td>☐ No</td></tr>
<tr><td colspan="4">Have staff and volunteers been provided with an opportunity to debrief and discuss the issue?</td><td>☐ Yes</td><td>☐ No</td></tr>
<tr><td colspan="6">Follow up action required:</td></tr>
<tr><td colspan="6">Signed: ____________________ Date: ____________</td></tr>
</table>

Task 8.3

INCIDENT REPORTING EXAMPLE

Brian notices a display jutting out into the aisle of his store. As he does so, a staff member walks past the display and hits her leg on the stock causing her to trip and fall over. She receives a bruised shin and complains of a pain in her wrist, when she caught herself before landing on the floor.

Brian must take action.

Firstly he deals with the hazard and the staff member quickly by going to her aid and directing another staff member to change the displayed stock around so that it does not stick out into the aisle. Brian then assists the staff member back to the office where he assesses her injuries and decides to provide first aid and light duties for the remainder of her shift.

Brian fills out an incident report with the staff member and includes a recommendation for ensuring that displays do not protrude into the walkways.

1. Did Brian do the right thing? Discuss this with your colleagues, classmates or trainer.
2. What would be different if the same injury happened in your workplace?
3. What procedures do you need to follow if you see someone injured in your workplace?

CONVEYING THE OUTCOMES

Safety is an ongoing concern in the workplace. In other words, things change and people need to be kept up to date with what changes have occurred—especially if it involves the safety of them or others. It is necessary therefore, to convey safety outcomes to co-workers from time to time in accordance with the WHS policies of your workplace. It is an obligation for employers to do so—and they may delegate the responsibility (at least in part) to you.

Ways of communicating the outcomes of incidents, hazard reports, and other safety suggestions and concerns include the following.

- safety noticeboard—staff notices and other information are often pinned to a staff noticeboard, usually located in a break room or back office. Safety notices can be highlighted on this board and rotated regularly to keep staff up to date. It is important that if this is the primary source of safety feedback, all staff are required to read the noticeboard as a part of their daily routine.
- safety meetings—scheduled staff meetings can be used to update staff on safety outcomes such as changes in procedures that may make a certain task safer.
- one-on-one contact—direct feedback can, and should, be given to people involved in the original incident or accident. This is a courtesy rather than a requirement under the law. Check your store policies with respect to this, as there may be a specific procedure for contacting customers or staff involved in a safety incident.

WHS consulting process

The state and territory legislation specifically requires the workplace health and safety process to be *consultative.* This means that you or other staff *must* have input into the health and safety of the workplace. This is in place to develop a safety culture that extends to every person working in the business. Looking out for the safety of people in the workplace should become a habit and not just another workplace task.

The consultation process may include the use of a health and safety representative.

THE IDENTIFICATION AND ASSIGNMENT OF HEALTH AND SAFETY REPRESENTATIVES (HSR)

A HSR can be elected by co-workers to represent their safety interests. If requested by an employee, the business owner must arrange for the election of the HSR under the Act.

The responsibilities of a HSR include:

- attending WHS committee meetings
- consultation on health and safety matters with management
- inspecting any part of the workplace where a member of their work group works and particularly immediately following an incident or when serious risk is identified
- accompanying a WorkSafe inspector during an inspection if requested
- attending health and safety interviews if the worker gives permission
- representing employees outside their workgroup if there is an immediate health risk
- issuing a Provisional Improvement Notice (PIN) if a safety issue is identified. This directs the employer to make improvements to the task, environment or conditions to reduce the level of risk to employees
- power to direct work to stop if there is an immediate health and safety threat
- distributing minutes from staff meetings and WHS committee meetings so that staff can become familiar with WHS processes and gain vital feedback on the progress of WHS issues
- receiving informal and formal suggestions from staff for improving tasks and procedures. Retail owners *must* act on safety suggestions from staff through a negotiation with the staff member or their elected HSR. A suggestion might prove to be an important change to a process or procedure that makes for a safer work environment. Failing to act can result in the employer and its representative (manager) facing a fine under the Act.

Due to extent of the responsibilities of the HSR, the role usually requires additional occupational health and safety training in order to understand and meet these responsibilities.

Modelling the implementation of WHS

As a proponent of a safe and healthy workplace it is among your roles to model the behaviour expected of someone working in such a workplace. This simply means 'do what you say'. By consulting, providing information and reinforcing the various store safety and emergency procedures, others will look to you to act with integrity. Integrity can be demonstrated most clearly by:

- following existing safety and emergency procedures. This may include:
  - completing hazard reports regularly
  - completing incident reports accurately
  - acting on safety concerns within an appropriate time
  - participating in the WHS process
  - keeping records in accordance with workplace policy.
- offering assistance to others with respect to WHS
- ensuring WHS policies and procedures are being followed by others
- providing opportunities for others to participate in the WHS process
- providing feedback to other team members on the outcomes of WHS issues
- identifying the need for further WHS training.

Consider how you do this now and what changes *you* could make to better model a positive workplace health and safety culture.

Participating in the WHS process

A requirement of this unit is to demonstrate your ability to participate in WHS procedures according to workplace policy. In order to demonstrate participation you will need to:

- be involved in either a group or one-on-one consultation with another worker, supervisor or manager
- actively contribute in a consultation process. *Actively contribute* means that your views, opinions, ideas and feedback are provided to the supervisor or team that you are consulting with.

It is not enough to just attend these meetings. The intention of the Act is to ensure *everyone* in the workplace is involved to actively seek out, report and rectify hazards and potential health concerns in the workplace. The assessment for this unit will require your active involvement.

IDENTIFYING THE NEED FOR WHS TRAINING

The purpose of participating in and improving upon WHS systems is to ensure that foreseeable and repeat incidents do not occur. In some industries, this goal is referred to as 'zero harm'.

Zero harm, used predominantly in the construction and mining industries, is the aim of reducing all work-related injuries and illnesses to zero, so that no worker feels unsafe in their role. You may be thinking that this is a very optimistic goal, but the proof that having such a goal improves the standard of health and safety in the workplace can clearly be presented in a report from the Queensland coal mining industry. Between 1882 and 1994, the rate of fatalities to workers was approximately one in every 1000 workers every year. In the three years from 2007–2010, that rate had dropped to less than 1 in 20 000. (This is better than the road toll that sits at approximately 1 in 10 000 drivers per year.)[3]

The single reason for this improvement is training. Training provides information and information increases awareness. In the retail industry, training can be:

- formal industry training—such as completing the Certificate III in retail through a recognised training organisation
- formal workplace training—such as receiving specific on-the-job training regarding WHS policies and procedures or
- informal learning—such as receiving and passing on information in the workplace or at a social occasion.

Deciding on what type of training is needed will depend upon the situation.

- New workers *must* receive an induction that covers basic WHS procedures and policies for the particular workplace. This is the obligation of the employer under WHS legislation.
- Workers who change work areas for example, go from working in the storeroom to working in the delicatessen, must be given training regarding the WHS procedures for the new work area, as they will undoubtedly be different.
- As a result of an incident retraining or more specific training may be required to rectify the issue and to prevent repeat incidents.

ARRANGING WHS TRAINING

Individual policies will identify what types of WHS training are used in your workplace. There may be a separate training policy, or it could be written within the business's WHS policy.

As mentioned, training may be formal or informal. Informal training can occur ad hoc, and as determined under the existing systems within the store (for example, regular safety checks for individuals or departments).

Formal workplace training can include:

- awareness training during scheduled team meetings
- systems training, for example, filling out reports and recording hazards
- induction training, both for new employees and those changing work areas
- retraining where needed.

Formal industry or accredited training can include:

- Certificate/diploma-level training
- vocational short courses run by a third party

- on-site traineeships and apprenticeships
- distance and face-to-face training.

Arranging the training may include:

- organising time off for staff or changing existing rosters so they may attend any face-to-face training
- contacting and arranging payment for external (third party) training providers
- ensuring that there is sufficient notification for staff, managers, supervisors and training providers
- ensuring that costs and provisions are in accordance with the store's policies and procedures.

Task 8.4

For this role play exercise you will need a group of three or more people. If that is not possible discuss alternatives with your trainer.

Conduct a WHS meeting to discuss current hazards or recent hazardous situations in your workplace. The meeting should follow this agenda and the outcomes should be summarised in the space provided.

WHS meeting minutes		**Date:**
Attendees (names)		
Agenda	Discussion points	Recommendations (if required)
What hazards have been identified in the last month?		
What were the outcomes associated with each hazard?		
Have there been any injuries? If so, what have been the outcomes at this point?		
Other comments		

This task consolidates the learning regarding communication of workplace hazards, reporting the hazards, acting upon the hazards and making recommendations. You will gain the best outcome by participating enthusiastically in meetings such as this.

ELEMENT 2
APPLY BASIC EMERGENCY PROCEDURES

Emergencies are incidents that occur rarely, but which have the potential to cause multiple injuries or even fatalities. Under WHS legislation, employers have an obligation to provide a safe workplace for their employees and visitors. Employers must have effective and compliant emergency procedures in place, and ensure that their staff are fully aware of their obligations, rights and responsibilities.

- 2.1 Follow fire and emergency procedures, including store evacuation, according to store policy and legislation.
- 2.2 Identify designated personnel responsible for first aid and evacuation procedures.
- 2.3 Accurately identify safety alarms.
- 2.4 Maintain WHS records

LEARNING OUTCOMES

Emergency procedures

Retail businesses operate in the public domain. That means they are subject to the workplace health and safety laws that affect everyone working in and entering their premises for any purpose. It is not possible or practical to spend time inducting everyone who enters the premises in the store's emergency procedures; however there are many other options available to you and the business to provide adequate information under your duty of care. These include:

Figure 8.3 Be aware of your evacuation routes and muster points

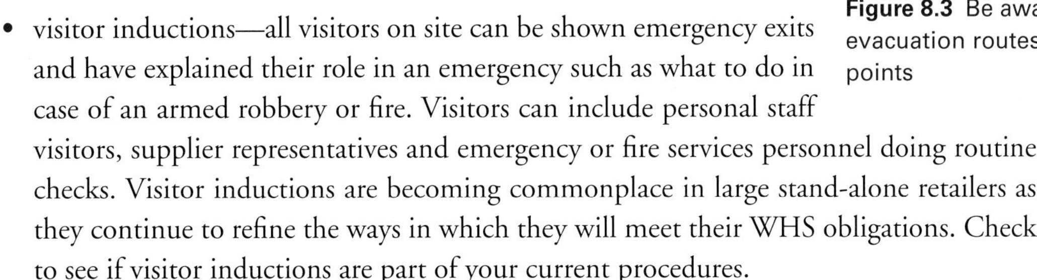

- visitor inductions—all visitors on site can be shown emergency exits and have explained their role in an emergency such as what to do in case of an armed robbery or fire. Visitors can include personal staff visitors, supplier representatives and emergency or fire services personnel doing routine checks. Visitor inductions are becoming commonplace in large stand-alone retailers as they continue to refine the ways in which they will meet their WHS obligations. Check to see if visitor inductions are part of your current procedures.
- attendance and participation in workplace meetings—the meeting forum can be an excellent opportunity to share and be shown current emergency procedures and to update information if changes have occurred.
- calmly explaining emergency procedures to customers in the event of an emergency—you are similar to an airline flight attendant in that you are the person customers may look to in an emergency to lead them through the process as calmly as possible. Panicking in an emergency will cause further distress to others and should be avoided.
- ensure that signage and emergency equipment is current and accurate—there are several requirements under building and fire codes for the position, number and location of

emergency exit signs, evacuation plans, fire extinguishers and first aid cabinets. If the signage is damaged, inaccurate (perhaps the floor plan has changed but the emergency plan hasn't), or equipment is not serviceable (fire extinguishers have not been checked and the first aid kit is half empty) you are potentially putting people in danger. Having these things in good order can allow customers, visitors and co-workers to access and interpret them correctly.

DEFINING EMERGENCY PROCEDURES

Emergency procedures are specific procedures over and above the basic safety procedures, such as hazard reporting and WHS consultation. Emergency procedures are designed to deal with unusual and drastic circumstances. Essentially, these procedures include those for fire, earthquakes, floods, cyclones and other natural disasters, bomb threats and armed robberies.

These events are identified as emergencies as they are not regular occurrences and are, in all cases, undesirable. So let's look at how you can become familiar with each procedure and what you should do under your duty of care for those you work with and who may enter your store during any given day.

FIRE EVACUATION

Having a compliant fire evacuation procedure is a legislative requirement for all 'bricks and mortar' businesses in every state and territory in Australia. Retailers operating online businesses will also need to maintain a fire evacuation procedure for their offices and storage or warehousing facilities. Fire evacuation plans include the fire evacuation diagram (to be located in clear view around the premises in specified locations) and a procedure that includes:

- building owner information
- the person or company responsible for administering the fire safety plan
- contact details for the fire safety advisor
- evacuation coordinators or wardens and the dates they were appointed
- written description of the evacuation procedure, including fire fighting and muster point details
- records of evacuation practices and fire training.

The fire evacuation diagram may also be used for other evacuations, such as gas leaks or earthquakes. It *must* include and easily identify the following basic information:

- exits
- accurate plan view of the premises
- emergency muster points
- evacuation route/s
- fire extinguishers, hoses and fire blankets (type and location)
- fire alarm locations (manual call points)
- other relevant information for that location.

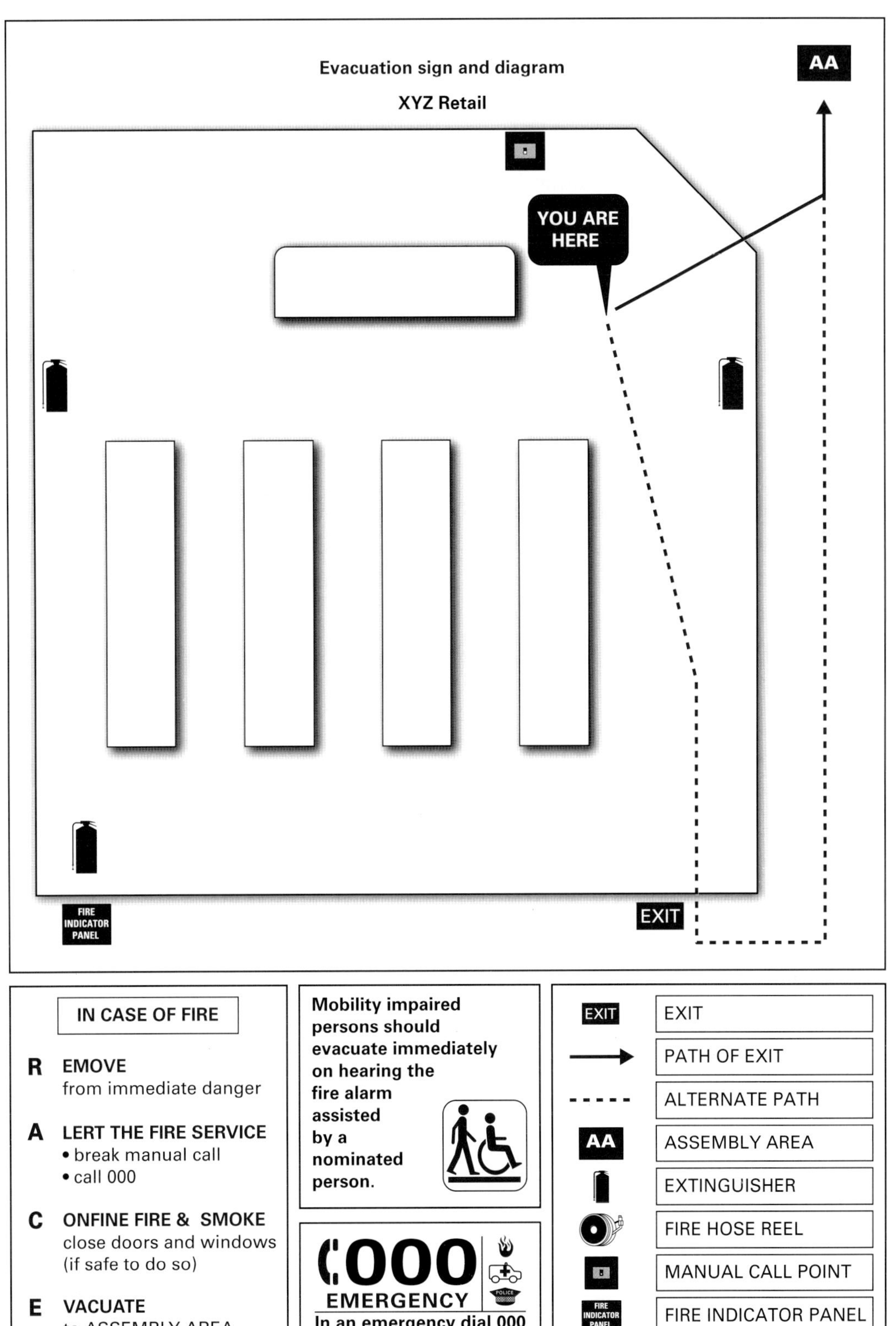

Figure 8.4 Evacuation sign and diagram

Fire safety

Fire safety for public premises is often regulated in accordance with the Australian Standard AS 3745. Some of the basic requirements for the building owner or operator under this standard include:

- appointing an emergency planning committee (for large workplaces)
- establishing an emergency control organisation (for large workplaces)
- preparing emergency plans and procedures (all properties). Emergency plans must show a floor plan of the store with the viewer's location, plus the evacuation route and muster point in the event of an emergency
- establishing roles for key personnel (all properties). The roles of workers in an emergency need to be understood, such as the fire or emergency warden
- establishing education and training requirements (all properties). Fire evacuation practice drills should be held on a regular basis (usually annually, depending on the facility).

Retailers residing in a managed facility like a shopping centre or shopping strip will have access to the building owner's safety procedures that should, in most cases, cover these requirements. Stand-alone retail outlets will need to be compliant depending on the size of the building and number of employees.

Fire services recommend this checklist to assist your small business in preventing damage that could be caused by fire:

- avoid storing or stockpiling flammable materials such as packaging materials or waste where they could be accessed by the public, including areas immediately outside your business premises
- make sure that all equipment is serviced as recommended by manufacturers and is kept clean. If possible, switch the equipment off when the business is unattended
- secure all doors, windows or other access points when the business is unattended, and make sure your business has adequate lighting to deter trespassers
- ensure that your business has an adequately serviced and functional fire alarm system that is suitable to your small business, for example remote-serviced alarm systems, sprinkler systems, or thermal or smoke alarms.
- store and use any dangerous goods in adherence to legislative requirements
- have a written and practised fire escape plan that includes full staff lists and designated meeting points.[4]

Useful websites:

Fire & Rescue NSW

www.fire.nsw.gov.au/page.php?id=73

Building Fire Safety Regulation 2008

www.legislation.qld.gov.au/LEGISLTN/CURRENT/B/BuildingFireSR08.pdf

Fire alarms

A fire emergency can be raised in two ways. First, upon seeing a fire you should yell out 'Fire, fire, fire!' This immediately warns those people within the vicinity that a fire is in progress. If someone yells out, human nature is to be inquisitive so people will usually stop to hear what is going on. Yelling out 'Fire' three times gives people the opportunity to firstly direct their attention towards the yelling—*then* to understand what is being said. Some workplaces do not use this first warning as it may cause panic in busy malls and centres, so be sure to find out what your specific process is.

Secondly, you need to locate and activate the alarm. This is denoted on the fire diagram as the 'manual call point'. Note that it is an offence to unnecessarily interfere with fire safety equipment, including the alarm, so only activate the alarm if there is a fire hazard or excess smoke that you believe is caused by fire.

In Australia, the evacuation alarm sound is described as a 'Slow woop woop'. Smoke alarms may also activate. They are usually a high-pitched and very loud 'slow beep'. You need to be aware of both of these sounds and react according to your workplace fire evacuation plan.

Next, you should attempt to contain the fire. If the fire is small, in most workplaces you may be required to use a fire extinguisher to put it out. If the fire is aggressively growing, it is always safer to evacuate and close any windows and doors on your way out. This reduces the amount of oxygen the fire can use.

Fire extinguishers

There are several common fire extinguishers used in public buildings. There are also more specialised extinguishers for industrial and commercial use. Each extinguisher is designed to put out a fire by removing the oxygen, heat or fuel. In the information provided in Figure 8.5, the water extinguisher removes the heat, while the foam, CO_2 and dry chemical extinguishers all smother the fire and therefore starve it of oxygen.

You must be able to use a fire extinguisher in an emergency. Regular fire training can be provided by your retailer or the store's landlord (shopping centre owners), however, you may need to know the information sooner. Here are some important pointers to remember under the mnemonic **IPASS**:

Inspect the extinguisher to ensure that it suits the purpose
Pull the pin
Aim at the base of the fire
Squeeze the trigger
Sweep from side to side.

Only fight fires you are confident you can put out. In all cases, refer to your in-store emergency procedures and never use an extinguisher for any other purpose than for fighting a fire.

I	Identify the right extinguisher for the fire. They include:

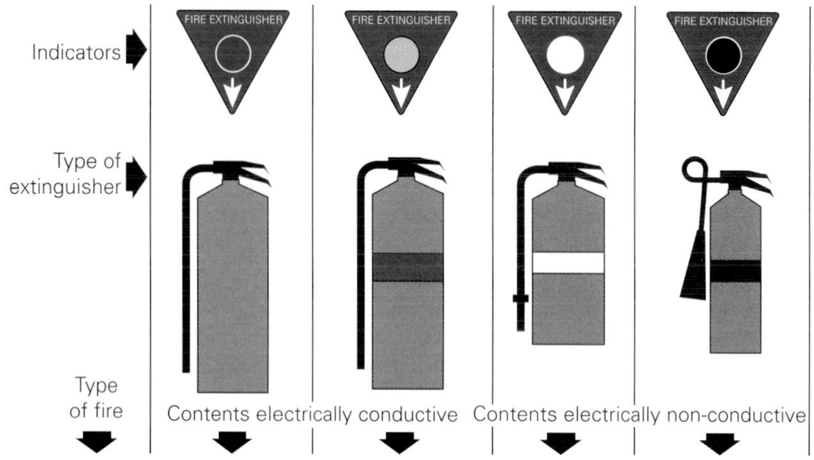

Indicators / Type of extinguisher / Type of fire	Contents electrically conductive		Contents electrically non-conductive	
	Water	Foam	Dry Chemical	CO_2
Ordinary combustibles wood, paper, etc	YES	YES	YES	YES
Flammable liquids	NO	YES	YES	YES
Flammable gases	NO	NO	YES	YES
Live electrical equipment	NO	NO	YES	YES

P	Pull the pin on the extinguisher
A	Aim it at the base of the fire
S	Squeeze the handle (trigger)
S	Sweep across the width of the fire

Figure 8.5 Extinguishers

More information:

Basic extinguisher training excerpt

www.youtube.com/watch?v=XQrdZG0cNUs

FIRST AID

All states and territories have regulations or codes of practice relating to first aid. These fall under the work health and safety legislation, so some codes and regulations are pending due to recent national changes. The codes of practice do (or will) outline the following:

- contents of first aid kits for workplaces depending on level of risk
- requirements for access to a person with a first aid qualification
- contents of a first aid room if the workplace meets the criteria for including such
- managing the risk of exposure to biological hazards from blood, disease or body substance.

First aid training is compulsory for many workers around the country. In the retail sector employers may select people or positions for which a first aid qualification is required. However, it is the employer's duty to ensure all staff have access to a qualified first aider. In shopping centres or retail strips this responsibility may be shared between a few shops or with the centre management. Larger shopping centres may choose to have qualified medical staff on hand. The key requirement is that they are accessible in an emergency.

The time spent waiting for a first aider might be the difference between life and death. You may wish to consider the cost and benefits of gaining a first aid qualification if you do not already have one.

Useful website:

DRSABCD first aid demonstration

www.youtube.com/watch?v=Pe4CmkJ4Jqk

EARTHQUAKE AND NATURAL DISASTER PROCEDURES

Australia and New Zealand have shared many natural disasters over the last few years including devastating floods in Queensland and northern NSW, bushfires in Victoria and Western Australia, and of course the devastating earthquakes in Christchurch. Retail businesses can do little or nothing to prevent these disasters occurring, but having a procedure in place in the event of such an occurrence can help staff and customers deal with the event more readily.

A disaster plan is similar to a fire evacuation plan and is often contained in the same documentation. The plan will include:

- muster points for assembly after the emergency is made known
- instructions for what to do and what *not* to do in the emergency (for example, during a cyclone, stay inside and turn off all electrical appliances)
- procedures and pathways for evacuating the premises safely
- roles for staff such as warden (the person who coordinates the people throughout the evacuation and at the assembly point) and first aider (a trained emergency caregiver to injured people)
- contact details for SES (State Emergency Services) and public emergency services such as police, fire and ambulance.

Task 8.5

Take a moment to identify the key areas, responsibilities and alarms in your workplace. Review the list above and write down the information below:

1. Location of my muster point ___________________________
2. Location of my emergency exits ______________________
3. The fire warden for our business _____________________
4. The local SES phone number ________________________
5. Who can provide first aid? __________________________
6. What does the fire alarm sound like? __________________
7. What is one thing I should *not* do in the event of an earthquake, cyclone or fire? _____ ___________________________________

BOMB THREATS AND ARMED ROBBERY

Unfortunately, bomb threats and armed robbery are realities in our society. The motives can range from an ill-conceived prank to genuine terrorism. If you are the recipient of a bomb threat either by telephone or written message, how would you handle it and what should you do? If an armed robber threatens you, what do you need to know?

These questions should be answered in an emergency procedures document. Businesses can have posters with checklists near telephone points or may have the procedure detailed in the store's safety policy. An example of a bomb threat checklist is provided in Table 8.5.

Table 8.5

Bomb threat checklist	
1. Stay calm	Take a deep breath and remain as calm as you can
2. Do not joke or threaten the caller	The caller may be very serious and this is not helpful
3. Write down as much information as the caller gives you	This can include their sex, approximate age (young, middle-aged), accent, background noises, key phrases they may use
4. Question the caller	• What is the threat? • When is the threat to be carried out? • Where is the threat located? • Why is the threat being made?
5. Keep the caller on the line	They may provide additional information which can help the police
6. DO NOT HANG UP	The call may be traced even if the caller has hung up
7. Alert your supervisor	If your supervisor is not available, call the police on a separate line if possible (ring 000)

For armed robbery events, your first consideration should be your safety and that of other customers and staff. You should never try to defend yourself against an armed robber, nor should you argue with or prevent the armed robber from gaining access to the store's merchandise or cash. Consider the following information regarding prevention and dealing with armed robbery.

Prevention

- Is your store an easy target? For example, is there easy access to an escape path such as a back alleyway or side street?
- Do you keep cash on the premises in large sums? Consider electronic payment methods as an alternative.
- Do you have well-signed and active security monitoring equipment? Detectors, CCTV cameras and motion sensors are commonplace in most retail outlets.
- Do you acknowledge everyone who enters your store? This can help you to identify potential robbers and even deter thieves, as they are aware that you have made a facial identification.

In the event of a robbery

- Try to remain calm
- If your store is fitted with an emergency alarm system, try to activate it, but only if safe to do so
- Do not enter into a conversation with the offender—simply answer their questions or demands quickly and without emotion
- Avoid direct eye contact—an armed robber may defend their identity with violence
- Take in as much information as you can about the event:
    - the offender's clothing, accent, age and height
    - the direction they left the premises
    - any specific information they divulged
    - if they leave in a vehicle, take down the registration number if you can.

These checklists and procedures should form part of a retail staff member's induction and training. See the example prepared by the Victorian Police Department for small business security by downloading the pdf (portable document file) in the 'More information' box below.

Useful Websites:

Australian Retailers Association—Free resources for retailers

www.retail.org.au/index.php/ara-article/Free_resources

Victorian Police bomb threat and other emergency checklist

www.police.vic.gov.au/retrievemedia.asp?Media_ID=11243

Maintaining WHS records

Safety and health can best be managed when hazards are known and controls are put in place. Without the benefit of historical records there is a higher chance of repeating mistakes or accidents. A well-maintained, accurate and accessible record system will help you and others to continuously improve the safety standards of your workplace.

Information from the records should be easily accessible to ensure that the risk control procedures in store are working and that hazards are being controlled within a reasonable time. The following are some ways in which this can be achieved.

1. Safety database—this is a computerised record of incidents. The benefit of using a computer database is that not only can you search for information more easily, but incidents and accidents can be easily categorised in order to assist the store manager, HSR or other stakeholders in better managing future risks.
2. Incident and accident register—this is a computerised *or* hard copy file of all the incidents and accidents in the workplace. They are usually sorted by date, allowing investigators and interested parties to access relevant information as it happened, and to review the improvement in safety over time.
3. Safety audits—regular audits can ensure the safety records are up to date, accessible and accurate. Safety audits usually involve the WHS processes and procedures for the entire store. Record keeping is one aspect of that.

Endnotes

1. *Lusk & Anor v Sapwell* [2011] QCA 059, Muir JA, Margaret Wilson AJA and Ann Lyons J, 1 April 2011.
2. WorkCover NSW, www.workcover.nsw.gov.au/healthsafety/healthsafetytopics/dangerousgoods/Pages/default.aspx.
3. 'Fatalities in Queensland Coal Mines 1882–2010', The State of Qld, Dept. of Employment, Economic Development and Innovation (2010).
4. www.fire.nsw.gov.au/page.php?id=73.

ASSESSMENT 1: REVIEW QUESTIONS

1. We use the hierarchy of risk controls to determine the most practicable control measure for reducing risk. What are the five levels of control? Provide an example of each for the following scenario:
   Overhanging signage in aisle two is currently held up by string and bulldog clamps. The string on one sign has recently broken, sending the sign crashing down onto a customer's head.
2. Complete an incident report for the above incident with the information you have available. Use today's date and time. Use the incident form provided in Chapter 8.
3. What type of fire extinguisher would you use on an electrical fire involving your POS computer? Why?
4. Describe three ways you could model WHS procedures in your workplace.
5. Conduct a hazard identification and risk assessment on the scenario illustrated in Figure 8.6. (Use the form layout provided on page p. 246.)

Figure 8.6 A hazardous situation

6. What hazards do the following symbols represent?

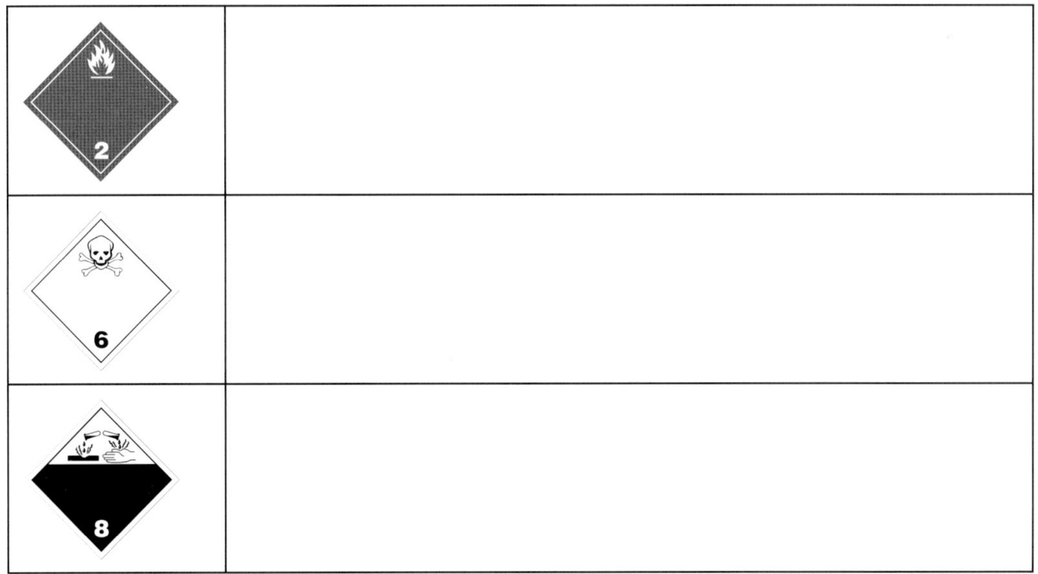

7. What is the name and common abbreviation of the document provided by manufacturers regarding the use and handling of a dangerous substance? What sort of information might you find in one (provide at least three examples)?
8. Which of the following is a hazardous substance? Why? Where could you store this item safely?
   a. Toothpaste
   b. Fly spray
   c. Used cleaning rag.
9. What are the five activities that can be considered 'manual handling'? Choose one from your list and describe how you would approach the activity safely. (For example, What would you wear? How would you do it? What else might you need to take into account?)
10. Draw a map of the emergency evacuation plan for your workplace (or the training facility). In the map, you must include:
    - emergency exits (all of them)
    - personal call box (alarm box)
    - exit path (dotted line)
    - emergency muster point
    - first aid cabinet or kit.
11. What is the name of the *current* state or territory WHS legislation for your store's location? What website could you go to in order to access this legislation?
12. Explain to your teammates how you would regularly provide accurate information on identified hazards and risk controls.
13. Explain how waste is disposed of in your current or previous workplace. What is one benefit of correctly disposing of waste?
14. Explain your responsibilities and the actions you would take in the following emergencies:
    a. You receive a telephone bomb threat.
    b. An armed assailant enters your premises.
    c. A small fire starts in a waste paper bin.

ASSESSMENT 2

Assessment instructions	**WHS meeting: role play** Conduct a meeting following the attached agenda. The meeting can be conducted in a real work environment, or as a role play in a simulated environment. Agenda 1. Explanation of the site fire evacuation procedure and where to find the information when on site (i.e. site diagram). 2. Conduct an emergency evacuation (you must physically lead the team through the evacuation procedure). 3. Explanation of what legislation and codes of practice this process aligns with. 4. Feedback from attendees about gaps in their WHS knowledge. What training would they each benefit from? 5. Explanation of how training might be organised for each team member. Be sure to take notes in the meeting as these will be used as evidence.
Evidence required	• Facilitator observation checklist • Minutes or notes from the meeting detailing the discussions for each agenda item.
Range and conditions	• Your meeting should take approximately 20–30 minutes • You must ensure that each member of the team has input.
Materials and resources required	• Minute pad or notepad and other relevant stationery • Access to a meeting facility • Access to site evacuation plan.
Assessor intervention	Your assessor will go through the assessment instructions with the class prior to commencement. You may ask questions at any point during the completion of the assignment prior to submission.
Reasonable adjustments	In the event that you have difficulty understanding the assessment tasks due to language or other difficulties, your trainer will attempt to make reasonable adjustments to the assessment paper in order to afford you every opportunity to achieve competency.
Decision-making rules	The facilitator guide on the McGraw Hill website provides benchmark answers and check lists.

ASSESSMENT 3

Assessment instructions	**Hazardous event: role play** There has just been a hazardous event in your workplace involving the spillage of a flammable liquid on the pants and shoes of a colleague. Your colleague had placed the liquid container on the floor while working, but accidentally left the lid off. They then kicked the bottle over, spilling the liquid on the floor and over their clothing. You are a witness and must now act in accordance with your workplace policy. The following steps *must* be demonstrated. 1. Take prompt action to deal with the event. 2. Complete an incident report. 3. Provide feedback to the employee on your recommendations to ensure that the incident does not recur.
Evidence required	• Facilitator observation checklist • Correctly completed incident report (as per the template from this chapter).
Range and conditions	• IMPORTANT—the spill is simulated only. DO NOT use a real flammable liquid in this assessment. Water can be a substitute for added realism • The event should take approximately five–ten minutes to deal with • Your report can then be done within a reasonable time following the incident (no more than one hour) • The incident can be conducted in the workplace or in a simulated environment.
Materials and resources required	• Copy of the incident report template from the McGraw Hill website.
Assessor intervention	Your assessor will go through the assessment instructions with the class prior to commencement. You may ask questions at any point during the completion of the assessment prior to submission of the incident report.
Reasonable adjustments	In the event that you have difficulty understanding the assessment tasks due to language or other difficulties, your trainer will attempt to make reasonable adjustments to the assessment paper in order to afford you every opportunity to achieve competency.
Decision-making rules	The facilitator guide on the McGraw Hill website provides benchmark answers and checklists.

COMPETENCY MAPPING

Element and performance criteria		Task	Assessment	Refer to page
1.1	Follow safety procedures to achieve a safe work environment, according to all relevant WHS legislation, including codes of practice relating to particular hazards in the industry or workplace.	8.1	1, 2	244–246
1.2	Identify and report unsafe work practices, including faulty plant and equipment according to store policy and procedures.	8.1	1, 2	246–247
1.3	Manage dangerous goods and substances according to store policy and relevant legislation.	8.2	1	247, 251–253
1.4	Identify potential manual handling risks and manage manual handling tasks according to store policy.	8.1	1	253
1.5	Report work-related incidents and accidents to designated personnel.	8.2, 8.3	1	254–256
1.6	Participate in consultative processes and procedures for WHS.	8.4	2	257–259
2.1	Follow fire and emergency procedures, including store evacuation, according to store policy and legislation.	8.5	1, 2	261–266
2.2	Identify designated personnel responsible for first aid and evacuation procedures.			267
2.3	Accurately identify safety alarms.			264, 265

Element and performance criteria		Task	Assessment	Refer to page
1.1	Clearly and accurately explain store policy and procedures in regard to WHS and emergency procedures to team members.	8.3	2	261
1.2	Ensure access for team members to store WHS policy and procedures.	8.4	2	249–251
1.3	Clearly and accurately explain relevant provisions of WHS legislation and codes of practice to team members.	8.4	2	260
1.4	Regularly provide clear and accurate information on identified hazards and risk control procedures to team members.	8.2	1, 2	246, 250–251
1.5	Model the implementation of WHS and emergency procedures to reinforce information.	8.3	1, 2	257
2.1	Provide opportunities and processes for team members to consult and contribute on WHS issues according to store policy.	8.2, 8.4	2	257–259

continued

Element and performance criteria		Task	Assessment	Refer to page
2.2	Promptly resolve issues raised or refer to relevant personnel according to store policy.	8.3, 8.4	2	245–251
2.3	Promptly convey outcomes of issues raised on WHS matters to team members.	8.4	2	249–250, 256–257
3.1	Implement store policy and procedures with regard to identifying, preventing and reporting potential hazards.	8.1	1, 3	246
3.2	Take prompt action to deal with hazardous events according to store policy.	8.4	2, 3	247–249
3.3	Investigate unsafe or hazardous events, identify cause, and report inadequacies in risk control measures or resource allocation for risk control to relevant personnel.	8.1, 8.2	3	249–251
3.4	Implement and monitor control measures to prevent recurrence and minimise risks of unsafe and hazardous events according to store policy and hierarchy of control.	8.4	3	247
3.5	Handle and store hazardous goods according to store policy and WHS regulations.	8.2	3	251–253
3.6	Maintain equipment according to store policy and WHS regulations.		2, 3	251
3.7	Monitor team performance to ensure use of safe manual handling techniques.	10.1		253–254
3.8	Implement store emergency policy and procedures promptly in the event of an emergency	8.4		257–259
4.1	Identify WHS training needs, specifying gaps between WHS competencies required and those held by team members.	8.4	2, 3	259–260
4.2	Organise and arrange training according to store policy.			259–260
5.1	Complete and maintain WHS records regarding occupational injury and disease according to store policy and legislative requirements.	8.2, 8.4	2, 3	247, 270
5.2	Use information from records to identify hazards and monitor risk control procedures according to store policy.	8.4, 8.5	2, 3	247, 270

Required skills and knowledge	Task	Assessment	Refer to page
Required skills:			
Communication and interpersonal skills to:	8.1	2, 3	246, 247, 249, 258–260
• report unsafe work practices, faulty plant and equipment and incidents and accidents through clear and direct communication			
• share information		2, 3	
• use and interpret non-verbal communication	8.4	1, 2, 3	
Literacy and numeracy skills to:	8.2	3	247–253
• estimate weights, size, quantities and mixtures			
• interpret symbols used for WHS signage	8.5	1	
• read and interpret instructions	8.1, 8.2, 8.3, 8.4, 8.5	1, 2, 3	246, 255–256, 263
Technical skills to:	8.4	1	251
• identify broken or damaged equipment			
• identify hazardous goods and substances	8.2	1	252
• locate and use safety alarms, fire extinguishers, and emergency exits	8.5	2	261–266
• dispose of waste appropriately	8.1	1	
• handle broken or damaged equipment	8.1, 8.4	1	251, 253
• identify hazardous goods and substances	8.2	1	252
• locate and identify emergency exits and use safety alarms and fire extinguishers	8.5	1, 2	263
• store and use chemicals and hazardous substances	8.2	1, 2, 3	252
• use personal protective gear and equipment	8.2	3	253
• report unsafe work practices, faulty plant and equipment and incidents and accidents through clear and direct communication	8.1, 8.4	2, 3	252–253

continued

Required skills and knowledge	Task	Assessment	Refer to page
Required knowledge:			
Strategies for controlling risks through the hierarchy of control, including:	8.2	1, 3	247–248
• appropriate use of personal protective clothing			
• eliminating hazards	8.1, 8.4		
• isolating hazards	8.3		
• using administrative controls	8.1		
• using engineering controls	8.1		
• first aid procedures	8.5		
Identification of hazards in the workplace, including:	8.1	1, 3	245–246, 249, 251
• fire, chemical and electrical hazards			
• managing broken or faulty equipment	8.1, 8.4		
• slip, trips and falls	8.1		
• spills and leakage of materials	8.1		
• storage of dangerous goods and hazardous substances	8.1		
• waste	8.1		
Hierarchy of risk control:	8.1, 8.5	1, 2, 3	247–248
• elimination of hazards			
• engineering controls to reduce risk			
• administrative controls			
• use of personal protective equipment			
Job role and responsibilities	8.3	1, 2, 3	241–243
Location of nearest first aid assistant or facility	8.5	2	267
Manual handling and safe lifting techniques	10.1	1	253
Possible fire and safety hazards	8.1	2	246, 252
Principles and techniques in interpersonal communication	8.4	2, 3	249–251, 256
Relevant WHS legislation and codes of practice		1, 2	243–244
Sickness and accident procedures	8.1	3	254–255
Store policies and procedures in regard to:	10.1	1	253
• manual handling			
• WHS emergency procedures	8.5	2	254–255, 261
• unsafe or hazardous goods	8.2	1	252
• handling and storage	8.2	1	253

Required skills and knowledge	Task	Assessment	Refer to page
Required knowledge:			
• disposal		1	252–253
• bomb threat procedures		1	261
• store evacuation		1	263
Management of WHS, including:	8.4	2, 3	256–258
• communication and consultation processes			
• interpreting symbols for WHS signage	8.2	1	252
• manual handling procedures	10.1	1	253
• reporting procedures	8.1, 8.4	1, 2	246, 254–255
Store policies and procedures in regard to:	8.5	1, 2, 3	268–270
• rights and responsibilities of designated personnel responsible for health and safety in the workplace			
• WHS emergency procedures		1, 2, 3	261–270
• relevant industry codes of practice		1, 2	243, 252
• state and territory legislation and regulations		1, 2	243–244
Critical aspects for assessment and evidence			
Applies safe work practices, in all areas of the store, according to WHS and codes of practice	8.1, 8.2, 8.4, 8.5	1, 2, 3	243–270
Applies appropriate store policies and procedures and legislative requirements in regard to following basic safety procedures and reports faults and problems to relevant person, department or committee	8.1, 8.4	1, 2, 3	243, 250–253
Identifies hazardous situations and rectifies where appropriate, or reports to the relevant personnel according to store policy and procedures	8.2	1, 2, 3	246–255
Reads, interprets and applies manufacturer instructions for using and storing hazardous goods	8.2	1	252–253
Applies store policies and procedures with regard to emergency situations, evacuation, or accident and illness in the store.	8.1, 8.3, 8.5	1, 2	254–255, 270

Chapter 9

SIRXFIN201

Balance and secure point-of-sale terminal

In retail, the **point-of-sale (POS)** terminal is where the transaction for goods or services is completed. This area has undergone significant changes over the last thirty years with the introduction of more streamlined technologies and higher security measures to assist both the store and its customers in meeting their needs.

In an online environment, the point-of-sale is usually represented by the shopping cart's checkout facility. Like a traditional terminal, the checkout facility must be secure and easy to interact with. Online vendors have the added threat of hackers to consider when developing their security protocols.

In this chapter, we will cover the general approaches to balancing and securing a POS terminal in a bricks and mortar retail outlet, as well as the common approaches used in online checkouts. As the technologies vary to such a great degree, we will use several examples to illustrate how the basic theory is put into practice.

ELEMENT 1

BALANCE AND SECURE TAKINGS FROM A REGISTER OR TERMINAL AND RECONCILE TAKINGS

Cash and other transactions at the POS terminal must balance at the end of your shift or the day's trading. Additionally, cash must be secured and transaction details must be accessed (often printed out).

LEARNING OUTCOMES

- 1.1 Perform register or terminal balance at designated times according to the store policy and procedures.
- 1.2 Separate cash float from takings prior to balancing procedure and secure according to store policy.
- 1.3 Supply change to register or terminal according to store policy.
- 1.4 Obtain and interpret register or terminal reading or printout.

1.5	Secure cash and non-cash documents according to store policy and procedures.
1.6	Count cash accurately.
1.7	Calculate non-cash documents accurately.
1.8	Determine balance between register reading and sum of cash and non-cash transactions.
1.9	Report discrepancies to relevant personnel.
1.10	Record store and individual department takings and file records according to store policy.

Perform register or terminal balance

From a management perspective, retailers must be in control of the cash that flows in and out of their business at any given time. In general, most of the business's cash and credit or debit transactions occur at the POS terminal: taking money from customers, giving the correct change, providing their tax receipt and ensuring that credit transfers have occurred correctly are all part of the terminal operator's duties. In addition, at this level you will also need to have a clear understanding of the procedures covering the register's use, including basic error corrections and end-of-shift balancing processes.

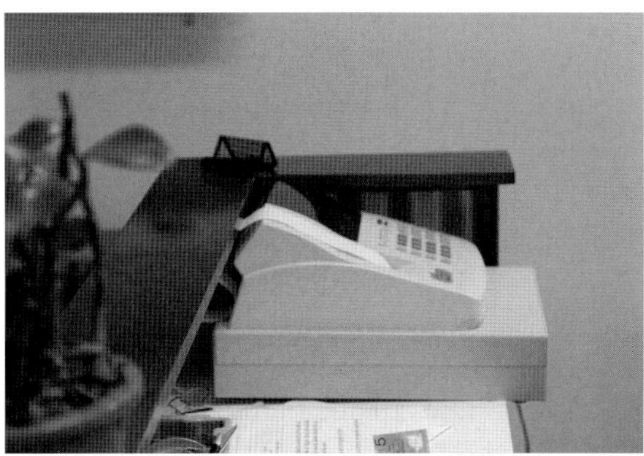

Figure 9.1 Small retail POS register

Balancing procedures vary in accordance with the accounting processes and cash management systems of the business. Accounting for the income and errors in cash handling is a requirement for all business owners. This leads to the development of effective cash management systems in line with the business's operational policies. As you will be involved in the handling, securing and frontline accounting of the retailer's income, you should be familiar with these systems and policies.

These systems and policies can include:

- cash handling
- register and terminal balance procedures
- store security policy.

It is very important that you ask your trainer, manager or supervisor to run through any specific policies if they have not already done so.

At the end of your shift or at the end of day, you may be called upon to complete the cash register consolidation. This is just another term for balancing or finalising the takings for that terminal at that time. One method is to complete a 'daily sales record'. The daily sales record (also referred to as the 'daily register report' or 'cash drawer report') allows you to summarise the information that is stored on the register and check it against the actual cash takings.

Take a look at the information in the sample below. You can see how the information takes all the cash and other transactions conducted during the day in the top part, and compares it to any refunds, voided transactions, and other sums paid out from the register, leaving a net amount that should equal the amount of money on the register reading. This information is used by the person or people responsible for accounting and forms a part of the business's cash flow records. More on this reconciliation process later in the chapter.

DAILY SALES RECORD

Cashier

_______________________ Date ________ Time ________

Cash (from cash count form)	$ ________
Cheques	$ ________
MasterCard	$ ________
Visa	$ ________
Diners/AMEX	$ ________
Store credit	$ ________
Other (Gift Cards etc)	$ ________
Starting float (subtract this amount)	$ ________
Deposit Total	$ ________
Returns	$ ________
Voids	$ ________
Paid Outs	$ ________
Other	$ ________
Total cash paid out	$ ________
Add Deposit Total & Total Cash Paid Out	$ ________
GST collected	$ ________
Register reading	$ ________
Difference (–/+)	$ ________

Figure 9.2 Daily sales record

Counting the cash

A standard way of counting cash is by denomination. Denominations are the various notes and coins recognised as currency in Australia. This also gives you the chance to report any foreign currency that may have made its way into the register through mishandling or a simple mistake. Denominations in Australia are currently 5 cents up to $2 in coins, and $5 up to $100 in notes. New Zealand currency is very similar in size to many Australian coins but its value is different. Be sure to segregate any non-Australian currency in the register and report it to your supervisor or manager.

A cash form may be used to assist you in counting the cash. For obvious reasons, it is important that the count is correct, so the use of these forms is often mandatory. Business may choose to incorporate the cash count form and the daily sales record into a single 'cash reconciliation form'. Regardless of the exact format, the intention of using these forms is the same—to ensure that the business's income is monitored and recorded correctly.

CASH COUNT

Cash on hand as at:
Time:
Date:

5c × ____ = ______
10c × ____ = ______
20c × ____ = ______
50c × ____ = ______
$1 × ____ = ______
$2 × ____ = ______

Figure 9.3 Cash count

Task 9.1

Counting cash

For this activity, you will need access to the float of a cash drawer, or a known sum of cash that includes at least one of each Australian denomination.

There are several techniques to accurately counting cash. The most accurate way is to use a counting device of some type (see www.vfj.com.au/ for some commercial examples). But if you need to count manually, here are some steps to improve your accuracy.

1. Ensure that the cash is sorted into the correct denominations before you start.
2. Start with the highest denomination and enter the quantity and total on the cash count sheet (you can take a copy of the example above). Repeat for all note denominations.
3. When you get to the coins, ensure that you are on a flat surface without a raised edge, like a counter or table top with no edging.
4. Hold your non-primary hand (left or right hand) below the lip of the surface.
5. Count the coins from each denomination into your hand using one or two fingers from your primary hand.
6. Stack each set of coins into easily counted totals of say ten or twenty coins.
7. Immediately record the total of each denomination as soon as you have finished stacking it.
8. Total the cash count sheet.

This may seem quite simple but, as we've determined, accuracy is key to profitability. Errors tend to pile up and cause larger problems down the line. Ask yourself if you have ever made an error counting anything before. Chances are you have—we all have! So take your time and ensure that the count is accurate.

Separating the cash float

A cash float is the amount of money present in the register till prior to trading. This amount is determined by the amount of trade that is expected to go through the register terminal during the day (or shift) and can range from as little as $100 up to thousands of dollars. For security purposes and as a theft minimisation strategy, most retailers keep the float at a minimum level to ensure that customers can receive the correct change when required, while maintaining a small amount in the till in the case of theft or burglary.

The cash float must be counted out first in order to accurately count the day's takings. Counting the float would incorrectly inflate the income for the store and could lead to accounting issues such as taxation mismatches and reporting anomalies.

Specialist staff may be appointed to 'top up' the float during the day. Front of shop managers (also referred to as line managers, register supervisors or cashier supervisors) often take the responsibility for opening, closing and topping up the registers. Alternatively, their position may require them to train the cashiers and sales staff to both use the registers and perform these actions on their own.

Topping up the float may occur in two ways. First, the float in the register is added to by some amount, say $20, in the denominations most required at that time, say $2 and $1 coins. This amount is noted on the register by 'adding' it as an electronic register function, or by simply writing a note and leaving it in a prescribed place in the cash drawer. Second, the float may simply be lacking in certain denominations—again, let's say $1 and $2 coins. You may decide to simply exchange a $20 note for more of the required denominations. This, in most retail operations, would not require any documentation; however some retailers do keep track of the various denominations and as such you would need to be aware of what process you may need to follow.

Registers may also be cleared at regular intervals throughout the day. This is to ensure that:

- the registers don't become overloaded with notes and coins
- the effects of burglary and theft are minimised
- burglary and theft are deterred.

When a register is cleared, the cash float is separated from the takings and replaced in the cash drawer. The remainder is sent to the cash office for reconciliation, storage and banking. (A cash office is a secured office location on the premises.)

Counting non-cash transactions

In today's world more and more transactions are occurring electronically. Electronic funds transfers at point of sale (EFTPOS) are a very popular form of transacting a small to medium dollar value purchase. In fact, over two billion EFTPOS transactions occurred in the twelve months to June 2011 (www.eftpospayments.com.au/) in Australia. EFTPOS and electronic credit card transactions are both considered here.

Among the purposes of electronic transactions are:

- personal financial security for the customer
- limiting fraud
- reducing time at POS—therefore reducing costs
- ease of use for the customer
- ease of reporting for the retailer.

After the cash component is separated from the list of transactions, how do you count the electronic transactions? Electronic transactions are intended to make things better and easier: one area where we can immediately see this is in the balancing of the cash drawer. Electronic transactions occur in 'real time'. That means that, like cash, the customer is handing over their money at the point of sale—only this time it is in ones and zeros (digitally). This means that the register records the transaction accurately in almost every circumstance. The only time this may not occur is if the system is not operating correctly for some reason.

Therefore, non-cash electronic transactions will be calculated correctly by the register and reported in the daily printout. You will simply need to transcribe what the register prints out onto any documents required by your employer.

Cheques

Cheques are a form of transaction that has all but disappeared. Some businesses and individuals, however, prefer to use cheques for large purchases as a means of accounting and keeping track of their cash flow. As such, you may receive cheques as a form of currency during your time in retail. If this is the case, be sure you follow the security processes in place at your workplace. These may include:

- scanning the cheque through an electronic authorisation machine
- verifying the customer's ID
- noting the customer's ID on the cheque.

If these steps are followed and your workplace accepts cheques under these circumstances, then accounting for them at the end of the day or shift is similar to counting the cash. The amount can be recorded on the daily sales record and the cheque is attached with the cash and record before sending to the cash office (or bank).

Other non-cash documents

Your store may use any of the following documents in its marketing strategy. We've attached a brief explanation of how each of these may appear and may need to be recorded.

Customer refunds

Refunds are a legal requirement under the following circumstances:

- the item is not fit for the purpose it is intended (also known as merchantable quality)
- the item is damaged or faulty (prior to sale without the possible knowledge of the customer)

- the customer was induced to buy the goods by misrepresentation
- the goods do not match the description given when purchased (or ordered)
- the goods do not match the sample
- store policy dictates some level above the points mentioned above (for example, 'all items purchased in December may be returned if the holder has the store receipt').

Documentation regarding the returns process may include register printouts where the customer must sign, as well as additional credits to the customer's EFTPOS or credit card. Documentation is usually stored in the cash drawer until the end of the shift or the day.

Gift vouchers

About 30 per cent of gift vouchers are never redeemed—in 2010 the total value was approximately $360 million.[1] Gift vouchers are sold like other store inventory, but can be claimed at some point in the future (usually up to twelve months). When a gift voucher is used to purchase an item, the 'credit' on the voucher is used. This may be accounted for electronically (as with the plastic credit card-type vouchers) or through the register by verifying the paper or cardboard voucher and storing it in the register. It is important that the voucher be valid. Check your store's policy for further information.

Hire-purchase, rent-to-buy, interest free promotion and lay-by

Products can be paid-off over time. This is a marketing strategy by retailers to make higher-cost items more accessible to people through a payment plan. Documentation surrounding the offering of store credit in this way is regulated under the law and must take the form of a contractual agreement. The agreement is a legal and binding document and must therefore be handled, counted and stored correctly. Many retailers combine online applications with hard copy contracts for the customer to take home and for the retail outlet to manage in-store.

Figure 9.4 Registers provide a daily sales summary either as a printout or electronic summary. Most retailers still prefer using the printout as a means of checking and balancing the terminal

Reconciliation of daily sales

Producing a daily sales record provides a reconciliation of the day's takings between the register's records and the actual cash and sales receipts in the drawer. Reconciliation is an accounting process where the aim is to balance the two amounts—that is, to end up with the same amount in both the register's records and the sum of the daily takings. If the amounts are not the same it is referred to as a discrepancy. If there is more in the drawer than the register records show, then it is a 'positive' discrepancy. If there is less than the register records indicate, then it is a 'negative' discrepancy. If the amounts match exactly, then they are balanced.

The Australian Taxation Office (ATO) provides a step-by-step process of daily sales reconciliation for small businesses. The ATO website also provides information on storage requirements for records such as register tape and cash sales forms.

Useful websites:

Australian Taxation Office

www.ato.gov.au/businesses/content.aspx?menuid=0&doc=/content/76494.htm&page=62

Electronic reconciliation

Many retailers link their cash registers to the business's information management system. This is the computerised system that monitors and reports on the information managers need to operate the business effectively and efficiently. Much of the information from the register, such as transaction amounts, line items being purchased and discounts, is sent electronically from the register to the information management system for analysis. Despite the use of this excellent technology, cash transactions will still require a manual interaction by a staff member to count and check against the daily (or shift) takings as reported by the register terminal.

RECORD KEEPING FOR SMALL BUSINESS

Blank forms

Cash payments books (PDF, 32 KB)

Reconciliation of daily sales (PDF, 33 KB)

Cash receipts book (PDF, 25 KB)

Summary cash payments and receipts book (PDF, 31 KB)

Cash flow projection (PDF, 40 KB)

Bank reconciliation (PDF, 35 KB)

Figure 9.5 Examples of cash forms and register documents can be downloaded from the ATO website[2]

There are numerous electronic systems in use throughout Australia that integrate retailers' inventory, accounting and warehouse ordering processes. These include (but are certainly not limited to):

- Pronto
- SAP
- Harmony Retail
- MS Dynamics
- Retail express and
- store-specific systems (designed in-house).

If your employer uses an electronic system, you will be trained in its specific use and if you are required to clear the register, the operations needed will be shown to you. For learning purposes, we've provided an example scenario in the following case study.

Supplying change to a register

Register tills (or cash drawers) are designed for the quick and secure temporary storage of cash. It is therefore relevant to ensure that the cash—coins and notes—is supplied to the register in an organised fashion. Typically, the coins run from lowest denomination to highest

CASE STUDY

Brea has just finished her shift at a busy fashion retailer in a suburban shopping centre. She counts the cash in the register and totals it by denomination as follows:

5c × 21 = $1.05	$5 × 6 = $30.00
10c × 8 = $0.80	$10 × 4 = $40.00
20c × 12 = $2.40	$20 × 17 = $340.00
50c × 9 = $4.50	$50 × 10 = $500.00
$1 × 16 = $16.00	$100 × 4 = $400.00
$2 × 11 = $22.00	

Brea adds the cash in her register and comes up with $1 356.75. Using the daily sales record form, she then enters the amount and adds the various other transactions as below. The store policy requires that sales people enter $0. when no transactions were recorded.

Cash (from cash count above)	$ 1375.00
Cheques	$ 0.00
MasterCard	$ 1012.00
Visa	$ 859.00
Diners/AMEX	$ 69.95
Store credit	$ 0.00
Other (Gift Cards)	$ 50.00
Starting float (subtract this amount)	$ –450.00
Deposit total	**$ 2915.95**
Returns	$ 25.00
Voids	$ 0.00
Paid outs	$ 0.00
Other	$ 0.00
Total cash paid out	**$ 25.00**
Add Deposit total & Total cash paid out	$ 2940.95
GST collected	$ $291.37
Register reading	$ 2940.95
Difference (–/+)	$ 0.00
The register balances!	

Note that Brea had to accept the return of an item valued at $25 (including GST). The amount is 'added' to the register total because $25 was in the cash drawer prior to it being returned to the customer, and therefore should be counted among the receipts for that day. Many register systems automatically cancel out voids and returns in the register read-out, so this will not need to be added to the total. Check your specific systems for more information.

denomination from the left to the right of the front part of the drawer. The notes follow the same logic in the compartments immediately behind the coins. Cheques and manual credit card receipts are often in a compartment at the rear, or sometimes underneath the cash drawer.

Regardless of the specific layout, the important thing to remember is that the individual denominations of coins and notes are not mixed. Doing so can result in the incorrect change being given, inaccurate counts, or excess time wasted to sort out the cash during the count.

Securing the cash and non-cash documents

Cash is an attractive item to thieves and it is never more vulnerable than when it is being removed from a cash drawer. Retailers usually have a store security policy in place that outlines the procedure for safe removal and transport of the cash and non-cash documents to the cash office and bank. Some interesting systems include pneumatic tubes and automated cashiers.

Pneumatic tubes transport the cash via a plastic tube by forcing air behind the capsule and shooting it in the direction of the tube. This system is popular in large retailers where crossing the floor with large amounts of cash is considered too risky. The system quickly and safely delivers the cash capsule directly to the cash office.

Figure 9.6 Pneumatic cash delivery systems

Automated cashiers are in operation where cash is stored in an ATM-like safe under the self-service terminal. The terminal is operated by the customer, and cash, credit cards or debit cards are used to complete the sale. The safe is cleared after hours or under armed guard during peak times. Use of these terminals is increasing in many popular Australian retail outlets. At this stage however, there is still need for cashier assistance in many cases.

Task 9.2

Carry out a basic cash drawer balance using the following information.

Your float is $100.

The cash in your drawer has the following:

5c × 8	$5 × 3
10c × 5	$10 × 4
20c × 10	$20 × 2
50c × 8	$50 × 5
$1 × 10	$100 × 1
$2 × 16	

Credit card and EFTPOS transactions total $131.10.

Your register printout lists all the transactions and totals $624.

1. Does this register balance?
2. If not, what is the discrepancy?

Report discrepancies to relevant personnel

Finalising the takings for a day of trading is a serious responsibility. Doing so incorrectly can lead to disciplinary action or, in the more severe instances, criminal charges being laid. If you become aware of any of the following, you will need to report it to your supervisor, manager or team leader at your earliest possible opportunity:

- a negative or positive discrepancy in the cash count
- missing manual credit card slips
- incorrectly completed credit documentation (including hire purchase, store credit card and lay-by contracts)
- counterfeit or unauthorised gift vouchers
- counterfeit cash
- cash of a foreign currency.

Filing records according to store policy

Every retailer records the store's daily takings in some way—it is an obligation under tax law. The methods and processes used can vary greatly, so it is vital that you are aware of the basic requirements as well as your store's specific policies.

Records may be stored electronically or manually.

Electronically stored records may be in the form of:

- digital records—reported via the information management system. These are data uploaded from each register to the retailer's main system for analysis and quality management

- RF downloads from portable sales devices—RF (radio frequency) tags and hand-held POS devices can transact, record and store sales data. These data are usually downloaded once the portable device is cradled in its charger. The system then detects the device and automatically downloads the sales data and reconciles it with store sales. These cannot be used for cash transactions
- email and other communications—Some retail outlets report back to central accounts departments through email or intranet portal—this is an internet site securely run by the company for internal use only.

Being familiar with the electronic storage requirements of your organisation should prepare you for meeting those requirements on the job.

Manual records such as the daily sales record, cash count form and so on, must be recorded accurately and then filed or handed to the right person in the right area. In many retailers, the cash office clerk is the person responsible for managing the money and documentation relating to transactions for the store. In smaller retailers, that could be the store manager or off-site accounts person. The two things to remember are that you must ensure that the documentation:

- is accurate
- is securely filed or handed on to the relevant person in line with the store requirements.

Accurate and secure record keeping is the backbone of a cost-effective retail operation. A great month in sales may not translate to a great month for the business if the records are not accurate and mistakes are made at the point of sale.

Task 9.3

Personal reflection

Take a moment to review the cash handling procedure in your store. Think about the steps and how you would complete them. Consider how the documentation and cash from the register is stored.

If you are satisfied that you know the process and could carry it out in accordance with your store's policies and procedures, carry on to the next topic.

(For security reasons do not write these steps down as they may be misused.)

Endnotes

1. John Rolfe, 2010, 'Un-used gift cards give 360m to retailers', *The Daily Telegraph*, 7 June 2010, www.dailytelegraph.com.au/money/unused-gift-cards-give-360m-to-retailers/story-e6frezc0-1225876166850, accessed 7 January 2012.
2. Australian Taxation Office, www.ato.gov.au/businesses/content.aspx?menuid=0&doc=/content/76494.htm&page=62

ASSESSMENT 1: REVIEW QUESTIONS

Instructions

Provide answers in full to every question listed below. If you are not sure how to answer the question, ask your trainer or assessor for assistance. If the information is commercially sensitive (your employer does not permit the information to be shared), please use a fictional or simulated workplace scenario.

Reasonable adjustments

The assessment may be carried out verbally and the answers recorded by your trainer or assessor.

1. What is the process for 'opening' and 'closing' your register? (You may describe this in point form.)
2. In point form, list the steps required to balance a point-of-sale terminal in your workplace.
3. Describe the EFTPOS procedure for the following scenario:

   Your customer purchases an item for $100. She will be paying via her bank debit card. List the steps of the procedure from the moment you scan or enter the item into the POS terminal.

4. What is your store's policy in regard to cash handling? In your answer, be sure to note the 'roles' of people in your store (for example, what your role is and the roles of any other staff who may be involved in the processes).
5. What are four reasons for using electronic funds transactions?

ASSESSMENT 2

Assessment instructions	You are required to balance, secure and reconcile the takings from a cash register.
Evidence required	1. Facilitator observation checklist 2. A completed copy of a cash count form and reconciliation form.
Range and conditions	• The assessment should take place in a real work context where possible. A simulated workplace may be used if the environment resembles a retail context. • The assessment time limit is dictated by store requirements. It is envisaged that the process will take approximately thirty minutes.
Materials and resources required	You will need access to: • a cash drawer • an electronic register or terminal with actual and recorded takings for a day or a shift • access to relevant documentation such as dockets, slips, invoices, credit or debit card vouchers, tally sheets and gift cards, and • the site procedures for this process.
Assessor intervention	Your assessor will go through the assessment instructions with the class prior to commencement. You may ask questions at any point during the completion of the assignment prior to submission.
Reasonable adjustments	In the event that you have difficulty understanding the assessment tasks due to language or other difficulties, your trainer will attempt to make reasonable adjustments to the assessment in order to afford you every opportunity to achieve competency.
Decision-making rules	Facilitator guide/McGraw Hill website provides benchmark answers and check lists

COMPETENCY MAPPING

Element and performance criteria		Task	Assessment	Refer to page
1.1	Perform register or terminal balance at designated times according to store policy and procedures.	9.2	1, 2	281–283
1.2	Separate cash float from takings prior to balancing procedure and secure according to store policy.	9.1		284
1.3	Supply change to register or terminal according to store policy.	9.1		289
1.4	Obtain and interpret register or terminal reading or printout.	9.2		287–289
1.5	Secure cash and non-cash documents according to store security policy and procedures.	9.3		289–290
2.1	Count cash accurately.	9.1		282–283
2.2	Calculate non-cash documents accurately.	9.2		284–285
2.3	Determine balance between register or terminal reading and sum of cash and non-cash transactions.	9.2		282–283
2.4	Report discrepancies between register or terminal reading and sum of cash and non-cash transactions to relevant personnel according to store policy.	9.2		290
2.5	Record store and individual department takings and file records according to store policy.	9.3		290–291

Required skills and knowledge	Task	Assessment	Refer to page
Required skills:			
• literacy and numeracy skills to:	9.1, 9.2	1, 2	281–291
– balance the register or terminal			281–291
– count cash			281–291
– calculate non-cash transactions			281–291
– interpret documentation			281–291
– report on takings			281–291
– calculate discrepancies between reported and actual takings			281–291
– complete documentation			281–291
• planning and organising skills to complete tasks in a set timeframe	9.3		290
• technology skills to operate register or terminal	9.2		290–291

Required skills and knowledge	Task	Assessment	Refer to page
Required knowledge:			
Cash and non-cash handling procedures, including:	9.2	1, 2	281–290
• balancing point-of-sale terminal			281–290
• calculating non-cash documents	9.2		284–285
• change required and denominations of change	9.1, 9.2		281–290
• EFTPOS	9.3		284–285
• gift vouchers	9.3		281–290
• lay-by	9.3		281–290
• maintenance of cash float	9.1		284
• clearance of terminal and transference of tender	9.2		287–289
• counting cash	9.1		282–283
• credit and returns	9.2, 9.3		281–290
• credit cards	9.3		281–290
• opening and closing point-of-sale terminal	9.3	1, 2	281–290
• recording takings	9.1, 9.2	2	281–290
• security of cash and non-cash transactions	9.3	2	289
Store policy and procedures in regard to:	All completed in 1, 2		
• cash float			
• operation of equipment used at register or terminal			
• register or terminal balance			
• security of cash and non-cash transactions			
Critical aspects for assessment and evidence			
Operates register or terminal equipment according to manufacturer instructions and store policy	9.1	1, 2	281–290
Applies store policy and procedures in regard to handling cash and removing takings from register or terminal	9.3		281–290
Applies store policy and procedures in regard to cash float	9.1, 9.2, 9.3		281–290
Applies store policy and procedures in regard to reading registers and recording information	9.2, 9.3		281–290
Processes documentation and records responsibly and according to store policy and procedures	9.2, 9.3		281–290
Reconciles takings according to store policy and procedures.	9.2		281–290

Chapter 10

SIRXINV002A

Maintain and order stock

Figure 10.1 Warehousing is a critical element of stock maintenance. Too little stock and you affect sales, too much stock, and you affect cash flow

Stock is the collective word describing the goods you have on hand to sell to your customers. It includes those items on the shelves or hangers in the store, as well as those in the storage area. Having the wrong balance of stock translates to poor sales and having too much stock puts a strain on the business's cash flow. Maintaining the balance of correct stock items and volumes against the proposed or forecast turnover of the store is a valuable skill.

ELEMENT 1
MONITORING THE RECEIPT AND DISPATCH OF GOODS

Receiving and dispatching stock at a retail business premises is a detailed procedure. It involves ensuring that the quality and quantity is correct; the paperwork associated with the delivery is correct, acted upon and filed appropriately; and the stock received is relocated safely to an appropriate warehouse zone or shop floor area.

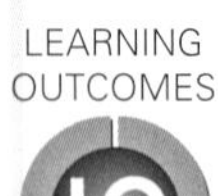

LEARNING OUTCOMES

1.1 Delegate responsibility for receipt and dispatch of goods to appropriate staff.

1.2 Implement store procedures in regard to receipt, dispatch and secure storage of goods.

1.3 Observe staff functions to ensure that store procedures are followed and documentation is completed correctly.

1.4 Implement store procedures to ensure that goods are inspected for quantity and quality on receipt.

1.5 Act upon variations to quantity and quality of delivered goods, according to store policy and procedures.

1.6 Supervise safe handling and storage of goods, according to store policy.

Delegating responsibility for the receipt and dispatch of goods

The procedures for receiving and dispatching goods will depend upon the size of the business and the type of retail business. Staff roles that may be responsible for this duty can include:

- frontline staff—such as warehouse and sales staff
- relevant managers—includes store managers, receiving managers, warehouse managers and dispatch managers
- stock supervisor, warehouse, receiving or dispatch supervisor—a role may be created for this task
- 'team leader'—this is another name for a supervisory role that focuses more on leadership than management. Regardless of the position title, a team leader may be in charge of the receiving and dispatch area at the retail site
- specialists in the area of warehousing—these are often placed in charge of this function as they are familiar with the storage and movement of stock in the store's warehouse area and have training in specific WHS (workplace health and safety) as a part of their warehousing training.

The delegation of this function is a communication task. Communication has been covered in Chapter 2 and relates directly to your interactions with those in the workplace who may be responsible for the function (as listed above). When communicating with staff in order to delegate a role such as this, you must consider:

- people from a range of social, cultural and ethnic backgrounds—always address people with respect and treat them as you would like to be treated. Always look for opportunities to 'ask' them how they should be doing things. Simply, put yourself in their shoes and consider the sort of language and attitude you would respond to best.
- people with varying degrees of language and literacy levels—similarly, respect that not everyone has the same level of proficiency in the English language as you do. Some may be more and some may be less proficient. Always use standard English and refrain from difficult concepts until you know the other person's level of proficiency.
- whether they are full-time, part-time or casual employees—this will affect the times that staff are available and the types of roles they are qualified to perform. For example, a part-time staff member may not be rostered on at the times when receiving usually takes place.

Implementing store procedures

The loading bay of a retail site can be a dangerous area. It can also be a very large door for thieves and burglars to use for their own self-service take-aways. Store procedures surrounding the receipt, dispatch and secure storage of goods are designed to minimise the risk of harm to those working in the area and to minimise the risk of loss through damage, theft or robbery. As these procedures vary, let's look at the generally accepted practice.

RECEIPT OF GOODS

Goods are often delivered by freight line for larger quantities or by courier for smaller quantities. Many stores have a specified loading area sometimes referred to as the **loading dock** or **loading bay** for freight carriers and couriers to deliver their loads. Store policies usually prohibit the delivery of stock items through the front of the store as this presents a WHS risk to staff and customers, and an aesthetic issue for customers (that is, it looks bad!). In some shopping centre locations this is unavoidable, so efforts should be made to schedule the deliveries outside of peak customer traffic times.

When the responsible staff member becomes aware that goods are awaiting receipt at the loading dock (usually via the ringing of a bell or chime), they must ensure firstly that the delivery is scheduled or is known to them. If there is no scheduled delivery at that time, the staff member must check the identity of the delivery person prior to agreeing to open the loading bay door. As mentioned, the loading area can be an easy target for criminals as there are usually few staff and no customers in this area.

The receiving process then usually requires the following steps:

1. Visually inspect the goods for quality—are they what you are signing for? Check for brand, description and colour (if applicable, e.g. if items come unpacked or in transparent packaging) against the delivery agent's paperwork (usually a delivery docket).
2. Count the number of cartons, pallets, boxes—do the quantities match the delivery docket?

   So far, if you have answered no to either of these steps and the delivery agent cannot account for the discrepancy, refer to your policies for rejecting or accepting the delivery. You may need to refer to a manager for authorisation.
3. Receive the delivery into the loading area. This is the vacant area at the door used to temporarily store the items while you carry out the remainder of the process.

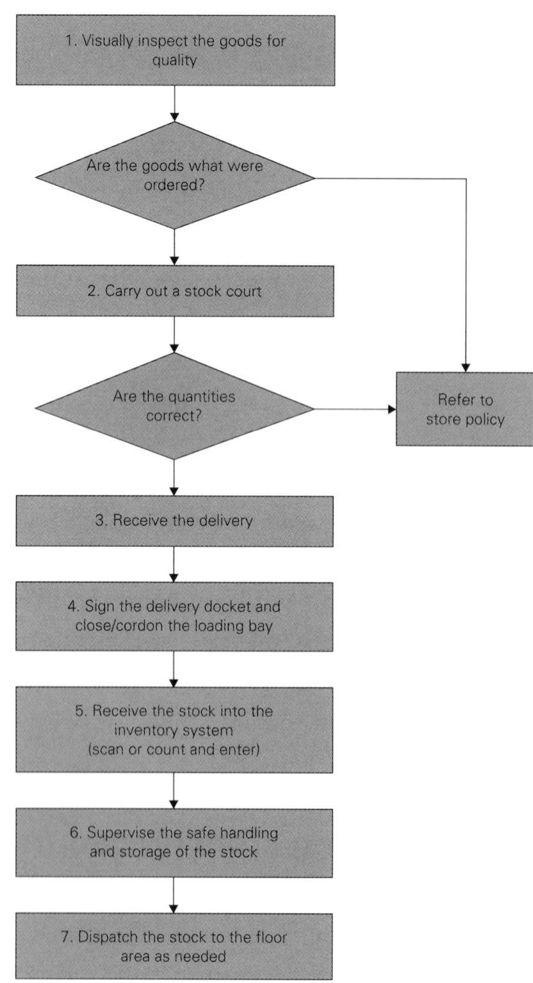

Figure 10.2 The receiving process

4. Sign the delivery docket and close or cordon-off the loading bay door. This is the last 'simple' legal opportunity you have to ensure you are signing for what you have received, so accuracy is essential. Always be sure *before* signing.
5. Scan the stock. If a barcode system is in place in your store, then scanning the barcodes of the items should immediately enter them into your inventory. As there may be several barcodes on boxes, you should identify the EAN or International Article Number barcode, as this is the current standard for identifying a stock item. (Believe it or not, EAN stands for International Article Number! It was originally termed the European Article Number, but the old acronym continued to be used when it became more widely international.)

   If you do not use a barcode or other electronic system, you will need to tick off the stock on the delivery dock against the dispatch docket and the store's order form. These should match. In other words, you should check that the stock you have received is the stock you have ordered.

   Once this is done the stock can be entered into the stock system of the store and be ready for storage, dispatch or display. Then simply follow the filing procedures of your store to ensure the dispatch docket, order form and check sheet (if you have a separate one) are stored in an appropriate manner.
6. Supervise the safe handling and storage of the goods as per the store policy. This may vary according to the stock characteristics (for example when handling furniture as compared with a box of cans of baked beans) and the codes of practice for the storage of particular items (for example paint cans and solvents must not be stored in direct sunlight).
7. Dispatching refers to the moving of stock from the storage or receiving area to the retail sales floor. This is the final step in the process, and like step 6, staff must move the items safely (see 'Safe handling procedures' below).

ACTING UPON VARIATIONS IN QUALITY AND QUANTITY

In the flow chart, you can see that if there is a discrepancy, you should 'refer to store policy'. This is essential as store policies will be in place and usually form a basis for the contracts with various suppliers and courier companies. In most cases, small discrepancies in quantities (say an extra carton was received or the stock was one carton short) can be sorted out with a correction to the order or an extra shipment by the supplier. In both cases, the aim is to minimise costs to both parties and to deal with the error quickly. If there is a larger discrepancy, or the quality of the order is outside of expectations (wrong product design, colour, damaged, faulty), then the contract with the supplier should be enforced. This can include refusal of the stock at the docking bay, refund of the order price, supplier credit or some form of compensation. The legal cost of delivery lies with the supplier (sender) as long as the shipment has not been signed for as complete and accurate.

SAFE HANDLING PROCEDURES

The final step in the flow chart is the safe handling and storage of goods. We have noted that this is highly variable due to the nature of the stock and the industry practices for storage. Regardless of these however, the requirements for manual handling have become standardised across most industries. The Australian Safety and Compensation Council (ASCC) declared the *National Standard for Manual Tasks* (2007) and the *National Code of Practice for the Prevention of Musculoskeletal Disorders from Performing Manual Tasks at Work* (2007) on 22 August 2007. In addition, a code of practice and regulations are now in place under state workplace health and safety legislation to ensure that employers have systems in place to reduce the likelihood of injury due to incorrect manual handling.

As such, you should be aware of what should and should not be lifted by one person without assistance (either mechanical or human). You should also be able to assess the risks and determine the correct control measures you should take before attempting the task.

Manual handling includes holding, pushing, pulling, lifting and carrying. Doing any of these tasks incorrectly can lead to injuries such as strains, overexertion and long-term back pain. If any of these injuries occur at work, an investigation will be made into the steps that led to the injury, with the correct manual handling processes being a central concern.

When assessing a task that may involve manual handling, consider these factors from the Manual Handling Code of Practice:[1]

1. Is there a requirement for frequent or prolonged bending down (where the hands are below mid-thigh height)?
2. Is there frequent or prolonged reaching above the shoulder?
3. Is there frequent or prolonged bending due to extended reach forward?
4. Is there frequent or prolonged twisting of the back?
5. Are awkward postures assumed frequently or over a prolonged period?
6. Is manual handling performed frequently or for long periods by employees?
7. Are the loads moved or carried long distances?
8. Is the weight of the object more than 15kg?
9. Are large forces involved in pushing or pulling the object?
10. Is the load difficult or awkward to handle?
11. Is it difficult or unsafe to get adequate grip of the load?
12. Is the task performed in a confined space?
13. Is the lighting adequate for manual handling?
14. Is the climate particularly hot or cold?
15. Are floor surfaces cluttered, uneven, slippery or otherwise unsafe?
16. Is the employee new to the work or returning after an extended break?
17. Are there age-related factors, disabilities or other special factors that may affect the performance of the task?
18. Does the employee's clothing or protective equipment interfere with their manual handling performance?

Useful websites:

Code of Practice—Manual Handling

www.safework.sa.gov.au/uploaded_files/resCOPManualHandling.pdf

Better Health: Manual handling injuries—Victorian Government

www.betterhealth.vic.gov.au/bhcv2/bhcarticles.nsf/pages/Workplace_safety_manual_handling_injuries

SafeWork SA manual handling safe work instructions

www.safework.sa.gov.au/uploaded_files/mh_booklet.pdf

Task 10.1

Workplace task

In your workplace or simulated retail environment, monitor the receipt of goods from a supplier in accordance with the policies and procedures for your store (or those of the training environment). Note down the following:

1. Brief description of the goods
2. The roles that you and other staff had in the process
3. Were the goods in line with quality and quantity expectations?
4. Did you and other staff apply correct handling procedures throughout the receipt and dispatch? If so, briefly describe what needed to be done.

Take your time to complete this task accurately to ensure you have applied the learning from this section.

ELEMENT 2
MAINTAIN STOCK RECORDS

By monitoring and maintaining effective stock records, a retailer can make better decisions as to what items should be stocked, put on sale or moved to a higher traffic area; storage levels; and reorder cycles. In this section we cover the specific actions you can take to ensure that stock records are maintained at the highest standard, and what to do when you detect various changes in stock performance.

Effective stock control systems work to minimise shrinkage—the loss of stock due to theft, loss, documentation errors or damage. Shrinkage increases the costs of the business and therefore the profitability.

2.1 Monitor and maintain stock at required levels.

2.2 Maintain, monitor and adjust stock reorder cycles as required.

2.3 Inform team members of their individual responsibilities in regard to recording of stock.

2.4 Maintain stock storage and movement records, according to store policy.

2.5 Record stock discrepancies and follow procedures according to store policy.

2.6 Monitor stock performance and identify and report fast- and slow-selling items according to store policy.

LEARNING OUTCOMES

Monitoring and maintaining stock levels

There are several techniques used in modern retail to monitor and maintain stock levels. A stocktake is one of the regular methods that we will discuss in the next section. In this section we will cover the everyday methods that you can use immediately.

- stock performance statistics—by using a computerised POS and inventory system, retailers can monitor the stock performance statistics in real time. As a product is scanned or entered for sale, the computer system records the transaction details such as time, price and register or sales person in order to give the manager or team leader a picture of the performance of that product. Stock levels are then adjusted and, if necessary, the stock is flagged for ordering. This means the store buyer will see an indicator (such as a flag, highlight, tick or cross) next to the item on the store's computer inventory system and determine whether or not a reorder is required.
- manual counts—manual counts such as stocktakes and cyclical shelf counts can be useful tools for correcting the errors that can occur when stock is misplaced, stolen, damaged (but not recorded) and returned (but not recorded). A manual count is as it sounds, a physical count of the products on the retail floor and in storage. The amount is reconciled against the stock-on-hand values in the business's inventory system. This is covered in more detail in the following section (Element 3).

Required levels can be set by any number of methods. These include:

- electronic data interchange (EDI)—the integrated computerised systems used by some advanced retail operators who have to manage very large or fast-moving stock levels. The system integrates the real-time data accumulated through the retail management system with the suppliers' stock levels, pricing and delivery schedules. These systems can monitor partial orders and only order when the amount reaches a certain quantity to ensure speedy delivery or efficient pricing. The system sets an appropriate level based on these and other inputs (see 'Considerations when maintaining stock levels' on page 303).
- planogram—a **planogram** sets the facing stock design for the shelves of the retail store based on the physical size, market share and sell-rate of the product. The quantities ordered may still vary based on local performance, but the idea is to replicate a consistent store look for customers across a number of outlets. For an example, see www.goplanogram.com/p-webplan.html.
- FIFO, or 'first in, first out'—the process of re-ordering stock as it sells. The **FIFO** style of stock maintenance is not particularly efficient. It demands that stock is reordered as it is sold. This can lead to excess quantities of seasonal stock and insufficient quantities for special events. The basic premise is sound for the ordering of commodity-based stock.

- local market preferences—where items are identified by the business manager as high yield or high turnover in the specific locality, they can manually set the stock levels accordingly. This is a gut-feel approach that may or may not work depending on experience and the person's approach to continuous improvement.
- **min–max levels**—a system where minimum and maximum stock levels are monitored and where orders are placed when minimum levels are reached. When the stock falls to the minimum level—say five units—then the inventory management system flags the product for reorder up to the maximum level—say ten units. Therefore, the buyer orders five additional units.

Manually adjusting reorder cycles may be required when unforeseen events occur, such as:

- supply shortages
- weather conditions
- highway closures
- unexpected supplier marketing activities
- community interest or personal referrals (for specific products).

Of course, manual reorders can be planned for events such as:

- holidays and associated sales such as Christmas, New Year and Easter
- traditional dates of note such as Mother's Day, Father's Day, Australia Day, Valentine's Day.
- expected supplier marketing activities such as competitions, new releases or mass-market advertising
- clearance sales and internal sales and marketing activities.

CONSIDERATIONS WHEN MAINTAINING STOCK LEVELS

There are a number of things to consider when you're maintaining stock levels in a retail outlet. These include:

- damaged stock—stock that, for one reason or another, has been damaged beyond a point where attaining full price is possible. **Damaged stock** is accounted for as a loss for the store and is usually thrown away or donated. Opened packaging may be replaced in some circumstances, and some retailers may choose to sell the item, along with soiled items, in a sale bin or seconds area (usually at a loss or close to cost price). Seconds are items that do not meet the general quality specifications of the originally specified item.
- lead time—this is the time it takes for goods to arrive once the order has been placed. Factors that affect **lead time** can include freight time and schedules, distance between the retailer and the supplier's warehouse, supplier stock levels, product demand by other retailers and natural occurrences like severe rain, flooding and earthquakes. Always ensure there is sufficient stock to meet demand while you are waiting for new stock to arrive. This can be determined by current sales rates and store experience.

- rate of sale—the **rate of sale** is a metric (measurement) of how fast an item sells during a given period. This may be per day or per month. For example, a can of baked beans may sell at a rate of 9.3/7—indicating that on average, 9.3 items sell every seven days. If your order cycle is weekly and your minimum stock level is ten, you will be ordering this stock every week if you want to maintain minimum levels.
- obsolete items—those products no longer produced by the manufacturer. As manufacturers and suppliers develop their products, or innovative products replace existing ones, you will inevitably be left with **obsolete items**. A valuable skill of a retail team leader or manager is the ability to identify and move the existing obsolete stock quickly and efficiently. Obsolete stock is less attractive to customers and therefore the price usually needs to be lowered to motivate the customer to buy. Reordering obsolete items is a common but costly mistake. Many computerised inventory systems now flag obsolete items so they cannot be reordered.
- seasonality—in most retail businesses, **seasonality** is a major consideration when maintaining stock levels. Seasonality refers to times throughout the calendar year when particular items are in high or low demand. For example, high demand seasonal items may include roses in February (Valentine's Day), Christmas cards in November and December, and floral summer dresses in Spring. Having seasonal products in stock when the season is drawing to a close, such as Christmas cards in stock on 25 December, means they will need to be cleared soon after. Clearance products, such as out of season or damaged goods, are usually sold at a reduced rate and are therefore less profitable than standard or peak seasonal items. Stock levels should reflect the seasonality of the stock items you are maintaining.
- shelf life—the **shelf life** of a product refers to the period of time during which a product can safely be consumed. For this reason, it usually refers to perishable goods like fruits and vegetables, dairy and fresh flowers; but it can also refer to products that become quickly outdated like some consumer electronics products and computers. The term 'shelf life' has therefore been extended to denote the period of time that any product is suitable for sale at its full price (i.e. no discount required). A computer may have a shelf life of just three months before a newer, faster model is made available—thus making it less attractive at the original price.

In marketing terms, this is referred to as the product's **life cycle**. As a retailer, you should endeavour to carry the highest quantity of a product when it is first released and plan to reduce the stock levels over the product's life cycle. Note that life cycles are dependent upon the type of product: computers have a short life cycle, while canned vegetables have a long life cycle.

- replenishment—stock **replenishment** is the act of adding stock to the display (shelves, end-caps, hangers) as product is sold. The reason this is a consideration when maintaining stock levels is to ensure that you have assessed all the stock on hand, not just that on display. For example, a corner store may have a milk fridge that is looking empty. There may be a crate of milk in the storeroom, but unless the stock is replenished as a regular activity, the store manager may accidently order more than is required.

- trends—these are noticeable increases or decreases in the sales of specific product categories over time. Like seasonality, current **trends** will directly affect the levels of stock you should maintain in order to meet customer demand and improve the store's profitability. Large retailers analyse local, domestic and overseas trends in order to forecast the products and quantities that will be required in the various outlets they control. On a local scale, you may be required to scan magazines, newspapers, industry websites and so forth in order to determine any specific trends which may impact upon the stock you order. For example, an electronics retailer in the late 1990s seized upon the upcoming digital music trend by reducing stock of portable CD players in favour of digital devices. As digital device sales grew, the retailer kept a sharp eye on the fashions in the industry to ensure they were ready for the convergent digital technology trend that followed.
- stock turns—this term refers to the rate at which stock sells and is calculated by the total cost of goods sold *divided* by the average inventory level during the period (usually one month). Average inventory is the stock at the beginning of the month, *plus* the stock at the end of the month, divided by two. This figure is compared with the return required for the space on the shop floor as a means of determining the success of the product. High **stock turns** demonstrate a good selling product.

TEAM MEMBER RESPONSIBILITIES

In a retail store, every team member is responsible for the stock—the way it looks on display, the quantities on display, reporting theft and clearing up any damage or spillage relating to stock. Given this responsibility, team members should also be encouraged to report any significant changes in the stock levels as this may be representative of an unusual sales occurrence or possibly a theft or burglary.

Your role may include informing team members of their responsibilities. This again is a communication task and should be handled with appropriate interpersonal skills in order to:

- give clear instructions
- explain policies and procedures as they relate to the staff member
- allocate tasks and provide directions for performance of the task
- liaise with other departments, buyers, warehouse staff and suppliers through clear and direct communication
- ask questions to identify and confirm requirements
- use language and concepts appropriate to the language and literacy levels of the staff you are addressing
- use and interpret non-verbal communication.

STORAGE AND MOVEMENT RECORDS

When stock is displayed it may have been moved from the warehouse or storage area, or from another part of the store. Some retailers record these movements to ensure that items are not misplaced. For example, a store having a sale on rice cookers may choose to move half the stock to the front entrance of the store and dress it up appropriately. If a stock count is done in the appliance department, the department team leader will need to be aware that some of their stock is at the front of the store.

Floor stock movement records are usually basic lists of the stock items and their temporary location. They are then posted on the office notice board or other appropriate area in order for the department team leaders to note any movements that affect their department's stock items.

When stock is moved from the warehouse or storeroom to the floor, the warehouse or storeroom supervisor is usually informed in order to account for the space in the warehouse. In most retail sites, space is at a premium, which means any wasted space is potentially costing the store money.

Inter-site stock movement

In multi-site operations, stock is often transferred to fill customer orders, clear stock or help stores with short supplies. Stock movements *must* be recorded in accordance with the dispatch procedures of the store. If the stock is not correctly removed from the store's inventory, it will create a discrepancy in the inventory system as well as during the next manual stock count.

Monitor and report on stock performance

As we've seen, stock maintenance is affected by a multitude of factors, yet it is one of the most crucial areas of financial control. For this reason, most retailers have invested in computerised systems of stock control and reporting to assist them with maintaining accurate and reliable records. Despite the use of these systems, discrepancies will still appear due to theft, damage, loss or errors in stock counts and documentation. To monitor and report on stock performance it is important to be aware of the following procedures.

STOCK CONTROL

The stock control system in your store has been developed to meet the needs of the business. The extent to which it is automated (that is, that there is no need for human input) will depend on the type of retail business, its size and business strategies.

A typical stock control system will monitor levels of the various stock items in store based on four main inputs:

1. cash register sales and returns
2. receiving and dispatch input

3. stocktake records
4. orders and order status.

Your role may involve any or all of these inputs.

Cash register sales and returns were covered in the previous chapter. You may remember that closing and balancing the register requires the physical input of information such as cash-on-hand and non-cash sales documents, returns, voids and daily sales record documents. This information assists the retail operation in ensuring that the recorded sales match the stock items that actually left the store.

Receiving and dispatch records add stock to the inventory of the store. As items are scanned or entered at the receiving dock they appear in the stock control system. Depending on the intricacy of the system these items may be marked for sale and dispatched, or marked as warehouse stock until dispatch. The more intricate the system the more variables can be associated with the stock items. Basic systems still allow for simple in/out stock control. This means that the stock shows as being on hand once received, then is removed from stock once sold through the cash register system.

Stocktake records provide the only physical means of determining stock levels. Spot checks, full stocktakes and partial stocktakes can all be used to assess whether the stock system is accurate (see 'Recording of stock information' below and the following section Element 3: 'Coordinate stocktake' for more detail on stocktake processes).

Order and order status information tells the retailer what stock is pending receipt into the stock control system. This information is critical for staff involved in ordering stock so that they are aware of what has and has not been ordered at any particular time. The ordering system relies on accurate stock counts for its integrity. This means that stock-on-hand in the stock management system should be accurate in order for staff to accurately order the correct quantities of stock as required. Automated ordering systems still usually require human verification. If you are involved in this step it is important to check for anomalies such as overly large orders, negative amounts or large price variations before authorising the order. A good understanding of the pricing of items is a great advantage when undertaking this task.

RECORDING OF STOCK INFORMATION

Recording stock information centres on one thing—accuracy. Whether you are recording the information as part of the receiving, dispatch, cash register sales or stocktake functions, accuracy is key to a robust and quality stock control system. When determining the accuracy of the records, you are paying special attention to the following:

- item quantity—what features are used to distinguish the item from others in the store? This may include clothing size, length, colour and gauge. Counting an item quantity that is not in line with the system's description will result in the wrong item being recorded and many errors occurring as a result—including pricing and ordering.

- product description—is the product that you are recording described correctly? If the system description is not the same as the item description on the packaging, outer box, or on the item itself, do not record it as that item. Check with the product buyer, store manager or department manager (as the case may be), as they may have to make changes to the order or the item description, or to contact the supplier for alternative courses of action.
- price—the cost or sale price of the item can be a good indicator that you are recording the correct item (see 'Pricing, labelling and packaging' on page 310 for more information).

PROCEDURES FOR INVESTIGATING DISCREPANCIES

Stock performance can be measured by sales rate, return on floor cost, return on item cost or other metrics, depending on the retailer's policies and procedures. These all rely on accurate levels of stock being maintained. So when a discrepancy is identified, how do you report and investigate it?

Reporting a discrepancy

Reports can be in the form of financial and other business documentation, informal verbal feedback or as a part of the stocktake procedure. The report should identify the stock on hand against the physical count number with a column for the discrepancy to be recorded. Examples of this are in the next section, 'Coordinate stocktake'. The discrepancy is then reported to the manager responsible for stock (usually the store manager) either via an electronic or manual summary report of all stock on hand.

Investigating a discrepancy

You may be instructed to investigate the discrepancy in order to determine the root cause. Remember, discrepancies can be caused by a number of things including:

- count errors
- product identification errors (during receiving, sales or stocktake)
- loss or misplacement
- theft
- damage (individual product damage or as the result of fire or water).

Your role is to determine the cause. In the event that an internal error is identified as the cause, the aim is then to prevent that same error happening again in the future. You have a few methods of investigation depending on the severity of the discrepancy and the policy of your workplace.

Some typical investigation methods include:

Observation

Is there an observable cause for the discrepancy? For instance, did you see someone move, damage or use the item, causing it not to be where it should be? Did you observe any actions leading up to the incorrect count that could explain the discrepancy? For instance, you may have seen a pallet of the goods being loaded onto a truck the day before—perhaps the count at the loading dock was incorrect? This gives you another line of enquiry.

Documentation

Analyse existing documentation. Are there any discrepancies that 'cancel each other out'? For instance, if you counted five size 8 tops and seven size 10 tops, but the system shows six and six respectively, the error may be that the incorrect size quantities were entered into the system. Again, this gives you an avenue for further investigation. Look for supporting documentation. In the example above you might go to the original order to see how many of each size were ordered, or to the sales report to see how many of each size were purchased. This will give you a clear indication as to whether or not the system quantities are incorrect and should be amended.

Interviews

The interview technique does not need to be as ominous as it sounds. It simply means asking people who may have better knowledge of the whereabouts of the stock or a reason behind a discrepancy. Asking others is usually conducted before searching the documentation as a simple answer could provide you with the information you need without the time you might otherwise take to go through the related documents.

STORE MERCHANDISING AND MARKETING

Stock performance has a great deal to do with the way the stock is presented and any marketing activities planned and conducted. The presentation of the stock in-store is referred to as 'merchandising'. Common practices include the use of:

- shelf-talkers—small cardboard or plastic information tags that protrude from the item or the shelf it is stored on
- endcaps—displays at the end of an aisle used to feature a product, brand or category
- floor stickers—marketing tools used in-store to guide a customer to, or provide information about, a particular brand, department, product or promotion.
- facing stock—where shelves or hangers are used as the primary method of displaying stock, the facing stock is that which faces the oncoming customer. Facing stock is also a verb, when retail staff bring stock forward from a hidden position to a more aesthetically pleasing and prominent position.

In retail, stock is usually ordered in advance of any marketing activity such as a promotion, sale, catalogue or other media campaign. Stock levels will be determined by forecast sales and stock availability. In recent times, some retailers have been investigated by the ACCC (Australian Competition and Consumer Commission) due to insufficient stock of advertised product being available in some areas. This can be construed as 'bait advertising' and contravenes the *Competition and Consumer Act* 2010.

Useful website:

Federal Court orders declarations

www.accc.gov.au/content/index.phtml/itemId/568383/fromItemId/465054

PRICING, LABELLING AND PACKAGING REQUIREMENTS

Stock performance also depends upon the items having the correct price, labels and packaging. In a retail environment, these factors can mean the difference between the item selling like the proverbial 'hot cakes', and not budging from the floor for the entire season.

When monitoring the stock in your store, check that items have the correct and current price. Pricing of goods at some retailers can change daily. It is critical to be informed and act upon changes immediately in order to give the stock the best opportunity to be sold. Additionally, ensure there are no 'mixed messages' being sent to customers by checking that the items do not have two or more pricing tags with different amounts on them.

If an item is on sale, the goods must clearly display the sale price. If the item claims to have a discount (like '20% off', 'was $20 now $10' or 'save $5') then the consumer must be able to identify the previous price and when it was that price.

Additionally, in some cases you will need to be aware of the pricing conventions for items such as grocery lines, fresh foods and cooked goods relating to price per 100g, per kg, per litre, and so on. These methods of pricing make it easier for the consumer to determine the best value purchase for their needs. So it is important that the pricing is accurate and does not unintentionally damage the sales rate of other items—say larger or smaller quantity packages.

Useful website:

ACCC Misleading pricing—was–now advertising

www.accc.gov.au/content/index.phtml/itemId/815334

Labelling in retail is becoming more and more regulated as a direct result of unscrupulous marketing practices of some businesses. Labelling of canned food, clothing sizes, imported goods, locally grown goods, health-related products, tobacco products, 'fresh' products, and more is regulated under federal and state law.

To ensure that the stock in your store meets the compliance standards you will need to be familiar with them and apply what you know within the current procedures and policy of your workplace. By doing so, you provide the best opportunity for customers to safely and legally purchase your products, thus affecting the performance of the stock you are managing.

Useful website:

Food standards Australia

www.foodstandards.gov.au/

FOR QUALITY CONTROL POLICIES AND PROCEDURES

Quality control in retail can mean two different things: maintaining and improving the quality of either the products, or the retail systems.

Product quality in a retail sense refers to the quality of the displayed merchandise. At a shop-level, you have the ability to ensure that the product looks its best in order to attract potential buyers. Goods that are in marked packaging, in damaged boxes or poorly stacked will generally sell more slowly than well-presented goods of the same type.

Quality systems start with a business charter or policy statement. When a business starts, the owners of that business will create a business plan and state what they hope to achieve with their newly formed business. They will then create policies in line with that statement that meet the needs and the legal requirements of the business. Quality control policies do the following:

- define the quality expectations of the business—this is the quality of the look and feel of the store, customer service, the store merchandising, the types of products stocked and the quality of the products stocked
- provide for training in quality control procedures—procedures can be drawn from the policy document that can describe how to:
  - assess the quality of the stock
  - identify areas where quality should improve
  - report on quality deficiencies
  - act on improving quality deficiencies.
- provide for a system of automation (where possible)—automation reduces the costs of labour for the retailer. For quality control, it is preferable that the bulk of the work to maintain or improve quality is done without the interjection of staff
- provide for a system for customer and staff feedback—this will assist the retailer to identify quality deficiencies that perhaps have not been noticed or identified within the day-to-day quality control process.

You can see that by adhering to stock control, accurate stock recording, discrepancy reporting systems, prescribed store merchandising and marketing, correct pricing and labelling, and finally, the quality control policies and procedures of your workplace, your ability to monitor and improve upon stock performance is enhanced.

Task 10.2

Access the stock records of your store and complete the following report. Alternatively, you can use the example provided.

1. List items that are in short supply.
2. List items that are on order but have not arrived.
3. What stock item is the fastest moving in your store (in the example) at the moment?

Stock control

PERIOD	
FROM	TO
8/08/12	08/10/12

ITEM			QUANTITY			DATE		
NO.	DESCRIPTION	STOCK TURNS	ON ORDER	BACK ORDERS	TOTAL	ORDERED	DUE	RECEIVED
88	White socks, short	5	15	0	15	8/08/12	10/08/12	
89	White socks, long	1	0	0				
90	White socks, ankle	6	0	20	20	2/08/12	7/08/12	
91	Blue socks, short	3	5	0	5	8/08/12	10/08/12	
92	Blue socks, long	2	0	0				
93	Black socks, short	8	20	0	20	8/08/12	10/08/12	
94	Black socks, long	3	5	0	5	8/08/12	10/08/12	
95	Black socks, ankle	2	0	0				
96	Red socks, long	2	0	0				
97	Red socks, short	4	5	0	5	8/08/12	10/08/12	

SIGNED ______________________

ELEMENT 3
COORDINATE STOCKTAKE

So far we have looked at the many options available to maintain adequate levels of stock in your workplace. Adhering to the procedures in-store provides your customers with a quality range of correctly priced and labelled merchandise, which leads to a more profitable store.

Irrespective of the retail business within which you work, a manual stocktake can be quite a daunting undertaking. Having a plan that includes a method for cyclical counts, rosters, clear directions and reporting can have a marked positive impact upon the task.

LEARNING OUTCOMES

3.1 Interpret policy and procedures in regard to *stocktaking* and cyclical counts and explain to team members.

3.2 Roster staff according to allocated budget and time constraints.

3.3 Allocate stocktaking tasks to individual team members.

3.4 Provide team members with clear directions for the performance of each task.

3.5 Allocate team members to ensure effective use of staff resources to complete task.

3.6 Produce accurate reports on stocktake data, including discrepancies, for management.

Stocktake and cyclical count policies

Stocktakes are undertaken for two main reasons:

1. Stocktaking is a compliance requirement under taxation law. Businesses with a turnover of more than $2 million per annum must conduct a full stocktake by 30 June each year in order to report their assets and liabilities correctly to the ATO. Smaller businesses may use simpler means.
2. The stocktake is a business performance monitoring tool. Regular or cyclical stocktakes will assist managers and supervisory staff in making better decisions about their business. For example, when a business that conducts monthly stocktakes discovers a large discrepancy in one line item, the manager can quickly investigate and act upon the discrepancy to ensure that it does not grow into a larger financial problem for the business.

Figure 10.3 Portable barcode scanners reduce the time taken for stocktakes

There are three types of stocktake: they are full or cyclical stocktakes, or spot checks.

FULL STOCKTAKE

A full stocktake is where every item in the retail store (including in the storeroom) is counted. The regularity of such a stocktake will depend on the business. A school canteen may choose to conduct a full stocktake each month, whereas a retail superstore may only conduct one per year.

CYCLICAL STOCKTAKE

This is a planned, regular stocktake of sections of stock throughout the retail outlet. The aim is two-fold: firstly, to identify any issues that could affect stock levels and profitability early; and secondly, to reduce the burden of a full stocktake (such as extensive labour costs and reduced trading times).

SPOT CHECKS

Spot checks can be carried out for a number of reasons. They may occur:

- at the manager's behest
- because staff have noticed irregularities in a certain section or area
- when stock has been moved to or from promotional areas
- if there is any doubt as to the accuracy of the stock quantities
- as a means of training staff
- in preparation for a full stocktake.

Figure 10.4 A manual stocktake may be required where merchandise is difficult to access with an electronic scanner

Spot checks are useful for identifying irregularities and issues in an isolated area.

Your workplace will have a policy that best suits its business model. It may include a mixture of full, spot and cyclical stocktakes, or a monthly count routine. You will need to be aware of the specific procedures used in your workplace.

Stocktake procedures

Stocktake procedures refer to the planning and execution of an accurate count of stock-on-hand. Let's look at an example of this—but remember, the procedure will differ from retailer to retailer, and you will have to be familiar with your specific procedures.

STEP 1: THE PLAN

The stocktake plan will include:

- staff requirements and allocation of tasks
- stocktake time constraints
- budget constraints
- recording and reporting procedures.

EXAMPLE: STOCKTAKE PLANNING

You need to take stock at a small suburban franchised grocery store called ITA's Groceries. You have a stock holding of $500 000 and an annual turnover of $2.4 million. You have three casual staff members and one full-time staff member who report to you and a store franchisee/manager. All other staff are on approved leave. It is approaching 30 June and you have been asked to coordinate the stocktake for the end-of-year reports. The following may be an accurate reflection of the stocktake process at this store.

Staff requirements, allocation of tasks, budget and time constraints

Your first consideration is the staff required to complete the stocktake in time and accurately. The store procedure is that all staff must contribute to the stocktake, so you ask your manager about the budget she has put aside for this. She informs you that you have one full-day's wage per person to complete the task. That is your budgetary constraint.

She also tells you that it must be completed by close of business (5 pm) on 30 June. This now provides your 'time constraint'. With this information, you start to plan the process.

You call a meeting with the staff to work out a roster. Because you have casual staff, you will need to make sure that they are available for the times you need them. During the meeting, you complete a stocktake roster with all the staff committing at that time. The roster looks something like this:

Table 10.1

Stocktake roster example

Stocktake roster				
Date	**Team member**	**Time on**	**Time off**	**Section**
29/6/13	Josh Hill	3.30 pm	6.30 pm	Dairy/deli
29/6/13	Brenda Lowe	3.30 pm	6.30 pm	Dairy/deli
29/6/13	Jody Renner	6.00 pm	8.00 pm	Aisle 1/2
29/6/13	Liam Harm	6.00 pm	8.00 pm	Aisle 1/2
29/6/13	You	3.30 pm	8.00 pm	Counter/front fridge
30/6/13	Josh Hill	9.30 am	2.30 pm	Aisle 3/4
30/6/13	Brenda Lowe	9.30 am	2.30 pm	Aisle 3/4
30/6/13	Jody Renner	11.30 am	4.30 pm	Aisle 5/6
30/6/13	Liam Harm	11.30 am	4.30 pm	Aisle 5/6
30/6/13	You	8.30 am	4.00 pm	Storeroom/ Discrepancies

Note that the roster only covers stocktaking duties. The store manager can choose to serve customers or close the store during the stocktake period. Running a stocktake while serving customers can present several issues regarding the accuracy of the count. It is often the case that casual staff will be brought in after hours to carry out the stocktake leaving the opening hours for trade. This is highly dependent on the size of the business, flexibility of staff and managers and the urgency of the stocktake. This will all need to be confirmed in your workplace. Let's get back to ITA's groceries.

You'll notice that the staff only work a maximum of eight hours each on stocktake duties as per the budgetary constraint. You have elected to work more hours, however you can account for this by involving the manager or conducting other duties.

Task allocation is a collaborative process and roles and times should be agreed to at that time. Alternatively, if staff are unable to attend a meeting, the schedule may be forwarded to them so that they may then respond as to their availability.

STEP 2: IMPLEMENT THE PLAN

Recording and reporting procedure

You will need to provide the staff with clear directions so they are aware of how to count, check, record and submit their reports. A sample stocktake report is provided below. We will use this to explain the process to Josh Hill, one of your casual team members.

EXAMPLE: RECORDING AND REPORTING

YOU: 'Josh, each item listed on your stocktake report needs to be physically counted, and the result of that count needs to be written in the 'Quantity on hand' column. Do you understand?'

JOSH: 'Sure.'

YOU: 'If you count fewer of any item than the sheet says—for example, you only count four when the column "Quantity on RMS" [that is, the "retail management system"] says there should be five, you need to write it in the "discrepancy column" as "negative one (–1)", OK?'

JOSH: 'What if there's no stock or I can't find it?'

YOU: 'Skip it and come back to it at the end. If you still can't find it, let me know and we'll try to find it together.'

YOU: 'For every item you completely count, ask Brenda to count it also to confirm your number, then stick one of these green sticky dots on the shelf price ticket for *that* item. OK?'

JOSH: 'Won't that take even *longer?*'

YOU: 'We need to be accurate so the business can meet its tax obligations, Josh. It always pays to have a second counter.'

JOSH: 'OK.'

YOU: 'Now lastly, when each sheet is completed—that is there are no blank lines—bring it to me. When all the sheets are done you can help Jody and Liam until your shift's over. Is that OK?'

JOSH: 'Sure—thanks.'

The process is now clear to Josh and his teammates. But the job is not done until discrepancies are investigated and the reports are finalised for management.

STEP 3: DISCREPANCY RECORDING AND REPORT FINALISATION

The sample stocktake report below has a column for the reasons for the discrepancies. This column can now be filled out by you, as Josh and the other staff hand their reports in. You use the investigation methods discussed in the last section to help you complete the form.

Table 10.2

Example stocktake report

Stocktake report (Example)					
Name	**Josh Hill**	**Date/ Time**	**29/6/2013**		**3.35pm**
Stock EAN	**Description**	**Qty on RMS**	**Qty on hand**	**+/–**	**Reason for discrepancy (team leader to complete)**
5905013868741	1L plastic bottle XYZ	2	2		
5905015322898	1.25L bottle, plastic, w/handle	4	5	+1	*Possibly stolen—no other errors*
5905016895724	500mL opaque plastic bottle RED	3	4	+1	*Incorrectly received as 'ORANGE'*
5905017659874	500mL opaque plastic bottle GREEN	4	4		
5905018528639	500mL opaque plastic bottle ORANGE	6	5	–1	*Incorrectly received as 'RED'*
5905019205819	500mL opaque plastic bottle BLUE	3	3		
5905010326985	600mL Sports bottle BLACK XYZ	6	6		
5905011857968	600mL Sports bottle RED XYZ	8	7	–1	*Bottle at counter—see counter ST report*
5358694765223	ECO Sandwich bags, small	7	7		
5358694765224	ECO Sandwich bags, medium	7	7		
5358694765225	ECO Sandwich bags, large	8	7	–1	*Used in store, not written off.*

Ensuring effective use of resources

Stocktakes can be labour-intensive and therefore costly to the business. There are a number of methods you can use to improve the efficiency of the process, including various scheduling and communication tools. Of course you will need to comply with whatever systems currently exist in your workplace.

Scheduling can be accomplished through the use of electronic roster software that calculates total time worked (daily or weekly), breaks, pay rates and so on. This software can be commercially available or developed in-house by the retailer. A manual roster, such as the one we've used in the example, can also be a useful tool to ensure you have staff available when necessary and only for the length of time you need them.

Efficiency is achieved through what is called a 'feedback loop'. A feedback loop is a cycle of continuous improvement such as that shown in Figure 10.5.

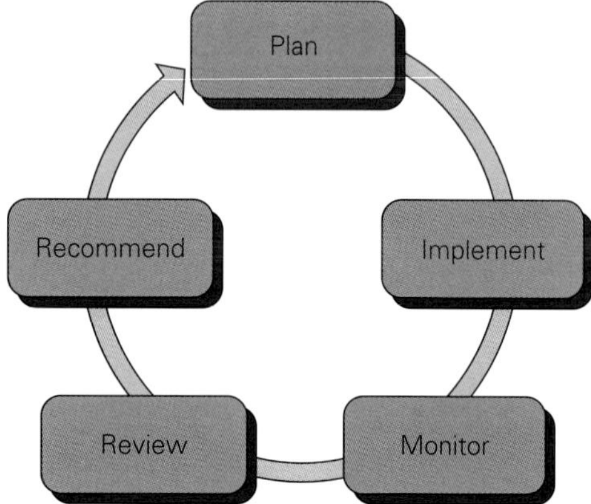

Figure 10.5 A 'feedback loop'

Each of these steps requires communication—feedback. The planning process only works if the team can agree to the schedule. Implementation only works when clear directions are given and stocktake records are collected and reviewed in a timely manner. Accuracy can only be monitored if team members are working together and team leaders are providing feedback. Review of the process and recommended changes can only occur with communication between you, the rest of the team and the manager responsible.

Task 10.3

Arrange a cyclical count of stock in a section of your store. To do this, you will need to complete the following:

1. a roster of who will be involved and when they will be required (date/time)
2. a report of the stocktake for the section. This should indicate overs/unders and reasons for any discrepancies, as per the example stocktake report in this chapter.

As this is a learning exercise, choose a small area of the store or even a single product line. At this stage, the focus is on the process of rostering and reporting.

Useful websites:

FairWork Australia award 2010 retail roster template

www.fairwork.gov.au/resources/templates/pages/industry-specific.aspx

Commercially available roster and scheduling software

www.timeandattendance.com.au; www.findmyshift.com/, www.rosterlive.com/; www.rosterportal.com.au/; www.madrigalsoft.com/, and many more.

ELEMENT 4
STOCK LOSSES

Stock losses are a cost to the business. These costs include higher insurance premiums based on a risk assessment, stock write-offs, ongoing security costs, reduced profitability on damaged goods and administration costs relating to the loss. Unfortunately shrinkage (as it is known) is a reality and therefore you will need to know how to deal with it in your workplace.

LEARNING OUTCOMES

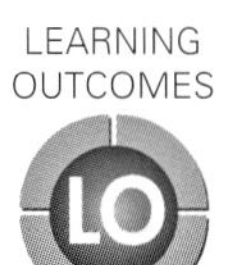

4.1 Identify, record and assess losses against potential loss forecast on a regular basis.
4.2 Identify avoidable losses and establish reasons.
4.3 Recommend and implement possible solutions.

Accounting for stock losses

Retailers generally work on an acceptable loss forecast figure of between 1 per cent and 3 per cent of total sales.[2] In this case, less is better. To put it in perspective, imagine if you had 3 per cent of your wage stolen each week. If you are earning $600 a week, that is almost $20 that you will not get to use. How would that affect you?

Losses are often unavoidable or at least difficult to control. In the first instance, you should identify whether the loss was avoidable or not. Losses fall broadly into three categories—errors, theft and waste. Examples of the causes of loss are shown in Table 10.3.

Figure 10.6 Monitoring store movement

Table 10.3

Stock losses

Avoidable loss	Type	Unavoidable loss	Type
Staff damage (during dispatch or movement of the stock)	Waste	Moisture ingress	Waste
Receiving errors—entering the wrong product, quantity, value or price	Error	Smoke or fire damage	Waste
Shoplifting, petty theft	Theft	Return where the goods are not in a condition that permit them to be returned to the supplier for credit	Error

Stock losses			
Avoidable loss	**Type**	**Unavoidable loss**	**Type**
Staff pilferage	Theft	The goods expire (such as fresh fruit, vegetables, meats, flowers and dairy products)	Waste
Customers opening packets/boxes in store	Waste	Goods are faulty or damaged but not detected on receipt	Error
Customers damaging goods in store	Waste	Armed robbery	Theft
Not maintaining stock	Error	Supplier theft	Theft
Not rotating stock	Error	Natural disaster	Waste
Incorrect change and pricing	Error	Unforeseen incident	Waste

You could argue that even the 'unavoidable' losses could be avoided if the appropriate control measures were applied. We will look at controls that minimise the threat of loss in both lists throughout this section.

RECORDING AND ASSESSING LOSSES AGAINST FORECAST

The retailer's loss forecast is a guideline only. It is intended to serve as a risk assessment tool for the business owners (investors), managers and insurers. Therefore, the intention at store level is to implement whatever 'practicable' controls are necessary to keep the loss total *below* the loss forecast.

The word 'practicable' is what differentiates between the lists of avoidable and unavoidable causes. The unavoidable causes are only unavoidable up to the point where it is no longer practicable to control them. For example, it is not practicable to fireproof an older structure as well as the surrounding buildings, over and above the fire safety regulations, in order to remove any chance of smoke damage. Nor would it be practicable (or legal) to refuse customer returns based on a specific supplier agreement.

Regular checks

It is recommended that cyclical stocktakes are conducted to monitor and react to stock shrinkage. Losses can be immediately identified against the stock control system report. This can be manually checked against a stocktake inventory list (see stocktake report example) or electronically, using a handheld barcode scanner. Electronic stock control systems often make use of mobile scanners to quickly check stock. Using a wireless stock control scanner involves the following steps:

1. Scan the barcode on the item's store-printed label (usually on the shelf or stuck to the product). This brings up the item on the scanner and you can check the quantity shown there. It also retrieves pertinent information about the stock, such as price and description, so you can double-check that it is the correct product.
2. Scan the items on hand. The scanner will make a distinctive 'beep' and can often display a red or green light to verify that the stock has been correctly scanned.

3. Enter the stock. On some scanners you will use a keypad to enter the stock quantity rather than scan each item.
4. You can now compare the computer's 'stock on hand' figure to the physical stock count that appears on the device screen.
5. When complete, you can download the totals into the stock control system by docking the scanner into its charger or attaching the USB connector (if applicable) to the store's administration computer.

Making an assessment

The results of the stocktake are assessed against a few different parameters, again depending on your workplace policies. These can include:

- actual quantity versus shown quantity (this is the computer system figure)
- actual loss versus forecast loss
- error rates (based on the outcome of investigating the losses).

> **IMPORTANT NOTE:**
> The loss forecast figure must be verified with your manager. It will be a specific figure written into store policy. The 1% to 3% range is mentioned as a learning tool only.

In this section we are concerned with assessing losses. As mentioned, retailers will have a loss forecast figure of somewhere between 1 per cent and 3 per cent of total sales. So, for a business turning over $2.4 million per annum, the forecast loss figure would be somewhere between $24 000 and $72 000.

So, in an annual stocktake, the losses at the end of the year must total *less* than the loss forecast in order to be on target with the financial objectives of the business. If the figure is higher, particularly if the losses fall under the 'avoidable' category, then the business manager must act quickly to further investigate the causes and rectify any issues that may be contributing to the unacceptable figure.

ESTABLISHING REASONS FOR AVOIDABLE LOSSES

It is never good enough to just say, 'well, stuff happens'. In every case, the loss should be investigated to a reasonable extent. But what is a 'reasonable extent'?

Remember the word 'practicable'? That is the key to deciding what is reasonable and what is not. If the cost of investigating a loss far outweighs the potential benefits over the next twelve months, then the investigation is not deemed practicable. For example, if you identify a –1 discrepancy with a can of asparagus valued at $2.40, and there do not appear to be any other missing cans in the vicinity of the asparagus, then you might limit your investigation to following the documentation trail and talking the staff responsible for that area. If the loss were a $2000 digital camera from a locked glass cabinet, then you would probably investigate further until you have found the item or filed a police report over the theft.

In all cases, large and small, your gaol is to establish a reason for the loss. The table of avoidable and unavoidable losses shown earlier is a good reference for the outcome you are trying to achieve. For instance, if you investigate the can of asparagus and find that it was thrown out by a staff member because it was rusted or badly dented, you would report on the stocktake report that the item was 'damaged but not detected at receiving'.

In this case it would not necessarily be practicable to view hours of CCTV video to determine whether a customer or staff member damaged the goods. In the case of the $2000 camera however, it may be worth establishing a time when staff knew the camera was there, and when they first noticed it missing. You could then establish through interviews or CCTV the reason behind the loss.

For more information refer to the investigation methods on pages 308–309.

The use of one or more of these methods, coupled with the aim of establishing and reporting a reason for the loss, will enable you to carry out this task competently. Be sure that you are aware of the procedure for reporting the loss in your workplace. It may be any of the following:

- provide a verbal or documented report to the department head or team leader
- provide a verbal or documented report to the manager
- provide a verbal or documented report to a committee
- enter the report into the stock control system (computer system)
- provide the information for another to enter it into the system or report it to relevant staff.

Recommending and implementing solutions

Your recommendations for improvement can significantly affect the profitability of the retail business. Positive steps to minimise stock loss are encouraged at all levels of business and are valued highly. We will now look at a range of recommendations and ways of implementing them:

Table 10.4

Losses and solutions

Type of loss	Example recommendations and implementation
Error	• Review the procedure that led to the error • Change the procedure to reduce the risk of recurrence • Retrain the staff responsible • Improve or rework store signage to better inform staff and customers • Run an information campaign for staff and customers (e.g. using flyers, webcasts, emails).
Waste	• Retrain staff in handling techniques • Review the waste handling procedure • Implement a sale bin for seconds • Donate damaged goods • Have a repackaging facility on site (shrink-wrap or boxing facility).

Losses and solutions	
Type of loss	**Example recommendations and implementation**
Theft	• Retrain staff in managing shoplifting • Review store security systems • Improve current systems to cover more of the shop floor • Implement new security systems with new technology • Review and upgrade the receiving and dispatch processes.

Implementing the recommendations may require:

- additional training (for you)
- coordination of contractors on-site (in the instance of updating security systems)
- coordination of rosters and training for team members
- meeting with managers or team members responsible for the area
- planning a new procedure
- assisting others with the implementation.

Task 10.4

Investigating a stock loss

STEP 1

You've identified a missing smartphone on your latest stock count. The item is valued at $650 ex-GST at cost. What steps would you take to investigate the loss?

1.
2.
3.

STEP 2

After investigating, you have discovered that the item was not checked off in the receiving area. What could be the possible causes for this, and what would you do next in each case?

Possible cause	Recommendations
1	
2	
3	

ELEMENT 5
PROCESSING ORDERS

Retail sales depend on having the right stock, at the right price, at the right time. The process of ordering takes into account all of these critical factors. Orders will need to be raised on a regular basis in order to maintain adequate stock; but what if the price has changed? Or seasonal items have run out? Or there is a new marketing push coming up? Ordering is an important process and those responsible must be aware of all the factors affecting what they order.

Note that in this unit there is a distinction made between ordering and buying. Ordering is a day-to-day function in-store, used to replenish stock and order new stock in accordance with the buying plan. Buying is a merchandising function and is usually specialised. Buyers have expertise in their products and can often plan out merchandise lines up to twelve months in advance.

LEARNING OUTCOMES

LO

5.1 Process and raise orders for stock as requested, according to store policy and procedures.

5.2 Maintain an ordering and recording system.

5.3 Ensure availability of sample range, according to buying plan.

5.4 Order pricing materials as required.

5.5 Record negotiated purchase and supply agreements and file for retrieval.

Raising orders

Retail orders are almost exclusively raised on the store's computer system. On rare occasions, faxed orders may need to be raised and sent, but these will still need to be entered into the inventory system in order to monitor and maintain the stock once it arrives.

Store policies regarding ordering vary greatly. In general, the policy will dictate:

- who is allowed to raise orders
- who must authorise the orders prior to sending
- the amount able to be spent per order or per day (often referred to as 'open-to-buy')
- submitting and filing of orders
- supplier agreements (or a link to the location of supplier agreements)
- process for receiving the stock.

Figure 10.7 Stock must be re-ordered based on existing ordering policies

Depending on the size of the store, orders may be raised by full-time sales staff, administrators, store managers or a specialised buyer. Orders can be generated automatically via an electronic

POS replenishment system, or manually as required. In both cases, the orders must be checked (and often authorised) prior to sending. This is to prevent errors such as:

- incorrect pricing—this can occur if the cost price changes since the last order, or there is a negotiated price in place for a specific order. The current price should be maintained in the computer system, but often there is a lag between negotiations and entry into the store's computer system.
- insufficient or over-order of stock—this can occur for a number of reasons. As we've previously mentioned, consider the impact of seasonality, trends, marketing and merchandising promotions, and lead-time, obsolete items, FIFO, shelf life and replenishment. In all cases, the order must be in line with current requirements with consideration given to future needs based on these factors.
- fraud—this can occur if the responsibility for ordering is too broadly allocated. It is an unfortunate fact that some employees will try to steal from their employers. Unmonitored access to the ordering system provides another way of achieving that end.

Once the order is verified it can be sent to the supplier. For a retail outlet the supplier could mean:

- off-site company warehouse—this is stock that already exists in the retailer's inventory system but is not at your particular site. You may hear the term 'cost centre' used to describe these different sites as they each operate to achieve profit and therefore actively work to reduce their costs. So when a store orders from its own company's warehouse, factors like freight charges (especially on small orders) need to be considered. The benefits of this arrangement include:
    - › secured stock (no competitor will be able to access the stock)
    - › a guaranteed price that matches the system price
    - › opportunity for bulk purchase discounts for the retail company.
- third-party warehouse—a multitude of distribution companies operate in Australia. These companies may be suppliers in their own right (that is they have trading agreements in place with the retailers), or they might be proxy warehouses for a manufacturer (where the agreement is between the warehouse distributor and the manufacturer). Pricing will vary according to negotiated deals between the retailer and the supplier and therefore ordering must be verified for accuracy. Buying groups and retail cooperatives often use this method.
- the manufacturer, grower or farmer direct—in some instances retailers may have an agreement with a local supplier to provide goods directly. This may be a local grower, farmer or manufacturer whose goods have some competitive edge (such as higher quality or lower price) over other suppliers. These arrangements are exclusively negotiated at the store level, and prices are usually set for specified periods (from one month up to twelve months).
- manufacturer's warehouse—where the manufacturer operates a warehouse distribution function, orders may be placed directly with the manufacturer, who will take care of

the distribution costs. The advantage is that there is less handling, and potentially fewer overheads. The disadvantage is that some manufacturers cannot distribute products as efficiently as professional distribution companies.

SUBMITTING AND FILING ORDERS

Orders are usually sent electronically. Many systems are now integrated with suppliers' systems in what is termed B2B (business-to-business) commerce. Submitting the order can be as simple as pressing 'ENTER' on the computer keyboard, or clicking on the 'SUBMIT' icon on the screen. Manually, orders can be printed and faxed or scanned and emailed. The supplier then enters the order into their system for dispatch.

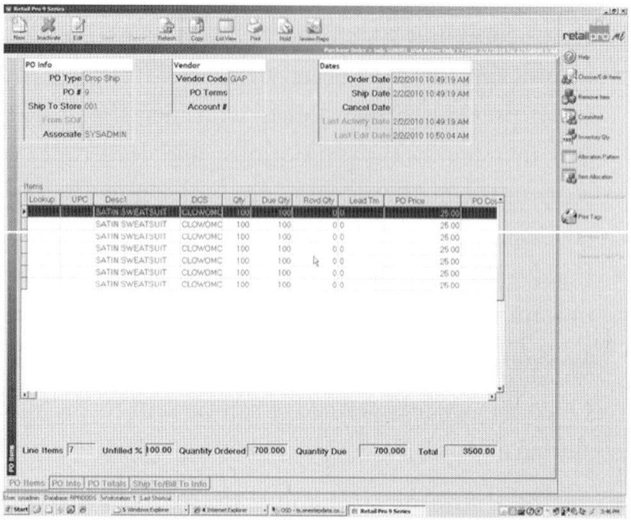

Courtesy of Retail/Pro

Figure 10.8 An example of a retail order screen by Retail Pro®

The electronic ordering system at your workplace will be set up with the stock information, supplier contact details and various codes to differentiate between departments, locations, supplier types and so on (see Figure 10.8).

In most cases, a hardcopy of the orders for each day or supplier is printed out and filed. When the supplier's order arrives, the dispatch docket (from the supplier) can be checked against the order to ensure that it is correct and accurate.

When the supplier's invoice is received, the hardcopy order is attached as reference and filed for accounting purposes. The hardcopies may even be scanned and saved in computer in order to save space. You will need to check with your workplace to determine the filing process for orders.

THE ORDERING AND RECORDING SYSTEM

As just mentioned, ordering can be electronic or manual. In order to maintain the system's integrity (in other words, how accurate and stable the system is), you must ensure that you follow the procedures for using the system. If the procedure requires authorisation, make sure that the order is authorised. If the procedure requires paper filing, then make sure that you print out the order and file it appropriately.

An effective system is one that works each and every time. The ordering process is no different. The factors affecting the ordering system's effectiveness are:

- accuracy
- records management—how and where the records are stored (online, or in a filing cabinet)

- process—a procedure should cover every task from the moment an order is required to the moment the stock is received into the store.

In order to remain effective, follow the current procedures, but also offer suggestions where you believe improvements could be made.

STOCK AVAILABILITY

Prior to ordering, it pays to check the availability of the stock and whether it is still featured in the store's buying plan. These two steps can be quite simple.

Where a B2B relationship exists, you will have access to the supplier's stock-on-hand quantities—usually in real time. This allows you to order with some certainty that the quantities on the system are those in stock. Remember though, they are susceptible to the same losses and errors as you, so variations may occur. So if it is a critical order—say, a customer order or stock for a promotion—it is worth checking with the merchandise buyer, supplier representative, or the supplier customer service person to be safe.

If the ordering relationship still relies on manual ordering, or there is no access to the supplier's stock-on-hand quantities, you can still call, email or otherwise contact those people mentioned above in order to confirm availability.

A buying plan, or open-to-buy (OTB) plan, is a short- to medium-term plan (one to three months) for the amount of money the store can spend on stock for that period. It is a figure worked out by using forecast sales, planned markdowns, and the starting and ending

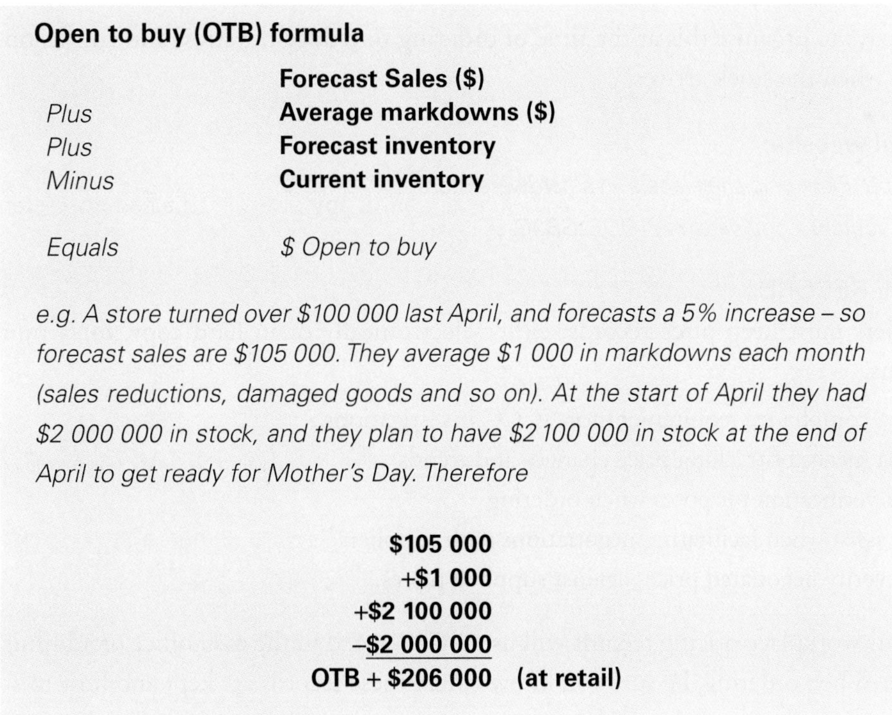

Open to buy (OTB) formula

	Forecast Sales ($)
Plus	**Average markdowns ($)**
Plus	**Forecast inventory**
Minus	**Current inventory**
Equals	*$ Open to buy*

e.g. A store turned over $100 000 last April, and forecasts a 5% increase – so forecast sales are $105 000. They average $1 000 in markdowns each month (sales reductions, damaged goods and so on). At the start of April they had $2 000 000 in stock, and they plan to have $2 100 000 in stock at the end of April to get ready for Mother's Day. Therefore

$105 000
+$1 000
+$2 100 000
–$2 000 000
OTB + $206 000 (at retail)

Figure 10.10 Example OTB plan

inventory levels to come up with a retail figure in dollars. It stands to reason that the sum of all orders for that period should be less than or equal to that amount, otherwise cash flow will be affected, which could cause a variety of problems for the retailer.

ORDERING NEW ITEMS

If you have been asked to order an item that does not already exist on your inventory management system, it will need to be added first. This is usually the responsibility of the merchandise buyer but in some cases, a single customer order may arise. Therefore, you may need to be aware of the procedure for entering in a new product into the system used at your workplace. As there are simply too many variations to show here, it is recommended that you become familiar with your particular process should this responsibility be given to you.

PRICING

Each store has a process for pricing stock when it arrives. This can range from a manually written price tag, through to a centrally generated company-wide shelf-price system. The order system may provide the pricing materials automatically, but if not, you'll need to ensure that you have ordered them in the relevant manner (as per your particular workplace). Shelf and stock labelling can also be electronic (see 'More information' below).

You may need to consider any other materials associated with the order. For example:

- sales signage
- promotional signage
- supplier- or company-provided stands, shelving or other promotional fittings.

It pays to organise this at the time of ordering to reduce the stress and confusion it may cause when the stock arrives.

Useful website:

YouTube 'Electronic shelf labels' in a hardware store

www.youtube.com/watch?v-/1QQEzGB2O-U

PRICE RECORDS

Retailers must keep price records, either electronically or in hard copy, for a number of reasons.

1. as a compliance requirement for ACCC investigations
2. as a means of tracking price changes and trends
3. for verification purposes when ordering
4. to assist when facilitating negotiations with suppliers
5. to verify negotiated prices against supplied prices.

Your workplace pricing records will usually be stored in the cash office or administration office. When ordering, be sure you know where these records are kept and how to store the records once they are generated.

Task 10.5

Raise an order for stock in your store's inventory system. You may need to do this under supervision, so be sure to get the authorisation of your manager or trainer before completing this task.

When completed, print a copy of the order for your trainer or assessor. You can, if required, block out pricing details or any other sensitive information in line with your store's policies.

ELEMENT 6
FOLLOWING UP ORDERS

To keep stock flowing smoothly through the store it is important to keep an eye on orders after they have been submitted. There are usually a few tools to help you achieve this with relatively little effort, but issues may occur that require your full and attentive involvement.

LEARNING OUTCOMES

6.1 Monitor delivery process to meet agreed deadline.

6.2 Handle routine supply problems or refer to management as required by store policy.

6.3 Maintain ongoing liaison with buyers, store or departments, warehouse and suppliers to ensure continuity of supply.

6.4 Distribute stock according to store or department allocation.

Monitoring the delivery process

It is the responsibility of the staff at the receiving dock to accurately receive, check in and dispatch the stock being delivered by suppliers. They will need access to the order relating to each delivery and need to know that the delivery is scheduled for that day in order to accurately mark off the goods and provide the resources to check and dispatch the stock.

DEADLINES AND STOCK FLOW

Deadlines are the specified future point in time by which stock must be received in order to meet the needs of the store. Deadlines may also be enforced under a contractual agreement with the supplier. For example, the contract may state that the supplier agrees to deliver stock within three trading days of the order being received. So whether the deadline is a store-related requirement or previously agreed to contractual requirements, you should monitor the receipt of the stock to ensure that it is met.

Monitoring the flow of stock can happen in several ways:

- computer flags and triggers—flags next to expected stock or triggers created when stock is late can be used to highlight concerns and prompt you to take action.

- regular impromptu checks—team leaders and managers gain an invaluable insight into the business's operations by regularly checking on various operational functions from cash register operation through to stock receipt. An impromptu check on the status of an order might highlight a concern that you are then able to follow up.
- meetings with supplier representatives—suppliers may have mobile representatives who move from store to store to merchandise, train and process orders for their particular brand or supplier. A brief meeting can provide insight into the availability of stock and any potential issues in the future.

HANDLING ROUTINE SUPPLY PROBLEMS

When a problem is identified, you may be able to deal with it effectively and efficiently yourself. There may be a need to refer the issue to management to gain additional support or to rectify the problem. Table 10.5 identifies some typical supply problems and possible solutions.

Table 10.5

Typical supply problems and possible solutions

Broad supply issue	Possible solution
Late delivery	Contact the supplier. If the shipment has left the supplier's warehouse ask for a connote (consignment notice) number and contact the freight company directly.
Unforeseen delays	If delays are unavoidable due to natural disaster or industrial action, notices around the store may need to be posted for customers and staff. If the delays are avoidable but unforseen (such as damage on the loading bay or during dispatch in store), recommend retraining in handling procedures or updating hardware such as trolleys and lifting equipment.
Incorrect delivery	Check the order and refer back to the supplier for follow up. If this causes unnecessary issues with store deadlines, involve your manager or buyer.

Being able to handle routine problems is a necessary skill in retail. Well-developed interpersonal skills and the courage to tackle issues and unusual tasks head-on are favourable characteristics to have.

MAINTAIN LIAISON WITH STAKEHOLDERS

If you are to be actively involved in the order process, you will need to maintain effective communications with the following key stakeholders:

- buyers—are responsible for the success or failure of their choices in merchandise for your store. They rely on feedback and two-way communication to regularly review their decisions and may be a very helpful ally when confronting difficult supply issues.
- suppliers' representatives—make yourself known to the 'reps' that visit your store. They are there to help you buy and sell more of their product, so they are also a great source of information and help should there be any issues with orders relating to their product lines.

- supplier customer service or sales/order staff—often, a sales desk staff member or customer service operator can be a great help in tracking down orders and investigating issues. Maintaining a good relationship with people in these positions is very beneficial.
- team mates—your fellow retail staff members need your feedback and should be the first to give you feedback about the ebbs and flows of stock within the store. They may be the first to raise a late order with you.
- team leaders, department and store managers—the store is only as effective as the communication between all members of the team. From managers to weekend casuals, written and verbal communication must be clear and regular. This consistency make anomalies easier to spot, so when stock issues arise, everyone who needs to know will be made aware quickly and the issue can be solved more easily.

DISTRIBUTION OF STOCK IN-STORE

Once orders are received and checked into the system, the receiving dock staff will contact the department managers to arrange for the stock to be allocated to specific areas of the store. In larger stores, this activity is coordinated based on the item's pre-loaded location. When the item is scanned on the receiving dock the intended floor location is attached to its unique barcode. For example, if a clothes dryer is scanned at the receiving dock, its barcode should already exist under the category of whitegoods/laundry/dryers and a location will be allocated.

For smaller stores, where a specific merchandising plan does not exist, refer to the current store layout and ensure that the items are dispatched to the correct area.

For online retailers, the warehouse areas must also be identified in the stock control system to ensure efficient picking systems and customer order fulfilment. So rather than distribute the products to a shop floor, you may only need to deliver the boxed product to a warehouse location—aisle, rack number and so on. To ensure order pickers can find the stock, there may be a need to unbox the products on the picking level, dependent on the products being sold.

USE OF MECHANICAL AIDS

As the majority of retail stock is delivered in boxes on pallets, there will be a number of options for you to choose from when dispatching the goods to the correct store location. They include the following:

Forklift

In all states the use of a forklift is regulated by WorkCover (or equivalent) and a licence may be required under law. *Do not* operate a forklift without an appropriate licence or without being under the supervision of someone with a licence, as you may be in breach of the law. If in doubt, ask your immediate supervisor.

There are different types of forklifts including order pickers (larger high-lift units) and smaller electrically powered units. In all cases, under workplace health and safety legislation you must receive adequate training prior to use.

Manual trolleys

Manual trolleys include pallet lifters and flat tray trolleys. These are relatively simple to use, but when a large weight is being shifted, the load becomes more difficult to handle and there is always the risk of injury. Again, you must receive training before using these or delegating the use of these to someone.

Ladders and mobile stairs

Stock may need to be stored in overhead shelving. You will need to be aware of the proper use of ladders and stairs in the workplace. For example, most workplaces require the following safety measures:

- Use the mobile stairs' grounding mechanism, which disengages the wheels to prevent stairs rolling while in use
- Do not move the stairs or ladder with someone on them
- Do not lift stock above your head (or, in some workplaces, above your chest)
- Do not over-extend yourself above or over the railing of the stairs or stock picker
- Do not climb on the railing of the stairs or order picker
- Do not climb above the second-last rung on the ladder
- Ensure that ladders are opened and locked correctly before climbing
- Do not climb a ladder that is leaning on stock or shelving.

There may be other specific safety instructions in your workplace, so be sure to observe them at all times and to direct others to do so to avoid injuries.

Task 10.6

You've just been informed over the phone by your supplier's representative that an urgent customer order, due today, has been delayed by two more days. List and describe the steps you would take to resolve this issue. Your customer is coming to the store in the next few hours to pick up her purchase.

Useful websites:

Forklift licence Sydney

www.forkliftlicencesydney.com.au/41/forklift-licence-faqs/.

NSW HSC online

www.hsc.csu.edu.au.

Endnotes

1. SafeWork SA, www.safework.sa.gov.au/uploaded_files/resCOPManualHandling.pdf
2. Mark Wrice, 2010, *First steps in retail management*, Palgrave MacMillan, South Yarra, Victoria

ASSESSMENT 1: REVIEW QUESTIONS

1. Describe the seven steps for the receipt and dispatch of goods.
2. What considerations must be taken into account when approaching a manual handling task? Describe at least five things you need to consider.
3. What is the FIFO method? (Ensure that you describe what it is, as well as what FIFO stands for.)
4. During a stock count you find a discrepancy of +4. What does this mean, and what could be one possible cause of this discrepancy?
5. What information does the 'Open to buy' figure provide when you are processing orders?
6. Stock losses can be investigated in three ways. What are those three ways and why would you use each one?

ASSESSMENT 2

For this assessment your immediate supervisor or assessor will need to observe you doing a number of tasks in a workplace or simulated environment. The tasks are listed in the 'assessment instructions' below. They will complete a checklist and provide feedback to you regarding your progress.

In addition to the observation, you will need to collect a few documents that demonstrate your knowledge and skills in the area of maintaining and ordering stock. These documents are listed in the 'evidence required' section below. All the necessary templates and forms will be provided to you. If you are unclear about any of these instructions, talk with your trainer or assessor before commencing.

Assessment instructions	This unit requires observation over a period of time necessary to evaluate the performance of the assessment candidate across a range of tasks. The tasks required are: • implement and monitor store policy and procedures regarding receipt, dispatch and secure storage of goods • monitor staff implementation of store procedures and documentation in regard to receipt, dispatch and secure storage of goods • monitor stock levels, storage, movement and re-order cycles on a regular basis • organise and coordinate a stocktake • raise and process stock orders and maintain record system • monitor delivery processes and distribute stock to ensure continuity of supply.

continued

Evidence required	• Facilitator/assessor observation checklist • Copies of relevant store policies/procedures regarding receipt and dispatch of goods and ordering processes (authorisation may be required. These are for assessment purposes only and will not be distributed to third parties). If unable to print these, provide a letter from employer stating that you know how and where to access this information • Completed stocktake report identifying discrepancies and recommendations • Completed store roster showing allocation of staff to the stocktake process • Print out or screen shot of at least two stock orders placed on two separate occasions • Third-party report from your supervisor or manager.
Range and conditions	• The evidence must be gathered in a work environment or simulated environment where all required stock maintenance activities can be replicated • You must use at least one presentation aid (electronic presentations, whiteboard, butcher's paper, handouts or any other presentation aids that are suitable).
Materials and resources required	Access to store/simulated ordering and stock maintenance systems and procedures.
Assessor intervention	Your assessor will go through the assessment instructions with the class prior to commencement. You may ask questions at any point during the completion of the assignment prior to submission.
Reasonable adjustments	In the event that you have difficulty understanding the assessment tasks due to language or other difficulties, your trainer will attempt to make reasonable adjustments to the assessment paper in order to afford you every opportunity to achieve competency.
Decision-making rules	Facilitator guide/McGraw Hill website provides benchmark answers and check lists.

COMPETENCY MAPPING

Element and performance criteria		Task	Assessment	Refer to page
1.1	Delegate responsibility for receipt and dispatch of goods to appropriate staff.	10.1	1, 2	297
1.2	Implement store procedures in regard to receipt, dispatch and secure storage of goods.		2	297–298
1.3	Observe staff functions to ensure store procedures are followed and documentation is completed correctly.		2	299
1.4	Implement store procedures to ensure goods inspected for quantity and quality on receipt.		2	298–299
1.5	Act upon variations to quantity and quality of delivered goods, according to store policy and procedures.		1, 2	299
1.6	Supervise safe handling and storage of goods,		2	299–301
2.1	Monitor and maintain stock levels at required levels.	10.2	2	301–302
2.2	Maintain, monitor and adjust stock reorder cycles as required.		2	302–304
2.3	Inform team members of their individual responsibilities in regard to recording of stock.		2	305
2.4	Maintain stock storage and movement records, according to store policy.		2	306
2.5	Record stock discrepancies and follow procedures according to store policy.		1, 2	308, 312
2.6	Monitor stock performance and identify and report fast and slow selling items according to store policy.		2	306
3.1	Interpret policy and procedures in regard to stocktaking and cyclical counts and explain to team members.	10.3	2	313–315
3.2	Roster staff according to allocated budget and time constraints.		2	315
3.3	Allocate stocktaking tasks to individual team members.		2	315–317
3.4	Provide team members with clear directions for the performance of each task.		2	316
3.5	Allocate team members to ensure effective use of staff resources to complete task.		2	316, 318
3.6	Produce accurate reports on stocktake data, including discrepancies, for management.		2	317

continued

Element and performance criteria		Task	Assessment	Refer to page
4.1	Identify, record and assess losses against potential loss forecast on a regular basis.	10.4	1, 2	319
4.2	Identify avoidable losses and establish reasons.		2	320–321
4.3	Recommend and implement possible solutions.		1, 2	322–323
5.1	Process and raise orders for stock as requested, according to store policy and procedures.	10.5	2	324–328
5.2	Maintain ordering and recording system.		2	326–328
5.3	Ensure availability of sample range, according to buying plan.		2	
5.4	Order pricing materials as required.		2	
5.5	Record negotiated purchase and supply agreements and file for retrieval.		2	328
6.1	Monitor delivery process to meet agreed deadlines.	10.6	2	329–330
6.2	Handle routine supply problems or refer to management as required by store policy.		2	330
6.3	Maintain ongoing liaison with buyers, store or departments, warehouse and suppliers to ensure continuity of supply.		2	331
6.4	Distribute stock, according to store or department allocation.		2	331–332

Required skills and knowledge	Task	Assessment	Refer to page
Required skills:			
Technical skills to:	10.5	2	297–332
• use store stocktaking systems			
• use electronic recording equipment			
Interpersonal skills to:	10.3, 10.6		
• inform team members of their responsibilities and give instructions			
• explain policies and procedures to staff			
• allocate tasks and provide directions for performance of tasks			
• liaise with buyers, store and departments, warehouse and suppliers through clear and direct communication			
• ask questions to identify and confirm requirements			
• use language and concepts appropriate to cultural differences			
• use and interpret non-verbal communication			
Management skills to coordinate stocktakes	10.3		

Required skills and knowledge	Task	Assessment	Refer to page
Required Skills:			
Literacy and numeracy skills to:	10.2, 10.3, 10.5, 10.6	1, 2	319–332
• prepare and present stock control reports and documentation			
• process orders			
• maintain delivery and supply records			
• maintain stock distribution records			
• maintain stock ordering and recording systems			
Negotiation skills to handle supply problems	10.6		
Required knowledge:			
Store policy and procedures in regard to:	10.1, 10.2, 10.3, 10.4, 10.5, 10.6	2	297–312
• stock control			
• store merchandising system			
• current and future stock levels			
• bar codes, labels and price tags			
• store stock recording system			
• stock replenishment and reorder procedures			
• inter- and intra-store and department transfers			
• reporting of stock discrepancies and damage			313–318
• identifying and recording stock losses			
• identifying and recording discrepancies			
• existing suppliers			328–331
• quality control procedures and requirements			
• receipt and dispatch of goods, including inspection for quality and quantity			
Relevant licensing requirements for moving stock mechanically	10.1		331–332
Relevant legislation and statutory requirements			309
Relevant industry codes of practice			300, 354
Relevant work health and safety (WHS) legislation and codes of practice			332

continued

Required skills and knowledge	Task	Assessment	Refer to page
Critical aspects for assessment and evidence			
Consistently implements and monitors store policy and procedures regarding receipt, dispatch and secure storage of goods	10.1, 10.2, 10.3, 10.5, 10.6	1, 2	297–332
Regularly monitors staff implementation of store procedures and documentation in regard to receipt, dispatch and secure storage of goods	10.1, 10.4		
Monitors stock levels, storage, movement and reorder cycles on a regular basis	10.2, 10.3		
Organises and coordinates stocktake, according to store policy and procedures	10.3		
Consistently raises and processes stock orders and maintains record system according to store policy and procedures	10.5		
Monitors delivery processes and distributes stock to ensure continuity of supply.	10.1, 10.2, 10.6		

Chapter 11

SIRXRSK201

Minimise loss

Theft of retail stock, known as shoplifting, accounts for an estimated $810 million each year in Australia.[1] This has a substantial impact on insurance and legal costs for business owners and staff, and while some of these costs are absorbed by businesses both large and small, the majority are passed on as higher prices to retail customers. With such a substantial effect on businesses, staff and customers, minimising loss requires a substantial focus for any retail operation.

For online retail operations, a significant effort must also be devoted to the maintenance of anti-fraud measures to prevent, deter and pursue criminals who might otherwise fraudulently acquire goods or services over the internet.

This section builds on the concepts you have learned so far in Part 3, including handling and securing cash, understanding store security, minimising theft and fraud and using stock efficiently to reduce shrinkage.

ELEMENT 1
APPLY ROUTINE STORE SECURITY

Effective store security is the result of a combined effort of staff, electronic monitoring and alarm systems, customer vigilance and effective store layout.

1.1 Apply store security systems and procedures according to store policy.

1.2 Handle and secure cash according to store policy and procedures.

1.3 Observe and deal with suspicious behaviour of customers according to store policy and legislative requirements.

1.4 Deal with internal and external theft according to store policy and legislative requirements.

1.5 Store products and equipment in a secure manner according to store policy and procedures.

LEARNING OUTCOMES

Implement store policy and procedures to ensure store security is maintained

Retailing, like most business operations, relies upon written policies and procedures to maintain consistency throughout various business practices. A store security policy includes the procedures for day-to-day security-related operations as well as information regarding special circumstances such as shoplifting, bomb threats (although this is often documented separately) and other emergencies. Security policies may also be referred to as, or included within, the store property policy, virtual security policy (for online businesses), access control policy, or by another name. It's important that you are familiar with the name and location given to your specific store's security policy.

Figure 11.1 You must know how and where to access store policies. These days, most policies are kept in electronic format

WHAT IS IN A SECURITY POLICY?

A **security policy** needs to consider a number of regular activities and specific issues. These include:

Handling of products

You may need to handle a variety of different products in a number of different contexts depending on the type of retail outlet you are working in. This part of the policy may specify particular handling procedures for certain goods, including giveaway items, staff purchases and discounts and lay-by items.

Offering of services

Staff may be permitted to offer certain services to customers such as free delivery, home installation or ongoing product support. The limits and processes under which staff must operate should be outlined within the security policy so that everyone is aware of their obligations under law, as well as those circumstances permitted by the business.

Cash handling

Cash is a particularly attractive item for thieves as it is relatively untraceable. Procedures for handling cash are therefore a mandatory part of any complete security policy. Cash is usually handled around the point of sale, including the cash register procedures and transporting cash from the register to the cash office throughout the day. Security procedures may also include who can gain access to the register and at what times.

Credit card procedures

Credit card procedures are designed to prevent fraudulent use of credit and to ensure that credit transactions are successfully completed prior to the customer taking possession of the goods. There are a number of security measures in place by banks, retailers and credit card companies to reduce fraud, however it remains as a growing criminal concern.

Funds transfer procedures (such as EFTPOS and cheques)

Electronic Funds Transfer at Point of Sale (EFTPOS) is a common method of payment preferred by many customers over cash. Instead of credit card transactions, customers may prefer direct debit transfers and may be entitled to receive a 'cash out' under the store's policy. 'Cash out' transactions are discussed in the section dealing with the use of cash registers.

Opening and closing the store

Unfortunately, many occurrences of robbery have been recorded while staff have been in the process of opening or closing the store. As such, security measures for these occurrences should outline cash security, key or access card security, applicable times and any other relevant measures that ensure the safety of both staff and property.

Staff property

This part of the policy may include information regarding access and maintenance of staff lockers, storage of food and other personal items, and staff purchases that are on hold.

Customers' property (including personal information security)

Retailers may be required to temporarily store customer or visitor property. This can include their personal information for electronic commerce or stock they wish to hold temporarily after paying a deposit or full amount. A detailed description and procedure for handling this information should be understood by staff handling customers' property.

Particular store hazards

Situations or things that may cause injury that are peculiar to a specific site should be identified and measures for how to deal with these hazards outlined in store policies and procedures. This documentation may be in the security policy or store work health and safety policy.

Visitor and contractor access

Suppliers, work contractors and visitors may require access to public and private areas within the store. The procedure for gaining access may include a site safety induction as well as a requirement for a staff member to be present at all times.

Armed robbery and shoplifting procedures

In the event of a robbery or theft, staff must be made aware of the procedures that can assist in their personal safety and any legal options for intervening in the event.

Cash office security

Most retail outlets handle cash. As a consequence, on-site cash storage may be required. Operating a cash office requires a number of security measures which may include secure access procedures (including passwords or security codes), staff authorisation levels and maintenance of the cash office.

Lay-by property storage and procedures

A separate procedure may be included that specifies the handling of lay-by stock and the payment procedures involved in initiating and finalising a lay-by purchase. For the purposes of store security, the procedures explained in this section of the policy will generally relate to handling, storage and receipt of lay-by items.

In addition to these, some policies may include a summary of customer rights, staff obligations and dispute resolution procedures.

Task 11.1

Identify your store security policy. Choose an activity that is described in the policy and summarise this in a paragraph. You may choose the cash handling process, shoplifting procedure or some other activity. Write a summary of the key points covered in that section of the policy. This helps you to understand the policy and where to obtain the information when you may need it in the future. If you do not have access to the policy, ask your trainer for an example.

APPLYING SECURITY PROCEDURES

Once you have identified the security policy and procedures for your store, you should become familiar with putting those procedures into practice. In Chapter 8 we looked at the various safety procedures for bomb threats, armed robbery and fire evacuation. These are known as '*emergency* procedures' as they are not likely to happen, but if they do, you must be able to follow the workplace procedures accurately and as calmly as you can. The other security procedures mentioned in this chapter will also be documented in the security policy and will therefore include a procedure for you to follow. Let's look at a few examples.

Example 1: Store-opening checklist

A small suburban clothing retailer uses a store-opening checklist for two reasons: firstly, to ensure the basic steps are followed each and every time the store is opened; and secondly, to have a record in the event of a security problem. The checklist is kept on a hook next to the staff entrance and is filled out by the staff member opening the store that day.

STORE-OPENING CHECKLIST			
Name	Date		
STEP	Required by	Completed (initial)	Time
Staff entrance unlocked	7.15 am		
Security alarm disabled (code: 2884 # ENTER)	7.15 am		
Store back office computer system on and logged in	7.20 am		
Cash box retrieved from safe (code provided to authorised staff only)	7.25 am		
POS computer system turned on and float distributed to cash register drawer	7.45 am		
Register drawer locked	7.45 am		
Housekeeping (shop floor is tidy and no trip/slip hazards are present)	7.55 am		
Staff pre-start meeting	8 am – 8.20 am		
Staff sign-in register has been completed and filed	8.25 am		
Register drawer unlocked	8.29 am		
Front doors opened	8.30 am		
COMMENTS/ISSUES			
Signed			

Figure 11.2 Example of a store-opening checklist

Note that the procedure covers the handling of cash, including access to the safe and cash drawers. Handling cash has also been covered in Chapter 10.

Example 2: Visitor access

The same retail store has a very strict process for visitor access. It was improved after a junior staff member let her friend stay in the store with her during the day to keep her company. While it seemed harmless, it drew the staff member's attention away from her job and potentially cost the retailer in lost sales and additional housekeeping. The process now requires the following:

1. All visitors MUST report to the duty manager or senior staff member on roster at the time.
2. The visitor's details must be entered into the visitor log (see Table 11.1).

Table 11.1

Example visitor log

Visitor log					
Date	**Name**	**Person visiting**	**Reason/Company**	**Time in**	**Time out**
23/5/2013	Dion Levi	Julianne Stocks	Clothing rep, Dreamy Clothing	8.45 am	9.15 am

3. If you do not know the person, ask for identification. Acceptable ID includes:
   a. driver's licence
   b. passport
   c. business card from relevant supplier.
4. Safety induction
   a. All visitors must be briefed on the safety hazards and procedures in the store. These are:
      i. evacuation procedure
      ii. any current physical hazards present in store
      iii. their obligation to report hazards to staff if identified.
   b. Complete the safety checklist located next to the visitor log (see Figure 11.3).
   c. Tear off the checklist, fold it and insert it in the plastic sleeve behind the visitor pass card.
5. Issue a visitor pass (orange lanyards and passes located on hook next to visitor log).

Surveillance of merchandise

Retail stores are set out in a way that maximises the customer's shopping experience. Whether online, or in a bricks-and-mortar outlet, this principle holds true. Retail owners report an average 20 per cent increase in sales after a store renovation.[2] An important consideration for store layout though, is ensuring that the store does not provide opportunities for shoplifters. Hidden corners, unsecured merchandise, goods out of the line-of-sight of the register and staff, and small items out in the open are all potential risks for loss.

Store surveillance includes the following:

VISITOR SAFETY CHECKLIST

Item	Covered (tick)	Visitors initials
Fire evacuation procedure		
Hazards present in store		

Visitor to read and sign:

I understand that I must report any hazards that can potentially cause harm to me, customers or others, as soon as practicable, to a staff member. Failure to do so could lead to a ban from entering the store for 12 months, and legal proceedings.

Name ______________________________

Signature ______________________________

Date ____________________

Tear off and keep with the visitor pass while on the premises

Figure 11.3 Sample visitor pass

Electronic surveillance

This is the use of a professionally installed Closed Circuit Television (CCTV) system. Most retailers use CCTV to monitor and record customers and staff in the store. CCTV recordings play a key role in the prosecution of criminals who steal from the store. A high-definition system allows for better identification and, due to the continuous upgrades in technology, is cheaper than the older tape systems of the 1990s and even the standard definition systems of just a few years ago.

Electronic surveillance also refers to the non-visual sensors used to minimise loss. Electronic article surveillance (EAS) includes electronic tags and stickers that attach to a product to monitor, report and deter theft. They use a range of technologies such as magneto-harmonic, radio frequency (RF), microwave and acousto-magnetic. While it is not important to understand the technology, it *is* important to know the way these systems work and how to use them in store. The magnetic range of stickers and tags react with sensors usually placed at the entrance of the store. The sensors will then provide an alarm for staff to respond. RF and microwave tags are proximity sensitive and will sound an alarm if the merchandise is removed from a specified area.

Lastly, there are micro-switch devices that can attach to the product that will open if the product is detached and thereby sound an alarm. These are common in mobile phone stores and electronics retailers.

Figure 11.4 Direct observation can include the use of mirrors and two-way glass

Observation

Direct observation is a greater deterrent than any electronic surveillance. Having a uniformed guard or vigilant staff monitoring the movements of customers will deter shoplifters more than a static tag or security camera. Surveillance can be carried out discreetly using mirrors or random floor walks (where a staff member casually walks around the shop floor at irregular intervals).

The negative for retailers is that overly observant staff can 'scare' customers away. A balance must be achieved.

Suspicious behaviour

If you observe a person acting suspiciously, what can you do? What are your rights and what are the rights of the person you suspect? Firstly, we need to determine what constitutes suspicious behaviour.

Suspicious behaviour is any action taken by someone that a reasonable person would construe as potentially unsafe, illegal, antisocial or unusual.

Any of the following may be considered suspicious depending on the context:

- behaving strangely—this may mean doing something unexpected—something that most people would not do, such as adding and removing layers of clothing for no particular reason, or repeatedly looking over their shoulder.
- excessive sweating (when others in the same conditions are not sweating)—in addition to keeping cool, this is the body's reaction to stress and nervousness. Of course, if the person is wearing gym clothing you might not be so concerned.
- whispering to others—why would people be whispering to each other in a retail store? There are not many good reasons for this behaviour.
- wearing dark glasses or a hoody with the hood up in store—hats, sunglasses and hoodies all serve as methods of concealing one's identity. This is not usual behaviour.

In all cases however, no single sign necessarily means the person has done or is about to do anything wrong. In fact, if you accuse a person without reasonable grounds, you can find yourself in trouble with the law.

It is generally not recommended to approach people behaving suspiciously as it could put you in a dangerous situation. A 'suspicious person report' is discussed in the next section, which details a process for dealing with this situation.

In some circumstances however, if it does not contravene store policy, you could reduce the likelihood of loss due to theft by simply making yourself known to the suspicious person or people by asking if you can help them, or if there is anything that is wrong. Remember, the person may not necessarily be acting suspiciously on purpose—they may have a health or behavioural condition.

Legal rights

The following information reflects the requirements under Australian state and territory law relating to criminal acts, privacy and confidentiality, anti-discrimination and civil rights.

Firstly, retailers have the right to set the conditions of entry to their premises. People may be excluded from entry based on things such as their previous behaviour in store or known behaviour in the community. You cannot exclude people generally—only known individuals. Retailers can also prescribe a bag check upon leaving the store. These and any other conditions *must* be displayed clearly at the entrance to the store. Permanent exclusion from the store can only be enforceable if the person has been informed in writing and there are witnesses to the letter being delivered. It is advisable to have copies of the letter for the store, the local police and for a witness. This is usually only done when there are documented behavioural issues such as theft, abuse, threats and unruly actions.

Secondly, the retailer has the right to detain someone if they believe that the person have committed an offence. While the right exists, store policy will outline the approach you should take, as there is a chance that you could put yourself at physical or legal risk. Here are some steps to avoid physical and legal ramifications if you witness a person concealing a product within their clothing or bag:

1. Confront the person by asking them to return the item to the shelf or pay for it. In most cases, being seen will cause the person to comply with your instructions. If they do not, go on to step 2.
2. Ask the person to allow you to check their bag. You need verbal approval as their bag is personal property and you cannot assume ownership of their property even for a moment without their consent. It is usually the case that store policy will direct you to have the person open and show you their bag so you do not touch it at any time. If they do not allow you to search their bag, you have three alternatives:
    a. Politely point out the conditions of entry and ask again.
    b. Ask the person to leave the store. Record their description and the direction they take after they leave the store and inform police.
    c. Detain the person if you have reasonable grounds to believe they have indeed committed an offence (that is, you have seen them hide the item and attempt to leave the store).
3. You cannot touch the person or their bag at any time—all bag checks must be voluntary. You cannot detain someone who does not show their bag to you.
4. Detaining the person is only an option if you have witnessed them attempting to steal something.
5. You can only detain the person while they are on your premises. Once they leave, you must turn over the task to the police as soon as possible.
6. Remember to be polite. You may have been mistaken, and threatening behaviour towards a customer is not only bad business, but often will not be tolerated by the retailer.

DETAINING SOMEONE—ADDITIONAL INFORMATION

Detaining someone whom you believe has committed or is committing a criminal offence is known as a citizen's arrest. If you decide to do this, you must be aware of the following:

- Detaining someone without reasonable grounds may result in *you* committing an offence.
- You cannot simply be suspicious of the person. You, or another staff member, have to see them actually take goods and conceal them *and* attempt to leave the premises without paying.
- You must be honest with the person and tell them why you are detaining them.
- Avoid physical contact with the person. Use an authoritative tone of voice rather than attempting to grab them in any way as this too can lead to *you* breaking the law.
- Physical force may *only* be used if you are defending yourself and even then it must be reasonable in the circumstances.
- It is better to avoid detaining someone. If you are in any doubt you should allow the person to leave and contact the police immediately.

See the next section for more information about dealing with people who act suspiciously.

Storing products and equipment securely

Consider how stock and other equipment is currently stored in your workplace. Have you seen examples of how other retailers store their products and thought it was smart or perhaps not so smart? There is no right or wrong way—there is only what is appropriate in the context of your workplace.

For example, a busy shopping centre store will have lots of customers inside and outside their store. With this increased traffic comes a higher risk of loss through damage and theft. So to combat this issue, shopping centres use advanced CCTV, roaming security guards and usually have a police station or kiosk within the premises or close to it. As such, individual store security is enhanced but not fool-proof. Having products displayed outside the entrance or in the mall-style walkways can attract customers, but it can also attract thieves. The threats in-store also remain.

One retailer in Queensland shared a story of theft from the front of his store in a large shopping centre. A 42-inch television was plugged in and running when thieves decided to unplug it, put it in their trolley and walk off. By the time staff had noticed, they were long gone. Fortunately, the criminals were known to police and were arrested a short time later once CCTV footage was examined.

Securing products and equipment can mean:

- having the products behind glass or in glass or perspex cases
- tying products down with chains, high-strength steel cable, locks or electronic devices (such as those mentioned previously). For example, lawn mowers being displayed on a street walkway can be chained for security

- using dummy cases, boxes or products. For example, mobile phone kiosks usually display dummy phones on the outside of their kiosk while keeping the real merchandise locked behind the counter
- keeping products out of reach. Have any small, portable or valuable products or equipment behind a barrier such as a service counter, so that it is out of reach of a potential thief
- removing components. Some products require key components to operate correctly—for example, battery packs, lenses, remote controls and drawers. Removing key components may make the product less attractive to thieves. This is really an additional measure and should never be considered as a primary method of securing property.

Task 11.2

Complete the following checklist to ensure that you are aware of store procedures.

Process	YES (tick)	NO (tick)
1. My workplace has an electronic security system	☐	☐
2. I am aware of the procedures for operating, entering and exiting the premises	☐	☐
3. I have been shown the correct cash handling procedures for my workplace	☐	☐
4. I know how to deal with theft at my workplace	☐	☐
5. If I observe suspicious behaviour, I know what my rights are and I know the rights of the person I have observed	☐	☐
6. I know how to secure products in my workplace to minimise theft	☐	☐

Reflection:

Pick two of the above processes and briefly explain how each is used in your store. This will demonstrate your understanding of each task and how it applies to you.

ELEMENT 2
MINIMISE THEFT

So far we have looked at some broad concepts and some specific methods for minimising loss. In this section we will look at putting these and other methods into action and actively minimising theft through taking direct measures.

Some of the concepts have been covered in previous chapters, so we will refer to these as necessary. See the mapping at the end of this chapter for reference.

LEARNING OUTCOMES

2.1 Take appropriate action to minimise theft by applying store procedures and legislative requirements.

2.2 Match merchandise to correct price tags according to store procedures.

2.3 Maintain surveillance of merchandise according to store policy and legislative requirements.

2.4 Maintain security of cash, cash register and keys according to store policy.

2.5 Maintain security of stock, cash and equipment in regard to customers, staff and outside contractors according to store policy and legislative requirements.

Applying store procedures to minimise theft

The store security policy outlines the procedures in-store. You will need to familiarise yourself with the specific procedures of your workplace. However, to give a general overview, we will look at some examples of store anti-theft procedures.

Figure 11.5 Anyone can be considered a potential threat to store security

REPORTING SUSPICIOUS BEHAVIOUR

In the last section we looked at your rights in relation to acting when you *see* someone stealing, but what about other suspicious behaviours? Store procedures usually include communication between staff to ensure a cohesive approach to minimising theft. This means that staff should relay information to others to collectively work against theft and other costly behaviours in-store.

The following example procedure covers reporting suspicious behaviour in a mid-sized grocery supermarket.

MATCHING PRICES ON MERCHANDISE WITH SYSTEM PRICES

Theft is not just taking stock without paying. It also covers the intentional attempt by a customer to defraud the retailer by changing sale or price tickets of products. This practice is becoming less concerning, with more and more retailers using electronic

REPORTING SUSPICIOUS BEHAVIOUR

If you suspect a customer or staff member of stealing stock or other property from the business, follow these steps	
1.	Do not approach the person.
2.	Take note of their behaviour including specific details such as: 1. Where they are in store 2. What they are doing 3. Personal actions that have caused you to be suspicious. Accurate details are very important. Only recount the facts and refrain from embellishment or drawing conclusions.
3.	Report the actions directly (in person) to the register manager immediately, before the person has left the store if possible.
4.	Register manager will assign store security to the area if appropriate by calling for 'S7' to the area (e.g. Aisle 3) over the store public address system.
5.	Register manager will inform store manager by relaying the exact information given by you.
6.	If security is not called, continue to observe the person if possible. Take note of any further behaviour that seems unusual or suspicious and update the register manager where possible.

Figure 11.6 Example procedure for reporting suspicious behaviour

price books (centralised pricing based on the product's EAN barcode). However, there is still room to defraud the retailer if there are markdowns on some products and local sale pricing has been applied.

To minimise this you will need to be aware of the correct price of the item. The correct price is the default price in the store's stock control system. If the items are priced manually, you will have to check against a manual price book or be aware of the pricing in store for each product. If the item has been discounted, the store should have a policy and procedure for monitoring these markdowns and reducing the likelihood of fraud.

Many markdown stickers (like older price-gun labels) now come with anti-removal technology. This simply means that the sticker cannot be removed without destroying or tearing it. The store's policy should be to never accept markdowns if the label is torn. Instead, the department should be notified and the markdown confirmed.

Online theft minimisation

With online retail purchasing growing in popularity, the concept of theft is changing. There is a level of trust that must exist between the customer and the retailer in order to exchange financial information for goods. Both parties have something to lose in the transaction if the other party is acting fraudulently. To minimise this threat, online retailers can:

- use verification techniques such as PIN (personal identification numbers) and credit card checking
- use a third-party payment agency such as PayPal or Merchant Protect. Most financial institutions also provide credit card assurances for online purchases.
- only ship the goods once payment has been confirmed.

Online buyers can:

- shop with reputable retailers
- shop at sites using secure payment protocols— look for sites that start with https://—the 's' stands for secure
- protect their own privacy—check the company's privacy policy and only proceed if you are satisfied.

In both cases, retailers and consumers should check for reported scams through consumer websites like www.choice.com.au and government sites including www.fairtrading.qld.gov.au/online-shopping.htm. By doing so, you are actively minimising loss from either perspective.

Maintaining surveillance

We discussed above the two main methods of monitoring the security of store merchandise: electronic security and observation. Let's now look at putting these into action.

ELECTRONIC SURVEILLANCE IN ACTION

Store procedures will cover what to do in the instance of an alarm being raised by the electronic surveillance systems you have in your workplace—yet you have probably seen cases where store alarms have sounded and staff do *not* react in a way that you would expect. This could be due to:

- apathy—not caring about the process or paying it little regard
- poor training—staff not being aware of their responsibilities
- attention—not paying attention to the alarm, or ignoring it due to other activities that currently require their attention
- inexperience—not being sure of what to do, and not wanting to appear silly or offend the customer in question.

A store policy will usually dictate the following in the event of a security alarm.

What to do when the front entrance alarm sounds

1. Immediately observe the entrance to determine who or what set off the alarm.
   a. If a person (staff member or customer) just entered the premises you do not need to do anything.

   b. If a person (staff member or customer) is leaving the premises, ask them to step back through the security sensors and ask to check any bags they have.
2. If the person does not return:
   a. in the case of a customer, take down any relevant personal identification information and the direction they took when they left the store and immediately inform your manager. Your manager may choose to call the police and the details you record will be important to their investigation.
   b. In the case of a staff member, inform your manager immediately.
3. If, upon checking the person's bag/s, you identify store merchandise, ask them to show you a receipt. If they do not have one, ask them to wait briefly and contact the manager.
4. If they leave the store, contact the manager and call the police. (Follow shoplifting procedures.)

What to do when the in-store merchandise alarm sounds

1. Observe the area and notify a department representative immediately.
2. If you observe someone (staff member or customer) attempting to conceal or flee with merchandise, follow the store shoplifting procedure.
3. If a customer has activated the system, wait with them until a department representative arrives with the key to de-activate the alarm.

MANUAL SURVEILLANCE IN ACTION

Nothing is quite as effective as having direct observation of each customer in store. Not only can you deter theft, you can also offer better service. However, the nature of retail businesses does not allow for such labour-intensive options. Instead, we can use some simple techniques that serve to both welcome the customer and to deter potential thieves.

Introduction to the store

As a customer arrives, if you acknowledge them with eye contact and a smile, you will achieve a great deal towards making their experience pleasant and reminding them that you are observant to their needs.

The store introduction should be genuine—that is, it should not be a forced task that comes across as awkward. While a genuine customer will appreciate a real smile, a potential thief will see it as a huge deterrent. Why? Because, firstly, human nature will tend to deter them from stealing from someone they see as friendly. Not always, of course, but in more instances than not. They may just browse and choose a different target unless a lot of planning has gone into their criminal activity. Secondly, by making eye contact you have demonstrated to the person that you can probably identify them if necessary. And, lastly, you have given the person reason to believe that you are watching them: a real deterrent to most thieves.

Random floor walks

We mentioned the idea of carrying out irregular patrols around the shop floor in the previous section. Here we acknowledge that this action can have a number of benefits. Firstly, you make yourself visible to potential thieves. Secondly, you improve your knowledge of the store layout and merchandise. This will help you to identify things that are out of place or not correctly merchandised. Lastly, you can offer assistance to other customers where necessary. A store walk-around needs to fit in with your daily duties, so be sure to confirm the procedures in place at *your* workplace.

In-store scams

You must be aware of potential scams.

- Flash attacks were recently reported in the USA, where organised groups of people 'attacked' retail stores en masse making it impossible and dangerous for staff to stop the damage and theft.
- Distraction techniques are used by thieves working in small groups of twos or threes, intentionally attracting your attention while another member of the group steals from your store. While it is important to provide excellent customer service, always be vigilant and notice if the customer entered the store with others.

Store security staff

Retailers may employ the services of undercover security staff who act as customers while closely observing the activities of others (including staff). For this reason, security staff are usually not known to all staff. If you report a security staff person for 'suspicious behaviour', your manager will usually clear the situation.

Cash-in-transit code of practice

Under workplace health and safety legislation, employees must not be placed in a position in which their safety is compromised. Retail business owners and managers are responsible for ensuring that personal security measures are in place to protect their employees. These measures cover the handling of cash.

We have dealt with the handling of cash in-store in Chapter 10, including the use of cash delivery systems and automated tellers. In this section we cover the responsibilities of those handling cash as it leaves the premises and is transported to and from the bank or security organisation.

This is covered in most states by a 'cash-in-transit code of practice' that falls under the WHS legislation. As an example, the Queensland code states that:

> *Workers have a duty to take reasonable care for their own health and safety and that they do not adversely affect the health and safety of other persons. Workers must comply with any reasonable instruction and cooperate with any reasonable policy or procedure relating to health and safety at the workplace.*[3]

In action, this means that the retailer and any staff member instructed to move cash to and from the premises must be covered under an existing policy and procedure, and that the procedure must not put the individual at an unreasonable level of risk.

Many retailers have reduced the risk to staff and managers by outsourcing the pick-up and transfer of money to armed security organisations. These organisations must comply with the code of practice and other relevant legislation.

Security of cash and goods among staff

Sadly, theft can be a crime of opportunity. That is, if the opportunity presents itself, some people will choose to steal where under other circumstances they would not. Theft of cash, goods and equipment by staff and contractors in Australia is estimated at $500 million per annum according to the National Retail Crime Prevention Council, and 80 per cent of fraud is committed by employees.[4] To minimise losses due to internal theft, consider the following tips:

- Staff background checks are conducted routinely as a part of the employment process. A police clearance can be conducted within a few days by contacting the local police department and lodging the application with the police on behalf of the employee. This can give a good indication of the employee's honesty and credibility
- Clearly outline the repercussions of being caught taking the property of the business. This can be in the standard employee contract and mentioned in the employee's induction training
- Always have at least two people close the shop at the end of the day (if possible). This is a proactive precaution for both internal theft and the safety of those leaving the premises after hours
- Use CCTV to monitor the whole store, not just the retail floor
- Keep a key register and ensure that keys have a 'Do not duplicate' warning embossed on them. Keys must only be trusted to employees who have demonstrated that they have, over time, earned the right to take keys on and off the premises. (This does not necessarily apply to internally-used keys for display cabinets.) Keys should be signed for when being taken out for use and when being returned. A basic key register should accompany a lockable key cabinet in a secure area of the store (usually the cash office)
- Don't pre-judge people. The most unlikely staff member could steal if the opportunity presented itself
- Have a staff purchase procedure. This procedure should cover who can complete a staff purchase and how staff purchases occur. For example: do not allow staff to process their own purchases—the manager must visually authorise every staff purchase, and so on.
- Look for behavioural changes or indicators such as that the staff member:
  - is moody
  - blames others readily
  - doesn't accept responsibility for their actions
  - seems immature
  - lives beyond their means
  - is seeking revenge for an alleged wrongdoing.

- Use cash register security measures such as:
  - having a procedure that limits 'no sales' or requires authorisation by a senior staff member (a cash register 'no sale' allows the drawer to be opened without a transaction being recorded)
  - limiting the authority to reset the register
  - not allowing the transaction numbers to be reset—they should simply continue from one shift to the next
  - having employee purchase receipts signed by a senior staff member or manager and then stapled to the merchandise or the bag
- Have all stock deliveries signed for by the staff member. That way they are vouching for the quantity of items received.

Task 11.3

Watch the fifteen second CCTV footage at http://youtube.com/EYcgERFYPVk titled 'Retail CCTV Cameras Ireland' *once* only.

Then write down the following:

1. What other actions could have been taken to reduce this theft?
2. If you saw this activity occur, what could you do within your legal rights and in accordance with your workplace policies?
3. What actions should you take now?
4. Lastly, what distinguishing features can you recall about the perpetrator? List as many as you can then check the video to see how close you were.

ELEMENT 3
USE STOCK EFFICIENTLY

The efficient use of stock reduces the loss due to wastage.

LEARNING OUTCOMES

3.1 Handle and store stock to minimise loss through damage or deterioration.

3.2 Ensure effective stock rotation to minimise stock loss through wastage.

3.3 Ensure correct stock amounts are prepared for individual transactions to minimise stock loss from over-supply.

Handling stock

If items are damaged they cannot usually be sold for full retail price. Worse still, if their shelf-life expires they cannot, in many cases under Australian food standards, be sold at all! As a result, they become a financial loss to the business and one that can cost dearly over time. Your role when handling stock or delegating the task to others, is to ensure that the process occurs without damage and without financial loss to the business.

Here are eight tips for minimising stock damage:

Figure 11.7 Effective stock rotation is a critical factor in the efficient running of a retail operation

1. Loading and unloading stock. Do so safety by undertaking a quick risk assessment of the weight and the manual task at hand. Remember, repeating an awkward task over a prolonged period can cause injury and can lead to mistakes. Look for the safe way to do it and do not try to move something that is too heavy or in an awkward position (such as too high, too low or in a confined space).
2. Know where you are going. Moving stock around the store is necessary at times. There may be a promotion or you may simply be dispatching stock from the storeroom. By mentally planning your route, you are less likely to change direction or accidentally come into contact with someone or something that can damage the goods.
3. Use two hands. Depending on the stock you are moving, don't try to save time by using one hand, especially if it compromises the grip you have on the item. Obviously this does not apply to smaller-than-hand-sized items.
4. Observe the correct handling instructions. If the item is large enough to come with handling instructions, make sure you obey them. Follow the instructions to the letter to remove yourself from any liability and to meet the manufacturer's directions. For example, does the item have a transport bolt holding a component in place? If so, is it in place to stop undue movement and damage?
5. Follow store policies and procedures. Workplace procedures will usually outline the steps for stacking products and displaying items. If in doubt, ask your immediate supervisor or the store manager. Over-stacking can lead to overbalancing or damage to items at the bottom of the stack.
6. Promotional displays. Promotional displays should first be planned and then executed according to that plan. Displays might involve hanging things from the ceiling or stacking products in creative ways. Ensure that the plan and the execution take into account customer traffic and the safe stacking heights of the items.
7. Keep your mind on the job. Handling stock cannot only result in unnecessary damage, it can also result in injuries if you are not concentrating on the task at hand. Where possible, avoid interruptions and finish the task at hand before starting another. Where you have to stop to serve a customer (this is the priority, after all), ensure that your workspace does not present a hazard to customers and other staff. If a customer trips over stock you have left on the floor, the loss can be a lot more than the cost of the stock.

8. Consider the customer 'fudge' factor. Lastly, consider the wide variety of people who will come into your store. When arranging stock, moving stock around the store or creating a display, think about how others might interact with what you are doing. For example, if you are moving a pallet of products using a trolley jack and a customer suddenly stops you to ask a question, can you safely park the trolley? Can you stop quickly enough? Are you going to hit anything or anyone? Is the pallet of goods going to block access or impede traffic in any way? People can get quite irate if they are blocked from selecting an item for purchase, and they might try to move the trolley themselves!

Deterioration and expiration

As we learned in Chapter 11, effective stock rotation is key to maintaining adequate stock levels. Stock that has reached its **expiration date,** or the end of its shelf life, can end up costing the business in forced markdowns. This cost, while inevitable in most retail environments, must be kept to a minimum in order for the business to stay profitable and financially healthy.

The best way to approach minimising the losses associated with expiry and deterioration is to have a stock rotation plan. The stock rotation plan works in two ways:

1. Items that are newer or fresher are placed *behind* or *underneath* the items that are older; thus prompting customers to buy the products in the order they are received into store.
2. Older stock is moved by a planned price reduction strategy.

People are quite savvy when it comes to retail stock rotation. Most, if not all, are aware of the practice and will reach to the back or bottom of the display to get the fresher goods if time is not a major problem. You can, in some cases, refrain from putting the newer product out on display until the number of items displayed falls to a predetermined level. This will be determined by store procedures and policies relating to stock merchandising.

The type of retail industry you are in will have a huge role in the way in which stock is rotated. The expiration dates in cellars and bottle shops are very different from those of a florist (see the following case study). Stock can sometimes stay on the shelves for a year, take up very little space, and sometimes even go *up* in price!

CASE STUDY

ABC Flowers receives new flowers in each day. The stock takes between an hour and five hours to prepare for display and usually has a refrigerated shelf life of five days before it can no longer be sold. ABC's owners have a very strict pricing and rotation policy. They provide only fresh flowers for orders (phone and specific orders) and older stock is used for display and walk-in customers.

To reduce the loss of deteriorating stock, they use post-harvest preservatives and *always* sell on a FIFO basis. Arrangements are often changed to use older flowers first, but to maintain quality they always discard flowers older than six days (depending on the flowers of course).

If you are retailing items where the shelf life is longer, such as fashion items, clothing, consumer electrical goods or stationery, having a planned price reduction strategy is a clever method of minimising loss over the period of the product's life cycle.

CASE STUDY

XYZ Appliances has a refrigerator on the floor that is four months old. Their pricing strategy includes a mid- and end-of-life reduction price, as well as a clearance price. The refrigerator has a GP (gross profit) percentage of 22 per cent and sells new for $799. Accounting for GST, this means that XYZ makes $159.80 in gross profit at full retail. The mid-life markdown occurs at three months, and the end-of-life at six months. Once the new models are ordered, the clearance price is applied. The mid-life price is a $50 reduction; the end-of-life reduction is $100, and the clearance price reduction is $150, allowing the sales people to sell the product at $649.

The pricing strategy removes commission from clearance item sales to motivate staff to sell the item before it reaches that age.

Recording stolen, damaged and waste stock

Items that are no longer for sale due to theft, damage or deterioration must be recorded in order for the retailer to effectively account for the loss. This can be carried out as part of a cyclical stocktake or as a direct response to a theft or accident.

Loss items are usually rectified on the store stock control system by overriding the stock quantity on hand and writing in the reason for the override. Systems will vary, so please make yourself aware of what is used in your workplace should you be involved in this task.

In addition to correcting the stock system, you may need to fill out a police report for stolen goods. A police report will be usually be written by the police officer you report the theft to in the first instance. The report may be given over the telephone. If this is the case, the officer will provide you with a report number for future reference and follow up. Be sure to write the number down and record it with the stolen item entry in the stock control system (or elsewhere as defined by your workplace procedures). Similarly, if you fill out a paper report, you will be given a copy for your records. Be familiar with where police reports are stored at your workplace.

Individual transactions

In some retail businesses (especially online retailers) it is possible to prepare stock for individual orders, thus removing the need to rotate stock and minimise losses due to wastage. This is based on a manufacturing system first developed by Japanese car manufacturers called JIT, or 'just-in-time' order fulfilment. In retail it is known as 'vendor-managed inventory'—with the retailer being the vendor. The benefits are that:

- stock doesn't sit on hand and take up valuable floor space
- customers get what they pay for—the items are generally new and therefore satisfaction is higher

- set up time is reduced as there is no need to keep displaying and replenishing stock
- employees can multi-task from sales to packaging to dispatch
- over-supply is virtually ruled out
- prices are set at the time of the order so there are no stock-on-hand price variations to deal with.

There are also disadvantages of this type of business model. They include that:

- there is a lead time to fulfil customer orders
- bulk-buying discounts will not apply
- there is no product for the customer to see, touch, smell or listen to, so the onus is on them to have researched what they want first—again this bodes well for online retailers
- supply shock, which occurs when you order the supplies to fulfil the order only to find out that there is a stock problem.

Task 11.4

The following items are for sale in your store. List at least two things you need to consider for each item in order to minimise loss in store. Where would you find the instructions for effectively handling this stock?

1. Flowers
2. Milk
3. Fashion shoes

Endnotes

1. Australian Institute of Criminology (AIC) website at http://aic.gov.au/publications/current%20series/crm/21-40/crm028.aspx
2. Hill, D, 2012, *Interviews with retail shop owners in Queensland*, December 2010, accessed 9/1/2012 at www.spectraining.com.au/clients-partners.ph
3. Workplace Health and Safety Queensland, 2011, *Cash in Transit Code of Practice 2011*, Department of Justice and Attorney-General, Queensland.
4. KPMG, 2010, *Fraud and Misconduct Survey 2010*, www.kpmg.co

ASSESSMENT 1: REVIEW QUESTIONS

1. What is the process for checking a customer's bag? In your answer, be sure to identify the legal requirements and rights of each party.
2. If you witness a theft in your store while you are on duty what should you do?
3. Provide three reasons why you should secure stock and equipment in store.
4. Explain how you would maintain surveillance of the merchandise in your store.
5. Who must you report any security issues to? Why?
6. What documentation could you use to ensure that contractors and visitors are monitored for both safety and security in your workplace? Explain how each document achieves this purpose.
7. Circle the correct price tag for this item and discuss the reasons for your choice.

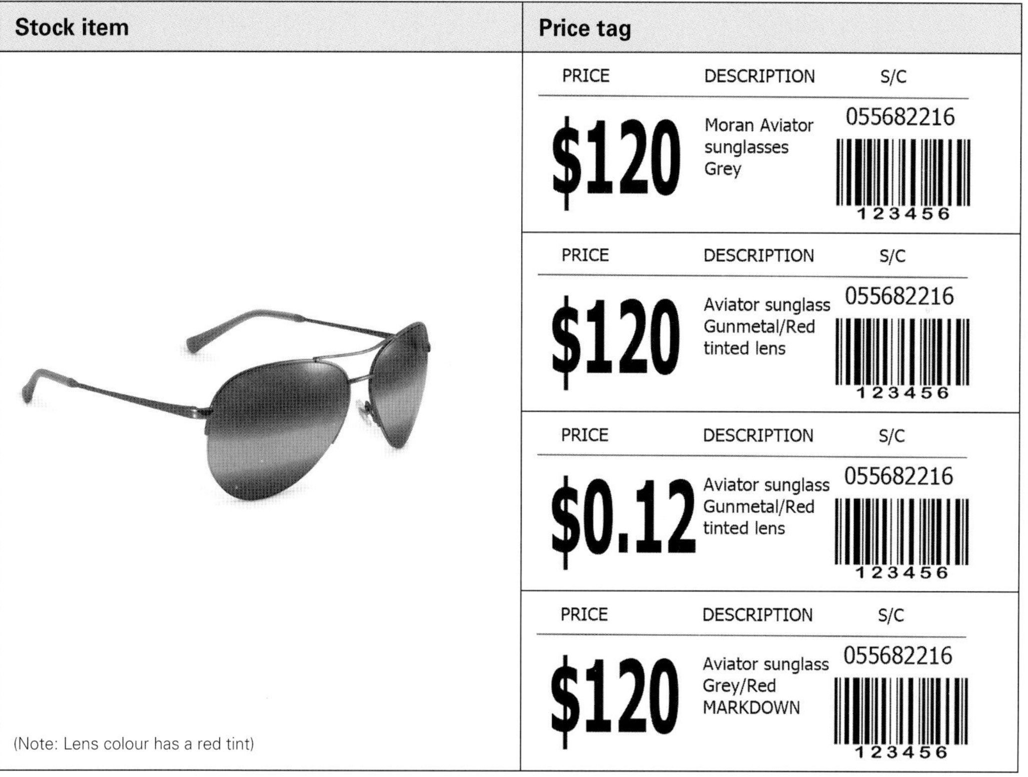

Stock item	Price tag
(Note: Lens colour has a red tint)	PRICE: $120 — DESCRIPTION: Moran Aviator sunglasses Grey — S/C: 055682216 — 123456
	PRICE: $120 — DESCRIPTION: Aviator sunglass Gunmetal/Red tinted lens — S/C: 055682216 — 123456
	PRICE: $0.12 — DESCRIPTION: Aviator sunglass Gunmetal/Red tinted lens — S/C: 055682216 — 123456
	PRICE: $120 — DESCRIPTION: Aviator sunglass Grey/Red MARKDOWN — S/C: 055682216 — 123456

8. Select a product sold in your store, or one you are familiar with from a retail outlet (e.g. a fashion item, electronic item or food item). Complete the following table as it relates to the efficient use of that item.

Handling of the item	How must you handle the item to prevent loss through damage?	
Storing the item	How must you store the item to prevent deterioration or damage?	
Stock rotation	How often would this item need to be rotated to ensure that you minimise loss due to wastage or age	
Supply	Assume that the item has six stock turns each month. What order quantity would be the most efficient to minimise over-supply? (circle your choice)	Order three every week Order three every fortnight Order three every month Order six every month

ASSESSMENT 2

Assessment instructions	Applying routine store security: role play 1. You will be observed reacting to and interacting with the following scenario. Roles: 1. Suspicious person/thief 2. Store manager/team leader 3. You • A person enters your store acting suspiciously. You are securing the cash from a register in preparation for delivering the cash to a senior staff member. • The suspicious person then takes an item off the shelf/hanger and attempts to hide it. They are on their way towards the exit. What do you do?
Evidence required	• Facilitator observation checklist.
Range and conditions	• The role play should be no more than ten minutes • You must follow existing store procedures or have the procedures for the simulated store environment explained prior to the assessment.
Materials and resources required	A real shop situation is ideal, however you can act out the role play sufficiently with minimal props such as a register and a few store items Access to the store's cash handling procedures and security procedures.
Assessor intervention	Your assessor will go through the assessment instructions with you prior to commencement. You may ask questions at any point during the completion of the assignment prior to its conclusion.
Reasonable adjustments	In the event that you have difficulty understanding the assessment tasks due to language or other difficulties, your trainer will attempt to make reasonable adjustments to the assessment paper in order to afford you every opportunity to achieve competency.
Decision-making rules	Facilitator guide/McGraw Hill website provides benchmark answers and check lists

COMPETENCY MAPPING

Element and performance criteria		Task	Assessment	Refer to page
1.1	Apply store security systems and procedures according to store policy.	11.1, 11.2	1, 2	340
1.2	Handle and secure cash according to store policy and procedures.	11.1	2	340–342
1.3	Observe and deal with suspicious behaviour of customers according to store policy and legislative requirements.	11.2	1, 2	344–348
1.4	Deal with internal and external theft according to store policy and legislative requirements.		1, 2	350–355
1.5	Store products and equipment in a secure manner according to store policy and procedures.		1, 2	341–342, 348–349
2.1	Take appropriate action to minimise theft by applying store procedures and legislative requirements.	11.3	2	350–351
2.2	Match merchandise to correct price tags according to store procedures.	11.4	1	357, 360, 361
2.3	Maintain surveillance of merchandise according to store policy and legislative requirements.	11.3	1, 2	352
2.4	Check customers' bags as required at point of sale according to store policy and legislative requirements.		1, 2	347–348
2.5	Maintain security of cash, cash register and keys according to store policy.	11.1	2	354–355
2.6	Maintain security of stock, cash and equipment in regard to customers, staff and outside contractors according to store policy and legislative requirements.		2	354–358
2.7	Deal with suspected or potential thieves according to store policy.	11.3	1, 2	346–347
3.1	Handle and store stock to minimise loss through damage or deterioration.	11.4	1	356
3.2	Ensure effective stock rotation to minimise stock loss through wastage.		1	301–302
3.3	Ensure correct stock amounts are prepared for individual transactions to minimise stock loss from over-supply.		1	357, 359–360

continued

Required skills and knowledge	Task	Assessment	Refer to page
Required skills			
Communication and interpersonal skills to relate positively to customers while conducting routine security procedures, such as bag checking	11.3	1, 2	347
Literacy and numeracy skills to:	10.3, 11.2, 11.2, 11.4	2	360
• count or measure stock			
• interpret manufacturer handling and storage instructions and store procedures		1	252, 299–301
• handle cash		2	281–291
• record stolen items		2	359
• report theft		2	359
Observation skills to identify suspicious behaviour	11.4	2	346, 347
Technical skills to manually handle and store stock	10.1, 11.4	1	281–291
Required knowledge			
Location and operation of store security equipment	11.2	1, 2	261
Reporting procedures for internal and external theft or suspicious circumstances	11.3	1, 2	346
Security procedures relating to cash and non-cash transactions	11.2, 11.3	1, 2	340–342
Store policy and procedures in regard to:	11.1, 11.2	1	347
• checking customers' bags and purchases			
• counting, measuring and weighing stock		1	360
• dealing with suspicious behaviour and actual theft	11.3	1, 2	346
• handling and storage of stock	11.4	1	297–312, 313–315
• reporting problems and faults	11.1	1, 2	317, 330
• security	11.1, 11.2	1, 2	330, 340
• stock rotation	11.1, 11.4	1	301–302

Required skills and knowledge	Task	Assessment	Refer to page
Critical aspects for assessment and evidence			
Applies store policy and procedures and legislative requirements, including industry codes of practice in regard to store security and theft prevention in a range of contexts and situations	11.1, 11.2, 11.3, 11.4	1, 2	340
Applies store policy and procedures in regard to following security procedures and reporting theft or suspicious behaviour to relevant personnel	11.1, 11.3	2	359
Monitors stock, work area, customers and staff to minimise opportunities for theft.	11.3	1, 2	340, 359

PART 4

Personal development

Units covered in Part 4:

12. SIRXMGT001A—Coordinate work teams

13. SIRXQUA001A—Develop innovative ideas at work

A career in retail can lead in many directions, but, as you gain experience and develop your competence in the industry, a likely direction is towards leading and managing a team. Your personal development and your commitment to learning new skills, both interpersonal and technical, will help you to be a success as you grow in your new role.

As a leader you now need to communicate effectively with the people you work with, and be prepared to motivate and support them in their own roles. This includes bringing new people into the team and ensuring that they are able to perform to the best of their ability and to the requirements of the organisation. At the same time, you will be managing the team so that the store is properly staffed when it needs to be, within the structure laid out by the policies of the store and the underpinning statutory requirements, and generating the required revenue. In addition, you will be required to report to more senior management, and to take some responsibility for the performance of your team.

Being a successful team leader involves developing a range of new skills

'None of us is as smart as all of us.'—***Ken Blanchard***.

In the highly competitive and fast-changing retail environment you will also be called upon to develop new and innovative ideas that will maintain and grow the business in which you work, improving customer service and the workplace, and generating greater sales. You will need the support and input of your team in order to do this, and the ability to evaluate and reflect on different ideas that will arise.

In Part 4 we look at these two key areas of personal development, as you move into a team leader or management role.

Chapter 12

SIRXMGT001A

Coordinate work teams

Figure 12.1 A work team in a pharmacy

The work team is the group of people who are employed in a retail store. Often the team is split between shifts, and made up of a mixture of full-time and part-time workers. Whether the shift consists of a single person at a register, or a number of people looking after different parts of a store, effective coordination to ensure that staff are present, that they know what they are doing and are motivated to provide the best service, and that both store policies and legislative requirements are being adhered to, is a definite skill that needs to be acquired by the new supervisor or team leader. There are many different facets to the coordination of work teams, and all come together to provide excellent customer service. As a team leader, supervisor or manager, one of your most important roles is coordinating your work team.

ELEMENT 1
MONITOR AND ORGANISE STAFFING LEVELS

In a business it is important to know what resources are required at a particular time to fulfil the needs of the operation of the business. Retail is an industry with increasing hours, but the demands on the human resources depend on the time of the day, the week and the year. Maintaining staff levels that are appropriate involves balancing a range of factors so that customers receive the appropriate service levels, but without there being too many resources present. Rostering in itself is an art, meeting the needs of customers, the business, and the staff members themselves.

1.1	Maintain staffing levels and rosters in designated areas within budget and according to store policy and procedures and legislative requirements.
1.2	Roster team according to anticipated sales peaks and statutory requirements.
1.3	Inform team members of individual rosters according to store policy and procedures.
1.4	Take corrective action as needed, according to staff availability.

LEARNING OUTCOMES

Maintaining staffing levels

The number of people needed to work effectively in a retail environment is subject to a range of influences and events. While the average day may seem predictable in terms of how many customers come through the door, there are many days in a year that will have a predictably higher number of people to serve.

FACTORS THAT AFFECT STAFFING LEVELS

Peak trading times

Peak trading hours vary according to time of day, day of the week and time of the year. If your retail outlet is in the city and mostly deals in lunches, then lunchtime on weekdays will be your busiest periods. Thursday night or weekend shopping may increase the trade through stores in a large shopping complex. The build-up to Christmas is traditionally a high period of sales in most retail environments.

Special events

A particular event such as a festival or street parade may mean increased trade through your retail store if in proximity to the event. This may be monthly or yearly, but can be an important time for your store to maximise its exposure to customers.

Promotion

Promotion of a new product or the announcement of a sale can increase trade for a length of time. Staffing levels need to be able to account for the increase as it happens, or lost business (through lack of service) represents a financial loss to the promoter.

Stocktakes

Stocktakes are an essential (though unglamorous) part of any retail business, and are needed to check and maintain stock levels. Because stocktakes often involve closure of the store, the time taken is lost to potential sales so staffing needs to be maximised to enable the stocktake to be finished as quickly as possible.

Refurbishment

Another internal pressure on staffing, refurbishment can mean that areas of a store are not usable for a period of time, and additional staff to assist may make the job happen faster. Alternatively, staffing may need to be minimised during this period as customer flow will be limited.

POLICIES AND PROCEDURES

Most retail businesses have policies and procedures that you need to follow in order to organise the right staffing levels for the right time. It is the combination of these factors, together with what is influencing the need for staff, that will allow you to decide on how many people to roster on to a particular period or shift. These factors include:

Figure 12.2 Busy holiday shopping crowds place extra pressure on staffing levels

Staffing requirements

How many people are required ideally to provide the accepted level of customer service for the respective period?

Business requirements

Consider how the budget allows for the number of hours allowed to be worked in a given period. This might not allow you to have all of the staff present that you believe is necessary.

On-the-job training

Do staff require training in their roles as they work? This may be new staff, or staff being asked to sell new products. Extra floor staff may be required while training is happening.

Maintaining staffing records

All appropriate records (discussed later in this chapter) need to be kept for staff who have worked in a set period. This may also affect budgeting as different staff members may be on different rates of pay.

Housekeeping

As well as serving customers, there are other routine jobs that need to be undertaken in every retail outlet from cleaning and stocking shelves through to balancing the till at the end of trading. Have adequate staff been rostered on to complete these activities?

LEGISLATIVE REQUIREMENTS

Overriding all of your rostering will be legislative requirements that may impact both on the staff that you are putting in place, as well as aspects such as their hours of work. These include:

WHS

WHS is of paramount importance both to your staff and to your customers. Staffing levels should aim to provide optimal workplace safety. This is not limited to the more obvious hazards such as ensuring that power cords are not left across aisles or that spills are cleaned up. Fatigue can easily result in accidents and mistakes, for example when performing mental tasks, such as adding up figures.

Equal opportunity

Staff need to be provided with equal opportunity to work at different times.

Anti-discrimination

Staff members cannot be discriminated against due to gender, age, religion or race when you are allocating particular working hours.

Workplace relations

It is important to bear in mind employer/employee relations.

Industry awards and agreements

This refers to the agreement or contract between employers and employees that is governed by legislation, and that defines the expected working conditions.

Task 12.1

1. Identify and list the relevant legislation that applies when considering staffing levels at different times in retail store, including:
   - workplace health and safety
   - equal opportunity
   - anti-discrimination
   - industry awards.
2. How did you find this information?
3. Why is it important to keep your knowledge up to date in these areas?

Rostering teams

Rostering a work team in a retail environment involves considering what resources will be required at particular open times, and then allocating staff to fill the required work places at those times. The number of individuals can vary depending on how busy it is expected to be, and also on how many staff are available and how many are budgeted to be on hand.

Work teams in a retail environment may be quite complex. That is, there will be few times when a whole team will be working at the same time. This is due both to the number of hours that a shop may be required to be open through a week, and also the different ways the employment relationship may be structured for individuals.

Teams are made up of individuals, and so the variances between individuals, both in terms of their employment relationship with the business and their own abilities and backgrounds, need to be taken into account when setting up rosters. Variations between individuals may include:

- whether staff are full time, part time, or casual
- whether staff are on a contract or permanent

- language and literacy levels of team members
- the range of cultural, social and ethnic backgrounds that may impact on when individuals may be rostered on
- the range of responsibilities and job descriptions that will occur in a retail store. The larger the store, the wider this range may be.

As well as looking at the members of the team itself, you need to be aware of any statutory (legal) requirements in respect to your team members. These include:

- minimum and maximum hours of work
- meal and other breaks—have you catered for breaks?
- leave entitlements—are people on leave when you want to roster them on duty?
- remuneration scales
- penalty rates that may be incurred by staff rostered on to times that are normally accepted as non-work times, such as Sundays
- relevant industry awards and agreements.

Being able to roster effectively and efficiently, both in terms of the business needs and the needs of your staff, will lead to a more motivated and satisfied work team. This in turn will help improve business performance and reduce staff turnover. Consider the following when setting up a roster, in addition to sales peaks and legal needs:

- Put the business first: that is, look at what is needed and when, and relate it back to estimated wage costs for each period. Then put names into the shifts. Doing it this way means that you are looking at the business first instead of individual requests around outside (social) needs. While it may sound harsh, it is fairer and you cannot be accused of favouring certain people.
- Remember to look at personalities and other less-tangible aspects of people, as well as simply filling in the spaces. It may do harm to the business to roster on two people who have difficulty working together. Dealing with those issues may be another part of your role, but in terms of the roster, do what you can to work with it.
- Make sure that harder shifts are equally shared by the team.
- The busier the shift, the better the staff you need. Do not reward good, experienced staff with the easiest shifts. While it works for them, it certainly will not work for the business.
- Leave and other requests for time off are not only a legal requirement. Sometimes you need to be flexible to cater for staff needs as well as business needs. This is also reflected in the fact that the standard work week gives everyone two days off. Even if a team member is requesting long shifts, and seven days a week, they can only maintain this intensity for a short period while still performing to expectation.
- Being able to determine the cost of a roster (in wages, etc.) will give you a much better idea of the costs of the shift and therefore how the business is performing than working it out afterwards.

Communicating the roster

These days there are a range of online systems to assist in both setting up rosters and communicating with staff. These systems reduce the time it takes to incorporate changes and deal with queries. The earlier a roster can be made available to your team, the sooner they can make plans for the rest of their time. This acknowledges the importance of the team members, and also allows more time for changes should they be necessary, either following requests from team members or through unavoidable things that may arise.

Note the range of people that may be present in a work team. Your communication must make the roster available to all members of the staff. Whether you ask staff members to access the rostering system online, or pin it up on a noticeboard in a lunchroom, or check verbally that each individual is aware of the times that they need to be at work, it is your role to both communicate the roster in such a way that all can access it, and ensure that each staff member knows where and how to find the roster.

Correcting the roster

When changes are needed, all of the above factors need to come into consideration. Importantly, staff may have made alternative plans and commitments and so may not be able to fill in where a gap has appeared.

One of the most efficient ways of allowing changes to be made to a roster is to allow the staff members to do it themselves, working in collaboration so that the store is appropriately resourced, but still allowing team members to have a say in how they are rostered on. However, at the same time it is vital for the team leader or manager to have oversight of changes for all of the reasons stated above.

ELEMENT 2
INFORM TEAM MEMBERS

Communication with team members is a vital part of team leadership. This communication starts when a staff member first joins the organisation through their induction, and carries on covering all aspects of their work, from behaviour through to performance and, on some occasions, discipline. Regardless, the more effectively the communication process starts and then consistently continues, the more informed staff members will be. There is also a sense of security in team members who clearly understand what is expected of them.

2.1 Inform team of expected standards of work and behaviour required by store policy in a manner and at a level and pace appropriate to the individual.

2.2 Implement staff communication and motivation programs according to store policy.

2.3 Compare store targets to individual and team results.

LEARNING OUTCOMES

2.4 Conduct staff meetings to address issues within area of authority according to staff policy.

2.5 Perform staff induction into teams, according to store policy.

Teams

Teams are dynamic groups of people. The stages of team development are worth considering here, as awareness of these can help you as you work with your team. Originally described in 1965 by Brian Tuckman,[1] there are generally five stages that a team goes through. These are:

1. FORMING

The team is new and individuals do not know each other. The role of the team leader is important and that person will set some rules and objectives to give the team purpose. As a manager of a new group of staff in a retail store you need to show confidence in what you are doing and saying.

2. STORMING

The team is clarifying the internal roles and responsibilities, goals, and who is the most influential. These are small power struggles with the potential to create early conflict. As the manager you need to again be confident and guide the team to work together to define and commit to its goals.

3. NORMING

The behavioural norms of the team are established, as is trust. The team begins to function cohesively and make progress towards its goals. As the manager you may encourage the new openness, especially in idea development, while at the same time cementing processes.

4. PERFORMING

The team is now working well to achieve its goals. As the manager, you now need to seek to improve the way the team functions, and—importantly at this stage—act as a coach to individual members of the team. A well-performing team is often a satisfying place for the members to work.

5. ADJOURNING

This occurs when the team goes through a major change, or when a particular project is finished. Team members need to separate and move on from this team. As a manager, you need to ensure that what has been learnt by the team, say in process development, is not lost.

The importance of understanding this team life cycle is its relevance each time there is a change in your work team. This may be as simple as new staff members coming on board, or more complex such as a complete roster change where people are working on shifts with people that they have never met before. If you are mindful of the team dynamic, it will help you in building effective team performance faster than if you simply assume that everything will carry on as before.

Standards of work and behaviour

Stores vary considerably in terms of the behavioural norms that may apply. While two of the primary goals are always to sell merchandise and provide excellent customer service, the means of meeting those goals can differ. Consider the following aspects of work and behaviour in a retail environment.

Selling

This can relate to the way customers are approached, either proactively (such as in an electrical goods store) or reactively (such as in many clothing stores), the way customers are spoken to, whether up-selling is encouraged, and any other aspect of contact with the customer.

Merchandising

In retail, merchandising is the way that products are displayed or presented to customers so as to encourage them to purchase. Some stores, such as high-end jewellery stores, display little merchandise but it is of very high value. Others, such as discount DVD stores, will display lots of product with large signs promoting the cheap prices.

Staff appearance

The appearance of staff, including personal grooming and dress code, is often to a standard set by the store. In some instances there will be a uniform, and the way that this is to be worn can also form part of a dress code. Further, whether or not jewellery may be worn, or the type of jewellery, may be specified. Staff appearance is often directly related to the type of customer that is expected. If a customer feels comfortable with the staff member they are more likely to purchase.

Housekeeping

Keeping the store clean and the shelves or displays tidy (or not) is also store-specific. There is often a requirement for staff to maintain the store when they are not busy serving customers.

Rostering

The amount of flexibility allowed in rosters will be determined by a store policy, as well as the hours expected for each rostered period, including meal and other breaks.

Maintaining equipment

An action as simple as replacing the roll of paper in the cash register if it runs out so that the register is immediately usable by the next staff member seeking to make a sale is an example of a small but vital piece of maintenance that needs to be carried out regularly. Stores may have policies for this or, more likely, will have an expected standard that will apply, as part of the behavioural norms of the organisation.

Stocktaking

A regular activity in every retail store, stocktaking often involves all staff members' participation, and the temporary closure of the store. Given that a closed store is unable to sell merchandise, quick and efficient participation by all staff is needed. An alternative is a stocktake after hours. This is a different cost burden on the store (in overtime wages), but the same level of participation is needed.

Note how all of the above aspects of work and behaviour are closely linked. There is often a common theme running through a retail store in terms of its staff appearance, sales process, layout and so on. In addition, many of these factors are related to the budget and cash flow of the store. In the jewellery store mentioned there will be a higher margin for each item sold, so fewer individual sales are required although the value of each to the store is high. In a fast-moving consumer goods (FMCG) store, sales volume is key, with each individual sale having less value. Many items are required to be sold for the business to be successful.

So, how are these standards best communicated to the work team? One way of seeking to ensure clarity is to remove ambiguity when describing expected standards. Although some standards will come under the heading of behavioural norms, and so be informal and unwritten 'rules', the best way to avoid confusion and disagreement is to have all important standards written down and provided to staff members when they begin. They can also be described clearly as part of an induction process.

Task 12.2

Visit the following websites and read the examples of some publicly available standards for particular retail stores.

- www.davidjones.com.au/images/For-Investors/Corporate-Governance/Code-of-Ethics-and-Conduct-2010
- www.davidjones.com.au/FAQ/Social_Networking_Policy.pdf
- www.jbhifi.com.au/documents/corporate/Code_of_Conduct.pdf
- www.target.com.au/html/careers/aboutus.htm
- www.bunningscareers.com.au/why-bunnings/our-culture.

1. Which would encourage you to seek employment with them?
2. Where can you see similarities between policies and expectations?

3. Why do you think there are differences between expected standards of work and behaviour?
4. At your workplace, gather as many policies related to standards of work and behaviour as you can.
   a. How do they differ from some of the examples here?
   b. Where do you think there are policies missing that you think would be applicable?

Staff communication and motivation programs

Communication with staff can take a range of different forms, often dictated by the size of the store. The most common forms of communication are face-to-face and written. Written communication can in turn be by letter or memo, via a noticeboard or by email.

Communication will be to individuals or to groups. The nature of the communication will often determine which is chosen. While a change of policy in a large department store may be communicated via an announcement posted on a noticeboard in a central staff area, for example a lunch room, or an announcement at a staff meeting, a disciplinary discussion will likely take place face-to-face in a private office. The latter may then be followed up with a written letter.

The style of communication must be considered in terms of the impact that it may have on the motivation of staff (discussed further below). The more personal a communication is, for example a face-to-face and public compliment from a senior manager, the more the recipient is likely to respond it. Conversely, a warning over poor performance may be embarrassing and so a low-key message may be best.

Contemporary workplaces exhibit wide diversity in staff, and many may be from non-English speaking backgrounds. Communicators need to be aware of this and tailor their communications to be readily understandable by all employees. For example, be prepared to back up written notices with verbal explanations and allow appropriate time to ensure that the recipient understands.

Individual and team targets

All businesses have targets, and in retail these generally relate to sales volume and turnover. While the team target is the one most closely aligned with the goals of the store, there may be individual targets set as well as team ones. Individual targets are often used for determining incentive payments (such as commission or bonuses) as well as monitoring the ability of the sales person.

Stores will vary considerably in their policies for communicating how individuals and teams are progressing towards store targets. Most commonly, the overall store target and results will be available, and can be communicated to staff at regular staff meetings, say on a monthly basis. Individual results are often dealt with on an individual basis. Much depends

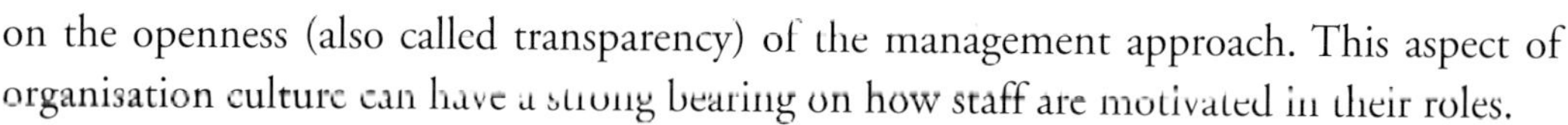

on the openness (also called transparency) of the management approach. This aspect of organisation culture can have a strong bearing on how staff are motivated in their roles.

Task 12.3

1. How are targets communicated in your organisation?
2. How are results communicated in your organisation, both individual and team?
3. As a manager, how would you communicate a poor result to a team member who has been working in the store for at least twelve months?

Staff meetings

Staff meetings provide an important forum for communicating with, motivating and listening to your team. For staff meetings to be effective, pay attention to two main factors, timing and discussion topics.

TIMING

Staff meetings can be held whenever you think appropriate, depending on the number of staff you have, how busy the store is, and what sorts of topics need to be raised. Informal and unplanned meetings can be had with one or two staff members during breaks, if there is something unexpected and urgent to communicate, or if there is a quiet time in the store. Where more staff members are involved, or when there is a range of items to discuss, a planned meeting is best.

Scheduled meetings can take place at any time that is suitable, and could be weekly, fortnightly or monthly. Ideally they will be timed for when the largest number of staff members are available, so that people do not have to make a special trip in to work, or miss the meeting entirely. Two common times for stores to schedule staff meetings are just before or just after opening hours. When the former time is chosen, the store may open a little later than normal to allow for the meeting to run its course and take advantage of the quietest period in the day.

The advantage of a regular, scheduled meeting is that all staff become aware of the timing, and can plan accordingly. A standard agenda then allows staff members to prepare to contribute, or be ready to raise issues at the appropriate time.

DISCUSSION TOPICS

As mentioned, having a standing basic agenda helps people know what to expect in the meeting, and lets them think about contributing. A basic agenda could look like the example on page 379.

EXAMPLE: A STANDARD AGENDA

Agenda

Midtown Store Monthly Meeting
23/7/13

1. Action points from last meeting.
2. Sales report
   a. Month just past
   b. Top performers
   c. Next month's targets
3. Upcoming store promotions
4. Policies and procedures update
5. New starters
6. Discussion topic (e.g. shoplifting)
7. Other business

In addition to the agenda, keep minutes of the meetings, which should record action points and who is responsible. This demonstrates that you are serious about taking on suggestions and seeking to continuously improve the business. Some other points to keep in mind for regular meetings are:

- Welcome new employees to the team.
- Celebrate success. At the meeting, recognise good performance.
- Maintain a positive atmosphere; do not allow the meeting to become a complaint session. Rather, if complaining is evident, turn the focus to finding solutions and invite participation as part of the action points.
- Choose a relevant discussion focus for each meeting. This could come from a range of topics such as shoplifting, goal setting, customer approaches, WHS, inventory, dealing with suppliers, dealing with complaints and dress code.
- Do not run over time and keep focused on the agenda.

Remember that as manager you are reflecting the overall business values and policies to the team. It is likely that you cannot solve all of the problems that are raised and you will have to seek input from someone higher in authority. When this happens make sure that you follow up on these issues and are able to report back to the team at a subsequent meeting. You will need to set the behavioural norm for taking committed action on what is raised in the store meetings.

Figure 12.3 Small teams can hold casual meetings, but there should always be an agenda and an outcome

Task 12.4

1. Obtain (if possible) a staff meeting agenda from your organisation.
2. What topics does it contain?
3. Do meetings in your organisation stick to the agenda? If not, how do they get distracted?
4. How would you as a manager bring a meeting back in line with the planned agenda?
5. If there is no agenda available, create one and discuss how it could be used with your manager or team leader.

Staff induction

An induction program is one of the most fundamental activities that a new employee will undertake in any organisation. Unfortunately, inductions are often poorly done, with a quick tour of where the toilets are and an introduction to an existing employee so the new person can be 'shown the ropes'. If the existing employee does not have enough time to train the new person properly, this can result in lost hours asking basic questions, relearning processes, and lost sales. The new person may also be taught bad habits, or simply ignored. Just as seriously, this can be demotivating for the new person and they do not feel valued from the start.

A thorough induction program provides a wide-ranging introduction to the organisation, its culture, working conditions, co-workers and the role the person will be undertaking. In addition, there is structured training in the tasks and processes that they will be doing. An induction program can be properly planned and executed, no matter what the size of the organisation. The result will be better able and more motivated staff members.

In the first week in a new role in a large retail environment, an induction checklist could contain the following:

The organisation

- Extent (are there multiple stores?)
- Organisational chart
- Mission statement and values
- Working environment
- Departments, functional areas, amenities
- Objectives and goals.

The role

- Position description
- Tasks and responsibilities
- Introduction to supervisor/manager
- Objectives and goals.

Terms and conditions

- Terms of employment, including leave, probation, pay details
- Hours of work/roster
- Dress code
- Smoking/confidentiality/conduct/grievance/IT and other policies.

Activities

- Introduction to 'buddy'
- Task familiarisation
- Introductions to key staff members
- Workplace health and safety briefing
- Security procedures
- Working with customers.

As you will note, it is likely that more than one person will be involved with staff induction. Often, in larger organisations, inductions are managed between the HR department, the line manager and co-workers. Usually the line manager will coordinate the induction, with time spent with HR to learn about the company, as well as certain policies and procedures. Co-workers may then be involved with training and support for the new staff member.

Training and coaching during an induction program is usually provided on a one-on-one basis, the goal being to have the new person able to be productive in their role as soon as possible. Sometimes there are also formal training programs that are necessary in the operation of particular pieces of equipment or in product specifics.

An induction doesn't finish after the first two or three days. An effective induction program will operate over two to three weeks. In week two there may be revision of week one, and skills coaching and mentoring. In week three there can be a skills review by the line manager, as well as clarification and questions from the new employee. Ideally, at the end of week three, the new employee, the line manager and the HR manager may be able to sign-off that the new starter is competent in their new role.

Task 12.5

1. Design an induction program for your organisation.
2. If one exists already:
   a. create a checklist and mark off all of the areas that it covers.
   b. Are there any areas missing? How would you address those gaps in the program?
   c. What different staff members around the organisation are involved in induction?

ELEMENT 3
COACH ON THE JOB

Coaching is all about helping people build their skills in the workplace, done in the workplace as part of their actual job. Coaching in the workplace is usually done individually, and is more closely aligned to both the needs of a role and the development needs that an individual may have. An effective coach is also a role model to other staff, and staff will follow the processes and procedures that they model in training: they will 'walk the talk'.

LEARNING OUTCOMES

3.1 Identify opportunities to coach team members who are unfamiliar with specific procedures.

3.2 Make team members aware of the work application of the competency or job being taught.

3.3 Use a systematic approach, including explanation and demonstration where appropriate.

3.4 Encourage trainees by positive comments and feedback.

3.5 Design feedback during instruction to help trainees learn from their mistakes.

3.6 Encourage and guide trainees to evaluate their own performance and diagnose it for improvement.

3.7 Evaluate trainee's performance, according to store policy and procedures.

Coaching opportunities

There are numerous ways to identify where coaching may assist in a person fulfilling the needs of their role. This starts as soon as a person begins with an organisation and continues throughout their time in that organisation's employment. While ideally the employee will have been given a grounding in the tasks that they are expected to carry out and the general procedures that apply to doing business in the store during their induction, there will always be areas in which a staff member is unsure, or is not fully competent, or simply needs encouragement or practice to perform better.

Some of the procedures that apply may include:

- communication modes and styles used in the store—for example, some employers will wish to have a direct phone call with a staff member who is reporting in sick. For others, a text message to the supervisor may be adequate. There will be accepted modes of communication for each procedure in the store.
- dealing with customers—this is a key part of the retail industry. All aspects of customer contact, from the initial greeting through to the sales process and the final sale may have a standard process for a store.
- job description and responsibilities—it is essential that each and every employee has their job description and is aware of their responsibilities. As their potential coach, you will also need this information.

- interaction with other staff and management—how a person interacts with other team members may also be an area for coaching, depending on the behavioural norms of the organisation. Poor interaction between team members will often be indicative of poor interaction with customers as well. Similarly, the organisation will have behavioural and process standards around expected interaction with management.
- workplace health and safety—possibly the most important area to look for opportunities to coach is in WHS. Although this should be covered properly in induction, many WHS policies and procedures become forgotten, or better ways are found. Remember, WHS is about both the employees of the store and the customers.

Linking coaching and roles

Motivating employees to accept coaching in the workplace involves many of the same demands as motivating anyone to learn a new fact or adopt a new process. The most important factor is that a person can see the reason that they are learning a skill. So the big advantage of coaching in the workplace is that it is very easy for the coach to align what they are doing to the work application.

When embarking on a coaching program it is important to know the job role and the responsibilities of the person being coached. Use every opportunity to link the training back to their job and what they will be doing on a day-by-day or shift-by-shift basis.

The coaching process

Effective coaching is done in a systematic and planned way. It is not an ad hoc process that simply involves telling someone what to do or showing them once and then moving on. For coaching to be effective, it is important that it follows a process such as the following.

1. Review the responsibility or task that requires coaching. Assume that the employee does not have any prior knowledge of the process. Remember, reviewing what they do know can be an effective way of showing why coaching is needed.
2. Choose a location or situation with as few distractions as possible.
3. Seek acceptance from the employee that they are being coached on a particular aspect of their role. This acceptance will engage them further in what is being done.
4. Explain to the employee the relevance of the task or process both in their job role and in the context of the whole store.
5. Explain the role or process, using clear and simple language. Break the task down into steps if necessary. Where appropriate, demonstrate an action and then ask the employee to repeat it. When demonstrating, explain why each step in a process is being carried out.
6. Include WHS aspects in your instruction and demonstration.
7. Check for understanding by asking questions or getting the employee to demonstrate back to you what they are doing. Allow time for the employee to practise.

GIVING FEEDBACK

Providing feedback helps a person to know when they are doing a job properly, or when (and where) they need to improve. Feedback can be in the form of praise when they doing well, or constructive comments for improvement when required.

It is important to know that all aspects of your behaviour can count as feedback to someone who is being trained.

- Appropriate and inclusive language should always be used. At no time should a coach belittle the efforts of a trainee. Positive language is always more effective than negative language. For example, 'try doing it this way' is more effective than saying 'don't do it that way'. Being mindful of how the trainee is spoken to will go a long way to helping them learn and become proficient in the skills being taught.
- Ensure that you are understood. Always speak clearly. Be aware if the employee comes from a non-English speaking background, and so may require you to use different words of explanation, or clear demonstrations and gestures to be clearly understood. Their understanding is your responsibility.
- Be aware of body language. Non-verbal communication represents up to 70 per cent of the message that a receiver gets. As with the language that you use, be mindful of your body language, attitude and tone towards the trainee. If you are providing feedback with your arms folded and while staring out of the window, it will not be as effective as if you have open gestures and are making eye contact with the trainee.

Constructive feedback is all about helping employees perform better. If a task is being undertaken to a satisfactory standard, you are aiming to have it undertaken to an exemplary standard! Remember to let the employee know that they are not doing it wrong. Rather, there may be a better way to do the task that will benefit both them and the business.

One very effective way of providing comment and feedback is to ask questions of the trainee while they are performing the task or process. This not only checks their understanding, but also involves them in decision making. For example, asking 'what do you think the next step will be?' allows them to think and better engage with the process. In particular, engage the trainee when they are unsure of what they are to do next or when they have made a mistake. Learning is more effective for a trainee when they take it on themselves.

Figure 12.4 Feedback and evaluation in coaching can often be done in an informal setting

SELF-EVALUATION

Building up a culture of self-questioning as to how a process works, what steps should come next and why the steps are the way they are also help a trainee to evaluate their own performance. Be aware of situations that may be impairing the performance of the trainee. For example:

- Are there aspects of the role that are creating difficulties, such as reading or maths?
- Is the person at ease with other staff, or nervous working with more experienced peers?
- Is too much being asked of the person too soon in the role?

As manager or team leader it is your responsibility to help the trainee improve their performance and to find ways to help them do it independently. It is important that a trainee can monitor their performance themselves, both for their own confidence and to alleviate some of the work pressure on you.

EVALUATING TRAINEE PERFORMANCE

There are numerous ways of evaluating a trainee's performance, other than simply asking them 'how are you going?' It is also useful to use more than one method to evaluate performance, so as to provide at least two different perspectives, which will in turn make identifying training needs easier. Typical evaluation methods include the following.

- Observation, or simply watching the trainee perform the task or process in the workplace. As the coach of the person, this is likely to be the easiest evaluation method available, and can be used for every instance from serving customers to operating the cash register. If it is not possible to observe in an actual workplace situation, a trainee can be observed in a simulated environment, for example, operating the cash register but after the store has closed so there is no interruption to business.
- Third-party reports such as a checklist or other form of report from a team leader, colleague or manager reflecting the trainee's performance. A third-party report will often be useful for providing an objective review of performance.
- Customer feedback potentially provides the most objective feedback of all, and can be completely anonymous. Customer feedback is often the hardest to manage unless it is done on an ad hoc basis. Best is a short questionnaire that customers may be invited to complete at the register, or a link on the store's website.
- Questioning whether oral or written, questioning to check understanding is probably the most traditional way of checking learning. While great for checking knowledge, questioning should ideally be done in relation to the workplace activity being carried out, so that relevance is clear. The most effective questioning will involve the trainee taking a practical, problem-solving approach within a process or task, to reinforce the learning.

Store policy and procedures need to be accounted for when evaluating trainees. For example:

- Can it be done during business hours or is it preferred that a simulated environment be used so as not the disturb customers?
- Does the budget allow for overtime to conduct training and evaluation after business hours?
- Is there a formal or online form of questionnaire that is used in practice by the store? Are results regularly collated and provided back to trainers and staff?

ELEMENT 4
MOTIVATE THE TEAM

The importance of having a team of people who are motivated to succeed in their roles cannot be overstated. However, motivation is often a very individual process, and there are many different motivators in a workplace. While remuneration is often simply regarded as the best motivator, this is rarely true, and it is important to know your team well in the workplace, and what is required of them, in order to provide the best motivation.

LEARNING OUTCOMES

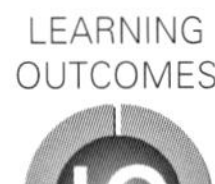

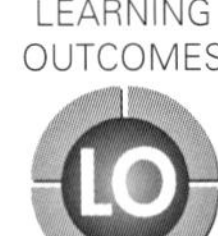

4.1 Identify strengths and weaknesses of team against current and anticipated work requirements.

4.2 Encourage individuals within the team to contribute to discussion and planning of team objectives and goals.

4.3 Update and review team objectives and goals on a regular basis in consultation with relevant personnel.

4.4 Develop positive and constructive relationships with and between team members.

4.5 Treat all team members fairly, equally and with respect.

4.6 Accept responsibility for developing own competencies and identify realistic objectives.

Team strengths and weaknesses

How do you know what the strengths and weaknesses of your team are? There are two ways—self-analysis for each person and your own observation. Often it is interesting to see how these two perspectives align.

An initial approach can be made using a simple table and comparing each member of the team against what work tasks are required now and what may be required in the future. Such a table is illustrated in Table 12.1.

Table 12.1

Team strengths and weaknesses

Person/ Task	Cash register	Stocktake	Customer service on floor	New product knowledge	Store open/ close	Store cleaning	WHS
Sarah	√	√	√	√	√	√	
Kim	√	√	√	√	√	√	√
Anthony	√	√			√	√	
Marcus		√				√	
Chantelle	√	√				√	
Rick	√	√				√	√

Task 12.6

Imagine that the staff described in Table 12.1 represent your team in a busy retail store. You need to divide them into two shifts in the lead-up week to Christmas. You will be open seven days with extended hours. The first shift will go from 9.00 am to 3.00 pm, and the second from 3.00 pm to 9.00 pm.

1. What are the challenges you will have in properly resourcing each team?
2. Where would you like to see urgent additional coaching or training?
3. Justify your training needs.

Inviting staff input

One of the simplest and most effective ways to motivate team members is to invite their participation in planning activities, and to listen to them and act on their input. Earlier we considered how best to structure and run team meetings. Meetings provide the ideal forum for team members to contribute. Often members of the team will have a different perspective on an issue or goal, possibly because they have prior retail experience or possibly because they are working on the floor and have more immediate front line experience. As a manager, do not disregard what others have to offer.

Some additional ways to encourage the team to feel confident to contribute include:

- recognising good ideas or input into goals at team meetings
- being available for less confident employees to talk to you privately if they choose outside the more public forum
- encourage creativity: do not dismiss any input without consideration or comment from other team members
- be positive about contributions, whether they are useful or not

- assign challenges to individual employees (or groups) to test whether goals and targets are achievable
- look for opportunities to add to training and development plans. Personal development is one of the key motivators in any work environment.

Reviewing goals

Team goals and objectives must be regularly reviewed. The mnemonic SMART to describe goals is useful. SMART stands for:

- Specific
- Measureable
- Achievable
- Relevant
- Time-based.

A SMART goal leaves little room for ambiguity, so an employee knows exactly what they (and the team) need to do. For example, consider the goal: 'Sell fifty units of product Y and twenty-five units of product Z by the close of business Friday next week'. The team knows exactly what they have to do and by when. The sales target needs to be aligned to the store target, and the number of units must be what people see as possible (there is no point in having a goal of fifty units to sell in two weeks if the accepted average is five units a week).

However, if the goal is related to a promotional activity, then the goal may be achievable. This is where consultation with management and with the team is vital. The team needs to understand the context of the goal as well as what is specified. Management needs to know that the goals are aligning to other business activities, to maximise the potential return on the costs invested in those activities.

As a store manager you provide the middle point between the team and the requirements of the business. Goals and objectives need to be tightly connected to what the business is seeking to achieve, and what strategies management is undertaking. In turn, employees need to understand and accept that the goals they are given are achievable, and why.

Task 12.7

1. Create five SMART goals for the next four weeks for your current role.
2. Create three SMART goals for each of your team members for these next four weeks.

Relationships with and between team members

Building a positive culture of cooperation and team cohesiveness is important to maintain and enhance the team's performance, and also to simply make the workplace a more satisfying place to work in. Constructive relationships between team members mean that people help and support each other, with a common sense of pride in their work.

Creating this environment is part of your responsibility as a manager and there are numerous ways to facilitate its development. Consider the following:

- Provide training opportunities for the team, helping them to develop skills as a team, rather than as individuals.
- Recognise good results and effort, showing that the team as a whole has benefited.
- Promote your team's success throughout other departments (if in a large department store) or branches (if a chain).
- Encourage participation in decision making and goal setting.
- Encourage innovation and provide a forum for new ideas to be openly discussed.
- Empower employees to use their common sense in decision making, and to discuss with and learn from each other.
- Identify and capitalise on different experiences, skills and abilities within the team. For example, have more experienced team members coach new team members.
- Where possible have tasks rotate through the team, so that everyone gets to experience the more boring, as well as the more interesting, aspects of working in retail.
- Ask members of other teams to present at your team meetings. For example, people from marketing may present on the latest promotional campaign and can discuss with your team how they can help make the campaign a success.
- Suggest that your team presents to other team meetings.

Most importantly, communicate consistently. Whenever possible ensure your team knows about what is happening in the wider organisation, its challenges and successes, customer feedback and marketing.

Treating people fairly

Treating your team members fairly, and with dignity and respect, is possibly the most important daily motivator that you can provide in the workplace. Treating people unfairly and disrespectfully has exactly the opposite effect. It creates a destructive culture and a poor team environment. Respect is also two-way, to receive respect from members of your team, you need to demonstrate a respectful attitude to those same members.

Some areas of respect are covered by legislation. These include:

- discrimination on the basis of race, religion, gender, age or sexual orientation
- having an explicit policy to maintain equal employment opportunity
- not endorsing bullying behaviour in any way.

Other, less tangible but equally important, behaviours that give a basis for a fair and respectful workplace are:

- Greet everyone at the start of a shift or work day positively and equally.
- Involve all team members in meetings or training. Do not sideline individuals.

- Listen to others when they offer ideas or opinions. Do not cut people off or dismiss them out of hand.
- Encourage ideas and suggestions. Where possible, instigate suggestions from people in the team.
- Give credit to people for good work or ideas.
- Do not insult, demean or criticise your co-workers. Handle poor performance professionally and privately.
- Share the jobs that are least popular.
- Be polite and kind. Set an example to others in the workplace.

Developing your own competencies

Moving into management is a difficult task for just about anyone. Generally, if you have just been in a line role without management responsibility, your move has been the result of strong performance, aptitude, enthusiasm or dedication. Often the move comes without initial effective training. By accepting responsibility for your own competency as a manager you will be able to perform more effectively and faster. You will also be able to set your own development objectives that are realistic for your situation.

Management competence is based around four key functions:

- planning—establishing goals and making sure resources will be available to meet those goals
- leading—motivating and guiding your team
- organising—roles and responsibilities within your team, and assigning appropriate work
- controlling—monitoring against the goals that have been set and identifying and solving problems and obstacles to the achievement of those goals.

New managers often fall into traps in one or more of these areas, for example:

- talking too much—do not assume that you know everything. As a leader you need to motivate, and therefore listen, to those around you.
- still doing your old job—you now have a wider range of responsibilities and it is important to delegate some (or all, depending on the size of your team) of those tasks. This is part of organising.
- not talking to your manager—part of controlling is reporting to your manager on how the team is performing against its goals. You are now assisting your manager as your team members are assisting you. Your manager can also be your coach and mentor.
- not worrying about problems—when planning goals for the next reporting period problems that are not addressed now will get in the way of achievement of those goals in the future. Problems may be lack of resources, poor processes or demotivated employees. You will not be able to solve all of the possible problems immediately, but you can flag them so that future planning takes them into account.

Above all, you are now responsible for the performance of your team. Good management and effective communication means that there will be few, if any, surprises both for your team and for your manager.

Task 12.8

1. As a manager, what are the areas that you feel you most need to develop?
2. Identify one problem area within your team or its performance, and describe what skills you specifically need to develop in order to solve it.
3. How (or where) will you seek assistance in self-development?
4. Obtain a copy of your organisation's training policy. What help can be provided by your organisation?
5. Develop lists of goals for the next month, three months and year for the management areas in which you most want to improve.

ELEMENT 5
MAINTAIN STAFFING RECORDS

Staffing records can be, in many ways, regarded as legal documents. They reflect the ongoing working relationship between the employer and the employee and are the formal and developing record of that relationship. Records are also a tool for team leaders, supervisors and managers. They allow a manager to see who is available to be rostered on to a certain shift, what pay rates are applicable or how much sick leave a person has taken. They are important for managing performance, and in the worst circumstances, can form evidence for dismissal. Proper attention should be given to the record-keeping system and your role in it, whether in a large or small organisation.

LEARNING OUTCOMES

5.1 Maintain staff records as required, according to store policy and relevant awards and agreements.

Maintaining staff records

Staff records represent a snapshot of an employee's time with a company as well as their history since their first interview. Beginning with their name and address, an employee's bank details, superannuation details, tax file number and other personal information such as emergency contact will be stored. This information is subject to privacy legislation and must not be made available. Records are generally maintained as either manual (print) or electronic systems, or sometimes both.

If electronic, records should have:

- password-only access
- a limited, and recorded, number of password holders

- anti-virus and firewall protection
- an electronic audit trail system so that previous users can be identified.

If print-based, records should be:

- stored in a locked office (for example, in HR)
- stored in a locked filing cabinet
- accessible by a limited number of (recorded) keyholders.

The best record-keeping systems are secure, reliable, easy to use and maintain, accurate and consistent. In addition to personal information, records will also contain:

- attendance records, including sick leave taken/available
- leave entitlements
- training records of courses undertaken and results. This is especially applicable for courses that are compliance-based, such as First Aid
- performance appraisals. These are especially useful for new managers and team leaders, and can be the basis for decisions about promotion or discipline
- grievances and disputes
- disciplinary steps that may have been taken in the past.

The current legal requirements in Australia for employee record keeping can be found at the Fair Work Australia.

Task 12.9

1. What staff records are maintained in your organisation?
2. What type of system is used?
3. Where are staff records located?
4. What do you rely on staff records for?
5. What do you contribute to staff records?
6. How do you access information when you require it?

Figure 12.5 A young work team in a clothing store

Useful website:

Fair work Australia

www.fairwork.gov.au/resources/fact-sheets/employer-obligations/Pages/employee-records-and-pay-slips-fact-sheet.aspx#obligations.

CASE STUDY

Gloria Jean's Coffees has opened over 480 stores in Australia: amazing when you consider that the brand was only brought to Australia from the US in 1995. (Gloria Jean's Coffees was founded in Chicago in 1979. Since 2004 the brand has been Australian-owned, and now operates across 39 countries worldwide.) The workforce is relatively young, seeking flexible working conditions and a youth-friendly workplace. How do you motivate such work teams across a business that also operates in so many different places?

Gloria Jean's Coffees tried an approach that illustrates lateral thinking in engaging with its essentially Generation-Y staff. They implemented 'The Battle of the Bands', a band competition that encouraged team members across the organisation's franchise partners' stores to work together. The winner was able to perform at the organisation's annual convention on the Gold Coast, and was given studio time to record a CD.

With the vision to be 'the most loved and respected coffee company in the world' (www.gloriajeanscoffees.com/au/OurStory/OurPeople.aspx), Gloria Jean's Coffees also demonstrates its commitment to community needs through its 'With Heart' program, integrated throughout the organisation's mission and goals. From a staff perspective, this represents the organisation recognising its social responsibility, and can provide a significant motivator for employees.

So Gloria Jean's Coffees seeks to engage and motivate team members in ways that are in addition to, but no less important than, say, providing effective training in barista skills.

Consider your workplace. What ideas can you think of that might motivate staff that have not been tried before?

Endnote

1. 'Developmental Sequence in Small Groups', *Psychological Bulletin*, May 1965.

ASSESSMENT 1: PROJECT

<table>
<tr><td>Assessment context</td><td>As a team leader or manager in the retail industry you will be responsible for the induction, rostering, coordination, coaching and motivation of team members according to your store policies and to statutory requirements. You will require strong interpersonal communication skills in order to successfully undertake these functions
As part of the assessment you will need to work with at least three other people in your workplace, and hold at least two training sessions for which you will need to produce a simple plan. You will also need to conduct one staff meeting.
You may need to ask for the cooperation of a manager or supervisor to undertake this project. For learners in a classroom environment–choose at least three partners for this project.</td></tr>
<tr><td>Assessment instructions</td><td>1. Develop a staff roster, and justify your decisions as to its structure, according to the following. The roster period is to take in:
a. The week prior to Christmas and the week following
b. The store will be closed on Public Holidays only
c. Trading hours each day prior to Christmas are from 9.00 am to 9.00 pm
d. Trading hours each day after Christmas are 9.00 am to 4.30 pm
e. There will be a post-Christmas sale for the week after Christmas
f. All staff are competent to open the store
g. Two staff members are competent to close the store
h. Three staff members are competent to close off the cash register daily
i. No shift can be longer than eight hours
j. One staff member has limited product knowledge.
To complete your roster you will need to know:
a. the Award details for each employee
b. who is competent in which area
c. when Public Holidays fall.
2. Identify two areas of development for coaching purposes that will allow the store to be staffed appropriately during the described period.
a. Outline the training required.
b. Develop a short training program for each of these areas.
c. Gain feedback from your colleagues as to the effectiveness of the program, and show where you would modify it.
3. You have been successful in your request to management for two new employees to join your team. They will start on 2 January.
a. Design a staff induction program for the new employees.
b. Conduct a staff meeting with your existing team and:
i. develop a set of goals for the team for the first three months of the new year
ii. ask your team to review the induction plan and suggest where they may be able to assist/contribute
iii. conduct a skills audit with the team and list areas for future training
iv. ask for feedback on your own performance as team leader and record where you can develop new skills.</td></tr>
</table>

Evidence required	1. Completed staff roster and justification. 2. Two completed training programs and feedback from team. 3. Completed staff induction program. 4. Minutes from team meeting including goals, skills audit, roles to be played by team in the induction program and a self-development summary.
Range and conditions	• As part of this unit of competency you are required to demonstrate that you can work through a detailed and considered process to coordinate a small team. You may commence work on the assessment once you are undertaking the subject, and complete the various parts through the course. The final report will be due two weeks after completion of the subject. • If in the workplace, you will require the cooperation a small group of colleagues, including your manager, in order to hold the team meeting requirement of the assessment. • If in a classroom, you can form teams with your classmates.
Materials and resources required	• Access to workplace policies and procedures. • Access to facilities in which to hold team meetings.
Reasonable adjustments	In the event that you have difficulty understanding the assessment tasks due to language or other difficulties, your trainer will attempt to make reasonable adjustments to the assessment paper in order to afford you every opportunity to achieve competency.
Decision-making rules	You will be assessed on your ability to: • roster staff according to a particular situation and limitations • identify training needs and plan for and provide simple coaching • identify key areas for an induction program • accept feedback from your team in a range of areas • collaborate with your team in key areas.

ASSESSMENT 2: REVIEW QUESTIONS

1. Outline the key stages of team development. How are they relevant when inducting new team members?
2. List seven records that you might find in an employee's records. Which are related to statutory requirements?
3. Why does staff input in goal setting increase motivation in the team?
4. What is a SMART goal?
5. Describe four factors that influence staffing levels in a particular shift period.
6. When planning a roster, what award and agreement requirements will you need to be aware of?
7. Define workplace standards and provide four examples.
8. What are the benefits of accepting feedback from your team members?
9. What is 'work' in a retail environment?
10. It is the responsibility of an employee from a non-English speaking background to be able to understand the roster that you have posted on the lunchroom noticeboard. True or false? Why?
11. What are the key legislative requirements in a retail workplace?
12. Outline three possible topics for discussion at a staff meeting in a retail workplace.

COMPETENCY MAPPING

Element			Performance criteria	Task	Assessment	Refer to page
1	Monitor and organise staffing levels	1.1	Maintain staffing levels and rosters in designated areas within budget and according to store policy and procedures and legislative requirements.	1	1, 2 (AQ 2, 5, 6, 11)	369
		1.2	Roster team according to anticipated sales peaks and statutory requirements.	1,6	1, 2 (AQ 2, 5, 6, 11)	371
		1.3	Inform team members of individual rosters according to store policy and procedures.	2	1, 2 (AQ5, 10)	373
		1.4	Take corrective action as needed, according to staff availability.	6	1, 2 (AQ5)	373
2	Inform team members	2.1	Inform team of expected standards of work and behaviour required by store policy in a manner and at a level and pace appropriate to the individual.	2	2 (AQ7, 9, 10, 12)	375
		2.2	Implement staff communication and motivation programs according to store policy.	6	2 (AQ7, 10, 11)	377
		2.3	Compare store targets to individual and team results.	3	2 (AQ7, 11)	377
		2.4	Conduct staff meetings to address issues within area of authority according to store policy.	4	1, 2 (AQ8, 10, 11)	378
		2.5	Perform staff induction into teams, according to store policy.	5	1, 2 (AQ1, 10)	380
3	Coach on the job	3.1	Identify opportunities to coach team members who are unfamiliar with specific procedures.	6	1, 2 (AQ10)	382
		3.2	Make team members aware of the work application of the competency or job being taught.		1, 2 (AQ10)	383
		3.3	Use a systematic approach, including explanation and demonstration where appropriate.		1, 2 (AQ10)	383
		3.4	Encourage trainees by positive comments and feedback.		1, 2 (AQ8)	384
		3.5	Design feedback during instruction to help trainees learn from their mistakes.		1, 2 (AQ8)	385
		3.6	Encourage and guide trainees to evaluate their own performance and diagnose it for improvement.		1	387
		3.7	Evaluate trainee's performance, according to store policy and procedures.		1, 2 (AQ10)	387

continued

Element		Performance criteria		Task	Assessment	Refer to page
4	Motivate the team	4.1	Identify strengths and weaknesses of team against current and anticipated work requirements.	6	1, 2 (AQ7, 12)	386
		4.2	Encourage individuals within the team to contribute to discussion and planning of team objectives and goals.	6	1, 2 (AQ3, 4, 12)	387
		4.3	Update and review team objectives and goals on a regular basis in consultation with relevant personnel.	6	2 (AQ4, 12)	388
		4.4	Develop positive and constructive relationships with and between team members.		1, 2 (AQ3, 10, 12)	388
		4.5	Treat all team members fairly, equally and with respect.		1, 2 (AQ3, 10, 11)	389
		4.6	Accept responsibility for developing own competencies and identify realistic objectives.	8	1, 2 (AQ8)	390
5	Maintain staffing records	5.1	Maintain staff records as required, according to store policy and relevant awards and agreements.	9	1, 2 (AQ2, 6, 11)	391

Required skills and knowledge	Task	Assessment	Refer to page
Required skills			
Interpersonal skills to: • inform team members of rosters • conduct staff meetings • coach team members, including explaining and demonstrating • provide feedback and encouragement through clear and direct communication • ask questions to identify and confirm requirements • give instructions and provide constructive feedback • use language and concepts appropriate to cultural differences • use and interpret non-verbal communication.	2, 3, 4, 5, 6, 7	1, 2 (AQ1, 3, 4, 5, 7, 8, 9, 10, 12)	373 377 378 383 384 387 389
Literacy skills to: • interpret workplace documents • report procedures.	3, 4, 5, 8, 9	1, 2 (AQ2, 6, 7, 11)	371 391

Required skills and knowledge	Task	Assessment	Refer to page
Required knowledge			
Store policy and procedures in regard to: • workplace ethics • work teams • staffing rosters • personnel records • trainee assessment • supervising new apprentices • staff counselling and disciplinary procedures • work and overtime periods • meetings • housekeeping.	1, 2, 4, 5, 6	1, 2 (AQ1, 2, 3, 4, 5, 6, 7, 9, 10, 12)	369 370 375 378
Store organisation structure	5	1, 2 (AQ5, 7)	371
Rights and responsibilities of employers and employees in retail workplace	1, 9	1, 2 (AQ2, 5, 6, 11, 12)	371
Award and agreement requirements, including employee classifications, such as full-time, part-time and casual.	1, 9	1, 2 (AQ2, 5, 6, 11)	371 372
Forms of work in retail.	6	1, 2 (AQ2, 7, 8, 9)	375
Major changes affecting retail workplaces.	7	2 (AQ7, 8, 9)	377
Principles and techniques in interpersonal communication.	7	1	377, 384
Relevant legislation and statutory requirements such as: • equal employment opportunity (EEO) legislation • anti-discrimination legislation • industry awards and agreements.	1, 9	1, 2 (AQ2, 5, 6, 10, 11)	371 389
Relevant Work Health and Safety (WHS) regulations.	1, 9	1, 2 (AQ2, 5, 6, 11)	370
Critical aspects of evidence			
Consistently and responsibly applies store policy and procedures and ethical behaviour in regard to the coordination of staff.	2, 9	1, 2 (AQ7, 8)	369–371
Consistently applies store policies and procedures in regard to monitoring, organising, maintaining staff levels, communicating with staff, mentoring, coaching and motivating staff.	2, 4, 5, 6	1, 2 (AQ4, 5, 7, 8, 9, 12)	370, 375, 383–388
Consistently and responsibly applies store policy and procedures in regard to the induction of new staff.	5	1, 2 (AQ1, 8, 12)	380–381
Consistently and responsibly applies store policy and procedures in regard to maintaining staffing levels and coordinating work teams within budgetary constraints.	6, 9	1, 2 (AQ4, 5, 7, 12)	369–370
Consistently applies state and local statutory requirements and regulations, including relevant industry awards and agreements.	1, 9	1, 2 (AQ2, 5, 6, 10, 11)	370–372
Consistently applies appropriate communication and interpersonal skills when motivating the team and informing staff of roles and responsibilities.	5	1, 2 (AQ10)	377
Reports suggestions for improvements in procedures to management.	8, 9	1, 2 (AQ12)	390

Chapter 13

SIRXQUA001A

Develop innovative ideas at work

Innovation is a cornerstone of all successful businesses. In the retail industry, already highly competitive and now facing increasing pressure from online shopping, innovation is essential. Innovation means *'a new product, method or idea'* and is a mix of both creative processes and the testing of the ideas, products or methods to make sure they are both workable and beneficial to the business.

ELEMENT 1
INTERPRET THE NEED FOR INNOVATION

The expert business researcher and strategist Michael Porter, a professor at Harvard Business School, said 'Innovation is the central issue in economic prosperity'. If there is no innovation in a business, then the business can't change, or adapt to changes around it. It is important to remember that all employees can have lots of ideas; the first challenge is to consider what parts of the business would most benefit from innovation, so that creative thinking is not misdirected or wasted, or money spent on ideas that may be impractical or not worthwhile. Also, you need to know what limitations there may be on areas of change or how to enact needed changes.

Figure 13.1 Everything that you see in a retail environment was once a new innovation

1.1 Observe the need for innovation within workplace context.

1.2 Challenge assumptions about products and processes to identify opportunities for innovation.

1.3 Project possible future contexts and environments for the innovation.

1.4 Define end-user requirements.

1.5 Identify resources and constraints.

1.6 Research factors and ethical considerations that may impact on the idea.

1.7 Access relevant organisational knowledge.

LEARNING OUTCOMES

The need for innovation

Innovation is all about generating new ideas or solutions, or developing new uses for old ideas and making them useful by means of improvement; and once the ideas are described and worked through, implementing those ideas into workable processes or products.

Innovation in a retail business is often about small steps or improvements (also relevant to the concept of continuous improvement, the Japanese word—*kaizen*). These steps can take place in any aspect of the workplace or workflow. While it is unlikely in a retail store that you will be able to affect the actual products that are being sold, there is a wealth of other areas to consider. For example:

- Are deliveries of products to your store done smoothly, and easily unpacked and stocked onto displays?
- Is there clutter on the counter? Can you always find a pen?
- Are there hidden parts of the shop that allow easy theft?
- Are opening and closing procedures easy and do all staff know and follow these procedures?
- Do your customer approach methods result in higher sales?

Figure 13.2 Sometimes the need for an innovation to simplify serving customers seems obvious

Any part of the workplace or workflow that does not seem to be working as smoothly as it could be allows for a potential innovation. Again, these innovations do not have to be giant leaps and they do not have to apply to major aspects of the store. A small change can be very effective, and when combined with other small changes the result can be a big improvement.

The expression that describes larger changes in a business is 'process reengineering'. This may apply to a complete shop refit, or a new customer relationship management piece of software. While these can all be important innovations, the small steps that impact daily behaviour and results are no less vital to a successful business.

The only way to know where to innovate in the workplace is to observe where an improvement could be made.

Assumptions and opportunities

Some of the biggest obstacles to innovation in any business or work environment are the assumptions that:

- there isn't a better way of doing things
- it is the responsibility of other people to think about innovation
- all the possible ideas will already have been considered
- a job is a job, and that is not part of mine.

When in the workplace, consider what isn't working properly. Many processes may appear to work but are cumbersome. Be aware of the phrase '*if it ain't broke, don't fix it*'. Just because a process works does not mean that it is the most effective or efficient way of doing something. This is where it can take courage to challenge what is assumed to be the 'right' way of performing a task, given that it may be the accepted **norm**.

Any process or product that might be able to be done differently, with a positive outcome, is an opportunity for innovation. The outcome may be time saving (on your or your customers' behalf), produce fewer errors or mistakes, increase sales, provide a more pleasant working environment (again, for both you and your customers), or affect any other aspect of your business. Innovations can work for you, your colleagues, your customers, or all three groups.

Task 13.1

Consider a retail store that you are familiar with. Look at aspects of the layout and service and reflect on the following questions.

1. Is access to the check-out counter easy, and is it easy for staff to make a sale to you?
2. Are the products you need easy to find?
3. Do you feel that staff are able to attend to your needs effectively?

CONSIDERING THE FUTURE

No business is static. There will be new products in your store, new technologies that assist with their sale, new competitors opening up nearby, new staff members joining the team, and different ways for customers to pay for their goods. The business may grow significantly, or it may grow slowly. There will be economic downturns and upturns.

Many products that are commonly available now (for example, mobile phones) were almost unheard of just twenty years ago. Other products have stayed much the same, but the ways in which they are sold have changed dramatically. A store that assists in kitchen design and equipment will still be selling ovens and benches as it has done for many years. However, there are now computer programs available that let the customer participate in the kitchen design, visualising and adjusting the final appearance. And possibly the biggest significant change in the retail sector is the growth of online sales and the challenges that online sales pose to traditional shop fronts.

Effectively planning for future innovation needs is challenging. Maintaining currency with trends in the market can be achieved through reading trade journals and newspapers, and attending trade shows. Simply visiting new competitors and seeing how they conduct business will give you a sense of what you may need to do in the more immediate future to operate effectively.

WHO IS THE END-USER?

The purpose of an innovation is connected to the person (or people) who will be benefited by the implementation of the idea. These are called the end-users, and their needs are directly related to what is being done. Think about the following questions in relation to these end-users:

- Why is a product or process needed, or why does the current product or process need improving?
- Who will be using the end product? Will it be staff or the customer?
- How will a product be used, or how will a process be implemented?
- What advantages will it provide, especially over a current product or process? Who will these advantages most affect?
- Where will the product or process be used? Is it on the shop floor, in a loading dock, at the cash register, or once the customer gets home?

By identifying the end-user requirements you put yourself in the context of what the outcome of the idea or innovation needs to be. This will be directly linked to how you select ideas to trial later on.

RESOURCES AND CONSTRAINTS

There are numerous factors that may act as constraints to innovation in a workplace. Sometimes they are simply resources, for example, there is not enough space to install a new display stand, or there are not enough staff to have four instead of three people on each shift. Other constraints are less tangible, such as attitudes. Look at the constraints under these two groupings:

Resource constraints

- costs—all businesses operate to a budget. Many ideas will simply be too expensive to implement, or to implement during the current year or financial period. However, remember that a good idea can be planned for, so it may be possible to reconsider for six or twelve months' time.
- equipment—are the tools present that are needed to carry out an idea? There might be enough business and enough staff to run three cash registers at the same time, but if there are only two cash registers in the store the idea cannot be carried out. Equipment is often aligned to costs; perhaps a plan to invest in a third cash register in six months will allow the original staffing idea to work as well.

- human resources—are there enough staff to carry out an idea, or to even allow effective planning? Again, staff numbers are related to costs.
- time required—can relate to whether extra hours have to be worked to implement an idea (and again, the costs of that) or whether a process might simply take too long to effectively allow smooth customer service.
- technology—related to equipment and costs, technology can represent a significant investment on the part of the retail store.

Other constraints

- work culture—the beliefs, behavioural norms and practices within the workplace define its culture. If a workplace does not have a culture that encourages new ideas (or even allows for them), then innovation will be constrained.
- management practice—the style of management of a workplace will be a significant influencer on its culture. Management that is open to change and encourages staff to think about ways of improving work process and procedure will always foster innovation in a way that rigid management practices will not.

One other factor with constraints is that sometimes it can be appropriate to challenge them. For example, if the resources to implement an idea are not available, then it may be possible for the business to invest in them. In order for this to happen, you may need to present a *business case* to management that will demonstrate how the investment will bring a return to the business, such as faster customer service and therefore higher sales.

ETHICAL FACTORS

While an idea may not actually involve doing something illegal (for example, contrary to the *Competition and Consumer Act*, such as misleading advertising), it is just as important to consider the **ethics** of an idea. This is a broad and sometimes subjective area; the important thing is to do what you think is right.

Examples could be:

- In a clothing shop, when finding a new line of clothing that presents well but has a significantly cheaper wholesale price from the supplier, you discover that the manufacturer uses sweat-shop labour in a developing country and is under investigation by an international human rights body. Would you still stock this line of clothing, even though you can make a greater profit with it?
- In your delicatessen you find that cleaning up is quicker if you use the same utensils for all of your meat products, ignoring the fact that some customers may not wish to have the same tongs used for chicken as for ham. Do you start using fewer utensils to serve all of your meat products?

Note that your ethical choices can also impact your customers' perceptions of your business. It is not only what you believe is right and wrong, but also what your customers believe is right and wrong. Customers will not shop where they feel that their own ethics and values are being challenged.

Ethical considerations are sometimes regarded as subjective. That is, people do vary on what they believe is right and wrong. The expression *caveat emptor* ('let the buyer beware') is used as a catchphrase to put the responsibility back onto the customer to be aware of being cheated, such as paying for a product that does not work. While these days legislation goes a long way to protect the consumer, there is still an ethical consideration when selling a product.

Other factors, both subjective and tangible

- aesthetic value or requirements—**aesthetics** are highly subjective, but, generally, in a retail store, the aesthetic value will be taken to mean than an object or thing is consistent with, complementary to or enhancing of its environment, both within a store and in its location.
- functionality—does the idea relate to a specific function or process, or add to one? And if yes, does it work?
- information available—how much can be learnt about the potential implementation of an idea before going down that path? For example, where has the idea (or a similar idea) been tried in the past?
- WHS—is the idea consistent with WHS principles?
- environmental considerations—of increasing importance is potential impact on the environment. For example, a new cleaning product may work effectively but at the same time need proper storage as any leaks could damage a nearby watercourse.

Task 13.2

Research the aesthetic requirements of a shopping centre or mall. To do this you may have to visit the Centre Management (if the centre is local to you), or check online. How do you think the aesthetics requirements might affect the implementation of an innovative idea in that particular shopping centre?

Using organisational knowledge

The knowledge contained within an organisation is not limited to what people remember. There are numerous sources of organisational knowledge within every business, and some of the more obvious ones are:

- technical knowledge, such as from product manuals that may accompany equipment that you sell or that are generally available on request from the manufacturer
- information gained from books or the internet
- knowledge from work areas that are different to yours. This could be particularly applicable in, say, a large department store

- information from work colleagues
- documented work processes, both current and historical
- the products that the retail store sells, on labels or cartons
- computer systems and records
- tools used by the store in the course of doing business
- working conditions for staff, and the policies that the store has for employees, such as grievance, leave or superannuation policies.

Often you may have an idea that has, in fact, been tried before and found to be ineffective or not worthwhile. There may or may not be records of this, so it is important that you find out if possible. Ways of accessing organisational knowledge include:

- discussing with your colleagues, especially if they have been with your organisation a long time
- asking your supervisor or manager
- looking through old process documents and operating procedures of the organisation. These are more likely to have been retained if you work in a bigger organisation than a small one, or one with multiple branches that seeks to standardise procedures across all outlets.

One point to be careful of is that innovation generally means change, and many people are not comfortable with change. Even if a process is a little arduous, if people are comfortable with it after performing it the same way over years, they may not want to have to learn a new process. They may therefore try to discourage you moving forward with your idea, even if it has not been tried before.

ELEMENT 2
GENERATE IDEAS

Creativity is the key to developing new ideas for your retail workplace. Even though it may appear that everything has been tried before, that is *not* the case, even in an industry with which everyone feels familiar. There is a wide range of ways to help with the initial creativity needed, and remember that all ideas may have value. Then once ideas begin to flow, it becomes necessary to choose the ones that seem the most worthwhile, from both the outcome and the realistic perspectives.

LEARNING OUTCOMES

2.1 Conceptualise ideas using a range of creative thinking techniques.
2.2 Apply relevant knowledge to explore a range of approaches.
2.3 Seek stimulation from alternative sources.
2.4 Test ideas against brief and other factors.
2.5 Select preferred option.

Creative thinking techniques

There is a wide variety of techniques to help thinking creatively about an issue or problem. Some are done individually, but most are done in groups, as people often can develop an idea more effectively when working together. Some commonly used techniques are:

- brainstorming—generating lots of ideas or solutions in a relatively short period of time, often before going through an evaluation process
- visualising—more exact than brainstorming, visualising allows you to 'see' what would be happening if a problem or issue didn't exist. For example, you might ask your team to describe how the process works when there is no problem. Then talk more deeply about it: 'How did you actually perform that step?' The outcome could be a solution that had never been considered because the problem was being thought of only as a problem, and not how things could work if the problem were not there.
- making and building on associations—seeking links between one part of a business or process and another, and then tracing where they can support each other
- building on associations
- telling stories and creative writing—allows people to express themselves in a way that they are not used to doing. That is, people can 'invent' a solution with their peers
- lateral thinking games—often used to freeup thinking. Lateral thinking often involves the posing of a problem which does not have an obvious answer. The manager (or supervisor, facilitator etc.) only reveals the answer at the end of the game
- mind mapping—involves 'drawing' the problem, firstly by writing the problem in the centre of the page and then surrounding it with each of the main issues or associations of that problem, and then doing the same for each of those. The idea is to break the problem down as much as possible, but not in a linear fashion
- six thinking hats—created by Edward de Bono in 1985, this process assigns the metaphor of a different coloured hat to each state of mind with respect to an issue. By rotating through the hats when considering a problem or solution, it means that each team member is approaching the issue the same way at the same time
- prompts—can be anything that facilitates clearer thinking or helps focus members of a team on a solution or issue. For example, in a camera store, the leader may place the highest-selling camera on the centre table and ask everyone to keep focused on it while coming up with solutions to improve sales. Or PowerPoint may be used to focus a group on a certain question.

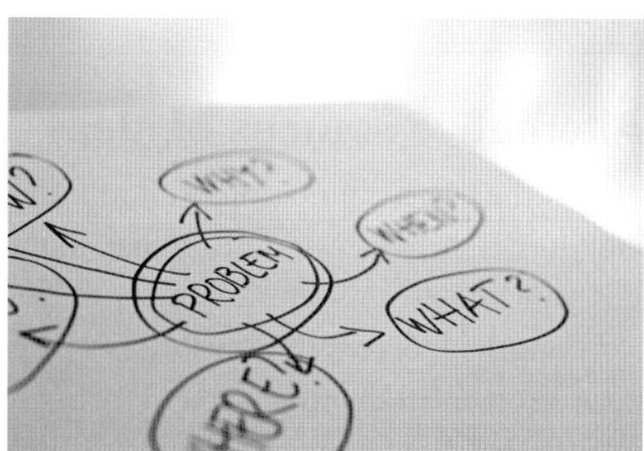

Figure 13.3 The start of a mind map

Task 13.3

Let's revisit the times when there are queues at the cash registers. Choose one of the conceptualisation techniques outlined and work in groups of at least three people to find as many ideas as possible about how to manage this problem. There is no limit to the creativity you can use, and the extraordinariness (or practicality) of the ideas. The key is to come up with as many ideas as possible.

Store knowledge

Once you have a range of solutions or ideas, you can begin to tease them out further, initially to see if they are even practical. It can be a very positive process to create as many ideas as possible. However, once they are there, you need to whittle them down.

Your store knowledge comes into play here. Some ideas will be dismissed immediately as impractical, or simply too expensive. For example, an idea may be to increase staffing levels significantly on Thursday nights for late night trading, and it is believed that doubling the shift would be ideal. While this may be theoretically possible, that is, you could simply hire more staff for Thursday nights, the cost imposition on the business would be such that the store would lose money. So an increase in staff to that extent may be dismissed, however, your knowledge of the wage budget could allow you to see that just one more staff member could be put on that shift. This, combined with an idea about more streamlined customer service, may mean that the pressure on Thursday nights is reduced.

Remember not to discount ideas too quickly. It can also be a good idea to 'park' ideas to one side in case they are of use later on.

Task 13.4

Taking the ideas that you came up with in Task 13.3, how many can you immediately remove from the list, how many will you 'park', and how many are worth evaluating immediately? Create three lists of ideas under these headings.

Alternative sources of ideas

One of the biggest limitations to finding solutions in the workplace is the workplace itself. Not only is there an assumption that all the possible ideas have been tested before, or that it is someone else's responsibility, but there is also a phenomenon known as '**groupthink**'.

Groupthink occurs in teams when everyone starts to agree on a solution or idea simply because others in the team agree. The best way to break away from this habit is to look for ideas from other sources. These may include:

- books and industry journals—see what others in the industry (or in different industries) are doing

- talking with colleagues and friends—other people may be able to give a more objective perspective, as they are not limiting by the immediate workplace
- art galleries and museums—can provide inspiration in a way completely disconnected from your workplace, and so help open up the creative side of the brain
- industry workshops—relating particularly to your industry, you may also be able to hear about how your competitors could be managing the same issues
- networks—an increasingly important part of input into your work can come from those you network with professionally or socially.

How do your competitors deal with the same problems? Retail is a highly competitive environment, and many processes are similar across many different retail stores. Don't be afraid to look at what other people do, and see if their ways of dealing with problems can be adapted to your own situation.

Testing ideas

Now you will have a range of ideas or solutions to the innovation need that you have identified. Not all of the ideas may be practical, but some may be easier to implement than others and may seem easy.

To test the ideas, write them down, and work through them, listing positives and negatives. For each idea, imagine what it would be like to implement it, and then how it would work in practice. Add every aspect that you can think of.

Using our example of queues forming at busy periods, let's say that you have three ideas to solve this problem.

Selecting an option

When selecting the best option try always to compare options against the same criteria, and as objectively as possible. While one option may be cheap, it may not provide the best customer service outcome, or the best working conditions for your team. A numerical

Table 13.1

Idea positives and negatives

Idea	Positives	Negatives
Install a third cash register for when needed	Allows flexibility for busy periods Potential to increase sales	Expensive Takes up space
Train all staff members on the registers	Can be done quickly Inexpensive Increases flexibility in how staff can be rostered	Makes it easier for staff to leave and work in other stores
Slow down customers so that they take longer in your store	Potential for higher purchase value per customer	Annoying for customers Difficult to do

guide is one way to indicate which is the best option to try. Apply a range of criteria to the list of options, such as:

- cost imposition
- resources availability
- importance (or urgency)
- likelihood of success.

Give a value out of ten for each of the criteria, and then add them up. This way you are looking at each option independently, and against each different criterion. The highest total may be the option to try first (even though it may not have been the most obvious).

Task 13.5

1. Take at least seven of the ideas that you thought worth evaluating from Task 13.4 and create a table as shown, listing the positive and negative aspects of each idea.
2. Now list the ideas again and apply a numerical value to each under the column headings of:
   - cost
   - resources availability
   - importance (or urgency)
   - likelihood of success.
   - Add the rows and see which has the highest value. Is this the solution that you expected? How does it align with the positive and negative comments?
3. How will you manage to address the negative comments?

ELEMENT 3
COLLABORATE WITH OTHERS

It is essential in a work environment to recognise that an innovation or change is going to affect other people. People may be affected directly (such as having their jobs actually change) or indirectly (the process helps the retail store as a whole), but either way they are **stakeholders** in the change. **Collaboration** means working with others in how ideas are developed, how they are implemented, and how they are used. Your colleagues are a source of information, feedback, and inspiration in innovating in the workplace.

3.1 Develop ideas in conjunction with the relevant people.

3.2 Seek and accept feedback from relevant people in an appropriate fashion.

3.3 Modify ideas according to feedback.

3.4 Maintain and utilise a network of peers to discuss ideas.

Who to work with

So who do you need to develop ideas with? Different people can be relevant to the problem or the store in different ways:

- colleagues and team members may have to also implement the idea
- supervisors may have to implement the idea themselves and will likely have to train new staff in the workplace if the idea becomes part of normal business process
- managers may need to add costs of including the idea into future forecasts and budgets, as well as accounting for set up, training or downtime costs if the idea is implemented
- the client is the one who will be ultimately most impacted by the idea, as innovation is all about how to provide better service either directly or indirectly.

Not all of these people have to participate in the creation of an idea, but all can participate to some extent in its development.

Task 13.6

1. List all of the people with whom you might develop ideas in your store.
2. What is the role each has?
3. How would you expect each to contribute to idea development?

Getting feedback

One important aspect of innovation, that is, introducing an idea or change in the workplace, is to understand that other people may want to have input also. While an idea may be good, there are often ways to improve it, or to recognise that its implementation will be different for different members of the team. An idea may in fact cause another part of a process to become harder.

Accepting feedback on an idea therefore can add value to the idea. Even better is to go one step forward: be proactive. Seek feedback from other stakeholders and look to make the idea better without waiting to see if new points are offered.

How you seek feedback will depend on the work environment. If an idea is likely to affect a whole team, but a team who rarely if ever see each other (for example, people are working different shifts), then it may be appropriate to introduce some way for people to provide written comments. This is likely to be more formal than simply asking colleagues casually for their input.

If possible, gaining feedback in a group setting can be better than via individual conversations. This allows people to hear what the others have to say, reduces the potential for duplicated comment and may also help the idea to develop further and faster for the reasons already discussed.

Task 13.7

Research and define constructive feedback.

1. What form would constructive feedback take in helping develop ideas for workplace innovation?
2. Provide some examples that may apply in your organisation.

Modifying your idea

Once the feedback has been collected it needs to be collated and the idea modified. Collating feedback helps identify where there are consistent points of view. This then gives you priority areas to reconsider as you develop the idea.

One way to effectively collate feedback is to list broad headings and write the headings down under the most relevant heading. For example, the comments:

'It's too expensive'
'The store can't afford that'
'There aren't enough staff members'
'We don't have the necessary tools and equipment'

can all come under the heading of 'Cost'. The third and fourth could also come under the heading of 'Resources'. Note that these comments are also quite negative, and don't provide much in the way of constructive comment for you to work with. One way to overcome this is to work with the person providing the comment and explore the context, to see if more information can be provided. For example, if the manager says that 'The store can't afford that', does that mean in this year's budget, or ever?

Questioning like this will help give you more valuable input for modifying an idea so that it is more widely acceptable.

Networking

Ongoing development of new ideas will contribute to the ongoing development and improvement of the business. Remember the concept of *kaizen*, or continuous improvement. One of the best ways to be aware of where new ideas can be valuable, and where they can help with the competitive position of your business, is to **network**.

Networking can take place through a range of means and in a variety of situations. Some common ways of extending your network can include:

- participating in forums or attending industry conferences
- attending industry training sessions
- attending workshops run by peak bodies

- joining an organisation that represents your industry
- using professional social media such as LinkedIn.

The value of a network of peers is that you are able to discuss ideas with people in similar situations (often similar roles). The hierarchical nature of the workplace is removed, allowing for potentially more open consideration of problems that affect your industry.

Task 13.8

1. Research the organisations that could help you build a professional network. List these organisations.
2. What sorts of events or information do they provide?
3. How does LinkedIn support a network? Are there other social networking sites?

ELEMENT 4
ANALYSE AND REFLECT ON IDEAS

Having arrived at a number of potentially workable ideas, and sought peer and management input, it is worth reflecting on how these ideas might work, and whether they will be successful. Reflection involves experiencing the implementation of the idea, and recording how you felt, and why. This process takes time, and is often forgotten in the need to implement new ideas and get on with business.

LEARNING OUTCOMES

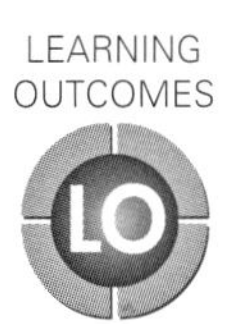

4.1 Analyse ideas from different perspectives.

4.2 Use appropriate strategies to capture reflections.

4.3 Examine ideas to ensure they meet context requirements, best practice and future needs.

4.4 Allow time for the development and analysis of ideas.

Reflection

As well as looking at ideas from different sources, and applying criteria to them that allows for a sound selection against other business priorities, it is also worthwhile to consider ideas from a range of perspectives. This analysis often involves **reflection**, based on your own experiences and senses. Reflection will help you to build an awareness of the impacts and effects of the implementation of an idea. Even better, reflect on the experience of the idea after you have trialled it, and then compare it with other ideas that you may trial.

There are three basic parts of reflection.

1. Consider what happened, both what worked and what did not, and how you felt. What did your senses tell you? Not only what you might have seen and heard, but also what you smelt, and your feelings. Discussing this with peers or team members allows you to build a picture as a group.
2. What did it all mean? This means taking the experience and analysing its context, why it was important, what you (or the group) learned, and what the impacts are. Within this part, three words that start with 'r' can be useful:
   a. reality—what really happened?
   b. reasons—what caused the reality?
   c. respond—how can you, or the team, react?
3. Consider the action plan for next time. Will the idea be modified or adopted? What learning has there been that will help with future ideas and innovations?

Reflection is a step that is often missed when implementing new ideas and processes. When an idea is adopted, the process can stop there, instead of continuing so that learning now can inform decisions made in the future. Remember again the concept of *kaizen*, or continuous improvement. Small steps forward that are based on learning from the past are far superior to unconnected ideas that follow one after the other.

CAPTURING REFLECTIONS

There are many ways to capture reflections, some of which mirror the ways of creating ideas in the first place that were discussed above. Importantly, you and your team members need to be able to describe feelings about the idea, which is quite different to simply writing up a brief report.

Figure 13.4 The idea of placing fresh tea in small bowls for customers to touch and smell has helped build a new interest in these products

Ways to help people describe the experience may appear to have little to do with the work environment, but are valuable tools in analysing the efficacy of an idea. Consider the following means of learning how people felt during a process. Ask team members to:

- write one word describing the experience on a piece of paper and pass it to the next person to also write a word and so on
- create a model out of play dough that says how they felt about the experience
- draw the experience, perhaps in the form of a mind map
- write a short story about the experience.

While getting this feedback is vital, just as important is having methods for retaining the knowledge. This can be in the form of a more traditional written summary, which can be derived from collective discussion following the period of creativity. To capture reflections in a way that will have ongoing meaning to the business, the following strategies may be useful:

- mind mapping—a collective mind map constructed though group discussion can record all of the information derived from the reflections in a way that is visual and so may appeal to many people
- assessing alternatives—can be used if two different ideas are being trialled or compared
- imagining possible outcomes—including best and worst case scenarios, is particularly useful for finalising an implementation plan. Not only does this allow the team and especially the manager to consider what a worst case may be, it also encourages the development of contingency plans for if that happens. Similarly for a best case. If a promotional idea for a store is extremely successful, problems can ensue—from servicing high numbers of customers slowly, through to not having enough stock on hand to meet demand. So the flow-through effects may also be noted.

Task 13.9

Consider a change that has taken place in your workplace as the result of an innovation or idea. The change might be in terms of a process, your role, or the way in which customers are managed.

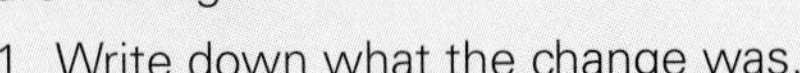

1. Write down what the change was.
2. Reflect on your experience of the change using the three steps:
   a. What happened?
   b. What did it mean?
   c. What action is being taken?
3. Either write a short story about the experience, or draw it in the form of a mind map.
4. Write down possible ways the idea could be modified. How would those modifications change your experience of its implementation?

Context, best practice and future needs

Even when an idea appears to work for the team, there is still one further step to take before implementing it as part of a standard process or procedure. That is, does it work in the situation and add benefit to the business? It is no use having doubled the breaks for staff during shifts to help them cope with the busy period in the store if customers are not being served or shelves are not kept stocked.

The **context** is the first area to consider. This relates to the type of store, its image and the image of the brands that it sells, the target demographic of the shoppers, the location (for example, in a large shopping centre or on a high street), the demographic of the staff, how busy it is and when, and any other factors that impact on the business. An idea needs to be *consistent* with the context of the store. That is, both the idea and its expression need to fit in to the store.

Consider a clothing store that aims at the teenage market. There are likely to be large posters on show, music will be playing in the shop, and staff will be wearing examples of the labels that are for sale. An idea might be to introduce a simple and contemporary uniform so that staff members are more easily noticed by customers. This may represent a financial saving for staff as the store management has agreed that it would pay for the cost of the uniforms. However, the concept of a uniform does not fit within the image of the store, nor does it 'advertise' its merchandise through its staff. The opposite might be true for a clothing store that sold practical work clothes to predominantly tradespeople. In that context, the uniform can not only promote the store merchandise, but the uniform concept may be more acceptable to staff and customers.

The second area is **best practice**. 'Best practice' refers to the acknowledged benchmark that delivers the best service or outcome. Best practice can be industry specific, or may cross many areas, depending on the process or outcome required. How do you know that an idea meets best practice? Research your industry sector, look at your competitors, and network. An example of relevant industry benchmarks from the Australian Taxation Office can be found at: www.ato.gov.au/businesses/pathway.aspx?pc=001/003/102&alias=businessbenchmarks.

Future needs are often forgotten when considering ideas, as problems tend to represent the here and now. All businesses should have plans for the future, whether the next twelve months or the next five years. An idea that is implemented now that can help meet future needs, such as expected demand for a product in a year's time, is always more sensible than one that only addresses a current problem (also often referred to as a crisis!). In addition, when you consider the processes that may have been followed in conceptualising, selecting and trialling ideas, it has the potential to be a large investment in time (and money). An idea that addresses future needs gives a long-term return on this investment.

Task 13.10

1. Review the ATO website (www.ato.gov.au) for information on retail benchmarks.
2. What other websites can you find that provide useful benchmarks for your organisation?
3. How would you use this information?

Allow time

Author of *The Seven Habits of Highly Effective People*, Stephen Covey, stated that even the creation of a mission statement for a business should be allowed to take six–twelve months. While obviously not every idea is going to take that long to consider and implement, some will. Even what seem like small ideas, if well thought out, require time to plan, reflect upon and implement for them to be most effective.

CASE STUDY

Ikea is a store and brand name synonymous with innovation. Ikea's business vision today is:

> to create a better everyday life for the many people. Our business idea supports this vision by offering a wide range of well-designed, functional home furnishing products at prices so low that as many people as possible will be able to afford them[1].

To meet this seemingly simple and unambiguous statement has taken many years of growth, development and, in the highly competitive retail furnishing market, innovation.

Founded by Ingvar Kamprad in 1943 in Sweden, Ikea has grown from a single person to a company operating 267 stores in 25 countries in 2009. One the of the best known product innovations at Ikea is the flat-pack supply of furniture to customers. Where did this idea come from? In 1956 competitors were placing pressure on suppliers to boycott Ikea, and, at the same time, an Ikea employee pulled the legs off a table to prevent damage while transporting the table in a car. The result? Ikea began designing its own furniture with easy transport in mind. The flat-pack now extends across a huge range of items, and allows customers to save on costs of delivery by taking the product home themselves, and costs of assembly by assembling it themselves. A simple idea has developed into a core product strategy.

Consider the range of other innovative ideas expressed in a single Ikea store, from the way customers move through the store, viewing different product areas, to the pads and pencils provided for customers to be able to record products that they are interested in, to the way floor staff provide assistance. Now visit the Ikea website—www.ikea.com/au/en/—and find and list the innovations that Ikea has for helping customers in the digital age.

Figure 13.5 Assembling flat pack furniture: a practical idea developed into a world-class brand

ELEMENT 5
REPRESENT IDEAS

Once an idea has been thought through, the actual implementation may still be determined by its acceptance after a presentation of some kind, say, to management. You may be the decision maker, in which case you will need to communicate the idea to a range of potential stakeholders, including staff, suppliers and customers. The communication style and medium that you use will be chosen to suit the people who are receiving the message. In return, you may have information conveyed back to you that makes you or allows you to modify the idea or change.

LEARNING OUTCOMES

5.1 Select an appropriate communication technique for the target audience.
5.2 Develop the presentation of the idea with the audience in mind.
5.3 Present the idea to educate and inform the client.
5.4 Modify the idea according to client feedback.

Communication techniques

THE AUDIENCE

The key to choosing how to communicate to an audience is first to understand the audience itself. In a retail environment, your audience may be made up of a specific group, or representatives from a range of groups. Each will have their own idea of what they are seeking to gain from the communication, and how they may interpret what you are trying to say about the idea or change. Most people or groups are primarily interested in how it will affect *them* as individuals and the business that they represent.

Below are some groups that may make up an audience in a retail setting, and the sorts of things that they will want to know:

External contacts such as suppliers

- Will the idea make the supply chain easier?
- Will it result in more of our products being sold?
- Might we get aid faster?

Peers, that is, your own team members

- Will we have to work longer (or shorter hours)?
- Will our job be easier (or harder)?
- Will we potentially earn more?
- Will our preferred shifts change?

Managers or owners

- Will the business turn over more?
- Can the idea fit within the budget?

Groups or individuals

- Will the team like the idea?
- How will the idea affect me?

People from diverse backgrounds

This includes people from a range of social and ethnic backgrounds, and with varying learning and comprehension styles.

- Do I understand the idea?
- How can I follow a new process?
- Do I understand the implications for me?

A little bit of analysis of the audience to whom you are representing your idea will go a long way to helping the people in the audience to understand and, more importantly, support your idea. There is a myriad of communication techniques that can be used, from simple through to highly involved. As a rule, the simplest is usually the best. Consider:

- writing a proposal—generally best when you are putting an idea to management or the business owners, and for when your audience may need time to consider the idea. A proposal needs to outline the idea and the benefits to the business, as well as the costs of implementation
- building a model—which may give a visual interpretation of an idea
- showing a film—does not mean making your own movie! There is a wealth of material on YouTube that can be used as part of a presentation or as a suggestion for people to see. A movie allows a visualisation of a concept or problem
- presenting a talk—when you have a group to communicate with, a talk can be as simple as just that, talking to a group, or with sophisticated aids such as a supporting PowerPoint presentation
- preparing a report—will often present the case for an idea rather than the idea itself. A report can also be used to report on the progress of the implementation of an idea
- drawing a diagram—as a visual cue, a diagram can be used as a prompt in a presentation, or as an illustration in a presentation, or as a standalone for others to view and comment on. A diagram will often overcome language barriers that may be present
- sending an email—or any form of electronic communication. Allows you to reach a range of people with the same message even if they are not available at the same time. This use of email, for conveying information, is the best use of this communication medium according to Bill Gates.

Developing the presentation

Having analysed the make-up of the audience, and formed the style of communication that you are going to use, you now need to consider the processes that you will need to undertake to gain the desired outcome of the presentation; that is, that the audience understands and accepts what you are saying.

Figure 13.6 Presenting an idea to a work team can take many forms

There are many facets to communicating an idea and gaining acceptance. Depending on the communication medium that you choose to use, the following points can assist:

- You want the audience to understand the idea and be able to visualise how it could work for the business and for them. The use of images, whether through a PowerPoint, in a diagram, or simply drawn on a whiteboard, can have a powerful effect in easing understanding. Images also help get past any language differences.
- Listen to your audience to understand their needs before you develop your presentation and while you are developing it. Listen actively, that is, engage with the audience members and clarify your understanding.
- Effective questioning will help you to better understand your audience before communicating with them, and questioning during and after will help you to see where the idea has been understood and what may need further explanation. Questioning improves with practice—don't limit yourself to closed questions that can only be answered with a 'yes' or 'no'.
- Open yourself to the opinions of others, incorporating feedback into the way you present your idea. If you question your colleagues and find that they would respond best to a discussion with a whiteboard so that all of the positives and negatives can be listed for all to see, then use this method and do not feel that it undermines what you are trying to do.
- When explaining a proposal, be careful not to assume a higher level of prior understanding in your audience than is the reality. If anything, provide too much explanation, in the form of some background. If in a written proposal, the reader can skim past that bit. If in a presentation, your audience may let you know that they already know this bit.
- Remember to clarify details. This can be in the form of summarising a set of key points, and works well when writing or speaking to an audience. If addressing a group of people directly, another way to clarify is to ask the audience for questions, or ask someone to paraphrase what you have just spoken about.

Presenting the idea

Remember, your goal in presenting the idea is to inform the audience, so that they are aware as individuals how the idea will affect them and the business. You are educating the audience, and this is not a one-way street. You should expect questions, requests for clarification and, sometimes, disagreement with what you are suggesting.

A key reason to inform people effectively is so that the potential consequences of an idea can be realised. These consequences may not always be visible to you as you develop an idea. But having a fully-informed audience means that other people will also be able to examine the idea. You could look at this as a process of lessening the risk of unforeseen negative consequences if and when your idea is implemented.

Using feedback

Having communicated your idea to an audience, you should now be prepared to modify the idea in light of any constructive feedback. Modifications can be large or small: in the worst case you may have to completely rethink the idea! Regardless, the feedback from your audience is vital to having the best possible innovations in your business.

ELEMENT 6
EVALUATE IDEAS

The final step in innovation, that is, evaluating ideas, is often the one forgotten. Evaluating ideas just before and after they are implemented is how you know whether or not the idea works, or whether it needs to be changed. Innovation is not a static process, and rarely does innovation halt after a single idea.

LEARNING OUTCOMES

6.1 Review ideas using appropriate evaluation methods to ensure they meet required needs.

6.2 Modify ideas as required.

Evaluating ideas

There are two times when it is necessary to review an idea. Firstly, check all of the details before it is implemented. Secondly, review and evaluate the success of the idea after it has been implemented. This second stage can of course happen more than once. And, as you review it, you can continue to improve the idea and its effectiveness.

Before the idea is implemented, review the following:

- Can the idea be implemented?
- Does it meet the needs of staff and customers? Will it result in better service, higher sales or a better work environment?
- Is the idea consistent with best practice principles?

- Can the idea be afforded, that is, does it fit in the budget?
- Are there adequate resources to implement the idea?

Once an idea is implemented, it is important to evaluate it after an agreed period (or periods). This evaluation can take the form of:

- using a checklist—this checklist may have been designed while you were developing the idea, and have formed part of your proposal
- discussing the idea—with peers, team members, or managers. Remember to record the results of discussions if possible
- writing a report—of the outcomes of the idea and submitting to your manager.

Modifying ideas

Many ideas require some form of modification after they have been implemented. This returns you to the notion of continuous improvement, and how it links to innovation. The two concepts together allow a business to develop its processes and procedures and to provide a better shopping experience for customers and a better workplace for staff.

Task 13.11

Develop a simple presentation that you can deliver to your work team about an innovative idea that you believe would aid customer service in your workplace. Although you can use any style of presentation, make sure that it is aligned to the needs of your audience.

After your presentation, obtain at least three pieces of feedback about your idea that allows you to modify and improve the idea.

Endnote

1. Ikea: Our business idea at: www.ikea.com/ms/en_AU/about_ikea/the_ikea_way/our_business_idea/index.html.

ASSESSMENT 1: PROJECT

Assessment context	When working in the retail sector you will need to be able to innovate and to develop new processes and procedures in order to sell new products, to keep up with competitors and customer needs, and to meet changes in the industry. As part of the assessment you will need to work with your supervisor and at least one other person in your workplace. For learners in a classroom environment, choose at least two partners for this project.
Assessment instructions	Choose three areas of the organisation that you believe would benefit from an innovative idea. 1. For each area describe: a. the nature of each problem b. assumptions that have been made that have meant that the problems do not yet have a solution c. constraints on innovation to find a solution for these problems d. what the end users need as a best outcome e. any ethical considerations or other factors that may relate to the problems f. how providing ideas to solve the problems may benefit the organisation in the future. 2. Hold at least three team meetings to: a. brainstorm for ideas to solve the three problems b. present a range of ideas to peers c. present final ideas after feedback and modification. 3. Design a final presentation of each idea: a. to management b. to staff i. including outlining the communication method to be used ii. describing how you will meet the needs of staff members from non-English speaking backgrounds iii. describing how implementation of the idea will benefit people in their roles. 4. Describe how you could evaluate the success of each idea.
Evidence required	1. Completed report providing details (as outlined above) with respect to the three ideas. 2. Minutes of any meetings held. 3. Suggested future modifications to the ideas, and why.
Range and conditions	• As part of this unit of competency you are required to demonstrate that you can work through a detailed and considered process to innovate in the business. You may commence work on the assessment once you are undertaking the subject, and complete the various parts through the course. The final report will be due two weeks after completion of the subject. • If in the workplace, you will require the cooperation of a small group of colleagues, including your manager, in order to hold the team meetings requirement of the assessment. • If in a classroom, you can form teams with your classmates.

Materials and resources required	• Access to workplace processes and procedures. • Access to facilities in which to hold team meetings.
Reasonable adjustments	In the event that you have difficulty understanding the assessment tasks due to language or other difficulties, your trainer will attempt to make reasonable adjustments to the assessment paper in order to afford you every opportunity to achieve competency.
Decision-making rules	You will be assessed on your ability to: • identify opportunities to innovate • generate a wide range of possible ideas • collaborate with others both in the development of ideas and in their analysis • communicate a selection of ideas to a wide range of stakeholders • refine ideas to produce workable and innovative solutions • present final ideas to management and staff.

ASSESSMENT 2: REVIEW QUESTIONS

1. What organisational documents would you look up to find information about:
   a. current processes and procedures
   b. innovations or ideas that may have been tried in the past in your organisation
   c. staff who may be interested in or affected by a particular innovation.
2. Define and explain how you could use the following idea-generating techniques:
   a. six thinking hats
   b. brainstorming
   c. creative writing.
3. What is a network? How could you use a network in the idea generating and testing part of innovation?
4. What role can your competitors play in helping you to innovate in the workplace?
5. Describe the process for reflecting on an idea? Why do you record reflections?
6. What is 'best practice'?
7. How does best practice influence your analysis of a potential innovative idea? Provide an example.
8. What communication techniques can you use in the workplace to inform your colleagues about an idea?
9. How would you present an idea to staff members:
   a. from a non-English speaking background?
   b. with a hearing disability?
10. Describe one appropriate evaluation method for seeing if an idea requires modification after it has been implemented.
11. Innovation is a quick process that should take no more than two weeks from idea creation to implementation. True or false?
12. Define innovation.

COMPETENCY MAPPING

Element		Performance criteria		Task	Assessment	Refer to Page
1	Interpret the need for innovation	1.1	Observe the need for innovation within the workplace context.	1	1, 2 (AQ1, 4)	401
		1.2	Challenge assumptions about products and processes to identify opportunities for innovation.	1, 5	1, 2 (AQ1, 4)	402
		1.3	Project possible future contexts and environments for innovation.	2, 5	1, 2 (AQ4)	402
		1.4	Define end-user requirements.	2	1, 2 (AQ4)	402
		1.5	Identify resources and constraints.	2	1, 2 (AQ1)	403
		1.6	Research factors and ethical considerations that may impact on the idea.	5	1	404
		1.7	Access relevant organisational knowledge.	5	1, 2 (AQ1)	405
2	Generate ideas	2.1	Conceptualise ideas using a range of creative thinking techniques.	3	1, 2 (AQ2)	407
		2.2	Apply relevant knowledge to explore a range of approaches.	3	1	408
		2.3	Seek stimulation from alternative sources.	3, 5	1, 2 (AQ4)	408
		2.4	Test ideas against brief and other factors.	4, 5	1	409
		2.5	Select preferred option.	5	1	410

continued

Element		Performance criteria		Task	Assessment	Refer to Page
3	Collaborate with others	3.1	Develop ideas in conjunction with relevant people.	3, 6	1, 2 (AQ1)	411
		3.2	Seek and accept feedback from relevant people in an appropriate fashion.	4, 6	1, 2 (AQ3)	411
		3.3	Modify ideas according to feedback.	7	1, 2 (AQ3)	412
		3.4	Maintain and utilise a network of peers to discuss ideas.	8	1, 2 (AQ3)	412
4	Analyse and reflect on ideas	4.1	Analyse ideas from different perspectives.	4, 9	1, 2 (AQ4, 5)	413
		4.2	Use appropriate strategies to capture reflections.	0	1, 2 (AQ5)	414
		4.3	Examine ideas to ensure they meet context requirements, best practice and future needs.	9, 10	1, 2 (AQ4, 5, 6)	415
		4.4	Allow time for the development and analysis of ideas.	9	2 (AQ5, 7)	417
5	Represent ideas	5.1	Select an appropriate communication technique for the target audience.	11	1, 2 (AQ8)	418
		5.2	Develop the presentation of the idea with the audience in mind.	11	1, 2 (AQ9)	418
		5.3	Present the idea to educate and inform the client.	11	1, 2 (AQ9)	420
		5.4	Modify the idea according to client feedback.	11	2 (AQ10)	421
6	Evaluate ideas	6.1	Review ideas using appropriate evaluation methods to ensure they meet required needs.		1, 2 (AQ3, 10)	421
		6.2	Modify ideas as required.		1	422

Required skills and knowledge	Task	Assessment	Refer to Page
Required skills			
Interpersonal skills to: • collaborate with others and represent ideas through clear and direct communication • ask questions to identify and confirm requirements • use language and concepts appropriate to cultural differences • work within teams.	3, 4, 5, 6, 7, 8, 11	1, 2 (AQ3, 8, 9)	403 407 411 418 421
Analytical and lateral thinking skills to examine self and external factors.	1, 2, 4, 5, 9, 10	1, 2 (AQ1, 2, 5, 6)	407
Required knowledge			
Relevant technical knowledge.	10	1, 2 (AQ4, 6)	403
Broad industry and market knowledge.	4, 8, 10	1, 2 (AQ3, 4, 6, 7)	408, 412
Organisational culture.	3, 4, 6	1, 2 (AQ1, 6, 9)	404, 405
Social, environmental and work culture impacts.	2	1, 2 (AQ6, 8, 9)	404
Principles of innovation.	3, 5	1, 2 (AQ2, 11, 12)	401
Critical aspects of evidence			
Interprets the need for innovation in the workplace.	1	1, 2 (AQ1, 4)	401
Identifies resources and constraints and researches affecting factors when generating innovative ideas.	2, 4	1	403–405
Generates ideas using creative thinking techniques.	3	1, 2 (AQ2)	407
Tests ideas against brief and other relevant factors.	4, 5	1, 2 (AQ4)	409
Presents and discusses ideas with relevant people.	6, 7, 8	1, 2 (AQ3)	411
Seeks feedback and modifies ideas accordingly.	7, 10	1, 2 (AQ6, 7)	412
Analyses and reflects on ideas to ensure they meet end-user requirements.	9	1, 2 (AQ5)	403, 413–415
Presents ideas using appropriate communication methods.	11	1, 2 (AQ8, 9)	418–421
Reviews and modifies ideas using appropriate evaluation methods.	11	1, 2 (AQ10)	421–422

Glossary

accessories items that can be used to enhance the products being displayed

aesthetics those aspects that relate to whether an object or thing is perceived as beautiful or nice to look at

allocated tasks refers to all the tasks that you have been given to complete within a given period of time

audience the market the display or promotion is aimed at

balanced appearance refers to the way in which the store is set up to provide an appealing layout for customers to browse in

basic principles of design steps to consider when developing a creative and successful display

benefit the reason why that product's features are attractive to the customer

best practice industry-acknowledged benchmark processes and procedures

body language the non-verbal signals we use subconsciously when communicating with others

budget the amount of money allocated to creating the display

business plans and strategies refer to the plans an organisation will put in place to achieve its objectives for the coming year/s. These plans outline the tactics, budgets and standards to be followed by all staff

buying behaviour refers to having an understanding of what motivates customers in their purchasing decisions

buying signals subconscious signals that the customer is ready to buy the product or service

call to action this is a marketing term that is used to encourage customers to buy a product by giving them a deadline or a specific reason for the making the purchase immediately

coaching developing the abilities of individuals in their roles while in the workplace

collaboration working jointly with others

communicating effectively refers to being able to interact with others in a positive and beneficial manner

confidentiality refers to the need to keep information about customers, staff and certain organisational facts private

conflict refers to a continuing disagreement between people that must be resolved in order to maintain an effective workplace

consequence the outcome of a hazardous event. A consequence is usually measured in terms of financial loss and the extent of personal injury

constraints issues that will impact on the plans you make and that have to be taken in to consideration

context the circumstances that surround the store and influence all aspects of its business

continuous improvement a system whereby an organisation ensures that it is always working towards offering better services and conditions to its customers and staff

control a control is something you put in place to reduce the likelihood of the risk occurring. For example, putting a safety cone and sign over a spilled product. Once you identify a hazard, you need to consider the best control measure to implement in order of the hierarchy of controls

customer service environment refers to an atmosphere in which customers will feel valued and encouraged to return repeatedly

damaged stock is stock that, for one reason or another, has been damaged beyond a point where attaining full price is possible

database a system of recording information about customers, products and sales that can subsequently be used to generate reports or information for marketing purposes

demography refers to specific knowledge about an area's population and could include information about their age, occupation, lifestyle, income and so on

detrimental work practices refers to all behaviours within the workforce that are contrary to, or in breach of, the company (or legal) policies and procedures

discrimination means treating someone unfairly or harassing them

display plan a document that provides clear details on how a display is to be constructed

diversity refers to all the ways in which people may differ from each other

duty of care your common law duty to take reasonable steps to minimise harm to others

Electronic Data Interchange (EDI) the integrated computerised systems used by some advanced retail operators who have to manage very large or fast-moving stock levels

enquiry survey a method by which you can gauge the success of a product or promotional campaign

ethical behaviour behaving in an open and honest manner and keeping the organisation's standards in mind at all times

ethics what is accepted as right and wrong

evaluating reviewing or taking a close look at something to ensure that it matches the organisation's or the customer's requirements

expiration date the date at which stock is considered 'unsaleable'

feature something a product or service has

feedback comments and suggestions received from colleagues and customers

FIFO, or 'first in, first out' the process of re-ordering stock as it sells

goals and objectives refers to the targets that an organisation will have set for the coming year (or years)

groupthink where members of a team agree with each other to preserve the team cohesion rather than risking conflict through disagreeing

hazard a thing or situation that has the potential to cause harm, injury or illness

hierarchy of risk controls types of hazard-control measures based on effectiveness of reducing the level of risk

incident reporting refers to the legal requirements for employers to report accidents in the workplace

industry code of practice refers to the guidelines provided by a given industry's member associations

IPASS the prompt for using fire extinguishers: Inspect the extinguisher to ensure that it suits the purpose, Pull the pin, Aim at the base of the fire, Squeeze the trigger, and Sweep from side to side

lead time this is the time it takes for goods to arrive once the order has been placed

legal requirement this relates to all legislative or organisational policies and procedures that you are legally obliged to comply with

loading dock or loading bay area in which stock is received and dispatched

loyalty scheme a marketing tool used to encourage long-term customer relationships

manual handling the act of holding, pushing, pulling, lifting or carrying

market demand refers to knowledge about whether customers actually have a need for a given product or service

market research refers to studies undertaken to understand your customers, products and business environment. This information can then be used to create effective marketing campaigns

merchandising refers to how products are displayed to encourage sales to customers

min–max levels a system where minimum and maximum stock levels are monitored and where orders are placed when minimum levels are reached

mutually acceptable resolution resolving a conflict or complaint so that all parties are happy with the result

network a formal or informal group of professional contacts

non-verbal communication the subconscious signals we send out when we communicate with others

norm a norm is an unwritten but generally accepted behaviour in an organisation

objection in sales terms, an objection is a reason a customer will give when they are not yet ready to buy your product

obsolete items those products no longer produced by the manufacturer

organisational culture refers to the way in which the organisation prefers to work with its staff and customers, and the standards they set

organisational hierarchy gives information about an organisation's management and staff structure

personal presentation refers to the manner in which you physically present yourself in the workplace—to your employer and colleagues

planogram a planogram sets the facing stock design for the shelves of the retail store based on the physical size, market share and sell-rate of the product

point of sale the point at which a transacted sale of goods is completed

policies and procedures refer to the standards and guidelines set by the organisation. All staff will be expected to abide by these policies and procedures

preferred products refer to products that your organisation will sell in preference to others. This may be because you earn a higher profit margin by selling those preferred products.

principals are the companies that manufacture, provide or produce the products that you sell through your organisation

profiling the market refers to developing a deep understanding of who your customers are, and who you could potentially sell to

profit the amount of money the organisation has left over, once all costs have been paid

promotional campaign refers to a specific and scheduled program of advertising and promoting a given product or set of products over a specified period of time

promotional material items used to attract customer attention and encourage them to buy an organisation's products or services

purpose the reason why the display is being created

quality assurance goes hand in hand with continuous improvement and sets the standards to which tasks must be completed

rapport refers to the relationship and good will that you build with your customers

rate of sale the rate of sale is a metric (measurement) of how fast an item sells during a given period

reconciliation the task of comparing daily takings with recorded takings in order to balance cash and non-cash records

records refer information that is stored by an organisation for marketing or audit purposes

referrals when a customer has recommended your products or services to others

reflection reviewing an idea and considering it from a range of experiential perspectives

refresh updating the look of the display on a regular basis to keep customers interested

replenishment stock replenishment is the act of adding stock to the display (shelves, end-caps, hangers) as product is sold

research techniques refer to the methods used by researchers to gather information

resources all the things that you will need to complete the plan and set up the display

Retail Award sets out the conditions under which retail assistants will work, and how they will be paid

revenue stream the methods and pathways your organisation uses to generate an income

risk the likelihood of an undesirable consequence occurring as a result of the hazard

roster a plan showing when individuals are expected to be working in an organisation. Rosters are usually weekly, fortnightly or monthly

sales presentation refers to structured methods used to promote products and services to customers individually or in groups

scheduled rotation a timetable of when displays need to be changed

seasonality refers to times throughout the calendar year when particular items are in high or low demand

security policy a policy outlining the operation's security procedures and responsibilities of staff

shelf life the shelf life of a product refers to the period of time during which a product can safely be consumed

staff roster a schedule that sets out who is due to work on what days and during what hours of the day

stakeholders people who may be affected by the change, including staff, customers and suppliers

stock rotation refers to the schedule in which products are moved around the store to comply with policies, or to generate new interest

stock turns a term that refers to the rate at which stock sells and is calculated by the total cost of goods sold *divided* by the average inventory level during the period

surveillance store surveillance can include electronic and direct observation. Surveillance deters crime and provides evidence in the event of a crime

sustainable refers to methods and practices by which the organisation can ensure its own successful future while decreasing its impact on the natural world

target market refers to the *specific* customers you are aiming your products and services at

terms and conditions (of a sale) the legal obligations that seller and purchaser must agree to for the sale to be completed

trends noticeable increases or decreases in the sales of specific product categories over time

wholesalers are companies that act as a *middleman* between principals and retailers

WOM, or word of mouth a marketing term that refers to how people find out about an organisation's products. WOM is when people you know tell you about their experiences with a product or service

References

Australian Institute of Criminology, http://aic.gov.au/publications/current%20series/crm/21-40/crm028.aspx.

Australian Bureau of Statistics, www.abs.gov.au/ausstats/abs@.nsf/mf/8501.0.

Budden, Michael Craig (1999), *Preventing shoplifting without being sued*, Quorum Books, Westport, CT.

City of Subiaco (2012), 'Rights of retailers if you suspect shoplifting', *Business Beat*, www.subiaco.wa.gov.au/fileuploads/businessBeat/retail_rights.pdf.

Covey, Stephen R (1989), *The seven habits of highly effective people*, Free Press, New York.

eCommerce Report, www.ecommercereport.com.au/tag/statistics, accessed July 2012.

Ikea, *Our business idea*, www.ikea.com/ms/en_AU/about_ikea/the_ikea_way/our_business_idea/index.html, accessed April 2012.

Forklift licence Sydney, http://forkliftlicencesydney.com.au/41/forklift-licence-faqs.

Gloria Jean's Coffee website www.gloriajeanscoffees.com/au/OurStory/OurPeople.aspx, accessed April 2012.

Hill, D (2012), 'Interviews with retail shop owners in Queensland, Dec 2010', www.spectraining.com.au/clients-partners.php, accessed January 2012.

Hoffman, Abbie (2002), *Steal this book*, Four Walls Eight Windows, New York.

KPMG (2010), 'Fraud and misconduct survey, 2010', www.kpmg.com.

NSW HSC online, http://hsc.csu.edu.au.

QLD government, 'QLD Coal mining fatalities report, 2010', mines.industry.qld.gov.au/assets/mines-safety-health/coal_fatalities_1882-2010_web.pdf, accessed January 2012.

Rolfe, John (2010), 'Un-used gift cards give 360m to retailers', *The Daily Telegraph*, 7 June 2010, www.dailytelegraph.com.au, accessed January 2012.

Smallbusinessnewz www.smallbusinessnewz.com/topnews/2010/09/16/offline-retail-vs-online-retail, accessed July 2012.

Tuckman, BW (1965), 'Developmental Sequence in Small Groups', *Psychological Bulletin*, May.

WHS Queensland, 'Cash in transit code of practice, 2011', Workplace Health and Safety Queensland, Department of Justice and Attorney-General.

Wrice, Mark (2010), *First steps in retail management*, Palgrave MacMillan, South Yarra, Victoria.

Index

J

K

L

M

N

O